W9-BYO-423

BOOKS BY THOMAS MERTON

The Seven Storey Mountain

The Sign of Jonas

New Seeds of Contemplation

Conjectures of a Guilty Bystander

Zen and the Birds of Appetite

The Collected Poems of Thomas Merton

The Literary Essays of Thomas Merton

Mystics and Zen Masters

The Hidden Ground of Love (Letters I)

The Road to Joy (Letters II)

The School of Charity (Letters III)

The Courage for Truth (Letters IV)

Witness to Freedom (Letters V)

Love and Living

The Monastic Journey

The Asian Journal

Run to the Mountain (Journals I)

Entering the Silence (Journals II)

A Search for Solitude (Journals III)

Turning Toward the World (Journals IV)

Learning to Love (Journals VI)

The Other Side of the Mountain (Journals VII)

Dancing in the Water of Life

THE JOURNALS OF THOMAS MERTON / Volume 5: 1963–1965 / Patrick Hart, O.C.S.O., General Editor

Thomas Merton

Dancing in the Water of Life

Seeking Peace in the Hermitage

EDITED BY ROBERT E. DAGGY

HarperSanFrancisco
A Division of HarperCollins*Publishers*

HarperCollins books may be purchased for educational,
business, or sales promotional use. For information please write: Special
Markets Department, HarperCollins Publishers, Inc.,
10 East 53rd Street, New York, NY 10022.

HarperCollins Web Site: http://www.harpercollins.com
HarperCollins®, ♨ ®, and HarperSanFrancisco™ are trademarks of
HarperCollins Publishers, Inc.

Book design by David Bullen

FIRST HarperCollins PAPERBACK EDITION PUBLISHED IN 1998

Library of Congress Cataloging-in-Publication Data
Merton, Thomas, 1915–1968.
    Dancing in the water of life : seeking peace in the hermitage /
Thomas Merton ; edited by Robert E. Daggy. — 1st ed.
        p. cm. — (The journals of Thomas Merton ; v. 5)
    "1963–1965."
    Includes bibliographical references and index.
    ISBN 0-06-065482-1 (cloth)
    ISBN 0-06-065483-X (pbk.)
    1. Merton, Thomas, 1915–1968—Diaries. 2. Trappists—United
States—Biography. I. Daggy, Robert E. II. Title. III. Series: Merton,
Thomas, 1915–1968. Journals of Thomas Merton ; v. 5.
BX4705.M542A3 1995b
271'.12502—dc21
[B]   96-48223

98 99 00 01 02 ❖ RRDH 10 9 8 7 6 5 4 3 2 1

Contents

Acknowledgments

As director of the Thomas Merton Studies Center at Bellarmine College in Louisville, Kentucky, for more than twenty years, I have long been aware of the interest in Thomas Merton's "personal journals" and the anticipation that awaited their release twenty-five years after his death in 1968. When the restriction against publication ended in 1993, I was pleased that the Trustees of the Merton Legacy Trust named Brother Patrick Hart as general editor for the publication of the *Journals*. I immediately accepted when he asked me to edit the fifth of the seven projected volumes. As I come to write these acknowledgments, I realize that all the people I wish to thank are special people to me, special beyond their help and support through the years of my tenure at the Merton Center. They are my friends and they have been a great grace to me.

Brother Patrick Hart's place in Merton studies was, of course, already assured. The general editorship of the *Journals* simply caps his already distinguished contributions to Merton studies. That he offered support and helpful suggestions in the preparation of this volume goes without saying, for he is supportive and helpful with every Merton project. Most remarkable to me is that in over twenty years of cooperating on Merton affairs no cross word or tense moment has ever passed between us – a tribute more to him than to me.

It has been my pleasure to work with the trustees of the Merton Legacy Trust – Naomi Burton Stone (Emeritus), Robert Giroux, James Laughlin, and Tommie O'Callaghan. Anne H. McCormick, administrator of rights and contracts for the Trust, has handled Trust business in which I was involved with efficiency and dispatch. I must say a special word about Tommie O'Callaghan, whom I met at a business lunch in 1973. It is she who, in her words and mine, "found me" and "gave me my great opportunity" at the Merton Center. Though I may not always have felt gratitude for that opportunity in moments of stress and distraction, it is quite true that I would not have had the privilege of editing this volume (or the Merton letters and other Merton material) if I had not eaten Kentucky barbecue with her many years ago. For all the good things, Merton-related and otherwise, that knowing her and her husband, Frank, have brought me, I have genuine gratitude.

Several people provided help with the editing of this volume of the *Journals*. Most significant is Gregory J. Ryan of Wall Township, New Jersey, who introduced himself to me at the Merton Conference at Columbia University in 1978 and became a charter member of my own "Merton web." He has helped with many projects since then, but his prodigious efforts in the preliminary transcription of this volume made my task of final transcription and editing far easier. His facility with Merton's handwritten English is remarkable, though he eschewed attempting to decipher Merton's difficult handwriting in other languages. For help with those transcriptions and translations I must thank other friends: Miguel Grinberg of Buenos Aires (for his own Spanish); Frank Donates of Chicago, sometime of Havana (Spanish); Lawrence S. Cunningham of Notre Dame University (Latin); and Beverly Marmion and Robert Wardell of Louisville (French).

Jonathan Montaldo, editor of Volume 2, *Entering the Silence*, entered my life when he wrote his master's thesis on Merton in 1974 and I am lucky he has not left it. He transcribed several of Merton's "Working Notebooks," including #17, several years ago. I am grateful to him for allowing that transcription to be used, in part, as an appendix in this volume. I appreciate the efforts of Rosalind Parnes, reference librarian at Bellarmine College, the first colleague with whom I lunched after coming to the Center and with whom I still lunch. She checked and rechecked databases and other sources to help identify the often obscure authors and books that Merton was reading as he wrote these journal pages. Finally, my sometime partner and long-time companion, Michael J. Drury, assisted me with computer entry of the text, allaying my doubts and soothing my frequent frustrations. For this and so much more, I am grateful to him beyond words.

Introduction

There was an old man of Whitehaven
Who danced a quadrille with a raven.
But they said: It's absurd
To encourage this bird.
So they smashed that old man of Whitehaven.

Charles Lear

Thomas Merton copied this Lear limerick into a 1964 "Reading Note-book" during the period when he was writing this volume of his private journals, dated "August 1963–End 1965." Written regularly (but not day by day) and without major interruption, the journal covers a period when Merton had been in the monastery of Our Lady of Gethsemani for more than twenty years, in which he passed his fiftieth birthday, and in which he began a new style of life and monasticism in what he called the hermitage. Merton is one of the most noted spiritual writers and masters of our time. While the journal offers abundant insights into and queries about the spiritual life, Merton lets us see that it is no easy task to find spiritual, or even physical, peace. His own struggle to accomplish the task is a consistent Merton theme and it provides the framework for this journal.

Charles Lear's limerick encapsulates in a fanciful, yet serious, way Merton's mood during these two and a half years. Merton, while undoubtedly amused by the limerick, probably copied it because he identified himself with the "old man of Whitehaven." We can imagine, first of all, that "Whitehaven" in Merton's mind is a play on "New Haven," a small town just over the knobs from Gethsemani. Next, Merton began in this period to think of himself as an "old man," stemming in part no doubt from his turning fifty but also from what he knew was diminishing physical well-being and energy. He was growing old, he thought, and yet resolution of the circumstances and activities of his life had reached only uneasy and uncertain solution. As he bobbed up and down the knob called Mount Olivet on his way from the monastery to the hermitage and back, Merton was, in the jargon of today's youth, "having a dance in his own head." Like the old man of Whitehaven, Merton found himself in a kind of cerebral "quadrille," whirling around seemingly without purpose or direction.

The raven has historically been a bird of ambivalent image – sometimes helpful, sometimes ominous, sometimes deadly. Ravens fed the prophet Elijah when he hid from wicked Queen Jezebel in the wilderness. Frequently depicted as a companion of St. Benedict, the raven acts as a protector of all who follow Benedict's monastic *Rule* (which Merton as a Cistercian of the Strict Observance did). On the other hand, the raven is also a bird of prey, one of the "birds of appetite" of Buddhist lore, a scavenger, a carrion eater, and often a precursor of doom. Certainly not graceful on the ground, the raven symbolizes the ambivalence and awkwardness that persist in Merton as he "dances" with specters of his own creation – the specters of anger, angst, agitation, and alienation that he cannot seem to exorcise from within himself. As he dances, he himself *ravens* (in another sense of the word), seeking and attempting to seize gratification as monk, solitary, and writer. He "rapaciously" indulges his own will through what he sees but cannot seem to stop as indecision, procrastination, drift, and vacillation.

Merton saw much in his life and in the world around him that was absurd. The word "absurd," in fact, recurs with frequency in this journal. In the limerick, "they" – that inevitable "they" who, we may assume, are the arbiters of what is proper and "normal" – think the raven is the problem and that the dancer's encouraging the bird is absurd. Yet, for Merton, the monk must encourage dancing with the raven in order to reconcile the absurdity in himself. "They" want to stop the quadrille, and they try to end it, not by doing anything to the raven, but by smashing the "old man of Whitehaven," he who encourages the protective yet rapacious bird to dance. There is no doubt that Merton continually felt "smashed" in this period, especially by his efforts to deal with the specters indicating that his writing, his vocation, his solitude were self-indulgent rather than genuine. Forces from outside the monastery continually smashed him: publishing business, visitors, peace movements, and ecumenical conferences. Merton may have perceived Dom James Fox, abbot of Gethsemani, as the chief "smasher" within the monastery, but disgruntlement with the monastic complex was almost equally as smashing. The continuing tension between dancing and smashing – between contentment and curtailment – helps to account for the highs and the lows, the joy and the despair, the enthusiasm and the carping that come through in this volume. Smashed Merton may have been at times, but the quadrille went on in his head and he could not seem to stop dancing with the raven. He could not stop the absurdity.

"Absurd" was one of the buzzwords of the 1960s and it is not surprising that Merton picked it up or that he was familiar with literature depicting the absurd. He delved into the French movement called the Theater of the Absurd, particularly in his reading of Eugène Ionesco. He said of Ionesco's play *Rhinoceros:* "To be the last man in the rhinoceros herd is, in fact, to be a monster . . . solitude and dissent become more and more impossible, more and more absurd" (*Raids on the Unspeakable*, p. 20). He read Paul Goodman's fairly popular book, *Growing Up Absurd*, which meshed in many ways with his own view of American society. Over and over in his journal, he speaks of what is absurd in the world, but more importantly, of what is absurd in his own life. In one entry (November 12, 1963) he says:

What a weary, silly mess. When will I learn to go without leaving footprints? A long way from that: I still love recognition and need to preach, so that I will believe in my own message, and believing that, will believe in myself – or at least consent to find myself acceptable for a little while. Absurdity, and very dishonest on top of it. I wish I knew how to be otherwise! Funny how I came to this, quite in spite of myself and in spite of everything, after several days of desperation (half-felt) and perplexity.

Events such as the assassination of John F. Kennedy he quite naturally finds "absurd" (November 23, 1963). He speaks of the "pompous absurdity" of pontifical masses at the monastery, which were too fussy for him (August 20, 1963). The war in Vietnam is, of course, "absurd" (April 27, 1965). He finds writing a text for the Vatican pavilion at the 1964 World's Fair "absurd" (February 2, 1964); finds it "absurd" that a solitary should be "accountable for what he says" (Appendix); and frets about "the absurd ritual of wastepaper," of producing too much paper as he cleans out his office when he "departs" for the hermitage (August 17, 1965). He finds wanting to be young again "absurd" (December 21, 1965) and even his own "nausea" (a word he picks up from reading the French existentialists) with things "absurd." Perhaps the most telling is when he writes on the eve of his departure to live in the hermitage: "The revelation of futility and interminable self-contradiction. What a poor being I am. If I try to conceive myself as, on top of all this, 'being a hermit' absurdity reaches its culmination. Yet I am convinced that I am on the right way" (August 17, 1965).

The narrative of the journal centers on the eventual move to the small concrete-block structure on Mount Olivet that Merton called "The Hermitage." The abbot of Gethsemani, Dom James Fox, gradually permits him to spend more and more daylight hours at the hermitage. He eventually allows him to sleep there and tantalizes him with hints of even more "privileges." Finally, late in August 1965, he replaces Merton as Novice Master and grants him permission to live "full time" on Mount Olivet. His first official day as a hermit was August 20, 1965. On the surface Merton had at last achieved the solitude for which he had searched, struggled, and prayed so long. To a certain extent, even in his own active and continually questioning mind, he had.

Merton loves the hermitage and its surroundings, though there are, of course, some "problems." He had said while spending only partial days there: "I talk to myself, I dance around the hermitage, I sing" (December 4, 1964). He revels in God's creation and in his creatures (particularly deer, squirrels, and birds) and enjoys being part of that creation with them. The journal is filled with descriptions of the weather, becoming at times almost daily reports from the hermitage porch. Weather itself constitutes an integral part of his solitude. He finds "peace," for example, "in seeing the hills, the blue sky, the afternoon sun." The rain, especially, intrigues him and surfaces as a theme in his writing – for example, in the superb essay "Rain and the Rhinoceros" and in "The Preface to the Japanese Edition of *Thoughts in Solitude*," written soon after this period.

Merton had finally accomplished his goals within the monastic structure without breaking his vow of obedience, but somehow he was not happy. He had been a monk for nearly a quarter of a century; he was a well-known and respected writer; he had "returned" to the world in his writings with renewed perspective and compassion. Yet doubts and uncertainties lingered. We encounter a Merton whose moods fluctuate, a man who is not always in a good mood. Is he a good monk? Is he using his solitude properly? Is he writing too much and is he writing the wrong kind of thing? Is his social commentary inappropriate and ill-advised? The journal does not depict a man who has come to rest, a man who is settled in his self-conceived and longed-for hermit role. He is still "dancing," performing, in one of his phrases, "mental gavottes" – trying to find his real *Auftrag*, or purpose, but finding it difficult to know what that is. Along the way, he expresses no little impatience and exasperation – with himself, of course, but also with others.

The hermitage is not the panacea he had imagined it would be during all the years he badgered Dom James about being a hermit. Lack of facilities inconvenience the urbane Merton at first, though he does question the extent to which a "hermit" should luxuriate in conveniences provided by modern technology. While this particular "hermit" may glory in the woods, he has little conception of "roughing it." He cannot see to read (extremely important to him); he has to carry water from the monastery; he has to go to an outhouse where snakes may lurk. He is grateful when Dom James starts improvements at the hermitage – wiring it for electricity; investigating the digging of a well; planning the addition of a bathroom and chapel. Yet, even as some improvements are being made and others planned, Merton, who suffered as much as any human from the "grass is greener" syndrome, has dreams about moving to a new location – Edelin's Hollow – which Dom James is thinking of accepting as a gift and where, he suggests to Merton, he might consider building more hermitages. So, Merton "dances" off to Edelin's Hollow and, while ostensibly scouting for Dom James, envisions sites where he might have a different hermitage and where, he implies, he might experience "better" solitude. One site that intrigues him is near an old, ruined dance hall where the people from the hollows roundabout had once come "to drink and raise hell" (January 6, 1965). As the Edelin's Hollow project falters, Merton turns to his life in the existing hermitage and by December 1965 settles into a reasonable, if still uneasy, acceptance of his life there and its meaning for him.

One "gavotte" that nags him is the recurring feeling of "growing old." Certainly we in the 1990s no longer consider fifty old, and I tend to doubt that people did in the 1960s – at least not in the sense that Merton means – so why does he have this consistent thought? One conclusion could be that the members of his immediate family were all dead and had died at early ages: his father at forty-four, mother at thirty-four, and only brother at twenty-five. But his American grandparents had lived into their seventies and, with the exception of his father, the genes of his New Zealand family produced extraordinary longevity – his grandmother and one aunt both lived to 101 and two other aunts lived into their nineties. If he were to live that long, at this point he would have lived only about half his life!

It was true that Gethsemani had probably seemed more youthfully vital in Merton's earlier years, particularly when young men flocked to the monastery after World War II. It is equally true that, as observers have noted, during and after the Second Vatican Council Gethsemani became an "aging community" (and he certainly does fear that the monastic life as he has known it may disappear in the wake of the council). Yet Merton was not among the oldest monks. The feeling of growing old, with attendant musings on death, stems, I think, from a different cause. During these two and a half years Thomas Merton simply did not feel good most of the time. During much of it he was in pain or extreme discomfort. Like all of us he saw his body deteriorating and he did not like it. In December 1965, a relative sent him a snapshot taken in 1937 and it reminds him of a different time and a different body – "a body totally assured of itself and without care, perfectly relaxed, ready for enjoyment." He wishes he could have that twenty-two-year-old rugby player's body back and "could start over again." But he quickly adds, "How absurd." This wish does launch him into a rare catalogue of his ailments, which lets us glimpse what a difficult period this must have been for him and why he so often grows peevish and feels old.

An arthritic hip; a case of chronic dermatitis on my hands for a year and a half (so that I have to wear gloves); sinusitis, chronic ever since I came to Kentucky; lungs always showing up some funny shadow or other on ex-rays (though not lately); perpetual diarrhea and a bleeding anus; most of my teeth gone; most of my hair gone; a chewed-up vertebra in my neck which causes my hands to go numb and my shoulder to ache – and for which I sometimes need traction.

Yet experiencing physical pain, feeling old, disliking his body, and even apprehending death could not stay Merton's natural energy in his writing. Granted, as he danced around in his cerebral quadrille, he continually questioned whether he should be writing; what he should be writing; whether he, a solitary, should be writing at all – but, despite these doubts, he kept on writing and it was a productive and prolific period. Five books – *Emblems of a Season of Fury, Seeds of Destruction, The Way of Chuang Tzu, Seasons of Celebration,* and *Gandhi on Non-Violence* – were published. More manuscripts were in the hands of publishers. Nearly a hundred articles and reviews were written and published in this period, including, in my opinion, some of the best things he wrote – such as "Message to Poets," "Day of a Stranger," "Atlas Watches Every Evening," "Rain and the Rhinoceros," and the "interpretations" from Chuang Tzu. Nearly all of this large output was inspired, in one way or another, by his *lectio* (or monastic reading) – a major activity as well as his inspiration and something to which he devotes major space in this journal.

As usual the range of Merton's reading is staggering, covering religious as well as secular literature. His reading is without plan or system. He admits that he often reads books simply because someone sent them to him or because he happened to pick them up from a pile. But, no matter why he reads them, the books of his *lectio* become a part of what is going on in his head. One can almost sense in his reading and in his recording of it in his journal that his "dancing" slows down, almost stops, as he finds comfort and a kind of resolution in this process. As he puts it, the process "situates" him. In a way it helps him transform his journal from the "private" to the "public." He says: "A journal is to keep one 'honestly situated'" (the private function). Then a journal "can be transformed into 'meditations' or *'pensées'*" (the public function).

This means more than just transforming the journal itself. It equally well applies to the writings, the "meditations" as it were, that grow from the process of keeping the journal. The process becomes an important factor in the production of Merton's public writings. It was in this way that Merton's "meditations" or *"pensées"* reached the world. In them we see the result and the distillation of the quadrille in his head, but the writings, mostly confident and assured, contain few hints of the "dancing" that produced them. The publication of the "private journal" does let us see how the dance in his head led to these writings, but the writings are not final answers – for him or for us. The dancing goes on. In one essay written in this period he invites us to join it. At the end of "Message to Poets," after warning against the dangers of technology, collective ideas, banality, and abstraction, Merton says to his readers: "Come, dervishes: here is the water of life. Dance in it." He answered his own invitation and he himself, the old man, despite "smashing," never stopped dancing. His journal lets us watch Merton dancing "in the water of life."

This journal was edited from four sources. First is the large ledger-type journal Merton dated "August 1963–End 1965," which comprises most of the volume. Second, "Reading Notebook #14" contained Merton's original account of the visit to meet D. T. Suzuki in June 1964 (I surmise that he did not take the larger journal to New York with him); this account was integrated with the shorter account in the larger journal. Third, the original, shorter, and angrier version of "Day of a Stranger," which had been requested as a "journal-like description of a typical day in his life," is inserted as he dated it: "Sometime in May 1965." Finally, the 1965 entries from "Working Notebook #17," called by Merton "Some Personal Notes, End 1965–Beginning 1966," are included as an appendix. Merton himself edited and shortened the larger journal for publication and readers will find sections of *Vow of Conversation* contained within this volume. Sections in Latin, French, Spanish, and German, mostly very short, are followed by English translations, some of them Merton's own. Complete names of people mentioned by Merton are given; books he was reading and his own writings are identified in the text. Footnotes have been kept to a minimum.

PART I

Living as a Part-time Solitary

August 1963–June 1964

August 3, 1963

From a prayer of Ambrose Autpert? ascribed to St. Anselm.

Intret Spiritus tuus in cor meum qui sonet ibi sine sono et sine strepitu verborum loquatur omnem veritatem tantorum mysteriorum (sc. missae). . . . Rogo te Domine per ipsum sacrosancti mysterium corporis et sanguinis tui, quo quotidie in Ecclesia tua pascimur et potamur, abluimur et sanctificamur, atque unius summaeque divinitatis participes efficimur, da mihi virtutes tuas sanctas quibus repletus bona conscientia ad altare tuum accedam ita ut haec caelestia sacramenta efficiantur mihi salus et vita. [Let your Spirit, who sings without sound and speaks without the clamor of words, bring every truth of such mysteries (i.e., of the Mass) into my heart. . . . I ask you, Lord, through the mystery of your most blessed body and blood, which daily we eat, drink, are washed and sanctified in your church, and by which we are made participants in your one and highest divinity, give to me your holy virtues by which, filled with a good conscience, I might approach your altar in good conscience so that these holy sacraments might bring to me salvation and life.]

Finished St. Anselm's dialogue *De Libero Arbitrio* today with great enjoyment. Clarity and strength of his dialectic. I have the sense that there is much more below the surface: a whole consistent doctrine and attitude in which this simple treatment of a *definition* is rooted. "*Potestas servandi rectitudinem voluntatis propter ipsam rectitudinem.*" ["The power of preserving the rectitude of the will on account of rectitude itself."]

August 4, 1963. Day of Recollection

Hot day, but dry and with breeze in the afternoon. Pleasant enough in the novitiate chapel.

I am wondering if I can perhaps begin to be more detached from my existence. Or to think of it, better to accept the unthinkable notion of it not-being. How insufficient are conventional meditations on death! I have the *responsum mortis* [answer of death] in me, and have spontaneously been aware of death as a kind of presence several times today.

Distinguish this from death-wish and frustration. It is at once an acceptance of not existing any longer (whenever I shall cease to exist in this state I am in) and a full acknowledgment of the good of existence and of life. In reality, it is the acceptance of a higher, inconceivable mode of life entirely beyond our own control and volition, in which all is gift. To resign oneself to not being what one knows in order to receive a totally unknown being from a totally unknown source and in that source.

My solitude is very real now, though I have more to do with other people than at any time in my life. I see the full irrelevance of so much useless communication, and have nothing to say – though I can speak and say nothing since it is expected of me.

What is said to reassure my novices is perhaps "nothing" but it has its meaning. They need not the words, but the voice, and the warmth of a heart in it. This is not nothing.

[R. J. Zwi] Werblowsky was here – professor from the Hebrew University in Jerusalem who has been teaching at Brown. Zalman Schachter sent him down. Had a lively and interesting visit. I wanted him to speak to the novices on Hassidism; he preferred to speak on St. John of the Cross. Used material from an article he has written in Hebrew for *festschrift* for some savant attracted to Cabalism. I thought this talk very good, very clear, insisting on the existential reality of faith as total emptiness and night. It was a very serious and valuable talk and has had a deep effect, at least on me, if only to remind me of my own center, which I have ignored more or less, that is, I have forgotten its supreme reality and confused it with lesser realities. Some complained of his theology, but though he did not dot all the "i"s and cross all the "t"s his talks were very good. He does not think much of Hassidism, but likes Bahya ibn Pakuda and says he will send *The Duties of Hearts.*

From an old *Dieu vivant luminaire:* it is clear that one must choose between people like [Emmanuel] Mounier and people like [Renato] Mori and [Louis] Massignon; between the progressives and optimists, à la [Pierre] Teilhard de Chardin, and the eschatologists. You can't be both. You can't be in every way fashionable. And presently the eschatological view is the least fashionable. But it is more my view and my choice.

"La solution des problèmes humains . . . diffère du tout au tout selon que l'homme se croit appelé à construire l'univers et lui-même par ses propres forces – même si cette tâche s'accomplit en nom du Christ – ou qu'il doit préparer par la souffrance, le sacrifice et l'adoration à recevoir de la plénitude de l'Esprit une 'terre

nouvelle' et de 'nouveaux cieux.' La parole du théologien ou du philosophe chrétien ne peut avoir d'efficacité réelle que si elle s'enracine profondément dans l'humilité de son début intime pour la sainteté." ["The solution to human problems . . . differs completely according as the man who believes himself called to construct the universe and himself through his own resources – even if this task comes to pass in the name of Christ – we whom He must prepare through suffering, sacrifice and adoration to receive from the fullness of the Spirit a 'new earth' and a 'new heaven.' The word of the theologian or of the Christian philosopher cannot have real effectiveness unless it takes root deeply in an attitude of humility from the beginning of his personal journey towards sanctity."]

August 9, 1963

Terribly busy yesterday. The whole morning went on a visit to the dentist (Joe Green) at Lebanon with Fathers Herbert and Bede and Brothers Giles and Pius. Felt that much was lost in the kind of time-wasting one gets into. Yet we had lunch with the Greens and that was nice of them, and I hope I was not too reticent. But really exhausted with talking. Would have much preferred a silent morning and some work. Then I would have been fresher for the afternoon – A[rthur] M[acDonald] Allchin from Pusey House at Oxford [University] being here. I like him and he has pleasant and interesting things to say and is a nice person very interested in monasticism. (I like his book on Anglican monasticism.)

He likes our *Monastic Studies*. Talks of Athos which he visited last year – its real decadence. Likes what he has seen of America. Was at the Faith and Order Conference at Montreal. Thinks American Protestant theology is lovely, which it is.

I am reading St. Anselm's *De Veritate* and the delight of the book is mysterious, clear, contemplative. It is very simple, deceptively so, and one is tempted to think he is arbitrary with his *debere esse* [ought to be] until one sees that the root is *esse* [to be] and not *debere* [ought (to be)], or that it is both, and he traces them both to the *esse* [being] of God which is the *debere esse* of everything else. The idea of *debere – devoir –* debt has been so wrung out and exhausted and so divorced from *esse* that for us it is a tired authoritarian command that has nothing to say but "You must because you must." Anselm is saying "You must because you are, and being what you are you must say what you are, by being and action, and whether you like it or not you must say you are in God and from Him and for Him, and for no other!"

My poem on the children of Birmingham is in the *Saturday Review* this week. (Dan W[alsh] showed it to me.) The article on the Black Revolution is (unofficially) approved by censors but may be stopped by [the Abbot] General. Dan Berrigan will be in the march on Washington with the Negroes.

August 10, 1963. St. Lawrence

Grey day, misty, cooler. After the Night Office, black veils of mist blowing over the middle cornfields and all the hills visible.

Allchin leaves today. I enjoyed his visit, and especially his dear sweet Anglican spirituality, orthodoxy, etc. He has got me interested in reading some of the Anglican divines, and this is important. I am also thinking of [John Henry Cardinal] Newman. What is important is the recognition of the deep worth of Anglican writings and of the elements of mysticism which Anglicans themselves ignore. He points to [Richard] Hooker on the Incarnation as a theological source. In a broader way it was good to have some of the light of Oxford here. He represents what seems to me to be the most excellent in the English universities, a breadth, a simplicity, a sane traditionalism, a purity of vision and an originality that can only be combined in a really mature and developed culture. (Other side of this coin is the Profumo case!) I keep thinking of the broad court of St. John's College at Oxford (if I had gone to Oxford I should really have gone there). It would be a joy to go to Oxford and stay at Pusey House: but immensely complicated. Not too complicated to *think* of, however.

Translated a talk of Dom Adrien Nocent of Maredsous [Abbey, France] in chapter this morning. Especially on Liturgy of the word as announcement and response very good ideas. But if this just means that on top of everything else we now *sing* the lessons and responsories of Vigils, it becomes meaningless. The longer and more difficult the offices are, the less it is possible to experience them as a dialogue with God. And one falls back into the interminable and indifferent performances that have killed Liturgy, and forced people into abstractionism and "validism" in order to make the whole thing bearable, if not comprehensible.

Have borrowed [Augustine] Baker's *Life* of Dame Gertrude More [*The Inner Life and the Writings of Dame Gertrude More*, 1910] from Stanbrook [Abbey] and like it very much. An important and original book.

August 13, 1963

Deus, qui omnipotentiam tuam parcendo maxime et miserando manifestas . . .
[God, who shows your almighty power especially in pardoning and showing mercy . . .] One of the most beautiful collects of the year, for this week
(today a final day after Tenth Sunday Post Pentecost).

Storms in the night – uninterrupted lightning for a long time and heavy
rain.

In the refectory last night was troubled by some things said about the
paintings in Egyptian tombs – the serenity and sanity of Egyptian life. Troubled by the fact that, after all this, serenity was not enough. The people of
God had to be chosen and *called* out of it. To a much less serene and sane life
in the Desert! And we have grown to equate Egypt with "iniquity," wicked-
ness, defilement. The good pagan life: are we not allowed to love it! Now we
try to by baptizing it. If we would get back to it, with divine blessing, how
happy we would be! Yet is the American concept of life so different? The
concept may be like the Egyptian one in some ways. The happy, comfortable
life, serene, joyful, expansive but the reality does not come up to the reality
of life in Egypt. There was, in all evidence, *real* earthly happiness in that
peaceful land, at least in the best dynasties, whenever they were!!

The Desert Fathers tried to resist this, turn it inside out, experience the
happy Egyptian past in themselves as diabolical and who is to say they were
altogether wrong? Yes – there is also the idea of stealing the gold of Egypt
. . . eating your cake and having it. K[arl] Barth said that if you try to steal
the gold of Egypt you simply take over the *idols* of Egypt. According to
Dom Burkhard [Neunheuser], who used to converse with him at Mari-
alaach [Abbey].

Dom Burkhard Neunheuser was here with Dom Adrien Nocent. Much
conversation and though I am tired of it, it is good for me. Both are very *sym-
pathique*. Dom B. at the hermitage yesterday with a small group, talking of
[Hans Urs] Von Balthasar, [Hans] Küng, Barth, etc. And of people who have
left the Benedictines to marry. A problem – the same for everyone. The
question of vows. I am for greater flexibility – a very long period under temporary vows, renewable every three years, and solemn vows only after about
fifteen years (normally – perhaps less, perhaps more). May write this out and
send to Paul Philippe,[1] who will be in Cincinnati at the end of the month.

---

[1] Paul Philippe, O.P., Titular Archbishop of Heracleopolis, was Secretary of the Vatican's
Sacred Congregation for the Doctrine of the Faith.

Question of Masses – much discussion with Dom N. and Dom B. They talk much of concelebration and of priests communicating at conventual Mass. And of not celebrating private masses daily or even frequently. There is something to be said for this. The important thing, however, is liberty for each one to follow legitimate aspirations. Naturally this whole trend is strenuously opposed by Dom James[2] and also, I understand by Archbishop Paul Philippe.

August 14, 1963

Proofs for *Emblems of a Season of Fury* have come in. The business with Macmillan is settled. They are returning the manuscript of *Prayer as Worship and Experience*. And the book (which I will not now release to anyone for publication) can be marked off as "experience." Experience of how little I am able to contend with a corporation intent on making money out of my books and my name – or two of them at once. Experience of Bob Giroux,[3] his reticences, suspicions, and specialized interpretations of my own statements – which he has now been scrutinizing from the point of view of a court of law, finding much that was not meant – and intent on blaming me over and over. It is a tiresome business, and finishing out the work for which I have contracted is probably not going to be fun.

Experience too of the fact that my tendency to make statements that are personal, impressionistic and subjective may be all very nice in a book for him to sell, but not in a letter to a rival publisher – or in the context of lawyers and lawsuits. In a word, he does not like to see himself through the eyes of one of his authors. And so he has to see me as a rogue, at times, and sees reasons why I should be declared so objectively. I am not too convinced by all this – and yet there does arise the significance of "objective" statements arrived at in lawsuits. They may not be "true" but there is a certain limited finality about them, and they are resolved and they have nothing to do with anybody's personal image of himself (unless a person is himself endowed with a juridical image). The truth of law and the truth of poetry. These are not neighbors.

I hope the affair is over, and it seems to me I have done the best I could to repair my mistakes.

---

[2] Dom James Fox was at this time abbot of Gethsemani.
[3] Merton's longtime friend and editor.

August 15, 1963

Cool. Cows lowing in the mist. Long but rich night office. *Maria optimam partem elegit.* [Mary has chosen the better part.] *Love* for the great responsories.

A seventeenth-century Carmelite attacked [Jean] Mabillon, [Thierry] Ruinart, etc. for their criterion of historical judgment.[4] They asserted that long familiarity with charters and manuscripts gave one a quasi-instinctive "taste" by which one could detect fabrications and falsifications. This, said the critic, was pure subjectivism. And the "objectivity" to which he appealed was that of accepted norms. What had always been regarded as genuine was genuine, because this was the tradition of the church and the work of God. So too the appeal to "law" sometimes.

Yet who can guarantee that he has developed the right "instinctive" taste for the real? So the accepted view cannot be disregarded. But it need not be blindly received as final.

August 16, 1963

A lovely cool, dazzling bright afternoon yesterday. Blue sky, clouds, silence, and the immense sunlit sweep of St. Malachy's field. I found a mossy turf under pines in that little island of woods, along which the Lespedeza hedge we planted ten or fifteen years ago is still growing. And yesterday it was blooming with delicate, heather-like purple blossoms and bees were busy in them.

An entirely beautiful, transfigured moment of love for God and the need for complete confidence in Him in everything, without reserve, even when almost nothing can be understood. A sense of the continuity of grace in my life and an equal sense of the stupidity and baseness of the infidelities which have threatened to break that continuity. How can I be so cheap and foolish as to trifle with anything so precious? The answer is that I grow dull and stupid and turn in false directions, without light, very often without interest and without real desire, out of a kind of boredom and animal folly, caught in some idiot social situation. It is usually a matter of senseless talking, senseless conduct and vain behavior, coming from my shyness and desperation at being in a bind I cannot cope with – and if there is drink handy I drink it, and talk more foolishly. This of course is rare – I was thinking of visits of

4 Jean Mabillon (1632–1707), French Maurist, partially in conjunction with Thierry Ruinart (1657–1709), laid the foundation for a scientific approach to documentary criticism. He is considered the founder of the twin sciences of paleography and diplomatics.

Father John of the Cross [Wasserman]'s people (other side of the field) when I was not true to myself. With him I suppose I rarely was. And now where is he?

[Romano] Guardini, speaking of [Jean Pierre de] Caussade, praises his clarity and adds that he is sometimes too clear – so clear as to endanger our religious integrity by short circuiting it. For his writings presuppose the order of convent life a bit.

"*On ne prend même pas en considération la possibilité que cet ordre puisse être lui-même en désordre, et qu'il puisse résulter de là un conflit que le concept d'obéissance ne suffit plus à régler.*" ["We do not even take into consideration the possibility that order could itself be in disorder, and that it could result in a conflict here in which the concept of obedience is no longer sufficient to apply."]

This is partly true. But Caussade does not have recourse only to obedience, and abandonment is not only more all-embracing but also can be more positive and creative than obedience. Obedience – acceptance of order and system. Abandonment – beyond system – direct contact with divine freedom.

"*La solitude d'un chrétien dans un monde détaché de l'ordre chrétien est un fait nouveau et décisif dont on ne rend pas suffisament compte, si l'on se contente de considérer ce monde comme étant dans l'erreur et d'ériger comme idéal l'état intérieur . . .*" ["The solitude of a Christian in a world detached from Christian order is a new and decisive reality to which we do not pay sufficient attention, if we are content to consider this world as being in error and to erect as ideal the interior state . . ."] In this context Caussade assumes the greatest importance. Frees man from dependence on a structure which is no longer there – to be a Christian *anyway*.

The responsibility of the individual called by what does not yet exist and called to help it exist in, through, and by a present dislocation of Christian life!!

Feast of the enigmatic Saint Bernard – whom we "know" so well that we do not know him at all. That is, in the Order we are satisfied with a very rudimentary image of him (not yet a decent ikon!) or, at best, with an aspect of him. I am unable to resist the brilliance of his writing, especially the early treatises – I do not mean his rhetoric, which I can very easily resist. I prefer the dialectic of Anselm. The personality of Bernard is, to me, difficult and unappealing. Yet I admit I have never really known him and agree with [Michael David] Knowles that it is very difficult to know B.

Reading William Owen Chadwick's excellent essay *From Bossuet to Newman* – idea of doctrinal development. Disturbed by the realization that since the late Middle Ages the Church has apparently lost her power of really creative assimilation (of non-Christian cultural values) and has on the contrary tended to let heresy be assimilated by secular forces. Reasons for this? And what does it mean?

A very grim portent.

Again – the pompous absurdity of Pontifical Mass. I don't usually even look at the sanctuary. Happened to glance at the throne, and the Abbot standing on his platform a little above the general melée – I saw his hands and his white gloves. What for? Along with all the other superfluities, the meaninglessness of white gloves and a ring (outside the glove of course).

There are many like myself in the community. The Abbot claims he loves simplicity, but in fact these masses are contrived largely because he wants them – along with Dom Vital[5] and the others who like a display, and much singing.

The hermitage – is a shame (I discover now) because I have been and continue to be tempted to *justify* it. Have a certain uneasiness about it. Better I come to accept it as "unjustified" (and not require justification: it simply is). Yet the mere woods, out "there" – anywhere – free – are "better" – they do not involve thought or attach moralizing explanations to themselves. Same thing about the community, the desperate, maddening obsession with explanation, formulation, declaration, justifying our excellence, infallibly defining our own rightness. What a disgrace! It is what makes me livid every morning in chapter. To all this I must obviously say "no" – and it is a virtuous "irresignation." Not a rebellion. At the same time I realize that my own struggle on this point is important for the integrity of others, and must be accepted especially for their sake.

During Mass (in novitiate chapel) silence, peace, "renunciation" of my own being, wanting only Him to be who is – and the rest in relation to Him.

Thanksgiving very quiet and peaceful, with a little bird I had not noticed before singing, clearly, definitely, seven or eight times (at wide intervals). Re-re-re-mi-mi-do. And with what beautiful finality, as if those three notes contained and summed up all the melodies in the world.

---

[5] Dom Vital Klinski was former abbot of Achel Abbey, Belgium, and monk of Gethsemani since 1927.

August 23, 1963

Yesterday was in some ways a rough day.

Discovery of what is apparently the key to the trouble over the Macmillan contract. A letter from Bob Giroux explicitly refusing to release me from the contract never reached me. Or was the letter really written? Was it introduced into the file after the trouble got to the point of a lawsuit, in order to cover Giroux himself? I don't know. But the whole thing was disturbing to me either way: the sense of helplessness in facing manipulations over which I can exercise no rational influence.

However, I had a good morning (yesterday) working on Baker's life of Dame Gertrude More – a very wise and beautiful book, and strikingly original. A fine, free, courageous spirituality, so unlike the hidebound continental manuals of piety. And really "monastic."

An intuition that may lead somewhere. Though the liberty of St. Anselm and the liberty of [Jean-Paul] Sartre seem poles apart, they may actually have a great deal in common. Both seek to transcend mere choice of predetermined objects – choice based on pragmatic offers of "happiness" in this or that – the choice which regards the fulfillment of the will as lying in something outside itself. For Anselm's *"justitia"* ["justice"] is *rectitudo propter se servata* [rectitude properly services itself] and this rectitude is in the will itself – and in God inviting the will to God and fulfilling the inner potentialities of the free being – making that being truly free. Thus for both Sartre and Anselm, the exercise of true freedom is demanded for a being to become what it *is*. Abdication of this freedom, and use of the will only for *commodum*, convenience, "happiness" – is the mark of the *salaud* (of the *salaud* [sloven] of Sartre and the *insipiens* [fool] of Anselm who makes a trifling and uncommitted use of concepts). However, Sartre is the freedom of Anselm with a short circuit, turned back upon itself in a ruined narcissism that cannot be anything other than nausea. *Nausée* [nausea] is then Sartre's *"rectitudo propter se"* without any root in being.

Both Anselm and Sartre have this in common. They are concerned with *"une morale de l'authenticité"* ["a morale of authenticity"]. But the great difference comes in that for A. the authentic use of freedom is measured by God's love, and for Sartre it is measured by nothing but the act itself. The great question is then how one looks at God's love. Not as an objective and exterior force, but as His indwelling Spirit. It is this that Sartre needs to be delivered from, the demon of his own meaninglessness. A. considers the divine will not so much an external force, as an inner ontological necessity in man made in God's image. (He can only be himself in serving God.)

August 26, 1963

Hot, damp days, though today was damp and cool.

Yesterday, my feast [the Feast of St. Louis of France], was a little nerve racking, as usual, but it was good. And I am really happy to be loved by the monks, and to love them, in an offhand and I think genuine way. The main thing is that I trust them and respect them, quite sincerely, and this they appreciate, and because of their appreciation I love them very much, though there is no need to go around making speeches about it. They gave me a wacky, funny card, with a cartoon of me, etc., etc.

Walked in the heat, yesterday, stood under big trees by St. Malachy's field and waited for air. But it was pleasant.

Dom Bede Griffiths was here – very good, ascetic, thin, quiet man. His ashram [Kurisumala in Kerala, India] sounds very genuine and very good. The Syro-Malabar rite (he said a Mass in Chapter for the Brothers) seemed to me to be magnificent liturgy. What must the real Mass be, with all the responses and bells! The texts were superb. Most serious and eschatological.

I do not know if I am well or not. Or what the numbness in my left arm means (it is always going to sleep). But in my case, health or sickness, or whatever else comes: I ask only to please God in life and in death, and for the rest there is precious little to think or worry about.

Tried to get some of my unfinished work together. With revision of several essays, etc. And revision of *The Inner Experience*. I have still four or five books on hand, not counting *Prayer as Worship [and Experience]*, etc.

August 28, 1963. St. Augustine

Altogether too many visitors this month. Not all of them mine, but I was involved in too many conferences, conversations, etc. Certainly not only for myself, and I must consider first of all the good of others. But also my own. Too much talking is simply futile, even though many good things are said, and good friendships are made. Yet I do not like to become intransigent and refuse absolutely. Yet I must refuse more (although I refuse much already).

One I did not see was Mrs. [Jeanne Cato] Nooijen, who sent her thesis on [Léon] Bloy, with a letter of mine photostatted in appendix [*A Study of Bloy*, 1963]. And on the back of Dorothy Day's new book [*Loaves and Fishes*, 1963] another letter of mine. I am glad to help, but – too many letters. My silence would really be of greater value to all these people, to the causes and to myself. Yet always there seems to be a reason to give in, and it seems to be, in each case, pleasing to God. But how do I know?

Offered the Mass of this Feast for all those in the great (Negro) march on Washington today. Dan and Phil Berrigan are in it. And for racial justice. For understanding and right actions.

Last two days – working on Baker. His ideas on examination of conscience.

Edmund Wilson's book *Apology to the Iroquois* is the kind of thing that moves me very deeply, more deeply than anything perhaps except the Old Testament Prophets. And in the same kind of way: sense of an inscrutable and very important mystery, the judgment of the white race and of "Christendom" by its acts and insensitivities. The centuries of blind willful cruelty and greed. The Iroquois have despaired of the whites almost as the Black Muslims have!!

August 31, 1963

August ending beautifully – bright days, relatively cool. Wonderful vista opened up at the end of the novitiate garden where I got Father Gerard to cut down the walnut tree that was doing poorly and hiding the valley, woods and knobs into the bargain. Now a problem – the young beech tree that I put there myself. I suppose I must have the sense to transplant it.

Some annoyances, but they hardly matter. Bulldozer on that dam built ten years ago across the road, and now beginning to fall apart. A lot of banging in the new waterworks. I think all the mosquitoes are coming from the new reservoir – never so many in the dormitory as this year! An awful lot of idiot letters. And so on.

September 1, 1963. Day of Recollection

Tu ipse elementer dispone me et omnes cogitatus et actus meos in beneplacito tuo, ut fiat a me et in me et de me tua semper sola voluntas. [Do you yourself in kindness dispose of me, my thoughts and actions, according to your good pleasure, so that your will may always be done by me and in me and concerning me.] *(St. Anselm, Orationes 1)*

September 2, 1963

After the Night Office – cool, and dark – mist on the low bottoms, a glow of red in the east, still a long way from dawn, and small, clear purple clouds in the glow. Sirius shining through the girders of the water tower and high over the building a star travels east – no sound of a plane, perhaps it is some spaceship.

September 3, 1963

News has come through about the great civil rights demonstration in Washington last week. It was impressive, orderly and successful. (Though hard to say precisely how.) The best thing about it seems to be the consolidation of the best Negro leadership. (Martin Luther King, etc.) The night before the march, W. E. B. Du Bois died in Ghana. He had recently become a Communist, which is sad. He felt that capitalism had no way of exorcising its inner contradictions – and there may be some truth in that.

[Robert Charles] Zaehner's new book, *Matter and Spirit*, is an attempted synthesis of Marxist Christianity with the help of Teilhard de Chardin. So far I am not sure I am impressed.

Today has been hot, stuffy, grey. Now it is at last beginning to rain lightly. My left shoulder hurts. My left arm keeps going to sleep. Have briefly reworked most of the rather fatuous manuscript on *Art and Worship*. It is perhaps a waste of time, but I don't like to leave it unfinished. However, if it comes to collecting more pictures, I don't see how it is possible. The whole question of illustrations is very muddled. There is no use in getting into another silly mess with Farrar, Straus. I don't know what I mean to do.

September 8, 1963

For several days now I have been having continuous pain, often quite severe, in my left shoulder and arm. The doctors from Georgia, who were here on this project, said it was not heart. No one is quite sure yet what it is. Heat pad does not help much. A couple of times I have sat in the sun. Aspirin makes me sick at my stomach. I am very tired.

Brother Denis (Phillips) made profession today and a postulant entered. (We sent away two others who were supposed to enter with him.) Consoled by Brother Denis' profession. I am fond of him and pleased with his simplicity and rectitude. Certainly one of the best novices I have had.

Still reading, or trying to read, St. Anselm, Augustine Baker, Edmund Wilson on the Iroquois.

Ulfert Wilke was here and gave me his fabulously good book of recent "calligraphies." Yesterday Father Bernard Häring came to see me, and it turned out that the reason was my writing about peace. He thought it was important for this to continue and said he would speak to the General about it. He said I should be writing about peace to make reparation for St. Bernard's preaching of crusades – and that if a monk could preach a crusade then a monk could certainly be allowed to write about peace. Needless to say I agree.

I hear Dom Walter [Helmstetter] is resigning as Abbot of the Genesee and coming back here. He is younger than I – we were novices together.

September 10, 1963

One of the things St. Anselm has to say to the modern age is that the *potestas peccandi* – the "power" to sin – is not a "power" and not an expression of freedom, nor does it even enter into the deprivation of freedom. This is the crux of the matter in comparing Anselm with Sartre. The point is that Sartre is groping for the kind of rectitude St. Anselm makes essential to freedom. The problem: to find a notion of sin that is not devout and meaningless, and which can be relevant to an existentialist! Not as hard as all that, when you approach it from the point of view of freedom and so sin as a capitulation, a renunciation of freedom and an abdication of personality – not its affirmation. It is in rectitude that the will finds its natural and perfect self-determination. To be redeemed by Christ is then to be freed from all servitude – but to be redeemed by a creature would have inspired servitude. We are redeemed by the obedience of Christ which is not an *obedientia describendi vitam* [an obedience describing life] but an *obedientia servandi justitiam* [an obedience which preserves justice] (i.e., of full liberty).

My shoulder is a little better today, but I am to go to Louisville tomorrow and see a doctor about it.

Spent an hour or more on Baker's *Inner Life of Dame Gertrude* carefully reading the chapters on "Divine Inspiration" (or part of them). I can see clearly how much I have failed in this attention where my active life is concerned – especially in my eagerness to publish, to make contacts, to spread messages. How wrong I have been! No matter how good the cause may be, I realize that my own silence and interior life come first, no matter how much anyone may say, no matter how good the results may appear to be. True, there is no essential conflict between interior prayer and exterior action: but more interior prayer is God's will for me and not so much exterior action. If I try to obey – and do not succeed in everything, that is another matter.

September 19, 1963

I have been in St. Joseph's Infirmary for a week with a cervical disk, and other problems, arthritis, etc. There has been some permanent injury to the vertebrae of my neck, but apparently I can escape an operation. I hope so.

Have had a certain amount of pain, especially at night. Daytime – lying in traction or going for massage – lately as I get better I can sit up and read.

Last Sunday was a terrible day in the South. A church was bombed in Birmingham and four Negro children were killed, and later two other Negroes were murdered in "rioting." It now seems that the racists in the deep South are trying to provoke violence so as to not have a general slaughter. It is quite evident that this was intended to provoke violent reactions. The Governor [George Wallace] seems to be expecting it with eagerness – rushing troops to the scene, etc. As if it had all been planned! And the poor people who are made to suffer from all this. It is utterly sickening and tragic. It is to me an awful symptom of the emptiness, nihilism and confusion of so much of American society.

We are perhaps going to have to face the same kind of decisions so many failed to face in Nazi Germany! What an awful and ironic commentary on our claims to be the chief apostle of democracy and freedom in the world!

In the hospital there were quite a few Negro nurses and tray-girls and I am happy to see them. They are lovely people. In Louisville we are better off. It is the best city in the south, for integration.

September 20, 1963

Still in hospital. Slow improvement. Effects of the disk still very noticeable in the left arm.

I have been able to do a lot of reading. Some on Barth's view of St. Anselm (very penetrating explanation of Anselm's religious sense of God in "the argument").

Wasted my time reading Morris West's *Shoes of the Fisherman*. Superficial and naive. A Ukranian Pope falls in love with Teilhard de Chardin! They talk earnestly. Teilhard de Chardin says: "You know, Holy Father, I think we are no longer reaching people!!" etc. Actually, this book is a nonentity. A pious, baseless hope for a renewal that would be comprehensible to *Time* magazine, and which indeed has already been dreamed of by it. Is this the best the Church can hope for? This folksy myth with its soap opera characters and its changes that change nothing. Here is the kind of prophecy that glorifies the status quo, and works only for a little glory in the Vatican.

Sartre's *Literature and Existentialism* on the other hand is powerful and convincing, though his historical synopsis is contrived and pontifical as are his pseudo-marxist conclusions.

Iris Origo's life of [Giacomo] Leopardi [*Leopardi: A Study in Solitude*, 1935] was a fascinating discovery (not new!). Leopardi is one of the few

Romantics I really like. Victor Hammer wants me to translate a few of his poems.

Finally – [Yevgeny] Yevtushenko's autobiography [*A Precocious Autobiography*, 1963]. Unquestionably good, lively, powerful. Here is *real* newness of life. Wonderfully encouraging in its sincerity. A powerfully moving description of the publication of *"Babi Yar"* in the *Literary Gazette* with the typesetter offering him vodka.

Some reflections – after recollection this evening.

1. I am going to be slowed down by this sickness. There is a permanent injury in the vertebrae of my neck, besides this disk. My arm is still very stiff and sore in spite of improvement. I will not be able to do a very great deal of writing and will have to be conservative in projects with the novices.

2. On writing and contacts:

I think it important to stick to – poetry, translations of poetry, contacts with poets especially in Latin America – not only [Ernesto] Cardenal, [Pablo Antonio] Cuadra, etc. but especially those like [Cintio] Vitier – also perhaps [Miguel] Grinberg and perhaps even *El Corno Emplumado* [a journal published in Mexico City].

Monastic articles and essays – but not an unlimited number of revisions.

My own creative work, whatever that may be.

3. For the rest the most important thing is the deepening of my grasp on spiritual reality. The renunciation of self in quest of freedom. More complete submission to the Spirit. In this I feel far from having begun to do what may be asked of me, and the final perspectives (if any) have not yet been opened up. I so easily let myself be bogged down in the "accepted" and the status quo – perhaps even in looking for futile reassurances from others, not explicit, but still gestures of acceptance. I am still too involved in the trivialities of my "place" and surroundings. Yet this must obviously be accepted, but I have not yet managed to do it rightly.

4. Cut down on the more superficial type of ecumenical contacts and especially on time-consuming palaver, and many visits.

September 23, 1963

Getting better.

Yesterday, sixteenth Sunday after Pentecost, I said Mass for the children killed in Birmingham, announced it to the few nuns and nurses and workers for the hospital who were in chapel and applied a few words from the Gospel to the situation.

The unreal enormous breakfast in the priests' dining room, and after that the banality of the Sunday paper and the far worse banality of *Our Sunday Visitor*.

In contrast I skimmed through Sartre's *Age of Reason* which at first (the other day) I had decided not to read at all beyond the first few chapters. But it is an important and well-written novel, and the theme is inescapable: the question of giving one's life a meaning by accepting the meaning of definitive commitments and not always evading them. It is a subtle and true study of the moral inanity of bourgeois life. But this is no guarantee that "socialist" life is any less inane. Quite the contrary! It is not social programs that give life the meaning it demands. The ending of the book is very effective.

In the evening Cliff Shaw and Mary Frances Dunne came and sang some songs in the Auditorium and I enjoyed it though my shoulder was hurting. Especially liked his arrangements of folk songs.

Last evening, too, in the quiet dusk, walked up and down under the trees along the fence of the deserted school playground, and looked at the last light of day beyond the school, over the low wooden houses. The sky suggested all the vast flat emptiness of the Ohio and Mississippi valleys! And trains going westward. A legendary America that sometimes comes back to enchant me though it no longer exists.

To accept my life in this context. Not to try to force Louisville into some arbitrary meaning or pattern. It is just that I am now in Louisville and last night I was under those trees, and I do not have to make sense out of it, still less to force it to "make sense," which would in fact be to insist on an illusion.

Two lighted planes, rising from Standiford Field [Louisville airport], came up low over the hospital and swung into the west.

Tonight at the grotto, after saying office, read some of the fabulous chapters of [St. Anselm's] *Cur Deus Homo?* (End of Book I, beginning of Book II). Now this is what seems to me to fit best the patterns of my life – that I should love such theological harmonies. Yet perhaps objectively this is less significant than I think. The *rectitudo* [rectitude] which I am capable of seeing in my life is far from being that which images in me the freedom of that divine mercy which is His *iustitia* [justice]. His fidelity to the reality which is His creation and reflects His hidden Being.

Proofs of Guigo's *Letter on the Solitary Life* reached me here from Stanbrook [Abbey] and they are handsome.

Read some new poems of Leopardi. He was at home with his *anima*.

September 28, 1963

Came home to the monastery Wednesday, shoulder hurting but glad to get back, especially to the novices. This is surely a much more rational life than anything to be found outside. Here at least there is a kind of order and tranquillity, and though there is plenty of noise, still in the novitiate everything is quiet and serene. And there is a real joy in the novices, a real peace. The goodness of the place is so evident – much more than ever before. It is certainly the best place in which for me to try to get well: I sleep in the infirmary when I need rest, have traction on the bed and a heat pad. Otherwise am in the novitiate. Not going to choir yet.

Sent some calligraphic abstractions to *El Corno Emplumado*.

Yesterday went up to the hermitage and sat on the grass and in the tall trees. The house quiet and cool. A few birds. And nothing. Who would want to live in any other way?

Today started conferences on Cîteaux and Cluny and was happy that everyone really seemed so glad to have me back. And probably they were so because they could see I was glad to be back with them.

September 30, 1963. St. Jerome

A magnificent line from Karl Barth. "Everyone who has to contend with unbelief should be advised that he ought not to take his own unbelief too seriously. Only faith is to be taken seriously, and if we have faith as a grain of mustard seed, that suffices for the devil to have lost his game" (*Dogmatics in Outline*, p. 20). What stupendous implications in that!

Always the old trouble, that the devil and our nature try to persuade us that before we can begin to believe we must be perfect in everything. Faith is not important as it is "in us." Our faith is "in God," and with even a very little of it, God is in us. "To believe is the freedom to trust in Him quite alone" (and to be independent of any other reliance) and to rely on Him in everything that concerns us.

October 2, 1963

Yesterday afternoon I finished a remarkable book [Martin Lings, *A Moslem Saint of the Twentieth Century*, 1961] – the biography of Shaikh Ahmad al'Alawi, who died in Algeria in 1934. One of the greatest religious figures of this century, a perfect example of the Sufi tradition in all its fullness and energy. This is one book that I want to read again. The excerpts from his writings are most impressive and I know I have not begun to appreciate their content.

Today (and all week) the frightful racket of the earth-moving machinery around the new waterworks. Impossible to stay in an infirmary room, and the novitiate is uninhabitable. Fortunately it is a brilliant sunny day and I can get to the woods.

I got off to a slow false start – a tape was played in the novitiate – some of Dan Berrigan's poems and then some Brahms. I was definitely in no mood for Brahms and seldom am. I could not listen receptively to the poems, though they were good. Yet there is something in the common run of Catholic feeling which is also ingrained in Dan Berrigan, a kind of facile and unserious eloquence . . . it spoils everything, though he's certainly trying to get away from it. But I was in no mood. And he's certainly by no means the worst offender. He just has that tone, which all have. The Irish Catholic pathos.

And I worked at the material I have to go over for the Liturgy book [*Seasons of Celebration*]. That too is unserious, it seems. What can I do with it? Is it even worth revising? I know I "must" try to revise it. Why? Because I expect myself to, and I am expected to. Is this honorable?

My shoulder still hurts. There has been small improvement in the week since I came back from the hospital, yet one thing I know: I am better off than if I had stayed in the hospital. I at least am not in a room where I can be trapped by visitors.

Read a little of the script of *Conjectures of a Guilty Bystander* which I dropped a couple of years ago (or perhaps in the spring of 1962). Most embarrassing. Such triviality and lack of perspective, though some parts (the least political) are lively. I begin dimly to be aware of my need to avoid (and very seriously!) this kind of trifling. One must be concerned about the events of one's time, yet there is a way of being so that is pure trifling, even though in some ways it may seem to be relatively serious, for the moment.

Yesterday there were eight woodpeckers at one time on the grass in front of the hermitage, playing and feeding – apparently at this season they feed very much on the ground. Six flew up when I went past now to get a T-shirt drying in the sun.

October 4, 1963

Two minds more different than those of Karl Barth and Frithjof Schuon would be hard to imagine, yet I am reading them both. Barth with his insistence on "God in the highest": completely unattainable by any human tradition and Schuon with his *philosophia humanis* [humanistic philosophy] (am reading his excellent book on Islam [*Comprendre l'Islam*, 1961]). True, Barth is a greater mind and there is an austere beauty in his Evangelical absolutism (closer to Islam than one would think!!) but there is another side to him – his love of St. Anselm and of Mozart.

Schuon naturally oversimplifies his "contrast" between Islam and Christianity. One has to know what he's really doing! I wrote this morning to Marco Pallis (who sent the Schuon book) about his *Way and the Mountain* (the other night I dreamed about the way).

I went to choir for High Mass today and my shoulder and arm are a lot better.

October 6, 1963

Dreamt last night of Italian Cathedrals (not real ones, dream ones). First I am with others of the community in a crowded Cathedral at "Siena." Confusion. I am trying to pray, turned toward a stonelike tabernacle beyond the crowd. (Is it the tabernacle?) I think of going to the "Shrine of St. Catherine." Then I am in another spacious well-lighted Cathedral "nearer home" and I am trying to "remember" the name of the city which should be very familiar. (Mantua?) I am struck and appeased by the airiness and spaciousness of the cathedral, the high shadowy vaults with paintings. A Nazareth nun walks through the cathedral and I am afraid she will recognize me. I pray. I cannot quite remember the name of the place where I am, a city perhaps beginning with "C"? Or "Mantua" perhaps? But no, Mantua is in the "North of Italy" and I am more in the center.

October 7, 1963

For some reason this day has been happy and rather exhilarated. Feast of the Holy Rosary, for one thing. Had a fairly good night's sleep, for another, and the shoulder seems to get better.

Read a good article on monastic silence by Dom Salmon in the *Mélanges Benedictines* (put out at St. Wandrille in 1947 – good!). Yesterday began Ida Göerres' diaries which are very lovely. She is one of the most alert and honest Catholic minds, not at all conformist, and very true. I am glad of course that she likes *The Sign of Jonas*.

Letter from Joel Orent with the usual about Hassidism, Yoga, etc., but this time also about a Susquehanna Indian "plot" to get back the land stolen from them.

Am planning to have enlargements made of some of my photos of Shakertown and Dant Station, and for some reason this is very satisfying.

Fine pages in Barth about God not being "pure power" in the sense of unbridled and arbitrary *potentia* – for this is really the power of nothing. God is *potestas*. The power of love and of truth, not an infinite and unbridled will purely arbitrary in itself and without responsibility to a creative plan. "Absolute power" is purely and simply the program of the devil. Strangely enough some excellent pages in Schuon's book on Islam say exactly the same thing.

The magnificent address of Pope Paul VI at the opening of the Second Session of the Council is being read in the refectory now. Certainly one of the greatest things of its kind, equal to that of Pope John last year and going beyond it (thanks to Pope John himself and to the first session).

October 8, 1963

Exciting news from France: not about de Gaulle or nuclear weapons, but about a man living in a village near Cordes in "my country," who has been discovering, unearthing and exploring the underground cultic labyrinths of the Albigenses. Places arranged in mysterious circles centered upon some town or hamlet, where the "perfect" fasted to death in the *indura* [endurance], where neophytes were initiated, where the fasters were cremated upon their death. The great and tantalizing thing about them: their silence. Even if what it hides may perhaps be trivial (will it ever be known?) the silence itself has its own question.

Other news: a "Freedom Now" party is being formed for positive political action by Negroes and it will undoubtedly become a force, and quickly so. May even seriously affect the 1964 presidential election. But in view of the non-entity and fatuousness of the existing two parties, there is no other way. This should have been done long ago.

Day after day bright and dry, hot afternoons over the bronze hills. We need rain to cut down the danger of fires.

Brother Denis is working this afternoon on the review of David Knowles' new book [*The Benedictines: A Digest for Moderns*, 1963] for *Monastic Studies*. This is something new and it gives joy to my heart. I hope he will do many such things well. Brother Basil has written good articles too, one of which is to appear in the *Collectanea [Cisterciensia]*.

When Schuon writes about Mohammed, one wonders to what extent he is surreptitiously using ideas suggested by the dogma of the Incarnation. For instance this: *"Mohammed c'est la forme humaine orientée vers l'Essence divine"* (127). *"C'est Mohammed qui incarné 'actuellement' et 'définitivement' la Révélation"* (p. 131). ["Mohammed is the human form directed towards the divine Essence," *Comprendre l'Islam*, p. 127. "It is Mohammed who 'actually' and 'definitively' incarnates Revelation," p. 131.]

October 9, 1963

Barth's concept of evil – that to which God has denied existence, and which we affirm by our choice. The world is grace, resting entirely in the word of grace which is creation. The world as the theater of God's glory (Calvin – from Augustine). Man as the witness of God's acts. "He has to express what he has seen."

With letters and additions to the "Black Revolution" (for the version to be in *Blackfriars* I hope!) I have typed about eight pages double spaced today and that is more than I have done since before going to the hospital – of course my arm is tired and sore, but it is evidently better. Letters to Dame Hildelith [Cumming, of Stanbrook Abbey] (lovely name) and Meg Randall of *El Corno [Emplumado]*.

Began [José María] Gironella's *One Million Dead*.

October 17, 1963

Still the same bright, parched, brilliant day without rain. The whole countryside is tinder. A grey squirrel runs very lightly over the dried leaves.

The last time I was in Louisville to see the Doctor I got two books on the Albigensians by Zoë Oldenbourg [*Destiny of Fire* and *Massacre at Montsegur: A History of the Albigensian Crusade*]. I have just finished *Massacre at Montsegur* – a deeply disturbing and moving book. One could find fault with it, in details, I suppose. But what would be the point? In general it is very honest and convincing and I think serious statement about the Church and the Inquisition, made without rancor, by someone whose real love for the Cathars makes her no doubt a bit partial.

Is there any getting away from the fact that the Dominicans invented the methods of the modern police state? The secret trial, with secret evidence, making it profitable for the witness to save his life by accusing as many other people (secretly) as possible – retaining his anonymity, etc. The denunciations that remain anonymous – same complaint today against the Holy Office. The clear fact that some very sincere, courageous and holy people went to their death convinced that the Church was acting as an instrument of Satan. Did they have, subjectively, really serious reasons to think otherwise? Is it not true that this has affected the attitude of whole generations and whole regions toward the Church? And all this in "my" country, near where I was born.

There are references to places near St. Antonin, Montauban, of course, one reference to Cordes, and one to the Penne that was near St. Antonin.

The Abbot is sore with me over the fact that Bellarmine College is starting a "Merton Collection." Today he is in town because Capt. Kinnarney died (aged 98).

In the novitiate the Zen (sand and rock) garden is coming along quite well and I think it will be quite meaningful – replacing the idiot tangle of flowers, weeds and trellises at that end of the terrace. It is a wonder we took so long to clear that place. But I wonder what will happen to the fill when we get a lot of rain.

October 22, 1963

Dryer than ever. Though the sky is clear and cloudless, a blue haze was drifting through the valley, probably from half a dozen fires in some other county. How long can we go without one here?

Zoë Oldenbourg's *passionate* religion, her admiration of the Cathars, it is beautiful and alluring, because there is truth in it. There is truth in everything. And she has cast her course on the particular, cold, burning, religious beauty which for her is a kind of quintessential protestantism, names of some of the rather richer and stronger elements that must have been in Catharism. How much is this beauty really stolen from the Church herself, and justified by a disturbed view of the cruelty and dishonesty of Catholics? The book *Destiny of Fire*, a novel, is far more powerful and "*bouleversant*" ["upsetting"] than the history. A fantastic religious Eros is at work there: this is her genius. It is her own self that is in the book, the beauty and fascination of her own religious aspirations. Really, there is all this passion – and nothing much after all of God: this sounds like an invidious judgment. Yet what you have is the beauty of religious passion in people hunted to death for heresy. And I have the feeling that God is very remote from that whole war, from either side of it. What mattered were the different kinds of passion. God was gone from it. Or no? But I don't want to have to fall into the usual Pharisaism that ends by saying – no matter how bad she looks, the Church is always right in the way the most corrupt of her clergy says she is, and so to obey them blindly is the only true test of love and faith! Sacrifice honor, desire, integrity, everything to plain orthodoxy!

A Franciscan from Louisville has come as a postulant. He is from one of the towns where Leander Perez, an excommunicated oil-man and politician, has been fighting school integration. Father M. says the south is full of evil – the murder of a Negro is not regarded as a sin – nor arson, bombing, etc. etc.

October 23, 1963

The rumor goes around that Maritain has been made a Cardinal. John Howard Griffin even declares he has seen this in print. The other day I finished a short preface to Julie Kernan's translation of Raïssa [Maritain]'s *Notes sur le Pater* [*Notes on the Lord's Prayer*, 1964].

Dead dry weather! The leaves tinkle like flakes of copper when the breeze passes over them. Haze. Wrote a little article on the Shakers at Pleasant Hill (yesterday) maybe for *Jubilee*.[6] Why were the Shakers first hated so much, then loved so much? Probably for their celibacy, or their mixture of celibacy and common life (both sexes in the same communities). And loved for their work? Not only that, for their angelic gentleness which, after all, was traced to their celibacy. Perhaps what underlay it all was the pioneers' panic at the thought of a kind of loss of virility involved in a man's living chastely with women and in a state of exaltation at that! "Unnatural!"

October 24, 1963

"To be a man means to be situated in God's presence as Jesus is, that is, to be a bearer of the wrath of God." Barth [from *Dogmatics in Outline*, 1949]. We need the shock of this sentence – which is of course immediately qualified by Barth himself. And the qualification is implicit, for Jesus bears that wrath and lives. But the wrath is on us!

And the Calvinist catechism: "What understandest thou by the little word 'suffered'?" "That He all the time of His life, but especially at the end thereof hath borne in body and soul the wrath of God against the whole human race." How powerful and how serious!

Catholic piety sees Christ suffering all His life, but in a different perspective. He is the bearer of all kinds of pains, but they are so to speak the pains of a person who has not been "struck," who is not under the wrath. They are quantitative, detailed, exquisite, etc. But the full enormity of sin is per-

---

6 "The Shakers," published in *Jubilee*, January 1964: 36–41.

haps not seen as well as here, for God seems to be pleased with this pain. No! It is His wrath!

And Barth's terrific chapter on Pilate. I think I will have to become a Christian. ("In this meeting of Jesus and Pilate everything is together that should be thought and said from the side of the Gospel regarding the realm of the *'polis'* ['city'].")

October 26, 1963

"One thing still holds, and only this one thing is really serious, that Jesus is the victor. A seriousness that would look back past this, like Lot's wife, is not Christian seriousness. It may be burning behind – and truly it is burning – but we have to look not at it but at the other fact, that we are visited and summoned to take seriously the victory of God's glory in this man Jesus and to be joyful in Him." *Karl Barth*

This is appropriate to what I was thinking about the grim and fearful seriousness with which Julien Green takes evil [in *Each in His Darkness*, 1961]. The fear that one's obsession with evil may be a sign of not being "of the elect." And Graham Greene too: in him evil is more serious than good. Certainly we tend to *experience* evil more than good – that divine good which is present to us in hope. But there is always the false Christian optimism which tries to "experience" the Kingdom in what is not the Kingdom. Nevertheless, the victory of Christ makes all joy possible even in the midst of evil, for what we experience as evil is no longer serious unless we insist on making it so for ourselves.

October 27, 1963

There! That seriousness again. Barth admits it: in the great pictures of the Last Judgment "one's glance remains fixed on those on the left!" But he also says that if we really want to understand the mystery of Christ's second coming we have to "repress certain pictures of the world judgment." And this is true (though "repress" is the wrong word). The real judgment is that our idea of left and right is not the true view, and that our hopes and fears, on the human level, have proved deceptive. (The visual imagination in Barth – like the Cathedrals. The odd and the humorous appears at the right moment.) "We (Christians) must not sit among them (non-Christians) like melancholy owls" [*Dogmatics in Outline*] (p. 132). "He that comes is He that previously offered Himself to the judgment of God." But this is what is not clear in Michelangelo's *Last Judgment*.

October 28, 1963. Saints Simon and Jude

The falling leaves, crowds of them, flying across the narrow novitiate lawn and the Zen garden (still unfinished – it needs the big rock). Last evening the sky was dark and it looked like rain, but they were only the "clouds without water" of Jude's epistle. There was, after supper, a momentary violent wind and a brief dust storm.

I have suddenly grasped the magnificent Chapter I.9 of *Cur Deus Homo?* [by St. Anselm]. Read it in the hospital and marked some of the right lines, but they had not struck deep. Here again, as in the *Proslogion*, Anselm's argument means little without an inner light that is spiritual rather than dialectical. Here it is a question of realizing that the Father did not drive the Son to death. Jesus was not "commanded to die" or "condemned to death" by the Father. He came into the world, was made man in order to love as man, to do all that was right. And to save His brothers. In doing "all justice," he comes to be condemned unjustly. He could justly have used His power to save Himself and to save man in some other way. He preferred quite spontaneously this way of saving man by the renunciation of power and undergoing death. The Father willed the salvation of man but left Jesus entirely free to specify the means. What is pleasing to the Father is not that the Son dies, but that He uses His will fully to choose what he deems best in saving man. Hence the Father's will is not that the Son suffer, but that He use His freedom as He pleases in order to save man. And Jesus, out of love for the Father, chooses the way of total renunciation of power. At the same time, the "will of the Father" is in fact the will of God, i.e., of the three divine Persons and so of the Word. Thus it is Christ's own will in so far as He is a divine Person. The will of God is then that the human will of Christ be free to specify by what means man is to be saved. And Christ, as man, elects to save man by the renunciation of power, by total poverty, annihilation and death since in this glory of the Father is manifest – the glory that leaves man free to choose, within the limits of truth. It is anything but blind and desperate subjection to an irreversible decree of death. And yet, nevertheless, Calvin's idea of Christ bearing all the "wrath of God" is also true. But that is another aspect.

Barth – believing in the Holy Ghost means, in fact, believing in man as "freely and actively participating in the work of God." "That this actually takes place is the work of the Holy Spirit, the work of God on earth which has its analogue in that hidden work of God, the outgoing of the Spirit from the Father and the Son . . . to take confidence in men for Christ's sake."

How can the idea of "Church" make any sense without this trust in man as capable of grace, capable of cooperation? Here's the real beginning of the idea of community. Individualism: the man hopes for himself alone, doubts or despairs of all others, or is indifferent to all others. "Few are chosen." Individualism is faith that there are a few individuals to be rescued from the general wreck. True community: hope in man. "All-Man." One in Christ with the dread that some may be lost, that individuals will fall out of the saved community, for whom there is hope because the Holy Spirit is powerful [enough] to work for all through all. The Christian way "is to hope for myself and for all others." And Barth is supposed to be one of those "Protestant individualists"? (Note hoping in all men is not by any means "hope in the human spirit," yet as for that spirit too "we must cherish it a little.")

October 29, 1963

A Baptist group from the seminary in Louisville were here yesterday.

Got a wonderful letter from Dame Hildelith at Stanbrook – about the little Guigo pamphlet[7] and other projects, but also the Swedish folk dances of the novices, and the strange moth they found, etc. Ruth Hollisey has entered that Benedictine convent at Ryde.

A meeting with the Junior choir monks yesterday, about their program and what is to be done. Father Flavian [Burns] is itching to put them into philosophy.

Again. Barth's bestiary. This time the Church is not a snail. "The Church runs like a herald to deliver the message. It's not a snail with a little house on its back and is so well off in it, that only now and then it sticks out its feelers and then thinks that 'the claim of publicity' has been satisfied . . ." *Dogmatics in Outline*, p. 147. Of the dog. Pilate is a dog. "How does Pilate come into the creed? . . . Like a dog into a nice room!" but the meanness is not toward Pilate but toward politics – the dog in the room is politics in the Church! Sometimes the Christian in the Church is like a bird in a cage, beating against the bars (trying to make the whole Gospel reduce itself to our own rite or our own preachments). "If you do not know this oppression, you have certainly not seen the real dynamic in this matter!!" (p. 147). But this invitation is to be patiently endured. We wait for the Kingdom "recognizing each other in longing and humility in the light of the divine humor" (148).

---

7 Merton translated *The Solitary Life: A Letter of Guigo*, published by Stanbrook Abbey Press, 1963.

It is clear and cool as if it had rained. But there has been no rain.

Ramparts [Vol. 2, Christmas 1963] came with my *Black Revolution* and Griffin's very moving dialogue with Father August Thompson – Negro pastor in a small Louisiana town (I met him here late one evening coming in from Louisville). New light on the South, again, and how impossible the situation really is. Actually it is quite a unique one for which new formulas must be sought and are being sought. But what will it avail? Whatever will happen if [Barry] Goldwater manages to get himself elected President in 1964!

Maniac letters from Joel Orent, the rabbi who went in for Tantrism, and whose most recent exploit is to have gone to receive communion at a New York Church – in a sort of dazed good faith! He is insane!

October 30, 1963

Parable of the Wedding Feast – an idea that some are called to the banquet, refuse and are replaced by others is given a cosmological significance by the Patristic idea of the fall of the angels and the replacement of the fallen angels by men. But the idea of the invitation to the wedding feast enters into the very structure of the universe, when looked at from this viewpoint!

New liturgies in the Juniorate. Dialogue Mass with parts sung in English, including now the Introit and Father [John] Eudes [Bamberger] preaches a Homily, etc.

Old Liturgies: in the Infirmary – Father Stephen, his own private rite, leaning on the altar, hanging on it, grappling with it, leaning sideways, ganging up on the book, and Brother Leo in strange places coming out with high-pitched "amens" and other responses in a language entirely his own (he is stone deaf). And the *plebs sancta* [congregation]. Brother John in a wheelchair with a red blanket over his shoulders and glasses on the end of his nose. Brother Jerome, leaning far forward. Brother Dominic, head bowed low. Brother Gerard solemn and slow . . . in the middle of it all the great aquiline powerful business frame of Brother Clement the Cellarer, at Mass there early so as to take the road on a big, mysterious errand in one of the cities. This early Mass in the Infirmary is unforgettable! And in many ways more moving than all the new improvements. (Father Raymond [Flanagan], facing the people at the new high altar, sings Mass angrily, and puts his fist in his stomach. –)

Finally getting into Zaehner's *Hindu and Muslim Mysticism*, a remarkable book. And convincing.

November 3, 1963

One of [Armand-Jean Le Bouthillier de] Rancé's arguments against study in the monastic life: it leads to wrangling – "contestation." Experience of twenty years of theological conferences in this monastery convinces me that the most intemperate, unreasonable and indeed uncharitable arguers in chapter are those who most vehemently support Rancé or live most explicitly according to his principles. Those, on the contrary, who have grown up with more intellectual interests not only are better informed and able to make sounder judgments, but are also more temperate, as well as more intelligible, and more objective, in their speech.

November 5, 1963

Please to remember the fifth of November! The Gunpowder treason and plot!

And St. Martin de Porres, and today's elections, and the southern priest who was beaten up by his parishioners because he had the white and Negro children go to the communion rail at the same time for first communion.

Rain was falling when we got up the other day for All Saints (I am still saying vigils privately though) and that night it began again at bedtime. This morning, still night, warmer, cloudy, wind, pale night over the Zen garden, cold in the chapel.

There is a wonderful therapeutic atmosphere about Eadmer's life of Anselm [*The Life of St. Anselm*, ed. R. W. Southern, 1962] because of the healing, tender, "motherly" quality of Anselm's concern. The dying monk who hated him found himself "in the arms of two wolves with their teeth at his throat." It is a grotesque medieval manuscript illumination! The two human wolves are dispelled by Anselm who is called from the cloister where he was correcting books while others were at their siesta.

November 7, 1963

The whole afternoon of the sixth it rained. I got over to New Haven to vote, before dinner – just made it in time for the last available ride. Voted the straight Democratic ticket, with the usual misgivings and sense of futility. The main thing was to vote against [Louie] Nunn [for governor of Kentucky], who has been playing on the racism and other prejudices of the people in the rural areas and small towns – big towns too! As far as I know [Edward] Breathitt got in, but by a very small margin.

Am getting far behind in correspondence. My mind seems to work more slowly and bogs down when I get close to that pile of letters. Especially when there are so many people, relatively, that just hang on to me for support – dead weight. I try not to carry on a correspondence with any such, as it is useless, even for them. What point is there in deluding them that they are "getting something" which their need imagines? Yet there are some in such trouble and danger that one has to give them at least a token encouragement, even if it is meaningless. On the other hand there is an equal meaninglessness in the business of getting myself published, or responding to people who ask for manuscripts and now (abstract) drawings.

Anselm's *Vita* and letters are a great support, however. How solid his letters are. How solid everything is in him, compared to our shifting, fluid ground in which there is no foothold.

Visited Brother Chrysostom's parents briefly at the gatehouse yesterday after dinner and it came out that Diem, the dictator in Viet Nam, had been murdered and the whole tribe with him. A miserable business. Sickened by these corrupt "Catholic" bosses hungry for power, cynical, greedy, slick, working with Church power, running little countries supported by American guns. What an appalling scandal and symptom of our own decay! What can be done? The lessons of Ezekiel – how inexorably true they sound! Our society is under stern judgment and we have no light! May God have pity on our darkness!

November 10, 1963

Ngo Dinh Nhu, brother of the President of South Viet Nam, husband of "that woman," and the real pawn in the country, assassinated with Diem on All Saints' Day – was a Catholic intellectual who had once nourished his mind on [Emmanuel] Mounier. He had studied at the École des Chartres and claimed he got the idea of his "strategic hamlets" there. His was an aggressive Catholicism, the kind we see so much of, friendly to the rich, rough on the poor and on non-Catholics, a Catholicism that consisted above all in militant anti-communism. The formula is much too familiar. It spells nothing but blindness, stupidity, obstinacy and disaster – especially where it operates with a semi-secret fascist party, a rigidly controlled police state, and a state Catholicism (in a state where all but 20% are Buddhist!). Universal horror of this regime in the U.S. because of the spectacular suicides of Buddhist monks. And the Catholic press trying to prove that Diem and Co. were "not doing anything wrong"! A sickening affair.

Finished some notes on Zaehner's Teilhardian pamphlet on *Matter and Spirit* which is good in intention, poor and hasty in execution. Have added

this on to the material on Zen for the winter _Continuum_.[8] Graham Carey
wired that he wanted some of _Art and Worship_ in _Good Work_.

November 12, 1963

Going over the Zen article has been a grace. It has brought me back to myself after a long while! A long, futile, round and round _peregrinatio_ [pilgrim-
age] all around nothing – just because I somehow got obsessed with a need
to get somewhere and do something (God knows what). In the first place,
too much writing, or rather too many useless projects. And my study has
been a bit absurd, due to my getting so many free books for review and
imagining it important to read most of them. In a word, my ailment is this:
I become anxious to keep up with all that is being said and done, and I want
in my turn to be "in there" . . . to play my own part, and contribute my own
words. Once in a while I get a glimpse of the folly that is really at the heart
of this "zeal"!

On the other hand I think that reading Sartre's _L'Être et le néant_ is going
to be important for me. (However, I did not read it.) Also, translating some
opuscula [short works] of Nicholas of Cusa (if I can keep at it. He gets away
from me when he seems too intellectual and dry). I will not abandon translations (hope of translation) of a few letters of Anselm, and maybe the article on Grimlaicus.

In the council: last week a piece of dishonesty on the part of some curia
officials was joyfully unmasked. The fools had simply cut out all the really
significant part of a schema, without the approval of the proper commission, and tried to push it through. I don't know the details – but anyway it
shows how these authoritarian characters, who always rant about obedience
and authority, are mostly "obedient" themselves only in so far as authority
sees things their way. I am glad someone is finally opposing them (without
Paul VI the opposition would not have any meaning).

What a weary, silly mess. When will I learn to go without leaving footprints? A long way from that: I still love recognition and need to preach, so
that I will believe in my own message, and believing that, will believe in myself – or at least consent to find myself acceptable for a little while. Absurdity, and very dishonest on top of it. I wish I knew how to be otherwise!

Funny how I came to this, quite in spite of myself and in spite of everything, after several days of desperation (half-felt) and perplexity. Peace in

---

[8] This article was eventually published as "The Zen Revival," _Continuum_ 1 (Winter 1964):
523–38.

seeing the hills, the blue sky, the afternoon sun. Just this and nothing more! As soon as I move toward anything else, confusion. Those asses and their active philosophy and their itch to get on every stupid bandwagon! Yet how I am influenced by them in spite of myself! They are so sure that is Christianity – that parading and gesticulating, that proclamation of ten thousand programs!

November 14, 1963

Yesterday – dark and cold, flurries of snow. All Saints of the Order. A delightful day. I moved out of the infirmary last night and the hard bed was good to get back to, also my own cell, the special stone one, at the head of the stairs to the novitiate dormitory, hanging in the air, a hole in the rock, a *caverna maceriae* [cave in the wall]. The traction affair was rigged up by Brother Anthony, and I have a reading light. *Paradiso* [paradise]. Blankets, quiet (except that corn blower roars in the daytime).

Nicholas of Cusa: opening up. Magnificent discovery. I have been on to him for a while, but not realizing how much was there!

Later – a telegram arrived today that Dom Gabriel Sortais, the Abbot General, had died last night – Feast of All the Saints of Order. I suppose he was exhausted from work, the Council, etc. and all his usual illnesses. He was in many ways a great man, a warm and generous person and I am indebted to him for many things though I certainly got annoyed at his arbitrary ways with the censorship of books. He was certainly not one of the "new men" in the Church: the old, authoritarian, absolutist, centralist type. Wanting a firm grip on every detail of everything that went on in the Order – and yet the General Chapter is the real authority in the Order, or it is supposed to be. But he ruled "his" abbots with a firm hand and gave them the devil if they did not do everything his way. Not to mention the mere subjects. He was often angry with me, and I must say I was often angry with him. He had the good grace to listen if I was in earnest, and sometimes when I was wrong he told me so without unkindness. I suppose in a way I was very fond of him, and my memories of the Beaux Arts, and his honest, Trappist spirit, and his acceptance of the Order in all its madness. He never caused a thousand hair-raising stories about the madness in our various houses. He and I lived in a different Order. I was annoyed at his encyclicals, and his pontifical reasoning, and above all his busy, bureaucratic little secretary. The King of all the censors. Yet after all I have managed to say a lot more than many writers in the Church have.

Well, now he is dead, and the Order will miss him. I can say I have lost a friend, and the Order has lost a great man, whose generalship will be significant in the Order's history. God alone knows how much good he did, or tried to do, and he certainly must have been a strong support to many people. It is out of place now to suggest that perhaps the support they needed was something different – not that of an all-powerful will in a high place, but that of more light, reason, understanding. In any case many will have cause to be grateful to him. It is due to him and Dom James that my attempt to leave the Order and go to Dom Gregorio was blocked, and perhaps not too justly or rightly.[9] I do not say I am grateful for that. Perhaps it was for the best, however. Who can say? He was strong enough to make a Roman Congregation change its mind. But that is not unusual, I imagine.

November 16, 1963

Yesterday, feast of the Dedication of the Church. Father Charles English, from Georgia (Conyers monastery) and formerly of *Catholic Worker*, spoke in chapter, warmly, and then had a heart attack afterwards. He is in Bardstown hospital.

First copy of *Emblems of a Season of Fury*[10] was handed to me by Brother Simon [Patrick Hart] just before High Mass.

Today, a solemn requiem mass for Dom Gabriel.

[Jean] Cocteau, dead. Did I already say this? Moved by a picture of a party, in 1930's or early 40's – Cocteau, Charlie Chaplin, Paulette Goddard, champagne, smiles, 1939 hairdos – a kind of gaiety that doesn't seem to exist any more. Another picture: National Guardsmen in Birmingham, marching: fat thugs, inexpressibly stupid and brutal faces. Even Nazis look more intelligent. Here these strong grown-up nitwits taking their bellies and muscles seriously as they have been taught by TV. What a piece of work is man!

November 20, 1963

All our students in Rome, except Father Chrysogonus [Waddell], have written letters about the death of the Abbot General, how he was taken with great pain in the cloister of Monte Cistello after supper, went to hospital and died a few moments after getting there. Long offices of the dead,

---

9 Dom Gregorio Lemercier's "project" in Cuernavaca, Mexico, seemed to Merton the answer to his quest for an eremitical lifestyle in the late 1950s.
10 Published by New Directions in 1963.

solemn masses, first for the General (yesterday) and for the November anniversary (today).

Yesterday a woman got through the authorities to visit me on the grounds
that she was a distant relative, which seems very doubtful. I cannot account
for her on any score. A remarkable, beatnik, Charles Addams, hair in the
eyes type who turned out, in the afternoon, to be a nymphomaniac. She
gave me a wild time – a real battle, at times physical, and finally, when I got
away alive and with most of my virtue intact (I hope!) I felt shaken that a
woman should still go to such lengths over me, even though a deranged
one. Only later did I realize how futile and insufficient were my own attempts to do something for her. Words sounded so foolish and absurd. Her
mode of communication was with her whole body and all her strength.

All kinds of feelings, of shame, confusion, bewilderment, resignation to
the final absurdity of it. Above all consternation at the awful ease with
which the situation produced itself. Almost unthinkable: here was temptation not in essence or in the mind, but in full existence, concrete, utterly
real, and yet behaving like a phantom. I can understand some of the Desert
Fathers' stories a little better after that! What can I say about sorrow and
pity for her – and my own complete and stupid helplessness to do anything
that would make any difference to her?

Began Anselm's *De Casu Diaboli* – not because of yesterday, but I have
been interested to get to it for a long time. Very profound book on freedom,
grace and sin.

November 23, 1963

There will be another solemn requiem Mass today, this time for the President.

When I came in from the woods yesterday, Brother Aidan met me at the
door of the novitiate and told me the president had been shot and died, in
Texas, an hour and a half before. At first I did not believe it. But there was a
notice on the board, and later I saw Father Abbot. Leo Gannon on the
phone told him, while I was there, that the gun and three empty cartridges
had been found in a building overlooking the route Kennedy traveled. It
was in Dallas, Texas. Of course it had to be some idiot place like that!

Again, the whole thing leaves one bewildered and slightly sick. Sick for
the madness, ferocity, stupidity, aimless cruelty that is the mark of so great a
part of this country. Essentially the same blind, idiot destructiveness and
hate that killed Medgar Evers in Jackson, the Negro children in Birming-

ham. I do not know what was the motive of this absurd assassination – whether it was over the race question or not, or just fanaticism. The country is full of madness and we are going to know this more and more.

As for Kennedy – what shall one say? He was a good president, vigorous, honest, fairly shrewd, with undoubted limitations, but trying to go in the right direction. Why should they hate him enough to kill him? Is a little honesty that dangerous? Basically I think the root of it all is the blind animosity of the rich and the greedy, influencing a lot of crackpots who are not so rich, but who want a totally selfish and irresponsible society to continue at all costs for the benefit of those who love money and power. The country is corrupted by the love of wealth, and the image of power. Men will do anything for this love, and nothing else matters.

Brother Colman just told me that the one suspected of the murder of Kennedy is a Communist, a twenty-four-year-old ex-marine, supposed to be pro-Castro. That puts a different complexion on the whole thing; at least it was not a fanatic ultra-patriot who would have a large following inside the country. On the other hand the super-patriots will turn this to their advantage against liberalism.

November 25, 1963

The curious adventure with nausea last Tuesday still stays with me, and sure. At moments I see it as no less absurd than anything else around me, for instance the talks in chapter and various celebrations or contacts in community. It shocked me most of all as a break in the safety and routine of the usual silliness: but such a shock is salutary, since it reminds me of the need to break out of all routines and molds – not arbitrarily or anarchically, but by grace and sense, which will be given and are "here" if my eyes can open to them.

This active sweatered body with hair in her eyes who came and went suddenly and changed my phantasm of one of the most pleasant fields, is a reminder not to people the whole place with sweet and solitary adventures (though it is comforting to be surrounded with contemplative animation). Contemplation is otherwise serious, and is in neither involvement nor void.

And the insanity of the country! Yes, the suspected murderer of Kennedy was a Marxist, had been in Russia, was on a Pro-Castro committee (Fair Play for Cuba), etc. But I say he "was" all these things because now he too has been shot. This time the super-patriots did get into the picture. "Jack Ruby, a prominent and anti-communist business man," shot Oswald in the stomach as he was being taken by the police to another jail. Everyone, so it seems, saw this on TV.

Later – gradually and in bits and pieces one learns news, as it gets from Leo Gannon's TV over the phone to Father Abbot or to Brother Colman and thence in one way or another to me and through me to the novices. The one who shot Oswald was called Rubinstein, a Jewish owner of two night-clubs in Dallas, and he was a friend of the police. Standing between two detectives he shot Oswald when he was about a foot away from him. In any case, a super-patriot.

I had to call Jim Wygal in Louisville, not at his office. He was at home watching the President's funeral on TV (Kennedy's body was being taken to Arlington). Everybody is terribly upset – the least upset are perhaps the Kennedys themselves. It is a real spiritual, moral, and emotional crisis for the entire country. I have never seen anything quite like it.

The speech Kennedy was to have read in Dallas is being read in the refectory. In Goldwater country it had to be a strong speech, and strong it was. All about our strategic weapons, our tactical nuclear weapons, our conventional weapons, our readiness to destroy any and every aggressor, our better preparedness to stop all attackers, saboteurs. Assassins were explicitly mentioned.

It took a German rifle and two bullets. (Plus one for the Governor of Texas.)

Hunters are all over the place, again. I chased some away on Friday, and another from behind the hermitage Saturday. They all turned out to be meek, apologetic men, and all claimed to have permission from prominent churchmen – (e.g., Father Mitchell, the assistant at New Haven, or Brother Frederic [Collins] in the farms building). But guns still bang merrily all over the place.

I picked up a cartridge box yesterday and on it read: "These copper-plated cartridges have a high velocity and increased pressure. They should be used only in a high-grade gun in first-class condition, certified by the manufacturer to be suitably constructed to withstand such increased pressure and velocity . . . *Caution – range one mile – be careful!*" I found it about three hundred yards from the monastery.

Everyone asks me if Dan Walsh went to the President's funeral – as if I knew!

How close is the *tricherie* [trickery] of Sartre to the *rectitudo* of St. Anselm? Is there any correspondence between Chapter XI of *De Casu Diaboli* (on the meaning of "nothing") and Sartre's *néant* [nothingness]?

I got back to the monastery and found death had built another nest in the news. This time old Joseph Kennedy, the rich one, the Ambassador and the President's father, had died of a heart attack, after the murder of his son.

November 26, 1963

But it turned out that Kennedy senior did not die after all. That at least was a false rumor.

Read Sartre's *Respectful Prostitute*. All I had ever heard about it ran it down, but it is a smasher! Best thing of his I have read, and one of the best on the race question. Certainly it is farcical, arbitrary, in a way "propaganda." And yet it is true. Simple: it has to be simple. And no Southerner has ever stated the Southern case as simply and blandly as his characters, the Senator and Fred. Maybe it is little more than a vaudeville act, but a very good one. The main thing wrong with it is that no signature would have been necessary to save the white man who shot the Negro.

The new President is of course Lyndon Johnson, former Vice-President. Sworn in hurriedly in a plane on the airfield at Dallas, shortly after Kennedy's death. Will he, like Truman, be the one left to carry out a momentous and destructive decision that may affect, and radically so, the whole future of the world?

November 27, 1963

A letter came from Cintio Vitier, written November 16, postmarked the 21st. I suppose it was censored in Cuba. A most moving letter, and with it another envelope containing poems of mine which he and his friends had translated into Spanish. A whole little group of most charming people. Cintio had translated "O Sweet Irrational Worship," Eliseo Diego the "Elegy for Thurber," Octavio Smith "Song for Nobody," Cintio's wife Fina [García Marruz] "Seven Archaic Images" and the young Negro poet Roberto Friol the whole "Early Legend" of which they sent me only Part IV, most touching to have chosen this – the meeting of the strangers. I feel they have profoundly understood everything and I love them. He spoke of them all busy translating when my letter of October 4 came. Referring to that (and the notes for Grinberg ["Answers on Art and Freedom"], from whom I have not heard).

"I think of what you say about the incommunicable manifestos of the poets of today, and their eagerness to preach a liberty made of drugs – or a justice made of slavery. I tell you that for me one of the worst demons is the demon of literature, in fact for many years I have felt the obsession of a writing that is tied up with evil. But lately I see even worse evils in the '*ente politico*' ['political area'], mixed up with literature."[11]

The cheese work is not yet great. Brother Clement and Brother Raphael are both in the infirmary, hobbling about after hernia operations.

November 30, 1963. St. Andrew

Cold, grey, a few flakes of snow swirling above the pines, and a crow fighting his way into the wind. Some ministers from Louisville, Baptist and Presbyterian Seminary. Jack [John H.] Ford, et al. from Bellarmine were here yesterday for some discussions and as usual I am dubious about it. At this time we seemed certainly to have much to say that was relevant. But what is more important is their being here – particularly ones like Glenn Hinson [from Southern Baptist Theological Seminary] who knows and loves the Fathers of the Church. Dale Moody [from Southern Baptist] kept referring to the wave of "charisms," "glossolalia," etc. which is sweeping through (Southern?) Protestantism. He is in favor of it. I regard it as a manifestation of spiritual insecurity and confusion.

Episcopalian nuns from Versailles [Kentucky], whom I saw briefly after lunch today, brought up the same thing. It is in some Episcopal churches, too!

After the Kennedy funeral, everyone is apparently calming down, with what seems to be a general impression of reassurance, based largely on the fact that Kennedy has suddenly become a giant in stature due to his death, and that there is a show of unity in support of Johnson. But my feeling of the unconsciousness of the whole thing persists.

1. The South has apparently accepted Kennedy's death with great satisfaction and absolutely no charity. On the contrary, some have openly regretted that Bobby [Kennedy] was not killed – there is real hate there. Flags are not being flown half mast (here of course they are, and in Kentucky), etc.

2. The question of murder, the motives, etc. is still extremely unsatisfactory, and though everyone believes the "evidence" discovered by the Dallas police, perhaps it is not all as solid as it sounds. (Apparently there is *no witness* of Oswald's shooting the patrolman, Tippitt, nor is it sure the man was shot with Oswald's revolver, etc.)

The whole thing is extremely grim, mysterious and much graver than people seem to believe, though God knows everyone was shocked. Our feds

---

[11] Letter from Cintio Vitier to Thomas Merton, Havana, Cuba, November 16, 1963 (Thomas Merton Studies Center, Bellarmine College, Louisville, Kentucky).

all have wanted a solution at any price and have taken the first one they could get. Is it good enough? Certainly Oswald shot the President: but it is important to know why. It is also very important to know more about this Ruby, and his endearing impulsiveness and the legend that he was just crazy about Presidents, always faithfully prayed in the synagogue, ran two highly respectable strip-tease joints and was the friend of all the cops.

December 1, 1963. First Sunday of Advent

Bright stars. I am still not going to the Night Office. Still need some traction to get the kinks out of my neck and shoulder when waking up. Take it again before going to sleep at night, so my time table does not quite jive with that of the community. But I love this season, need the hymns. Loved the responsories again yesterday in the snow-flaked mist. Yet the old liturgy itself recedes in a "past" which is itself being rejected, as if one were no longer allowed to cling to it, as if it were no longer sure to be there tomorrow. It is my own past and the past of my civilization and I must leave both, having them as though I had them not.

The seventeenth chapter of *De Casu Diaboli* brings up a very modern question – our creativity, that is, the creative power of our liberty is perhaps, as far as we ourselves [are] concerned, a non-destructiveness. If we can accept creation we concur in creating because we have the "power" to destroy. Our power to create is a power to consent in creation, or to work in common with the creative will that transcends both our freedom and our world. Our power to destroy seems more ours (and it is so) and more of a power. What is happening now is that we concentrate more and more on the power which is a rejection. Yet paradoxically, to have the power to destroy and not destroy is to "make." In this sense, by not destroying the world we seem to be creating it. We are said to make something "*cum possumus facere ut non est et non facimus*" ["when we could make something not be, and we don't do it"].

The problem is for people to see that the power to nurture and preserve which vanishes into the creative background of God's will is the only true power, and does not appear as power. Whereas what appears as power, the power to destroy, is not power but self-defeat. Strangely, this power is regarded as the one great reality in our world. It is the one on which everything else is built. And it makes our power to preserve also take the shape of an unnatural decision.

Now that my book *Emblems of a Season of Fury* is out, I discover by chance a curious and intriguing article on *Emblèmes Religieux*. Baroque books of direction, particularly Jesuit, based on stories and examples expressed in "emblems" which in turn inspired baroque preaching. There's a kind of negative baroque in some of my own poems, perhaps. There's certainly conscious parody of pseudo-moralism, and my "emblems" are baroque emblems turned inside out, as perhaps our society is a kind of bombed Dresden (morally).

December 3, 1963. St. Eligius[12]

Light rainy snow flying through the darkness, and the fields white in the gloom. I finished *De Casu Diaboli.* If a first reading can be said to finish such a book. Must go through it again. Especially for the difference between real freedom and mere determination. Perhaps the devil's sin was after all merely to substitute (arbitrarily and out of his own will) one for the other. Freedom is God's. He wills us to share it by *rectitudo* – willing according to the principle that is in reality itself – but the devil willed to have it regardless of *rectitudo* and reality, by his own arbitrary fiat. Hence he willed to be like God on his own (arbitrary and willful) terms – and by this he understood that the use of power in any way he chose was Godlikeness. Yet it was not. The devil's sin was then to put his own power against all contingencies and ultimately against all principles, too – so that the final word was open purely and simply to power. That this was not "Godlikeness" is shown by the Incarnation and Redemption, works not of power but of justice and mercy.

Father Charles (of Georgia) still in the Bardstown Hospital and I have not been to see him – as Father Abbot has always managed to arrange things so that I would not be able. Dorothy Day speaks of coming down to see him.

The boy from Chicago – artist, very amiable, not yet a Catholic who visited a few months ago was mixed up in dope – who is trying to get away from Chicago, jazz, and marihuana – was doing drawings when he heard of Kennedy's death and they instantly began to be drawings, in color, with angles and strange forms. His shock. It is easy for everyone but the right ones to declare themselves guilty of Kennedy's death.

Am well on the way to finishing Gironella's great book (*One Million Dead*). Great in size, and a very competent work. A picture of the Spanish war that is complete and objective, not pretentious, compassionate, detached, often very humorous, but real. It is really quite an extraordinary

---

12 This seems to be an error: St. Eligius's feast day is December 1, not December 3, as Merton has recorded it here.

book, rich in material, full of small touches, details, telling lines, full of people – characters all lightly drawn, the central one Ignacio in Spain, an impartial Spain – he has been on both sides, passed from one to the other through a kind of dynamiter's tunnel in Madrid – an aorta.

Everyone is not the crazy, humorous Catalan anarchists, the sour, efficient and brutal Communists (and André Marty running the International Brigade on Stalinist lines!). The idealistic Socialists, the English reporters (a very funny chapter on the two of them in Nationalist Spain) and then also the Falangists, the Casuists, etc. The Spanish Fascists are portrayed with accuracy and distaste – their gestures, their dramas, their slogans ("José Antonio – parasite!!"). Their relations with the Italians and Nazis, their speeches about the devil, etc. Very meaningful sketches – without comment. It is a very good, warm, humorous book, and basically a Christian one. A civilized book after all!! On the ancient model. Russia still tries to produce such – with what success I don't know.

December 5, 1963

Another Spanish writer – fourth-century Egeria (Etheria, "Sylvia") and her amazing Pilgrimage to Jerusalem, Egypt, Sinai and Mesopotamia [*Peregrinatio Aetheriae* (*The Pilgrimage of Etheria*), 1919]. I love her. Simplicity, practicality, insatiable curiosity, and tremendous endurance as long as she is riding her mule (laments a little when she has to go "straight up" the side of Sinai – any influence on St. John of the Cross?). All the holy women she meets – they must have been delighted with her and overwhelmed. This is a really marvelous book, one of the greatest monuments of fourth-century literature, and too few know it. Two English translations, the most recent being 1919. I am tempted to do it – but better not! Is she Spanish? Sounds like a Spaniard, with the simplicity, mixture of hope, humor, idealism and endurance. Or maybe some day she will turn out to have been Irish!

December 6, 1963

Etheria (Egeria, Eucheria) – is my delight! Have read and dug around: [Germain] Morin in *The Benedictine* on Jerome's Letter to Fusia (a veiled allusion to Etheria? – not too nice) and another letter, that of the seventeenth-century Spanish monk Valerius, on the "Blessed Etheria" – a beautiful document. She is one of "my saints" from here on!

December 9, 1963

Yesterday woke up with thunder rolling. Lightning and rain during Night Office (I said my Lauds and made a groggy meditation privately in novitiate). Cold afternoon of Our Lady's feast. Thought a little of Sung Ts'an among the shales and pines in a bitter lovely wind beyond the lake across the road. There was a little snow in the air from time to time. But this morning (4:10) it is snowing. Brother Martin de Porres is cleaning up the common box prior to going to the juniorate. He is now the only Negro in the community. Brother Chrysostom Castel will go over with him. Brother Bartholomew made simple profession yesterday and Brother Timothy his solemn vows and Brother Savio (Herrera), the little Mexican from Texas, will have to leave. His emotions get too wound up and he had a breakdown. I am sorry to see him go: a very simple and good person with much love for God, and a background of poverty and hardship, mistreatment by police, etc.

December 11, 1963

Obsolescence of a certain type of moral thought that deals _only_ in absolutes, that makes no room for change and for provisional situations. When dealing with nuclear war, this type of thinking proceeds immediately to the absolute, definitive conclusion which solidifies itself into an eternal statement _at once_ – and in so doing is already absolute, because by the time the discussion is over and the statement is arrived at, the facts are already different, and the whole problem has a new aspect.

Such people fail to see that the nuclear statement is at best unstable and provisional, that it represents a phase of a rapidly changing and revolutionary problem. But in order to safeguard a momentary set of interests, they evoke some eternal principle to justify (or condemn) nuclear weapons. In so doing they greatly risk canonizing nuclear power in a way far more definitive than even they themselves need. In "defense" of their thoughts, their values, their culture, they pronounce absolute determinations which seem to prescribe the use of the power that can destroy them. A clear sign of obsolescence!! The moral theology of bathos.

December 15, 1963. Third Sunday [of] Advent

Very cold (about six above this morning), bright sun. Cold sky. Yesterday the sky over the pines had an Apennine blue about it.

Began reading the Council's constitution on liturgy. (J[ames] Laughlin sent five pages of the _N.Y. Times_ containing the full text.) It is really remarkable. There is no question that great things have been done by the Bishops, and Pope John was truly inspired. When one reads quotations from some of the statements one is more and more impressed by their fullness of meaning.

Reading Tom Stonier's *Nuclear Disaster*. A frightful book. Descriptions of the destruction, death and suffering at Hiroshima and Hamburg are already far more genuine than Dante's Hell. It is benign and humane by comparison. And what would the big bombs do? The thing is that this is not the aspect of the problem one should get obsessed with. If he does he runs the risk of seeing no positive hope – and really things are still not bright. But one *must* concentrate on every positive step towards controlling this thing and getting rid of it, however impossible that may sound. Merely contemplating the possible horror is no use at all.

Interesting notes on New Testament anthropology in Werner Georg Kümmel [*Man in the New Testament*, trans. John J. Vincent, 1963]. I don't agree with his general thesis that man by nature has nothing whatever to dispose him for grace and life with God (no "image," "spirit," etc.). However, here and there profound meanings emerge. Especially in meaning of sin and man's "boasting" before God. Also this: "*Sarx* denotes the man who lets himself be *determined* by his actual historical existence in the world; it does not describe man in his fundamental nature but rather his membership in this passing evil age" (Galatians 1:4).[13] "In so far as he lets himself be determined by the reality of 'this age' and thereby denotes that he is yet *sarx*, so far he is a 'slave of sin and death'" (Romans 6:16), p. 62–63. But (the Christian knows) that "man is *sarx* in his very existence and is determined by *sarx*" (Romans 7:14–8:7). This is a judgment not of nature but of man's historic and existential relation to God. Yet this metaphysical language is impossible: "man is a historical being who derives his nature from his existence as a member of the present evil age and from his living in accordance with this historical existence," p. 70. This is an absurd "bind" that can only be opened up by a whole new creation that has nothing whatever to do with nature, the wicked cosmos, etc., etc. I do not follow him.

Of [Rudolf Karl] Bultmann: "Pauline anthropology is as a statement an act of the new life and not an anthropology in a general or obvious sense" (quoted by Kümmel, p. 71). He will end by rejecting Paul's Areopagus speech and Peter's "*naturae*" as Hellenistic and strange.[14]

---

[13] *Sarx* (or "flesh") is used by Paul as the opposite of God (*pneuma*, "spirit"). Humans as *sarx* are therefore "sinners."

[14] "Paul's Areopagus speech" refers to Acts 17. "Peter's '*naturae*'" refers to "partakers of divine nature" in 2 Peter 1:4.

December 16, 1963

The great value of the Kümmel book is its affirmation, conclusively proven, that in the New Testament man's sin has nothing to do with his bodily existence. It is not that bodily life = sinful life and spiritual life or "sane life" = good life. But that the whole man either accepts or rejects God.

December 17, 1963

Cold stars. Steam coming up in the dark from the kitchens into the freezing night. Father Leonard with his routine in the grand parlor, in the dim light. Creak of the wooden steps leading down to infirmary refectory. Flamingos on the Standard Oil Calendar in the kitchen. Tea. Frost on the side of the coal pile. Dirty bread lying among the stones, frozen, for birds.

Father Seraphim, Prior at [Assumption Abbey] Ava, Missouri, is here. He had written to me some time ago from Rome. Two years ago, or three, when there was a big question of several American Cistercians becoming hermits, and Dom Gabriel squashed it. Now Father Seraphim is planning a new kind of foundation in Alaska, and it looks reasonable. Simple, poor, austere. Certainly something of the kind is needed. The situation in the Order is such that a completely simple life is impossible in most of our houses, at any rate in America. Many of the American houses are confused, activistic, restless. There is a general air of restlessness in most of the houses. Ours is perhaps one of the most peaceful.

He says that Gethsemani is one of the only places in this country where one feels that there is some spiritual depth. On the other hand, nothing much is happening. The general impression here, he says, is that Dom James "has got everything screwed down so tight that nothing can happen" and consequently no one knows what really is in the house. This is probably true. The peace here is temporary at best. But I think nevertheless with this year of work with the two novitiates joined and the juniorate, there is something of a solid foundation. And we have a good prior (Father Flavian).

I find I still have great confidence in my community and my abbot though one thing is definite – I no longer have any questions in my mind about changing stability. I have no desire even to see the gatehouse of any other monastery of this Order, or of the Camaldolese, or of the Carthusians – though I would like to visit a Charterhouse perhaps. (Heard from our former Father Alberic Rackley – Dom Denys at La Grande Chartreuse.)

Father John of the Cross has been at Portsmouth Priory teaching this term but Dom Aelred [Graham] does not think he should stay. What will become of the man?

[Maurice] Merleau-Ponty says: "Nothing can be explained by way of man, for he is not a strength but a weakness in the heart of being, for he is not a cosmological factor but the place where all cosmological factors, through never ending change, alter their meaning and become history" (*Éloge de la philosophie* [*In Praise of Philosophy*, 1963]). In my Book Providence,[15] Merleau-Ponty is a radical and welcome discovery – he is like Zen, Herakleitos, much more radical and simple at the same time than Sartre, no need of any of Sartre's passion and programs, and no need of Nausea. Does not admit Descartes, radically anti-*cogito*, anti-Parmenides, anti-Plato. The anti-Plato in me has always been this and never Aristotle. The anti-Plato in me is Zen and Old Testament. His idea of metaphysical consciousness – aware that intelligibility is contingent fact, springing from man's existence and confrontation in history with being as *pour soi* [for oneself]. (The *en soi* [in oneself] is unintelligible.) This may seem radically antichristian (certainly anti-scholastic) yet I wonder if after all the Bible would not show it to be very Christian, cf. the approach of the W. G. Kümmel book.

December 21, 1963. Feast of St. Thomas

Very cold. Temperature has not been above freezing, even in the sun, and the snow stays on the ground.

Zwi Werblowsky has sent Bahya [ben Joseph] ibn Pakuda in the remarkable [Andrãe] Chouraqui translation. This is a very great book [*Introduction aux devoirs des coeurs*, trans. Andrãe Chouraqui, 1943]. The translation itself is classic. It was made in the time when the Nazis occupied France, and the furnaces of Auschwitz were in operation. Chouraqui was writing in occupied France. His rhythms in translation of the Psalms (the book is full of Biblical quotations) are superb. I think I have never seen such high religious quality in any translation of the Psalms except perhaps the Vulgate. But I think Chouraqui is even better.

Today I must go to town to see the doctors. I fell in the snow the other day – not a hard fall. The snow broke it, but my shoulder has been sore and the back may have been injured again.

Quite by accident I discover a reference to my old friend Jean Hering at Strasbourg [University, France] and find that he has been all along one of the earliest authorities on French Phenomenology and a disciple of [Edmund] Husserl – but I was only sixteen and he never talked about phenomenology,

---

[15] "Book Providence" is unclear, though this is what Merton wrote in his journal. He perhaps missed a word or words as he was writing. It could possibly read "Book [of] Providence," but that makes little more sense.

or if he did I was not interested. I wrote to him the other day – I wonder if he is still alive.

December 22, 1963. Fourth Sunday [of] Advent

Still very cold. The light snow has never melted.

Merleau-Ponty says: "*Je suis à moi au étant au monde*" ["I am to myself as being in the world"]. And this would appear to be the exact opposite of what I have been saying for twenty years – that I am my own by withdrawing from the world. Actually I agree with him profoundly. Everything depends on the meaning you give to "*monde*." If it means the delusions and clichés that stand between a supposed autonomous "I" and the world of phenomena, well, one does not want to belong to this and struggle for existence in it, thinking oneself to be now free, now not free. Who is this self? But if it means one's own situation, then how else can one be anything except by being what he is, and how can he be what and who he is apart from all that goes with him? What is with me? What am I *in?* That is one reason for a Journal like this, to keep honestly situated.

It is also a reason for taking pictures, for instance, yesterday, down at "The Point" in Louisville, with Jim Wygal, and along the river front. To withdraw from where I am in order to be totally outside all that situates me – this is real delusion. Hence the similarity between Merleau-Ponty and Zen. I am inevitably a dialogue with my surroundings, and have no choice, though I can perhaps change the surroundings. "*L'intérieur et l'extérieur sont inseparables. Le monde est font au dedans et je suis tous hors de moi.*" ["The interior and the exterior are inseparable. The world is created from within and I am always outside myself."]

December 23, 1963

Karl Jaspers says: "Today no philosophical insight is possible unless Socrates is present, if only as a pale shadow. The way in which a man experiences Socrates is fundamental to his thinking." It is curious that I "experienced" Socrates in school [at Oakham] as anything but what he was: I reacted to him with suspiciousness as to the bulwark of authority proposed by the "establishment" (the Headmaster [Francis Doherty]). Curious that the one who was in this case conventional was I, not Socrates. Happy if even at this late date Socrates can reveal to me that I am, or have been, to some extent a square, first when I wanted not to be – for in this matter good will is not enough.

December 25, 1963. Christmas

As usual, Christmas was a kind of spiritual crisis for me.

Christmas Eve was fine and quiet. Deep snow. Walked in some wind and snow in St. Teresa's Field. But the few days before had been hectic. Ambivalent about a terrible drawing I did for the Novices' Christmas card to Dom James. (Virgin and Child – strictly corn.) Also had to prepare sermon for Christmas Eve. It went well though (if that means anything).

Christmas night, after little more than an hour's sleep(!) went to Vigils and then had to be assistant priest at the Midnight Mass. Tired, frustrated and annoyed. I have to recognize that the new altar (facing the choir) is an improvement. But the sanctuary is now like a High School stage set.

Above all, all day long I was irritated by the "style" of the liturgy here. The constant effort to achieve new liturgical "effects," new vessels, new vestments, new decorations and yet the consistent mediocrity of the performance. Sincere no doubt in a way, but also vapid. No one is to blame, and the whole thing is relatively good, except that it lacks religious depth and seriousness. However, I will admit that at the Midnight Mass I was the one most lacking in these qualities. I was simply vexed and peeved, angry at the Abbot, finding fault with him and with all possible grievances against him simmering in my consciousness. This was in part due to the fact that I had a talk the other night with Father Prior (Flavian) and his observations in this regard. It is not just my problem: the whole house and the whole Order in America is a little sore at Dom James and his authoritarian manner (disguised under the most appalling sweetness), his solid position in the power group which, under Dom Gabriel, kept the Order "under control." (Dom Gabriel said when he was dying that he was afraid the Order was "getting away from him"!!) What an idiotic situation for one twenty-two years in a monastery – and yet how common, how "normal." This perhaps most of all infuriates me.

So with all that is said about liturgy, and I believe the Council, the fact remains that I cannot stay sane living on a level of "yes" and "no," and of opinion and of "correct thinking" and "right and wrong." This is simply absurd. My life makes sense only when oriented to a totally different level of consciousness: not an escape into false interiority, not a dilemma between interior and exterior, but the level of "no-mind" which gives some sense to "mind" if anything can.

But I am still afflicted with doubt and hesitation, even guilt – (This is a "Buddhist" trend! And how reprehensible, how frowned on by those who have no capacity to understand it correctly!!). This is the problem and it is here that truth and courage are needed, along with prudence – the gift of the Spirit of Counsel. The fact is that the choice between a kind of quiet interior contemplation and an outgoing liturgical piety is an illusion. Neither meditation nor liturgy can make sense for me unless I see them from the other angle – and my ability to do so depends (with grace) on *my* decision.

I hope I have once again made that decision.

December 26, 1963

I have to admit the truth that the particular frustrations of this life here are first of all not intrinsic to monasticism as such, and not essential to my own "way" by any means. And they are the product of social background and involvement in the economic and cultural pattern of the country (unavoidable). We are much more involved than we think, and my assessments of the Abbot are based mostly on this: that he is through and through a business man, and indeed even prides himself on his practicality and shrewdness, and yet he "gets away" with this by a formal unworldliness in certain spheres – discouraging correspondence, visits, recreations, etc. (He resents my involvement in the intellectual world.) (My frustrations are to some extent those of all intellectuals in a society of business men and squares.)

The great fault in my own spirituality is a negativism which is related to bourgeois sterility. What Sartre calls "right wing existentialism." Regarding *angst* as an ordinary, universal element in all life . . . (maybe this is to some extent true, however). Projecting my own frustrations and incapacities on the whole world. The fact remains that I here suffer from the sterility of my culture, and its general impotence. The optimism I reject is the optimism that denies this sterility. But where is the real optimism I should have as a Christian?

"The simplicity of the adult," says Mounier, "is won by long error, without miracles." Grace alone, the grace of the heights, sets the final grace upon the rejuvenation of the new man!

December 27, 1963

Yesterday afternoon was long, quiet, beautiful. Meditation by the field, sitting on dead branches, under low pines, sun and wind.

The determination to meditate right, and to seek "salvation." To concentrate on this, everything else worthless – except insofar as it helps clarify meditation.

Dark woods. The red squirrel in the tree top vanishes into his hole, which gets a little winter sun. A moment when the flame could be believed to be out, only the moon, the tall trees, the red grass, the wet snow under the boots. All of it cool, without the flame.

Utter madness of all life even here. Ferocity and desperation of Father Andrew's silly sermon, attacking everything, querulous, disoriented. How our community life really seriously maintains a flaming contagion of noxious and perverse thought! Cramped, violent, desperate, because always clinging to opinions of right and wrong in every smallest thing where no "certitude" is possible except by force, by doing violence to the truth.

After dinner (yesterday) I played the record (borrowed from Red Horn) of *Soeur Sourire* ["The Smiling Nun"] for the novices, etc. Pleasant in the sunlit room. Bright, genuinely pure, a good thing. This morning I drank my coffee with Dominique-nique-nique going in my ear. But remember the *albigeois*! It was not all that charming in Languedoc or in the days of Dominque, nor was all brutality and injustice on one side. One I like – "*Tous chemins mènent à Dieu.*" The first I heard on Wygal's car radio, outside "The Point" (East End of Louisville) again early afternoon (St. Thomas' Day).

Merleau-Ponty and the phenomenology of man's unfinished business (Herbert Spiegelberg) [*The Phenomenological Movement*] for whom "projects are loved in ambiguity," in the subject-object gestalt, where the subject does not withdraw into a given clarity of his own, where, on reflection, he can find all the answers or at least all the principles laid out before hand. We start from our "being-in-the-world" and not from pure being and our business is freedom – up to a point: life an existential (not intellectual) project "a polarization of life against a determined-undetermined goal of which it has no explicit idea and which it does not recognize until it achieves it." I like his sage philosophy of ambiguity, more sober and better tempered than Sartre's.

December 31, 1963

Yesterday this year drew to a quiet, curious end with an eclipse of the moon.[16] We all went out into the fierce zero cold and stood in the darkness of the garden while a last flake of light resisted for a long time the swallowing globe of

[16] Merton changes this entry to "January 1, 1964" in *Vow of Conversation*, which makes more sense.

dark. Then I went back to [Karl] Jaspers on Plato. Also we have a Japanese fish-kite and Brother Dunstan stuck up some bamboo poles in the Zen garden, so I hope we will fly fish and streamers to celebrate the New Year.

Spent some time running through the typescript of _Cold War and Black Revolution_[17] yesterday. It is testy, ephemeral and insecure. Can't do anything more with it now.

January 1, 1964

The year of the dragon came in with sleet crackling on all the quiet windows. The year of the hare went out yesterday with our red fish kite twisting and flapping in the wind over the Zen garden.

An ex-postulant (Tom Williams) sent a few pages torn out of _U.S. News and World Report_, some of them about the investigation of the Kennedy assassination, in which I read this curious sentence: "Oswald was a lone wolf whose background showed that he was inclined to nonviolence up to a point where his mind apparently snapped." He was a nonconformist – that in itself accounts for any crime. Inclined to nonviolence – this is new! How does one become inclined to a nonviolence that eventually ends in murdering someone? I can see that a "nonviolent" person could suddenly turn completely around and go against what he has professed. Here, however, the implication is that nonviolence quite logically and consistently leads to violence, and that the two are all of one piece. Nonviolence _is_ violence, according to the _U.S. News and World Report_. They have wonderfully transcended all opposites without benefit either of Hegel or of Zen. And in any case, this is the first I have heard of Oswald being _non_ violent. I suppose now any distribution of leaflets, etc. is called "nonviolence."

Cold grey afternoon, much snow, woods bright with snow loom out of the dark, totally new vision of the Vineyard Knob. Dark, etched out with snow, standing in obscurity and in a kind of spaciousness I had never seen before. The wide sweep of snow on St. Benedict's field. I furiously climbed the Lake Knob, wonderful woods! Slid down, tore my pants on barbed wire, came back through the vast fields of snow.

Sense of God all day. Now Bultmann's idea of God (evening, before Night Watch). Our care meets Him at the end of its capacity. He limits our care and cuts it short. Our love of beauty, our need for love, our desire to work, etc. Bultmann's God is the power who _limits_, who "sets a terminus"

17 Published as _Seeds of Destruction_, 1964.

to all this. "It is God who makes man finite, who makes a comedy of man's care, who allows his longing to miscarry, who casts him into solitude, who sets a terminus to his knowing . . . etc. Yet at the same time it is God who forces man into life and drives him into care, etc." Curious? But it is *a* Biblical notion of God, and very real! (*Essays [Form Criticism: Two Essays on New Testament Research*, 1962], p. 5). Not Christian yet! It could equally well be the devil! Yet belief is a "Nevertheless" embracing this power and the limits it imposes, with love and confidence. And it is *not* a *weltanschauung* [general idea]! "Real belief in God always grows out of the realization that being is an unknown quantity, which cannot be learned and retained in the form of a proposition but of which one is always becoming conscious in the 'moment' of 'loving'" (*Essays*, p. 7).

"Real belief in God is *not a general truth* at my disposal which I perceive and apply; on the contrary it is what it is only as something continually perceived afresh and developing afresh . . . Not a general cosmic purpose, etc." (p. 7). This will lead him back to say that there is no valid knowledge of God outside of Christian revelation (all other knowledge of Him is *weltanschauung*). But is this true? Are they merely "general ideas"? (We can see in the longing for a *weltanschauung*, an escape from the enigma and from the decisive question of the moment . . . etc. But he has apparently not learned the religious and existentialist quality of Buddhism, Taoism, etc.)

Yet he admits that such a belief, genuine though it may be, *need* not be any more than a belief in man. And it does not yet have the "right" to speak to God (which Christianity assumes through the Word). Christianity fully exercises this right in acknowledging the fruit of lovelessness and this by positive recognition of existence "for the other" (person) and the "claims of this moment in love." What does this involve? A constant crisis in belief! Hence "Belief in God is never something we can have as a possession." Momentous consequences for our concept of *time*. Time is given us not to *keep* a faith we once had, but to acquire a faith we need *now*.

Let me therefore inscribe this at the head of a New Year, not of the dragon but of the Lord: "If in Christian belief in God we understand the claims of the 'moment' to be those of the 'thou' and of the demand to love, then it is clear that this crisis is in the constant struggle of hate against love and that this crisis becomes acute in every encounter with the 'thou' which thoughtlessly or selfishly we would disregard, maintaining our own rights and our own interests, in contempt or in undisguised hate." *(p. 15)*

January 3, 1964

Warm wind, bright sun, melting snow, water off the roof flashing in all the buckets. A good letter from Ernesto Cardenal came today – he has been with the Cuna Indians on the San Blas Islands off Panama, speaks very highly of them, loves them very much.

[Martin] Heidegger's notion that the realization and acceptance of death is the guarantee of authenticity in life and existence is very close to Rancé and probably a better formulation of what Rancé himself saw and wanted to say. It is in short a very monastic intuition. And I find much in the existentialists that is monastic. In any case, Heidegger is also fully Socratic – (his idea of "Nothing"). "Knowledge is in its very validity a form of untruth because it conceals the ignorance which it does not abolish."

([Harold John] Blackham, Six Existentialist Thinkers, [1959], p. 104)

January 4, 1964

The monks in Georgia think they are going to have the choral office in English *immediately* – and their Bishop is behind it. I don't know what the General Chapter (in two weeks, for the election of the new General) will do about this.

I got a letter from Jean Hering this morning: he is still in Strasbourg, retired, living in the old city, so it appears (Ovai des Bateliers). It was a very good letter and he sent some bibliographical references. I want to look up some of his articles.

A hunter, a fat-bottomed Robin Hood in a green outfit, was blasting into the treetops up at the end of the field to the east of the hermitage, too far for an edifying shout. But he went away.

The French nuclear deterrent shows something of the ridiculousness of this theory of war.

1. It can never really protect France against a serious determination on the part of an enemy to destroy it. Only make the enemy "pay for it" – and think twice in consequence before wiping the place out.

2. The payment? Cities. Cities *only*. There is no intention whatever of "counterforce" strategy, not even a pretense. It would be totally useless. Not that the destruction of cities would be "useful." This is the tactic of the elder daughter of the Church, and the land of St. Louis. It is possible St. Bernard would have approved. The late Abbot General certainly did.

3. If missiles are used, the country *may* have five minutes warning. That is to say it will take the missiles five minutes to arrive. Nothing is said

about how long it will take the computers to figure out whether or not they are missiles.

4. Planes will take fifteen minutes from Russia. But how to identify them? The sky is always full of all kinds of planes.

5. *The decision will be determined by computers.* Machines will decide whether Christian France is menaced and ought to wipe out a few Russian cities. It is taken as an article of (Christian) faith that the menace will come from Russia. This does not seem to be questioned even for a moment. With five minutes in which to ask questions, who will think of a good one? At any rate, only the machine can answer, and probably only the machine can ask one!

January 6, 1964. Epiphany

All day yesterday I was trying to remember the name of the affliction I got in my eyes and which was slightly bothersome recently. Could not get the word. This morning in demi-sleep, before awakening it came to me clearly, "conjunctivitis." And yesterday also in the field I could not remember the fourth member in the "Noble Eightfold Path" and today I looked it up: "Right *conduct*." So much for that!

Bultmann's *Essays* have been a revelation to me, so powerful, so urgent, so important that every sentence stops me and I don't seem to get anywhere. I am snowed under by it. The extraordinary grasp of Greek thought which he has and which he always transcends in order to end in a Biblical and eschatological freedom. The seminal influence of Heidegger, whom he appropriates and develops in a fully New Testament and Kerygmatic way. Fantastically good. How many of my own old ideas I can now abandon or revise. He has revealed to me the full limitations of all my early work, which is utterly naive and insufficient, except in what concerns my own experience. He says: "Grace can never be possessed but can only be received afresh again and again."

"Man comes into his present situation as in some way under constraint so that real freedom can only be received as a gift." One of the great temptations of an over institutionalized religion is precisely this: to keep man under the constraint of his own and his society's past so that this "safety" appears to be freedom. He is free to return to the familiar constraint, but this interferes with his freedom to respond to the gift of grace in Christ. This raises the whole problem of outward forms of worship, etc. and I think Bultmann is so far weak in his concept of the Church. But this is nevertheless a great truth which *must be* brought in to our view of the Church. Otherwise, where is the Holy Spirit? Where is the soul of this Body? He is perhaps extreme in denying that freedom can be a *quality* in us, and is only an *event* – only comes to us in an encounter. This may be hyperbole, and apply to grace. But man has a natural faculty to will freely, surely! This is not absent.

The "dread of being oneself" (as the great obstacle to freedom, for freedom is being oneself) – flight to authoritarianism and approval. Contrary: ability to make decisions as though they were not subject to the comment of other men – true solitude! Solitude of the poet in his decisions (quote from [Thornton] Wilder's *Ides of March* – I ought to read this!). Bultmann has a very real notion of tradition – not a past which provides refuge.

"True loyalty to tradition does not consist in the Christianization of a particular stage in history . . . always criticism of the present before the tribunal of tradition but also criticism of tradition before the Tribunal of the present day." "Real loyalty does not involve repetition but carrying things a step further" (p. 315). And this: "Freedom from the past does not result in a denial of the past but in the positive appreciation of it" (p. 321).

January 7, 1964

Thick, curious icy mist – vile weather for a cold (which I have). The mist had made a wonderful abstract pigment out of the silvery mass of manure in the night pasture. And the dry weeds too, silver with it!

One of the most striking and in some ways frightening events (at least as narrated in the news stories that have been read in the refectory) has been Pope Paul's visit to Palestine. After landing in Jordan and driving to Jerusalem he tried to make the Via Crucis. First he was met by people with palm branches: "recalling Christ's triumphal entrance into Jerusalem" said the United Press man – then there were women veiled in black on the housetops, clapping rhythmically. Then the crowd of 100,000 got out of control – not hostile, not friendly, just out of control, all rushing at the Pope, some with reason, some without. Some shouting in Arabic "The Father, the Father!" Then the crowd became "hysterical," the Pope was rushed through the first Stations of the Cross without being able even to see them, let alone stop and pray. At the Station of Veronica's veil he took refuge in the entry of a convent and "his face was ashen." He finally got to the Basilica of the Holy Sepulchre. A TV cable over his head caught fire while he was trying to say Mass. All the lights were out most of the time of his Mass. The whole narrative of his first day or so was of him being hustled by huge crowds, carried through mobs by Arab policemen, or having a way beaten for him with clubs!

As I was leaving the refectory early I heard something about his plan to go by car to Nazareth, meeting high Israeli officials at Meggido, "the Biblical Armageddon." This whole story had the most ominous and urgent sound about it, and it seemed to be fraught with a symbolic seriousness I could not interpret or fathom in any way: as if somehow the passion of Christ in the Church were being definitively announced, or something else more strange – perhaps put the disappearance of the Church in a huge whirlpool of confusion! Coming on top of the mass trauma following Kennedy's assassination and with the explicit terror that the Pope himself might get killed, and the general background of unreason, this gives the impression that the world is slowly going completely mad and no solemnity, no gesture of civility, pleasantness, good will, can prevent the unknown fury that is breaking – without explanation.

A youth (?) in California sent a manuscript of a book he had written saying I had advised him not to write it (I did not remember) and that I would not be able to resist the urge to read it. I resisted the urge without difficulty and sent it back by return mail. I would not care if he were the Shakespeare or the Dostoievsky of the new generation. I am just not reading any more manuscripts that people send in. Not that I have in the past. But now I will not even hesitate.

Yesterday Reverend Father announced the officers for the year – he was away at New Melleray with the Abbot of Mount Melleray on visitation for New Year. Friday he leaves for the General Chapter and the election of the new General.

I got a good note from Père Placide [Deseille] at Bellefontaine thanking me for my card which complimented him on his draft of the new Directory. He said there were quite a few objections: from Dutch abbots that it was "too traditional" and from American abbots that it was "too favorable to eremitism."

January 9, 1964

Dom James is saying Mass for all the novices, getting ready to leave tomorrow for the General Chapter and the election. The question has arisen: will Dom James himself be elected? I think not. He has acquired great prestige and power in the Order, certainly enough to warrant his election – but he cannot speak good French, does not really know the Order or the houses in

France and I would add he is not really aware of the genuine monastic traditions. He has his own rather short-sighted, oversimplified view of monasticism. (Keep them locked up and silent. What they don't know won't hurt them – No letters and contacts, or only the minimum – make them obey rules, etc.) Yet his view is popular among the Abbots. If he were elected it would be a victory for conservatism and the status quo. On the other hand – Dom Willebrord [Van Dijk] of Tilburg (Holland) represents a certain type of progressive outlook. Dom Edward of Westmalle in the middle. The new school is represented by Dom André Louf of Mont des Cats who is too young to get it – and too advanced.

Nevertheless the question also arises: if Dom James is elected, who will be elected *here?* I don't think there will be any problem, because Dom James will not be elected. Yet anything might happen. Who are the possible candidates? Father Flavian, Father Eudes, Father Baldwin, and myself. Perhaps a few votes for some one of the old guard or an abbot of a foundation. However, most of the chapter know of my vow not to accept an election – and hence would probably not vote for me – again no problem. Dan Walsh, Jim Wygal, and Father Gerard my confessor have all urged me to reconsider the whole thing. I do not see any reason to at the moment. My vow still stands, though it was made "into the hands of Dom Gabriel" who is dead. It still seems to me to be a greater good *not* to accept a position fraught with artificialities and stupidities, with things I do not believe in, and cannot. Things I cannot change, or even try to. I would get into an official and institutional harness which is to me totally suspect. I am urged to do it in order to change things, to be a "discerning force," etc., etc. Is this really possible? There is no point in considering it unless an election happens and I am really *ordered* by a higher superior to accept – and I still retain the power to refuse and still think I ought to. Yet I will reconsider if there is a *real* indication that it might be God's will for me to do so. I see no such indication anywhere at present. All I can say is that I will not be obdurately closed in on my own preferred solution. There is very little likelihood of the problem arising and it does not disturb me in the least.

January 10, 1964

Ad Reinhardt sent all kinds of fine paper, especially some thin, almost transparent beautiful Japanese paper on which I have found a way of crudely printing abstract "calligraphies" which in some cases turn out exciting – at least to me.

Fine afternoon after yesterday's rain. The snow has been washed away. The hills are purple and cold, sharply outlined.

Dom James left today for Rome. Three of us separately had told him he might be Abbot General himself – I – Father Prior (Flavian) and Father Eudes. Apparently it worried him enough to keep him awake last night. I should not be so unkind. Yet there *is* a slight chance.

Half the community seem to be making up new offices, reorganizing the liturgy, planning new ways of prayer. After a thousand years of stillness now it is every man for himself.

The Pope's short visit to Palestine, his talk with Patriarch Athenagoras, seem to have been after all something quite magnificent – a great thing, a sign of real life, full of hope and meaning.

Father Reinhold gave my manuscript on *Peace in the Post-Christian Era* to Bishop Wright,[18] who apparently is reading it with interest and seems to like it. I think he is taking it to Rome soon.

January 11, 1964

Moved by David Kirk's notes on Patriarch Maximos of Antioch, obviously one of the greatest men in the Church today. He is doing a lot for the monastic life. Maybe get Kirk to write some notes on this for the *Collectanea [Cisterciensia]*.

Much as I disagree with some of Bultmann's statements on non-Christian religions I cannot help being swayed and moved by his basic argument which is completely convincing – and most salutary. "God's grace is to man grace in such a thoroughgoing sense that it supports the whole of man's existence, and can only be conceived of as grace by those who surrender their whole existence and let themselves fall into the unfathomable, dizzy depths without seeking for something to hold on to" (*Essays*, p. 136). The great hope of our time is, it seems to me, *not* that the Church will become once again a world power and a dominant institution, but on the contrary that the power of faith and the Spirit will shake the world when Christians have lost what they held on to and have entered into the eschatological kingdom – where in fact they already are!

From a certain point of view my monastic life brings me "close to God," but this closeness is an illusion unless I see it also in some sense as *conflict* with Him and therefore as dread. Monastic Peace or Monastic Dread?

[18] Bishop John J. Wright, then bishop of Pittsburgh.

Both! Monastic life as a "sure thing," as answer to everything, can become a prevarication.

Bultmann again. "It is not just what is transitory in man that is given over to death – not just what is subject to fate, so that his will to love now triumphs, and his old ego is perpetuated in his indomitable will to love. On the contrary man is given over to death in his entirety so that he has become a new man in a radical sense. But that means that his will has become a new will and that in the security of his possession of immortality he is not relieved of all claims and he cannot enjoy his new life with a mind set at rest."

(Essays, p. 146)

Blackham, writing of Sartre, says wisely that "popular wisdom" easily accepts extreme views but not disturbing ones. The extreme view that to live well is impossible, and the other extreme, that to live well is easy: this they will accept. But Sartre's claim that to live well *is difficult and possible* they reject as despair. Sartre's courage is laudable, his stoicism is insufficient. His seriousness is the kind that makes possible the conflict and contact described by Bultmann. *In hoc laudo.* [Praise for this.] But his dogmatic humanism has no point except as a useful illusion.

January 13, 1964

Yesterday it snowed and there was sleet, wind and cold, queer frozen surface on the new snow, sleet like the manna in Exodus, but useless. And after I had ploughed my way around among the pine trees in a walk before Vespers, with snow flying into my eyes, my neck began to hurt. But Saturday was a bright day, even warm, and the Hammers [Victor and Carolyn] came over.

Saturday evening I got a call from Msgr. [William J.] McCormick in New York. He had been down a month ago to get me to write a short script for something in the Vatican Pavilion at the New York World's Fair. I did ["The Church Is Christ Alive in the World"], and it was mostly about charity, peace, racial justice, etc. Now he calls and evidently the script has been to [Francis Cardinal] Spellman and back in the meantime. The indications are that all this must be replaced by an apologetic text-book piece on the Church as the one true Church, "what we have that is different from the Protestants and the Orthodox" to dispel any confusion that may have been created "by all this ecumenical business." I suppose this was to have been expected. I asked him to send down notes of what he wants and I will try to do something. I am a bit doubtful of getting anything worth while out of this – perhaps a few lines that will have meaning for someone outside the Church. The rest? Will it even support Catholics in their convictions – or just be another four minutes of familiar jargon?

Jaspers talks of the "Augustinian turnabout." At one moment Augustine is saying "let none of us say he has already found the truth. Let us look for it as though we did not yet know it on either side" and then later he advocates using force against those who do not accept our faith. And apparently without feeling there is any problem. As the greatest of Catholic Doctors he has bequeathed this mentality to the entire Catholic Church – and to the Protestants as well, because he is as much their Father as ours! This is the mind of Western Christendom.

If in my Vatican Pavilion script I give the impression of openness and ecumenism will this not be a deception? The temptation is deliberately to write a closed, impassive, inattentive series of declarations and let the heathen draw their own conclusions!

January 14, 1964

I learned this morning of the death of Paul Hindemith. It is about ten years since his visit here, and I remember he and I and his wife took a long walk to the woods at the foot of Vineyard Knob, and talked about many things. He had just directed the first performance of the *Harmony of Worlds* at Minneapolis. He was talking about his collaboration with [Bertolt] Brecht (very funny) and about the "*Ite angeli veloces*" of [Paul] Claudel. A great person. I have not heard half of what he has written.

It is zero weather – the novitiate thermometer which is quite conservative registered ten above but others were claiming that their thermometers were ten below. The snow is deep, sparkles in the sun under the trees.

I wrote a few final pages for *Art and Worship* – on the Council Constitutions, and a Preface.

January 16, 1964

5:10 a.m. At Cîteaux it is noon – we may already have a new Abbot General – and may learn his name even before the singing of the conventual Mass of the Holy Spirit, "for the Chapter."

Notes that come to mind in connection with Merleau-Ponty. When men speak we assume they have something to say and know what it is. How often are these assumptions well-founded? Ambiguity of man who tries to emerge from his own darkness – and yet wants not to emerge. How often is speech an excuse for remaining within, on the grounds that one "has communicated." (Has "done his duty" – been to the toilet.)

The artist who recognizes and loves his own style – *au grand dommage de son oeuvre* [to the great detriment of his work] – the style being imagined as "himself." At this point he begins to know and will his style as it were without contact with the world, whereas in reality the style is only a by-product of that contact. Emblems – equivalences. Finding my own system of emblems. Picture of the back of [Georges] Braque's white head surrounded by his own bird emblems. He looks, sitting in a corduroy jacket. (Braque is dead.) Finding figures of being, or seeming to – when the painter no longer seems to himself to find these – he is dead. That is, he does not encounter the world, for the figure is his encounter. ("*Des groupes de beffrois assistent les idées des peuples*") ["Some groups of belfries assist the ideas of the people"] Rimbaud. Response to the past – one's own previous work, the work of others – reviewing the life that was in them.

I have an obligation to Paul Klee which goes deep even into the order of theology, an obligation about which I have done nothing. Knowing he is there in some museum or in the Skira [art] books is not enough. Nor is mimicry. My obligation is to seriously question him, and reply to *his* question addressed to me. To justify, in some sense, the faith in me which he never knew he had (for how would he know *me?*).

The artist has not been demonstrated to be a failure because of his neurosis appearing in his work. He may have *succeeded* in using all his experience (even sickness) to interpret the world ([Merleau-Ponty] *Signes*, p. 80).

January 17, 1964. St. Anthony

Yesterday at the beginning of the afternoon work, as I was settling down to change a typewriter ribbon and rewrite the script for the Vatican Pavilion, Brother Denis came and told me Dom Ignace Gillet, Abbot of Aiguebelle, was the new Abbot General. Later Brother Denis wanted to know if I thought the new General was a "return to sources" man and I said I thought probably not. Father Prior (Flavian) thinks this means a "strong Chapter" (or stronger at any rate than it was when under the massive power of Dom Gabriel). Dom Ignace is a Dom Gabriel man, and will probably hark back to him as the hero and model for all, without trying himself to do all that Dom Gabriel did.

For Merleau-Ponty our body is not an apparatus which, directed by the Spirit, makes use of pre-existing signs to express a meaning which is "there."

It is on the contrary a living instrument of its own life, *making sense*, by all its acts, of the world in which it is. The whole body is art and full of art. Corporeity is style. A deeply (religious) spiritual concept!! Corporiety – a sense and focus of intelligent convergences. "*Le propre du geste humain . . . d'inaugurer un sens.*" ["It is proper for human signs to make sense."] *(Signes, p. 85)*

All gestures part of a universal syntax – the proportion of monograms and inscapes. History as "horizontal transcendence" becomes a sacred cow (*Signes*, 88). That is to say an external power bearing down on us inexorably and demanding the immolation of the present, the recognition of our nothingness in the presence of what "Man" will "one day be." (For as yet he is not.) (Ibid.)

He sees more rightly than most Christians that in fact Christianity abolished subordination and revealed a new mystery in relation of man to God that is *not* vertical only or horizontal only, for "*le Christ atteste que Dieu ne serait pas pleinement Dieu sans épouser la condition d'homme*" ["Christ gives witness that God would not be completely God without embracing the human condition"] in whom we find God as our other self "*qui habite et authentifie notre obscurité*" ["who lives and verifies our obscurity"]. (Ibid.) The whole mystery of the Ascension is here!

(Stalinist) Marxist history – a newness of the future, a non-philosophy. History – the judgment not of *intentions* only nor of *consequences* only, but of the measure in which values have passed into facts by virtue of free action. (Hegel.) Hence the maturation of the future in the present, not the sacrifice of the present in the future. Brilliant diagnosis of the evil of our time: a dialectic between the pessimism of the neo-marxists and the laziness of the non-marxists, in complicity with each other to produce the "*puissance de mensonge et d'échec*" ["the force of untruth and of failure"] which stifles the whole world in self-deception and transforms everything into futility – because it makes us blind to the "grace of the event" and strangles expression, therefore history, for history is language, i.e. dialogue. A dialogue in which the speakers (artist, politician, etc.) lead each other to new values which they can recognize as being their own.

January 18, 1964

I wonder if anyone reads the monastic letters, etc. of Abelard. They are full of fine traditional material, in the manner of Jerome, clear, precise, and among the best monastic writings of the twelfth century. I am reading them now for the course on Bernard, in connection with *De Conversione*. Ought to do an article on them but I don't have time. Unable to buy [Franciscus Salesius] Schmitt's edition of Anselm. We have two volumes on interlibrary loan from West Baden – I have them until Easter and went to work on some of his letters too. A question of order, and of making time.

The great impact of Walker Percy's *Moviegoer* is that the whole book says in reality what the hero *is not* and expresses his awareness of what he is not. His sense of alienation, his comparative refusal to be alienated as everyone else is (not successful), his comparative acceptance of the ambiguity and failure. Book full of emblems and patterns of life. (The misty place where they fish, or rather his brother fishes, like a vague movie too.)

"*Le romancier tient à son lecteur, et tout homme à tout homme, un language d'initiés: initiés au monde, à l'univers des possibles que détient un corps humain*" ["The novelist converses with his reader in a language of initiates and every man to every man, people initiated into the universe of possibilities contained in the human body"] (Merleau-Ponty, *Signes*, p. 95). This describes exactly the awareness that is alive in Walker Percy's book – of the scene with the crippled child. "*Ce que nous voulons dire n'est pas devant nous, hors de toute parole, comme une pure signification. Ce n'est que l'excès de ce que nous vivons sur ce qui a été déjà dit*" ["What we want to say is not right in front of us, outside of every word, as a pure signification. It is only the excess of what we live over what has already been said"] (*Signes*, p. 104).

Real expression – a spontaneous elucidation of what we do not yet know rather than a final statement of what we have "acquired." But we go at it the other way: we pretend to say what we know. Our genuine surplus is what we do not know, and what will come to be known in our saying it to someone who will reply. For instance I am not now saying something I alone know, but what I have not fully comprehended in Merleau-Ponty, and what *he* did not know because it is my response, and what will (or will not) be elucidated in the response of some other. (And yet, awareness of this reader is also irrelevant.) But if this response is merely "objective" it is as yet nothing and it is as if I too had said nothing. To this I have no particular objection; someone else may hear what is here.

January 19, 1964

Last night I dreamt I was speaking to a kind and friendly Benedictine and saying to him with confident happiness and abandon that I *deserved* punishment for my sins (deserved and accepted it gladly) and he was apparently deprecating this, as if it were a "too extreme" spirituality – yet as though he half knew

I was right. Then this morning in Anselm's Meditations and Orations – I find his *"Digne, certe, digne!"* ["Fitting, certainly, fitting!"] (Med. 2).

Anselm's meditations and prayers are musical compositions. He can use his themes without inhibition. Themes on which we are condemned to be inarticulate, for if we tried to say what he says we could not be authentic. Those forms have been worn out by tired monks and no longer say what he wanted them to say. Yet how close he comes to existentialist nausea for instance in prayer 8 (on St. John Baptist!). Yet there is always the hope, the presence of the compassionate Christ (not permitted to the existentialist!). I love Anselm. I love these prayers, though I could never attempt to use such language myself.

Merleau-Ponty again – from Husserl – *"Penser n'est pas posséder des objets de pensée, c'est circonscrire par eux un domaine à penser, que nous ne pensons donc pas encore."* [To think is not to possess objects of thought; it is to use them to demarcate a domain of thinking that we never again think about.] *(Signes, p. 202)*

The appointment of a person called Thomas Mann – not the novelist but a Texas lawyer and politician – to run the country's Latin American affairs may be the first step towards serious troubles, and is perhaps the first indication (after the Texas beer party with Erhard) of President Johnson's limitations.

January 20, 1964

Importance of that solitude, which is a solitary, spiritual-material rehabilitation of the sensible not as *en soi* which I can relate to others, and *see* is relatable, as part of a narrative or an explanation, nor as object which I understand in any such sense, but as "self" known in and through me, knowing not only my own *"Einfassung"* ["setting"] (Husserl) but the sensible around me being conscious of itself as me – allowing nature to return this virginal, silent, secret, pure, unrelatable consciousness in me. The reality "before all thesis" before the beginning of dialectic and *en soi*, the singular and timeless (not part of any series) mutual exploration of silences and meanings with which my consciousness never manages to be quite simultaneous, but to which my body is present or in which it is present. The self-awareness of the great present in which my body is fully and uniquely situated ("my"? – not as "had" by me, though!!).

January 23, 1964

The retreat – brings up again the problem of my resentments, my frustrations, sense of being unfairly treated, cheated in fact and to some extent exploited. There may be from a certain point of view some truth in this, but if I attempt to treat Dom James as guilty or to see the indications in him of perverseness and failure of which he is himself unconscious, it does no good to anyone. I have no need to judge and no capacity to (Father Miller had a good conference on judging). What matters is the struggle to make the right adjustment in my own life, and this upsets me because there *is no pattern* for me to follow, and I don't have either the courage or the insight to follow the Holy Spirit in freedom. Hence my fear and my guilt, my indecisions, my hesitations, my back tracking, my attempts to cover myself when wrong, etc.

Actually it is a matter of deciding what limited and concrete view to take so as to fulfill my duty to God and to my community – and to obedience – and thus be the monk I am supposed to be and seek truth according as I am called to do so. If I were a man of love and spirit I would have no problem. So my job is to advance with the difficulty of one who lacks love and yet seeks it – and the realization that I am not supposed to solve all my problems for myself.

Hence a good, fruitful, though anguished meditation in the wood by St. Malachy's field. The paradise smell under the pines, the warm sun, the seat of branches. I need to find my way out of a constructed solitude which is actually the chief obstacle to the realization of true solitude in openness, inner subjectivity. (False solitude – built on an artificially induced awareness of unrealized possibilities of inner subjectivity. One prefers to keep them unrealized. Leads to a short circuit.)

Magnificent ending of Merleau-Ponty's essay on Husserl (*"Le Philosophe et son ombre"*). Must translate and meditate [on] this. All is there – (I mean all of Merleau-Ponty).

January 25, 1964

The year of the dragon has so far distinguished itself by strong, lusty winds – great windstorm the other night, some trees blew down in the woods near the hermitage (one across the path going up). Pine cones and bits of branches all over the lawn. And last night too, great strong winds fighting the side of the building. I still hear them grumbling around outside like friendly beasts. Moon at 3:30, over the cold garden full of wind.

Father Miller the retreat master, an O.M.I. trained in Texas, the most American of priests, middle aged, greying hair, tired, handsome, full of all the known intonations and insinuations, he embodies now in himself all the people he has talked to and pleased, all the groups of women he has comforted and made to laugh, all the service men, all the prisoners. With us he started on a military swing – we were in battle. Next we were sailing in the Gulf. And so on. He has given us mostly psychology, and that is par for the course. The community is disgruntled.

Things are more humane in the infirmary refectory this year as Brother Thaddeus has replaced Brother Wilfrid. (Wilfrid has left with his vines and his statues and his little games and gone to the library where a non-cook creates no problems.) Brother Theobald is still there in the kitchen, a patient, devoted brother from Florida whose charity edifies me. Honest and simple. He and Thaddeus seem very aware of themselves as a team, and they are perhaps the two children in red robes and false haloes in the unexplained picture on their notice board. (That notice board! The fragment of brown paper on which is scrawled "cheese for mixt and eggs for supper *always*" and after it in large print LEO. Deaf and irascible Brother Leo!)

Still on Anselm's Letters – and now too Caesarius of Arles.

"C'est la ruse majeure du pouvoir de persuader les hommes qu'ils gagnent quand il perdent" ["The major trick or deception used by power is to persuade men that they are winning when they are losing," *Signes*, p. 272], says Merleau-Ponty, commenting on Machiavelli. And he commends the honesty of Machiavelli for admitting that social conflict is the *basis* of all power. Also that the prince must not become the prisoner of a virtuous image of himself that would obstruct action made necessary by a sudden new aspect of the struggle for power. *"Véritable force d'âme puisqu'il s'agit, entre la volonté de plaire et de défi . . . de concevoir une enterprise historique à laquelle tous puissent se joindre"* ["True strength of soul is needed, since in between the will to please and defiance, it is necessary to conceive an historic enterprise in which all can join," *Signes*, p. 275]. On this historic magnanimity and altruism (everyone gets in on the power project) Merleau-Ponty bases his defense of Machiavelli as a realistic moralist. It establishes a genuine relationship, while the moralizing politician remains aloof. The realist *accepts* distance but mediates through it.

The need for constant self-revision, growth, leaving behind, renunciation of yesterday, yet in continuity with all yesterdays (to cling to the fact is to lose one's continuity with it, for this means clinging to what was not there). My ideas are always changing, always moving around one center, always seeing the center from somewhere else. I will always be accused of inconsistencies – and will no longer be there to hear the accusation.

January 26, 1964

"What makes us afraid is our great freedom, in face of the emptiness that has still to be filled." Jaspers. And again these concluding words from the arresting little pamphlet on *The European Spirit*. "The philosophically serious European is faced today with the choice between opposed philosophical possibilities. Will he enter the limited field of fixed truth which in the end has only to be obeyed; or will he go into the limitless open truth? . . . Will he win this perilous independence in perilous openness as in existential philosophy, the philosophy of communication in which the individual becomes himself on condition that others become themselves, in which there is no solitary peace but constant dissatisfaction and in which a man exposes his soul to suffering."

January 31, 1964

I begin my jubilee year, not exactly clear what I am doing, for everything is always beginning again. If everything in my life remains indefinite to some extent (though it is superficially definite) I accept this as a good thing. As a serious and perhaps troubling thing always faced with possibilities, I must recognize that many of the "possibilities" are so illusory or so impossible as not to be worth considering. And at times I will not know which to consider, which not.

The new *Monastic Studies* is out, only one copy in the house, in the Chapter Room. A long review takes in that Italian collection of monastic conferences in which Dom [Benedetto] Calati discusses me as – precisely what? As utterly out of his world. And of course he is right. I do not belong to his monastic world at all, am no part of it – the world where the status quo is just all right. On the other hand I do not rebel against it either, I am just not concerned with it. And thus from many points of view I am "not a monk." In general that is all right with me, since I need only to be concerned with loyalty to my own graces and my own task in life, not with being recognized by "them" in "their" categories. Unfortunately I must meet them somewhere in order to be true to myself and I don't know where. Perhaps never will.

Ambiguities here – 1) I know I should equally well read Sartre and Ammonas or Theodoret on Julian Saba. *Both* are relevant to me at the same time. To pretend otherwise would be to lie.

2) I suppose I still worry about disapproval, incomprehension. And tend to meet the problem in some wrong way. I must remain open to any legitimate criticism and suggestions, and not dress up the truth to make it ap-

pealing to some imaginary judge. To say God is my judge is to be closer to Sartre than to Calati . . . and this is the scandal (i.e., that there is humanly speaking *no* judge. Only the Holy Spirit!). I do find in Sartre a modesty, a gentleness, a concern for humanity, a simplicity that are too good not to acknowledge. At the same time there is the fact that if I give other monks nothing more than an example of frivolity and dilettantism, due to my fears and rebellions, my refusal to get to grips with what is really there . . . this would be bad, and Calati is right to see the danger. There is no one, however far left, I could appeal to against him if I were really frivolous – and unfortunately I am.

Hence the real enemy and danger are my lack of seriousness, my triviality, my dilettantism. These are deep in me, and have to be negotiated. I cannot escape them altogether. The point is that I have refused to simply merge them in a triviality and false seriousness that are general and canonized by the fact that they are common to many and officially approved. It is the old question of justification – not now theological but human. The thing is not to waste time justifying trivialities.

February 2, 1964

Purification. *Magnum haereditatis mysterium! Christus pro nobis homo factus, ingreditum in templum.* [Great mystery of inheritance! Christ made man for us goes into the sanctuary.] A marvelous, Greek-sounding line from the tenth responsory.

Getting to grips with my reality – (as if this were not going on all the time) coordinating, incorporating in a living regime all that I can reach to make relevant my presence here, on its way to ending. The religious depth of Ammonas, the perspicacity of Merleau-Ponty, even the tedious subtleties of Sartre, and always the Bible. Meetings of opposites, not carefully planned exclusions and mere inclusion of the familiar. A life of clashes and discoveries, not of repetitions: and yet also deep dread before God, and not trivial excitement.

One of the worst things I have ever done – the absurd enterprise of writing that text for the Vatican Pavilion. Nothing whatever to do with a movie. I must learn to refuse these baits. Yet how marvelous to really and competently do a movie! Merleau-Ponty's essay on the films – have important implications for the new liturgy. Liturgy on *"comportement"* [behavior]! Translating language of movies into Liturgy. *"(La liturgie) s'addresse à notre pouvoir de déchiffrer tacitement le monde ou les hommes et de coexister avec eux."*

["Liturgy addresses itself to our power to decipher tacitly the world or men and coexist with them," *Sens et non sens*, p. 103.] This is either so right or so utterly wrong as to be blasphemous. But in that case . . . ? Liturgy is to be experienced, and it is a film. Not past thought or willed. Experienced by the presentation of conducts. *"Non pas . . . chaque conscience et les autres, mais la conscience jetée dans le monde, soumise au regard des autres et apprenant d'eux ce qu'elle est"* ["Not . . . each conscience and the other consciences, but the conscience thrown into the world, submitted to the view of others and learning from others what it is"] (*Sens et non sens*, pp. 104–105). This needs interpretation (danger of the Fascist application, or the Soviet application of it!) but in the right sense it is "liturgy." Or is it? *"Engagement de la conscience dans un corps."* ["The engagement of a conscience in a body."]

February 4, 1964

Father Abbot got back on the first. Brother Finbarr made his profession on the [Feast of the] Purification. There were slight changes in the Liturgy (distribution of candles by Sacristan). I was late and was in the back – in fact in the Abbot's Matin stall, with the brothers. The Abbot has said little or nothing about the Chapter. He arrived home ahead of a letter dictated on tape, which is coming by boat and contains all his news. It is evidently news at which he is immensely pleased and I know from other sources (Father Gregory Borgstedt, O.S.B., who has come from the Prairies Monastery in Manitoba) that the plan to put all the brothers in white habits exactly like the choir has gone through – or has gone through *again*. I am not exactly clear as to where these things go when they "go through." Last time apparently it was "accepted" and now it is to be "presented to the congregation" or something. But in any event the cellar full of white habits which Dom James ordered two years ago will now be put on. And the brown habits which are falling to pieces will be put off and away. In my opinion this change is really silly.

In the first place many of the brothers themselves do not want it. And those who do, have perhaps a strange reason for wanting it. I do not really know where the idea originated and the reasons for it have never clearly been given, except the cliché about "all one family" which is used to explain anything that does not have a more specific explanation of its own. I have no objection whatever to the "one family" idea. On the contrary I think that in reality the white habit is going to defeat this purpose more than help it. It is simply resorting to blanket uniformity, a kind of totalizing, a reduction of differences, rather than an integration. In point of fact, I think the difference in habit, as the difference in schedule and manner of life between the two groups, had a profound importance for *unity*. Psychologically and spiritually the effect of "complementarity" – of two groups needing one another, completing one another by definite and useful functions, had and has a great deal of meaning both for brothers and choir. It made possible a sense of relationship, of mutual interdependence, which had great significance for unity. It produced an *organic* unity, living. It is being replaced by a juridical unity, a unity on paper. And it certainly seems that the whole thing will go further and that the two lives will be reduced to a uniform observance, with the brothers more and more involved in choir and withdrawn from work. This is what more of them, or more of the real brothers, actually want – quite the contrary. The impression I get is that the serious and very earnest desires of those who have genuine brothers' vocations are being ignored, and that a very beautiful way of life – a very monastic way, perhaps a more authentic monastic life than that of the "choir monk" – is being quietly done away with.

February 7, 1964. St. Romuald

Cold wind, dark sky and sleet. I emerge at the end of Sartre's involved meditation on Baudelaire [Eng. trans., 1950], like coming out of darkness underground into daylight with the last sentence: *"La choix libre que l'homme fait de soi-même s'identifie absolument avec ce qu'on appelle sa destinée"* ["The free choice that man makes of himself is absolutely identified with what one calls his destiny"] (p. 224). This is really just what, to the superficial observer, Sartre's liberty seems *not* to mean. For those who think this liberty is arbitrary and subject to no restraint or limit, his portrait of Baudelaire is the most clinical and exact condemnation of a liberty misused, inauthentic, steeped in "bad faith." In fact, for Sartre, Baudelaire is guilty of the primal sin of forcing together *en-soi* and *pour-soi*, willing the impossibility of their union. It is "original sin" in a very real sense for, in Sartre's philosophy, if *en-soi* and *pour-soi* could be identified their union would be God. To seek to identify them in oneself is to seek to be God – i.e., static (for Sartre) excuse, pure nature, subject as object for eternity. The sterility of Baudelaire's life ("going into the future backwards") is never for a moment justified by the beauty of his poetry.

Sartre is right in seeing the puerility and unreality of Baudelaire's supposed Catholicism. This is a very hard, honest and objective book. One has a hard time not agreeing with it – and I do whenever I understand it. It is tiresome in its sustained, uninterrupted intensity not even broken into chapters, barely into paragraphs. Existentialism and Zen are here at one in condemning subjectivity and self-contemplation and I am with them too. It remains to be seen how much of himself Sartre was analyzing in Baudelaire. A recent autobiographical piece of his may show. Show what? That we are all to some extent alike in our failure to be free. And some start more handicapped than others.

Curious that I have more (good) reactions to the article on the Shakers in the January *Jubilee* than to almost any such thing I have written. Also quite a few (well, three or four) references already to the letter on "Ecclesiastical Baroque" in this week's *Commonweal*.[19] One woman thought that because I was against covering priests with lace, I was attacking women.

3:15 p.m. Right on time the SAC plane from the base in upper New York flies low over the hills, slowly, ponderously and lightly as a shark in water, making the wide turn, in relative quiet, pretending we are God knows what city in Russia. Or whatever else it is they pretend to do. Perhaps they are looking for strange things in our afternoon sky where there are only a few pale grey and blue clouds (clouds as there used to be over the Channel at tea time when the Boulogne boat pulled into Folkestone).

Brother Alcuin with his frightened calf look ready to leave, ready to tear off into any field, has decided to try to make it in the Laybrothers and so took the brown habit today, and is more pleased, a little more relaxed, wandering about, hoping for approval. I hope he makes it.

Simone de Beauvoir in her ethic of ambiguity (a harsh ethic where faults are never expiable) sums up Christian ethics thus: "The divine law is imposed on the believer from the moment he decides to save his soul." But that is exactly the opposite of the truth. *Justis non est lex posita*. [Laws are not made for those who keep them.] Let us see whether Paul is not as good an existentialist as she is! And do we "decide to save" anything? If we do we soon find out how much we are capable of saving. To save one's soul (object) is in fact to seem to have it as an object to save ("He that would save his soul must lose it"). I find considerable moral beauty in the idea (if I have grasped it rightly) that man who seeks vainly to "be" in the fullest sense, and *to exist* in default of perfect being, merely coincides with himself in existence, in that his existence becomes a *revelation of being* for others. This is a very pure

---

[19] "The Shakers," *Jubilee* 11 (January 1964): 36–41. "Ecclesiastical Baroque," *Commonweal* 79 (February 7, 1964): 573–74.

notion. It is the function of liberty to make this acceptance. There is a very Christian temper in this existential attitude. We would say in sacrificing his desire to be absolute, man reveals the world to itself as the place of man's meeting with the glory of God in freedom. (The "glory of God," the Shekinah, not *as an object*.)

February 8, 1964

When lists are being made of sheep and goats in present-day Catholicism, [Georges] Bernanos is always sheep and angel, at least if you are liberal and forward looking. But the trouble is that in politics one may doubt that he was at times more liberal than anyone on the right wing. Actually, he is complex, inconsistent, *"un imaginatif"* ["an imaginitive person"], and though his *"grandes lumières"* ["great lights"] are, certainly, against Franco, much of the time he is singing lamentations over the modern world and harking back to a medieval and monarchic Europe. I can certainly sympathize with his lamentations – I have sung a few myself – but lamentations are useless. They say nothing. They are laudable expressions of feeling but one gets tired of them if one does not share the exact woe: and Bernanos' woes are all of ancient date, and have much concentrated on his will and daily manifestations of iniquity (real enough, if you like). I have here his *Chemin de la croix des armes* – written about France in World War II. It is often tedious. Perhaps something to refer to. So much vehemence, so much overflowing anger, over the daily misdeeds of a futile, deluded old man like Pétain. And yet he is right – and really on the side of the angels in denouncing the impotence of the old guard who did not believe in man, after what man had sacrificed under him at Verdun (p. 139). His *"goût du malheur"* ["unfortunate taste"] – a fine analysis! After years of being passed over, he takes his bitterness for strength. Bernanos is accused of being merely anti-democratic. But is this true? This is not just lamentation, or archaism. Maybe his ideas of honor, etc. are not so crazy as they seem! It is a question of paying for things with ourself and not with one's money – or someone else's.

"*Toute la liberté de l'homme est dans l'honneur, et c'est l'honneur qui nous faire libre.*" ["All the liberty of man is in honor, and it is honor which makes us free."] Is this just theater? Not at all. In the context ([Neville] Chamberlain and Munich) it is sober realism. And his criticism of the French hierarchy for supporting Vichy? It is aimed at Cardinal Suhard, remember![20] Bernanos may not be a great "liberal" but he is there to remind us of the

---

[20] Emmanuel Célestin Cardinal Suhard (1874–1949) was archbishop of Paris (1940–1949) during the Nazi occupation of France.

complexity of life and the uselessness of labels. A couple of pages he wrote in January 1942, on General de Gaulle and on the whole situation are not only honest but prophetic. I am sure he would no more be a "Gaulliste" today than he was then, but he had the situation summed up as well as anyone could have done it. And in the very middle of it all he declares himself a royalist.

February 10, 1964

Thick wet snow – with occasional thunder of jet planes above the snow clouds. Forty hours. Some faculty and students from the College of the Bible [Lexington, Kentucky] were here last evening, and then I was up with the novices for night adoration – quiet, peaceful, an untimely mosquito in the dark, well-warmed church.

Simone de Beauvoir has this to say, which corrects so many of the clichés about existentialism: "It is not true that the recognition of the freedom of others limits my own freedom. To be free is not to have the power to do anything you like; it is to be able to surpass the given toward an open future: the existence of others as a freedom defines my own situation and is even the condition of my own freedom." *(Ethics of Ambiguity, p. 91)*

The question is the "open future" in Luther's telling critique of religious vows. He is right, if the vows are not lived fully and freely. Simply to enclose oneself in the "given" is no glory to God.

February 11, 1964. Our Lady of Lourdes

Crisp snow, cold happy stars. Reading an ad about caffé espresso with rum in it, lured by delights! Tomorrow is Ash Wednesday. Thought of caffé Ronricco is a Mardi Gras indulgence. Deliberate, too!

Brother Alcuin seems happier in the Brothers. Brother Denis unwillingly and under compulsion writes rather good book reviews. I learn more and more to respect the mystery of other people's hesitations, so I will not push him to write more. He is translating a piece by [Irenée] Hausherr on Hesychasm. The other day I got a fine letter from Sister Prisca at Regina Laudis [Abbey, Bethlehem, Connecticut] about a visit she and another Sister had made to the Shaker Community at Sabbathday Lake in Maine. It was a very touching and beautiful meeting, full of authentic religious meaning and deep charity.

The warmth and beauty of Anselm's early letters are most helpful and salutary to one. How I need such *exempla* [examples]. Yet how impossible ever to be quite even that any more. Our charity must have a different style, as warm, but with less amplitude I suppose, a simpler expression.

My own letters – the result of harassed efforts to respond to all kinds of strangers everywhere. Of course there are too many to write to, or even to get Brother Dunstan to write to. To some, and to friends, and to publishers, and to magazine people, I must write, but it is hard to make sense in every letter, and typing is difficult because of my numb left hand, and sleepy arm. All the people who send books. I have several books Etta Gullick sent from Oxford and have not got to any of them yet (except to look at the selection from Anglican texts by P[aul] E[lmer] More). Then there is the tract on ecstasy Zalman Schachter sent [Lou Jacobs, *Tract on Ecstasy*, 1963]. He wants me to mark it up and pass it on to Gerald Heard. I have not begun to read it and have a kind of distaste for the idea of it. I am glutted with books and with a million trifles besides – articles on this and that. I balk at reading about Panama. I have had enough. (Yet I will read it because I am obliged in conscience to know at least vaguely what is happening.) Panama, Zanzibar, Cypress (Costas Papademas wrote from there, he flew back at Christmas). Kenya (Joy French wrote from there today – first time I have seen the new stamp of the independent nation) and then "the freeze" (on nuclear weapons) and various iniquities in Washington, and nonsense in Viet Nam (new dictator), so on and so on. Does one read about all this? Enough! Thank God tomorrow is Lent. I am glutted.

However, we are having (at my suggestion) a good article on the miners at Hazard, Ky., read in refectory. Father Raymond does not read it seriously, hams it [up], is a bit foolish with it. But it is a good article, witty, objective, compassionate, and not deluded by the revival of myths out of the old days, the thirties. A much more sinister problem. Not the old simple forthright business of miners and operators and union. The union is on the side of big operators against small operators – and miners have everyone against them.

Father Gregory Borgstedt was here from Mt. Saviour last week and today a week ago I wrote out notes that Dom Damasus [Winzen] will take personally to Pope Paul. Dom Damasus asked me for them – ideas on monastic reform.

Today constant snow, ever so blinding, pale-bright-blue sky such as I have sometimes seen in England on rare days in East Anglia. All the trees heavy with snow, and the hills hanging like white clouds in the sky. But much of the snow has melted off the trees and there is a slight mist over the sunny valley. No jets, for a wonder! Only a train off towards Lebanon.

Quiet afternoon! Peace! May this Lent be blessed with emptiness and peace and faith. (The woods echo with distant crows. A hen sings out happily at Andy Boone's, and snow falling from the trees makes the woods sound as though they were full of people walking through the bushes.)

An honest statement. "No action can be generated for man without its being immediately generated against men. This obvious truth, which is universally known, is however so bitter that the first concern of a doctrine of action is ordinarily to mask this element of failure that is inimical in any understanding. . . . In order to deny the outrage it is enough to deny the importance of the individual." *(Simone de Beauvoir, Ethics of Ambiguity, p. 99)*

February 13, 1964

St. Stephen of Grandmont today. A saint in whom no one is interested, and who will probably disappear from the new calendar.

One of the great discoveries and graces of this year has been Abbot Ammonas. A magnificent primitive spirituality, the best of the ancient Egyptians (with Anthony, whom he succeeded as Abbot of Pisgar). We have him in the *Patrologia Orientalis*, printed in 1913 – no one has done anything with it. Ammonas is not even in the dictionaries (except *Dictionaire d'histoire et de géographie ecclésiastiques* [Paris, 1912–]). Hausherr refers to him frequently, however. He should be translated and I might write an article on him. Grace of Lent. Thinking this morning of the meaning of *covenant* in my life. Ammonas on striving for the gift of the Spirit.

St. Anselm, to a monk – to meditate on death and then: "*Ab inceptis ergo nulla lassitudine deficias, sed potius quae tibi expediunt et quae nondum es agressus, in spe superni auxilii pro amore beati praemi incipias, ut ad sanctorum beatum consortium Christo ducente pervenias.*" ["Do not let laziness stop you from what you have begun; rather, begin doing what you need to do, and what you have not yet done, out of love for a blessed reward, and in hope of divine help, so that, with Christ as your guide, you may arrive at the blessed fellowship of the saints."] *(Epistle 35. Schmitt III.143)*

February 14, 1964

"*Adeo namque vilis mens mea quasi quadam naturali arctatur angustia bonaeque voluntatis languet imbecilitate, ut uni quamlibet parvae curae ceteris exclusis tota non sufficiat, et cuislibet oneris tentationisque gravedine victa succumbat.*" ["My poor mind is, as it were, shut up by some natural anguish and languishes in the weakness of good will, so that my entire mind does not suffice, all other

things being neglected, even for those matters of small moment, and my
mind has succumbed to the pressure of every burden and temptation."]

(Anselm, Epistle 50, [Schmitt] p. 163)

I feel the same *"naturalis angustia"* ["natural tension"], not that I am as
busy as Anselm. Fasting clears the head and lessens the *angustia*, also brings
order into one's life. I think I will try to work on Chuang Tzu finally, but all
my resolutions about work go out the window. I never seem to do what I
plan. Yesterday though, I finally finished going over the material to be
typed for *Seasons of Celebration*. Don't know whether it is good or not. About
on a level with the *New Man*.

February 17, 1964

After a rainy weekend, warmer days (first week of heat). Yesterday there was
a meadowlark in St. Edmund's field (broad sweep of grass and alfalfa with a
few oaks against the cloudy sky, on the distant hillside). Today, song sparrows around the beehives. (Daniel Rops book, *another* one, in the refectory,
mentioned medicinal qualities of honey and its part in the diet of the
promised Land). Wrote to Manuel Mantero in Madrid and Costas Papademas in Cypress – and Naomi Burton [Stone] in New York (she is worried
about that World's Fair text). I have been reading [Edward] Schillebeeckx
and he is really remarkable! Best theologian writing today, I believe.

A group of students from Asbury [Theological Seminary] was here today
and I saw them briefly before None.

February 18, 1964

"Ut apud te mens nostra tuo depideris fuequat quae si carnis maceratione cangiat."
[Merton's loose translation follows.] The desire and need to be clothed in
the light of the Spirit when in fact I am clothed in shame (and yet I see the
shame itself also as grace!!). The wonderful power of the Letters of Ammonas and his mystical doctrine. It is to me impressive, beyond all the others, beyond John of the Cross and [Meister] Eckhart, not to say the lesser
ones. It is the pure doctrine of Christian monastic mysticism.

It is my day of recollection and I am finally reading the unpublished and
strictly confidential "Schema" of Dom André Louf on *"Cistercian eremitism."* It is really a very careful and judicious study, and solid in theory,
though I do not agree with his theoretical solution – which was doubtless
tempered to be totally "safe" and acceptable to Dom Gabriel (which it was
not). His solution is that since the Cistercians occupy a definite place in the

ordo monasticus [monastic order] and should provide a quasi-solitude in community, an institutionally recognized eremitism on the margin of this life would be confusing and undesirable and therefore hermit vocations should transfer to the Camaldolese. This of course depends on whether the Cistercian community fulfills its proper function of providing a "quasi-eremitical solitude in community" by virtue of silence, poverty, seclusion, etc. In actual fact, with the uproar and activity, machines, etc., our monastery does not do this – as everyone realizes. Hence a marginal "eremitism" – which, however, is not serious or thorough – mostly a matter of walks in the woods alone. (But this is a *real need* and only thus can we meet something of our requirements.)

In my mind then the only solution here is – more of this "marginal" eremitism – and places where people can go for a day – even a week – alone. The "danger" is not terribly great. There are few who really want more than an afternoon's solitude. André Louf is very good about the naive self-assurance of cenobitic declarations that "all the solitude you need is found right in our own Order." He refers to St. Bernard and Blessed Guerric (already courageous enough!) but I am sure he meant Dom Gabriel who was utterly definite on this point. Later in the article he returns in practice to "marginal solitude" – *"une grande souplesse sur le plan concret"* ["a great flexibility in the concrete plan"] – and has very good suggestions all along the line. Father Prior, who spoke of this paper in Chapter when Dom James was gone (much to the latter's irritation), omitted the second part which is the best – the practical part. The theory alone is misleading and can be "used" against those who need solitude.

Dom André brings out this criterion of a fully solitary vocation, in a Cistercian. *"La fidelité soutenue du sujet à choisir spontanément, dans sa vie de cénobite, toujours les situations qui l'établissent dans un grand dénuement matériel, intellectuel, ou spirituel, l'obligeant à une vie de foi de plus en plus pure, entièrement suspendue au bon volonté du Seigneur."* ["The sustained faithfulness of a person in choosing spontaneously, in his life as a monk, always the situations that establish him in great material, intellectual or spiritual destitution, compels him to a life of faith that is more and more pure, entirely dependent on the good will of the Lord."]

How evident it is that this denudation has been lacking in my life. I have kept myself safely provided with lots of cushions (books, indulgences, etc.), yet I know that my way too is and must be a way of faith – I wish I had been more loyal to its graces! Yet in the long run I have tried to face contradictions and to let myself be caught in the seeming intolerable grip of conflicting opposites (to find there is no conflict when you face it!!). I have been slow and fearful, but God has kept pulling me in that direction nevertheless, and from time to time I see it! I will go on, with His grace. All the same, this accounts for a fantastic and humiliating ambiguity in my life, an ambiguity so great that I must forever give up trying to justify my course in the eyes of men, or even sometimes in my own. Sometimes I seem to be so wrong that it is frightening – yet there is always the realization that the apparently "right" course would in some mysterious way be even more wrong. And I cannot explain it. The only solution is, in all dread and humility, to accept not to be "right," and leave the consequences in God's hands.

André Louf has a fantastically accurate statement about the masked call to spiritual liberty that may go with a humiliating infirmity. One's vocation, one's incapacity becomes itself that liberty (it humiliates totally) – and we don't have the courage to see and admit it. Then we deprive ourselves of our joy. He does not say all this – the conclusions are from my own experience. How *good* God has really been to me! And through fear I have been ungrateful.

February 22, 1964

Today is the twenty-second anniversary of my reception of the habit. And in all sobriety and honesty I must admit that the twenty-two years have not been well spent, at least as far as my part in them has been concerned, although from God there has been nothing but grace and mercy. Rather twenty-two years of relative confusion, often coming close to doubt and infidelity, agonized aspirations for "something better," criticism of what I have, inexplicable inner suffering that is largely my own fault, insufficient efforts to overcome myself, inability to find my way, perhaps culpably straying off into things that do not concern me. Yet in the heart of it is a kind of standing aghast at the situation, the ambiguity, in which I find myself. In the depths of my heart I do embrace the Cross of Christ but I fear to verbalize about it, and wonder if this failure is a failure of faith . . . and so on. *Nescio, Domine, Miserere mei!* [I don't know, Lord. Have mercy on me!]

I do know this – that after the first half year or so (beginner's consolations!) I ran into years of false fervor, asceticism, intransigence, intolerance, and this lasted more or less until I was ordained. I am trying to get back now to a little of the asceticism (how awfully little!) without the intolerance and uncharity, yet I am still not broad and warm as a monk this long in the monastery ought to be. All this, I know, is useless talk. Better to find refuge in the psalms, in the chanted office, the Liturgy. That is deep and real, and one thing I have learned to trust – though I am suspicious of the nonsense and "projects" that always surround it.

Yesterday there was a building committee meeting. We are about to move into the renewed South wing (temporary library on third floor). The new abbatial suite is nearly finished. In about a year I suppose the refectory will move there (temporarily) too. I do not like the concrete shaft that is supposed to run down the middle of the facade, but having had my say against it I have nothing more to do. The waterworks has been running for a couple of months, or rather for about six weeks. When was it – end of retreat? – that the water suddenly got good again.

Is [Joseph] Lortz too severe on Erasmus? Reading him after dinner today I wondered about this. Erasmus was "hardly a Christian," etc. A scholar, an individualist, not enough sense of the Church, etc. Yet his piety is so clean, so simple and so real. It is a breath of fresh air after so much of the late M. G[ilmore]. In a way I like it even better than Thomas More's "Moralism." But was this not *needed* at this time? And it is completely Evangelical. Erasmus is perhaps one sided, perhaps lacking in the full Catholic spirit, was perhaps a danger in many ways, but how can one read him today without joy and agreement? He is a splendid writer and to my mind a deeply pious one. And his satires, are they after all too bitter, too extreme? One feels that his Catholic critics almost begrudge him his fidelity to the Church, as if, to satisfy them, he ought to have apostatized and given them an open and shut case against him.

February 23, 1964

Brother Benet (Leo Denoncourt) is back. A professed brother who went on leave of absence to a seminary to study for the priesthood, came back to choir novitiate last summer for a few weeks, left for New Hampshire in confusion on six months leave of absence, returned here to give it another try last week, but lost all his desire for it on the way down. Now he is in the guest house, confused, small, thin, tired, anxious. I am sorry for him and do not know how to help him. If he came in now he would last three days. He has apparently lost everything. Yet he was a good and seemingly happy brother. How does one explain these things? He entered too young? And so on!

February 24, 1964

There is going to be revolution all over Latin America. This revolution is *inevitable*. It can be either violent or non-violent. It depends on the comprehension of the U.S. whether the revolution is non-violent, reasoned, democratic, gradual and effective. The U.S. must *want* and *participate in* the revolutionary reforms that are demanded. It must share the difficulty and the sacrifice. Is it capable of this? The Panama crisis (now quiet) makes me think not. There is a total lack of comprehension of our involvement in Latin America and of Latin American needs and grievances. *Dire* needs, *just* grievances. The high wages of U.S. industrial workers are due in part to low wages of South American miners and agricultural workers. The profits of U.S. business are due in great part to the captive economies of one-crop states in Latin America. Hence the probability that the U.S. will support military oligarchies that support the mine owners and landed gentry in South America. Hence the probability of violent revolution. It will be an American revolution, hemispheric – in which the U.S. as a whole will figure as an upper-class oppressor and antagonist – class and national issues being thoroughly confused.

Today I said Mass for Latin America – not that the revolution should not happen, but that there may be a truly just social order, established not through chaos and violence, but solidly and in true equity. The Mass of the day was appropriate – especially the Lesson from Daniel 9. *"Propter peccata nostra, et iniquitates patrum nostrorum, Jerusalem et populus tuus in opprobium sunt omnibus per circuitum nostrum"* ["Because for our sins, and for the iniquities of our fathers, Jerusalem and thy people are become a reproach to all that are about us"], etc.

February 25, 1964

An unpublished great monastic dialogue in the *Missale Romanum* for 1956 has fine things in it. About prayer the last question (31) says that when we have done an injustice to another, his grievance stands between our prayer and God and prevents it from reaching God. Apply this to the world today, and to our American Church: our fellow man cries out to God against the injustice our system is doing to him. We prosper at his expense. Our concern for him is well meant, but illusory. It cannot be efficacious. It can only be a gesture. Yet the communist power system is in many respects worse. This too is cried out against. Our prayer is not valid unless we are willing to work to change the systems we now have – as *Mater et Magistra, Pacem in Terris* [papal encyclicals] have plainly said.

February 29, 1964

[Rolf] Hochhuth's *The Deputy* is in New York and everything explodes with it. Someone tucked under my napkin in refectory a couple of tearsheets from the *Herald Tribune* of last Sunday, by Hannah Arendt, on this play. (Probably Matt Scott.) The *Commonweal* is full of it (best article is by Friedrich Heer). Hochhuth apparently justifies his play as perfectly fair and not anti-Catholic because it is directed "only at Pius XII" and not at 260 other Popes. On the other hand it seems to me that this is precisely the injustice of the play. If there is responsibility, then the responsibility is the Church's and is not to be laid at the door of one Pope.

Pius XII was a complex and perhaps tormented person (who knows?), but at any rate he was the captive of his own idea of the Papacy and that was the Church's idea, the curial idea. Indeed he was prisoner of his own idea of the Church – even though he was the author of *Mystici Corporis* and *Mediator Dei*. Idea that the Church can by power politics and diplomacy achieve ends which are essentially charismatic! And this view unsensibly shades off to another: that the ends achieved by political means are in fact spiritual and sufficiently spiritual and for the good of all, for the glory of Christ, etc. Hence that political success in fact covers the neck of the Church and of souls in a critical situation. That which serves Papal policy is in fact the best for everybody and that which hinders it is evil.

But the Pope can see reality in *political* rather than in human and religious terms. He can favor people like Franco, Mussolini, even Hitler, and he can regard the Communists as the single incontrovertible menace to the Church, etc. In point of fact the fascist tendencies in the political thought of Pius XII enabled him even to neglect the Jews who had become Catholics and for whom he was responsible. Though of course he did try to intervene *unofficially* and non-politically for some Jews. Effect of the separatism of political reality from the rest of human reality.

Meanwhile the Church at large – Catholic Press, hierarchy, etc. – continues with much the same concept that dominated and guided Pius XII (it has not been radically changed even by the example of Pope John). Now that the question of the Jews has come up in the Council exactly the same roadblock is met with: one cannot go further because to defend the Jews even on religious and spiritual grounds has political implications that are disadvantageous!

The other day – a horrible afternoon. [James] Wygal was out here, it rained, we sat in the hermitage and made sandwiches for lunch, etc., wandered in the woods and I came home finally with flu. I felt that the whole thing had been a complete waste, an absurdity in which I had been pretending and had been untrue to myself, my life, my own vocation to solitude etc. [Four lines crossed out here.] I have nothing against consulting him once in a while and being on friendly terms in town, but something revolts in me when it comes to having him out here when no one else has such freedom. It is as if I were lying, as one often must in social life but for me there is *no reason* to do so, and no real excuse. [Four lines crossed out.]

I had somewhat the same feeling about Naomi Burton last summer. She is a good friend, too, and an old one, but she is not my sister or anything like that, and I got myself upset after acting more or less as if she were, when I knew I would not mean any such thing. I don't like this business and don't understand it. Perhaps largely a deficiency in myself, but in view of my situation, I think not, at least not altogether. There is more than a mere personal eccentricity here.

March 1, 1964

Returning to the problem of (useless) "social contacts," what is wrong is not so much the fact that they are social but that they are not *meaningfully* social in the context of my monastic life. An empty conviviality with people not of my own community, or contacts not demanded by charity, do not signify the confusion of a life that is uncertain of its commitment. This is intolerable. (It is *my* Billy Cosgrove–Father Urban situation!)

March 2, 1964

Dom Damian, Superior of the Trappist Monastery in Japan, has been here. I had to translate for him in Chapter Saturday (his French is very hard to follow). Main thing that impressed me in his talk was his fear of the new Japanese religion Soka Gokkai – fanatical right-wing religio-political movement that is growing faster than any other movement in the world today. Someday it may cause a lot of trouble.

Stay with Chuang Tzu, [César] Vallejo, etc. Be true to your afternoon and learn poetry and experience.

March 3, 1964

I had been hoping to republish the few articles on nuclear war which had been permitted by Dom Gabriel – thinking that it was enough that he had permitted them once. Not so. The new General, Dom Ignace, dug into the files, held a meeting of definitors, and declared that there was to be no republication of these articles. Thus I am still not permitted to say what Pope John said in *Pacem in Terris*. Reason: "That is not the job of a monk, it is for the Bishops." Certainly it has a basis in monastic tradition. *"Monachi plangentis non docentis est officium."* ["The job of the monk is to weep, not to teach."] But – with things here: our cheese business and all the other "plangent" functions we have undertaken, it seems strange that a monk should be forbidden to stand up for the truth, particularly when the truth (in this case) is disastrously neglected.

A grim insight into the stupor of the Church, in spite of all that has been attempted, all efforts to wake her up! It all falls into place. Pope Pius XII and the Jews, the Church in South America, the treatment of Negroes in the U.S., the Catholics on the French right in the Algerian affair, the German Catholics under Hitler. All this fits into one big picture and our contemplative recollection is not very impressive when it is seen only as another little piece fitted into the puzzle. The whole thing is too sad and too serious for bitterness. I have the impression that my education is beginning – only just beginning and that I have a lot more terrible things to learn before I can know the real meaning of hope.

There is no consolation, only futility, in the idea that one is a kind of martyr for a cause. I am not a martyr for anything, I am afraid. I wanted to act like a reasonable, civilized, responsible Christian of my time. I am not allowed to do this, and I am told I have renounced this – fine. In favor of what? In favor of a silence which is deeply and completely in complicity with all the forces that carry out oppression, injustice, aggression, exploitation, war. In other words silent complicity is presented as a "greater good" than honest, conscientious protest – it is supposed to be part of my vowed life, is for the "glory of God." Certainly I refuse complicity. My silence itself is a protest and those who know me are aware of this fact. I have at least been able to write enough to make that clear. Also I cannot leave here in order to protest since the meaning of any protest depends on my staying here. Anyway I am definitely *silenced* on the subject of nuclear war.

The letter [from Dom Ignace] also seemed to indicate that the whole book (*Seeds of Destruction*) was stopped, but this must be a mistake as the *Black Revolution* is appearing this month in France.

I have a splitting headache.

Later. In a way I am content. It certainly is a big step toward being less public. There *is* a great good in drying up and vanishing into the sand. Not into *this* kind of sand, however.

Instructed by Sartre. I know this is not an adventure, and it in no way has the mode of happening that belongs to an adventure. I too have never seriously had adventures or even "experiences," that "happen," that "arrive." I don't have the slightest objection to regard this prohibition on an "event" that has slowly "arrived" here from Rome and reached the point of happening as it were a puff of smoke, signalling the explosion of a non-lethal missile in my immediate neighborhood. (That is one of the things that most sickened me last Wednesday, Wygal's conviction that we were having "a wonderful time" and that some kind of event was taking place, which gave life a meaning. What actually happened was meaninglessness in the shape of an "Event.")

"Mais il faut choisir: vivre ou raconter" ["But one must choose: to live or to narrate"], says Sartre.

March 4, 1964

Raconter . . . but this is not a story. It is not an event and I am certain that I need to write in order to stay relatively honest or to become relatively honest. Not all writing is narration and one must also know when to stop. Certainly one thing is true – much of my writing is useless (and dishonest perhaps?) and the General's mind (not altogether crazy) is rightly armed against a kind of agitation and intellectual activism in the Order. I know that to some people I give a distressing impression of agitation and rambunctiousness. That is more their problem than mine, I believe. But I have to be careful to look for the greater good that goes with all obedience, and is hidden in it. And to see that this care truly does give honor and glory to God – otherwise we doubt His wisdom and His power. At the same time I must also have a care for the other aspects of His will, that justice be done and truth be defended – leaving to Him the manner in which *I* am to attempt these things.

Hence the thing is perhaps now to cut out unnecessary and hasty projects for magazines. Looking back on the Peace articles, the truth is they were ephemeral. There is no need for them to be published in book form now anyway. And a monk should not be writing mere editorials. Again – less writing for quick publication, less writing in debate on immediate controversial issues, more creative writing, deepening of thought, etc.

South wind. Thunder and lightning. (There was a cat running in the windy dark, through the light cast by the boot room window.) Last night when I came in to my room before going up to bed there was a copy of a new form of Compline, in English, by Brother Basil, waiting for me to examine and approve and support *apud abbatum* [with the abbot]. Liturgy and politics. I am not too eager to get involved in either one.

Proceeding in peace in the line of God's will – perhaps a deeper Biblical base for such solid views as I may have. A Protestant writer, A[mos] N[iven] Wilder, says: "The solitude of the Christian to the world and its institutions will be based on the word of the Cross, upon the Good News of God, upon the revelation of the righteousness of God, upon the post-resurrection faith of his disciples . . . (not) a social ethic based primarily upon the . . . Sermon on the Mount, or on natural law, or the inner light or the Holy Spirit. Rather the grace of God discloses itself to us in the Gospel message and impels us to what we should do to further the purposes of redemption in the world around us." (The Background of the New Testament and Its Eschatology, *pp. 5–7)*

On the other hand Ida Göerres writes that under pretext of "openness to the world" monastic and religious spirit is simply being extinguished in Germany and that last year a Dominican was crowned King of Fools at Mainz, in a carnival, on TV. She says her friends in convents who take the ascetic life seriously are "The Last of the Mohawks" (sic).

March 6, 1964

Dom Damian left for California and Japan yesterday – a good, simple, sincere man. He was held up a long time at the airport and there met and conversed with another visitor who had been held up on his way here. The Czech Protestant Theologian, Jan Milic Lochman. Quite providentially, due to a sudden change of plans, he came to Louisville instead of Richmond, Va. and John Heidbrink arranged for him to see us.

I had a good conversation sitting up late with him last night. About Barth (impressed, of all things, with Catholic "psychology"). He said Barth's book on Anselm is one of Barth's own favorites. Barth, like most Protestants, was profoundly impressed by Pope John and said of him that he must make Protestants take another look at the Papacy. He is an admirer of Bonhoeffer, naturally. Twice quoted Bonhoeffer as saying that to qualify to sing Gregorian chant under Hitler one had to identify himself with the Jews. But he does not go along with a one-sided enthusiasm for Bonhoeffer's plunge into the world, with no roots in Bonhoeffer's "concentration."

Theology in Czechoslovakia and East Germany seems very alive because it has to be a complete expression of life lived in confrontation with, in dialogue with godlessness. But a confrontation without the privilege of any battlements behind one, or without the benefit of a drawbridge, in fact without a crusade. This is the most important discovery of the Church in those countries. (I say "The Church" though Catholicism is being slow to discover it. There are still plenty of battlements in Poland.)

We agreed completely on Hochhuth.

It was a very moving and Christian conversation in which we agreed on Christ's word in the world, manifested in the problems that face us, found in the problems themselves (not in evasion). He spoke of the marvelous way in which a monk of Chevetogne had come to his place in Prague, and of the discussions of Catholic and Protestant laymen there and of the great openness that is beginning and of "In the confusion of man is the providence of God." At one moment I felt we were sitting in Emmaus, and when I left he gave me an offprint on Bonhoeffer signed "in the joy of the fellowship of pilgrims."

March 7, 1964

I am coming to see clearly the great importance of the concept of "realized eschatology" – the transformation of life and of human relations by Christ *now* (rather than an eschatology focussed on future cosmic events – the Jewish poetic figures to emphasize the transcendence of the Son of God). Realized eschatology is the heart of genuine Christian humanism and hence its tremendous importance for the Christian peace effort for example: the presence of the Holy Spirit, the call to repentance, the call to see Christ in Man, the presence of the redeeming power of the cross in the sacraments: these belong to the "last age" which we are in. But all these do not reveal their significance without a Christian Mission to peace, the preaching of the Gospel of unity, peace and mercy, the reconciliation of man with man, and so with God. The duty, however, does not mean that there will not at the same time be great cosmic upheavals. The preaching of peace by a remnant in an age of war and violence is one of the eschatological characteristics of the life of the Church. By this activity of the Church the work of God is mysteriously accomplished in the world.

March 8, 1964

Yesterday Dom Aelred Graham came and in the evening Miguel Grinberg from Argentina and Ron Connally from Washington with his little blonde baby in his arms and his wife in the Volkswagen family bus.

First copy this from the remarkable "Message to the Cronopios" of Grinberg. "How" – in what sense? Not "the latest" which will immediately be left behind.

"Se va más allá del poema suelto . . . para buscar la unidad poema-poeta." ["It goes further than the free poem . . . in search of poem-poet unity."]

". . . el oficio de poeta sigue siendo un asunto de fe y de fidelidad creativa. El poeta auténtico es primeramente fiel a sí mismo, única manera de no tracionar a quienes ama." [". . . the role of the poet continues to be a matter of faith and creative fidelity. The authentic poet is first of all faithful to himself. It is the only way not to betray those whom he loves."]

"Vivir la poesia es el ejercicio global del acto de existir, un desafío a la vanidad actual, un rechazo a la búsqueda del exito . . ." ["To living poetry is a global exercise of the act of existing, a challenge to vanity everywhere . . ."]

"La poesia: – alerta pennanente . . . un rechozo de la mentira . . . una proposición de solidaridad hacia hermanos más débiles . . . una manera de participar de la realidad y de trabajar por la paz . . ." ["Poetry: – Piercingly attentive . . . a rejection to lie . . . a proposition of solidarity with the weaker brothers . . . a way to participate in reality and work towards peace . . ."]

"El poeta es . . . un agente de paz, un ser solidario y creador que no fabrica respuestas masivas, sino que se presenta como respuesta, existiendo en la medida total de sus possibilidades. Redescubre permanentemente el mundo y hurgo constantemente su capacidad para hacer emerger todo lo que late en sus profundidades." ["The poet is . . . an agent of peace, a solitary being and creator, who does not fabricate massive answers, but presents himself as the answer, existing in the complete realm of his possibilities. He permanently discovers the world and constantly stirs up his capacity for allowing all that exists in his depths to surface."]

". . . un poema . . . un puente hacia otro ser . . . un acto de amor." [". . . a poem . . . a bridge to another being . . . an act of love."]

"Saquémonos la careta, dejemos de aspirar a la inmortalidad." ["Let's unmask ourselves, let's stop aspiring towards immortality."]

"Al margen de la indignación o la saturación resulta indispensable cesar un momento tanta avalancha de letra." ["At the margin of the indignation or saturation, it is indispensable to stop for a moment before the avalanche of words."]

"¿Y sinos nos planteamos seriamente la posibilidad de dejar de escribir deuna vez y para siempre y hacemos de nuestra propia vida un acto poético?" ["And what if we were seriously to pose the possibility of stopping writing once and for all and making our life a poetic act?"]

March 10, 1964

Heavy and steady rain with high winds for two days on end – and much rain before it. The Ohio Valley must be flooded. Here there is water everywhere, streams come from everywhere, and all night the air is full of the rushing of water and of wind. Wonderful black skies over the woods, great strong expectancy of spring in all the wet, black trees. Yellow waterfall over the new dam at the waterworks.

Last night I dreamed that a distinguished Lady Latinist came to give a talk to the novices on St. Bernard. Instead of a lecture she sang in Latin, with meters and flexes and puncta, what must have been a sermon of the saint – though I could not quite recognize it. The novices were restive and giggling, and this made me sad. In the middle Dom Frederic [Dunne] entered.[21] We stood. The singing was interrupted. I explained in an undertone that I had just now remembered the violation of enclosure and would remedy matters as soon as possible. Where did she come from? "Harvard," I said in a stage whisper she must have heard. Then the novices were in a big semi, loaded on the elevator (how?) to go down from the top of the building and instead of the Latinist coming with us, I left the novices to escort her down safely by the stairs, but now her clothes were soiled and torn, she was confused and sad, she had no Latin and nothing much of anything to say. Is this my dream of the Liturgical revival and of Anglicanism, etc. Perhaps some Anglican *anima* of my own?

Good talks with Dom Aelred on Sunday. He is very open and sympathetic and one of the most pleasant, understanding people I have ever run into. A lot has gone under the bridge since the *Atlantic* article[22] (which in any case was not so far wrong!). This is something to be grateful for and a real manifestation of the life of the Church in us.

With Miguel Grinberg yesterday. Rain. We could not go out. Mostly exchanging ideas and addresses. People I must find out about like Julio Cortazar and Witold Gombrowicz – and all those new poetry magazines in South America. Wonderful initiative and courage with which people start magazines and publish books (publishing is cheap and people *read* poetry: people, that is, not Mandarins). I think the *Nueva Solidaridad* is one of the most hopeful signs of life in the hemisphere.

---

[21] Frederic Dunne was the first American abbot of Our Lady of Gethsemani (1935–1948). He died in Knoxville, Tennessee, on August 4, 1948, en route to Gethsemani's new foundation at Conyers, Georgia.

[22] "Thomas Merton: A Modern Man in Reverse," *Atlantic Monthly* (January 1953): 70–74.

Last night as I was finishing my turn on the night-watch, the fire alarm went off and the signal indicated the calf barn. But there was nothing there except a lot of bewildered calves and a lot of hay. Everyone turned out in the rain – Brother René got there extraordinarily fast, and the fire engine dutifully traveled forty feet to be right on the scene. Nothing but rain.

Miguel Grinberg in Washington wrote a fine long poem about three windows (about the whole country). His apostolic account of the meeting of poets in Mexico, and Raquel Jordowsky who sold her piano to come from Peru, and the Venezuelans of St. Techo de la Ballena, etc.

March 11, 1964. Stephen of Obazine

John Harris says he is going to the Lot and Tarn area – and can he do anything for me there? It is still cloudy and rainy (only one dim star tried to look momentarily through the covering). Floods in Louisville and Cincinnati. Dan [Walsh] says that in Louisville the water is up to Market Street.

I finished the letters of St. Anselm this morning (volumes of Schmitt to go back to West Baden). Miguel Grinberg left yesterday, after we had walked a little in the cold, dark hillside to the south of the farrowing house taking pictures, talking of Nicanor Parra, Manuel de Cabral, and the unkindness of Vicente Huidobro to Vallejo.

At a building committee meeting yesterday it was decided to transfer the library to the Novitiate building.

March 14, 1964

The other day I saw the floods in Shepherdsville – a drab little town, almost a non-town – small houses and dark trees standing in the water of the Salt River. The turnpike was not covered and all the cars and trucks of the town were parked on embankments and overpasses where the water could not reach. Absence of people. The people had vanished and were nowhere except in the newspapers.

I read Camus' *Discours de Suede* in the University of Louisville library. Fed up with Louisville. Wish I did not have to go there.

Am reading the life of Christina of Markyate (recluse near St. Albans in the twelfth century) and find it marvelous [*The Life of Christina of Markyate, a Twelfth Century Recluse*, 1959].

March 15, 1964. Passion Sunday

Still cloudy and rainy. Two dogs yesterday worrying a dead woodchuck in the fields, disturbed me when I was writing a review (book on Protestant

Monasticism) [François Biot, *The Rise of Protestant Monasticism*, 1963]. Brother Finbarr who had a wisdom tooth out has been in the infirm[ary] refectory for a couple of days. The Abbot is getting rid of Finbarr's pigs, and our meat business is shutting down. Calendar in the infirm[ary] refectory shows now the Temple of the Emerald Buddha in Bangkok – a "top tourist attraction." Buddha too is in the tourist business in spite of himself, along with St. Peter, and the Christ of Corcovado, and Niagara Falls and Islands in the Sun and old Vienna and the Alps, etc.

To insist on living by the Law is to annul and reject the gift of God in Christ (Galatians 3:15–21). It is a refusal to live in and by Christ. It is a refusal to *be* Christ in nakedness and simplicity before the Father. "Death" is in "living" by the Law which constitutes me as separate, isolates me in my own judgment and justification, and confirms my isolation by giving me a "standard" with which to judge and reject others.

March 19, 1964. St. Joseph

Moved by the antiphons and music of this Feast which means more to me as years go on. Jan Lochman said Barth was much impressed by the studies of Catholic theologians on St. Joseph. I am beginning to be glad I learned (barely) to read German in school, and regret that I have let it go for so long, because it is a very rich language. The perfect language for an existential theology. And how much language has to do with expressing a particular facet of reality? Things can be *discovered* in German, that can be perhaps reproduced afterwards in other languages.

Deeply moved for instance by [Heinrich] Schlier's magnificent article "Eleutheria" [Freedom] in Kittel. A superb investigation of the relation of sin, death and works – which explains for one thing my disillusionment and exasperation with the proofs of my new book (*The Black Revolution* again). I am wrong, and wrong over again to expect some definitive meaning for my life to emerge from my works. All it points to is the end: death. It leads others to deception and hurries them along to their own death, yet even in this I must witness to life. Monastic implications of this fine article.

". . . self and others consumed in the Death Might in the ownmighty life!" The forfeited *Dasein* [being present] – forfeited to self and death, driving from Law to own life and therefore to death. Law awakens works which establish one in "ownlife" and therefore make one a gift to death, one draws death to himself in the works that establish one in "ownlife."

Ambivalence of obedience as a "work" which makes me "something" – a prey of death, as does ambition! Obedience presented as a "work" that is pure, that justifies, that is disinfected of self. But what obedience? Obedience to a *collective will* to power, to assertion, a collective might.

March 21, 1964. St. Benedict

The relic of St. Benedict not exposed. Hushed rumors going about that this is due to a letter of Father Chrysogonus from Rome who "cannot see how any relic of St. Benedict can be genuine." (It was exposed later.)

Today I finished after several days of continuous work, Schlier's splendid article "Eleutheria" in Kittel. Amazing how much Zen there is in these insights which are nevertheless so far beyond anything Buddhist, or passive, or negative. The fullest and most positive concept of freedom from death in our death-forfeited *dasein* (!!) in which the Flesh slavishly works to attain Lordship over itself. Emphasis on the works of love and freedom, of self-forgetfulness, that show us as free from death because free from concern with self-assertion and self-perpetuation and entirely open to others.

March 24, 1964

The frightful novel of Piotr Rawicz. *Blood from the Sky* is a true descent into hell, so much so that it seems to be a voice of Christ – that is, of the not damned – often innocent – even from hell. The innocence of the work, in all its honor, comes from its realization that all is sin and horror in the absence of mercy. The relentless, seething, objective, existentialist revelation of the betrayal of the Jews by the leaders of the people, by all the wise, all the just, all the capable, all the intelligent, all the holy – picture of the total degradation of everyone and everything, and totally fruitless. Conclusion – the stripping off of the desire for survival and "love of life" and showing it as horror, nausea, hatred, death-dealing selfishness, headed inexorably toward its own extinction. A terrible and honest revelation that pulverizes the silly optimism of those Christians who do not take those realities into account. (Imagine any one of our "movements" addressing itself to those people in the Ukraine and in that situation!!)

March 26, 1964. Holy Thursday

"All the moral wretchedness as we see it about us is *our* wretchedness and *our* weakness," says Hromadka, in a powerful article about the Christian's concern for the (godless) man of today. From such a one I am willing to learn. He says the obligation of the Christian in socialist society is first to understand that society, to love it and serve its spiritual needs, and to bring up children in truthfulness and reliability for the sake of helping in the task of building a new world. "Not with groaning but with joyful love for the man of this modern world of ours we want to bring a service which no one can bring in our stead."

March 27, 1964. Good Friday

Came up to the hermitage at 4 a.m. The moon poured down silence over the woods, and the frosty grass sparkled faintly. More than two hours of prayer in firelight. The sun appeared and rose at 6:45. Sweet pungent smell of hickory smoke, and silence, silence. But birds again – presence, awareness, sorry idiot life. Idiot existence, idiot not because it has to be but because it is not what it could be with a little more courage and care. In the end it all comes down to renunciation, the "infinite bonding" without which one cannot begin to talk of freedom – but it must be renunciation, not mere resignation, abdication, "giving up." There is no simple answer, least of all in the community. The ordinary answers tend to be confusing and to hide the truth, for which one must struggle in loneliness – but *why in desperation?* This is not necessary.

March 28, 1964. Holy Saturday

Nimis amara [exceedingly bitter] – these two words jumped out at me from the Improperia on Good Friday afternoon. We have all been a most bitter inheritance to our God! (The shameful injustices of South America, especially Northeastern Brazil!) More and more I see that we in the Church are deluded and complacent about ourselves. How much there is in our Liturgy that puts all the blame on the Jews – so that we ourselves enter the universal guilt without realizing it. But the improperia are clearly addressed to *us*. And yet St. Paul says this: "What if some were unfaithful? Does their faithlessness nullify the faithfulness of God? By no means: *Let God be true though every man be false!*" (Romans 3:3–4).

My bitterness is the savor of my own falsity, but my falsity cannot change the fidelity of God to me and to His Church. Hence I must forget my bitterness and love His fidelity, in compassion and concern for all who are, without knowing it, gall and bitterness in His world that His joy may change us all and awaken us to His truth. And that we may live His truth in fidelity and eliminate injustice and violence from the earth. If we seek this, at any rate, He will live in us. The results are not in our hands.

April 4, 1964

Saturday in Easter Week. The Hammers were coming but did not. Just as well, for it is cold, dark, windy, threatening. Last Thursday workmen began on the sunporch for infirmary and novitiate and there is much noise around there. Hats, pipes, sweaters, striding around in the center of unassembled concrete forms. The foundation is poured.

I have been reading [Konstantin] Paustovsky with pleasure [*The Story of a Life*, 1963]. It is a great book with wonderful warmth and reality. But Kafka is now read, I hear, in Russia and the official people don't know what to make of him now that they understand it is bad form to call him decadent. Formally and aggressively accused China of selling out the revolution (which must, when all the chips are down, be a violent one). The Russians drift home toward the west. Paustovsky is thoroughly European (he loved Latin and you would be hard put to it to find anyone in America so willing to admit it!). Yet Russian too.

Have borrowed [Henry Robert] McAdoo on Caroline Moral Theology [*The Structure of Caroline Moral Theology*, 1949] from Rev. [William K.] Hubbell (Episcopalian) in Lexington. I like it.

Yesterday under some pressure finished a piece on mercy which Abbé [Alphonse] Göettmann requested for a Festschrift to Albert Schweitzer.[13]

April 10, 1964

Sun, warmth, quiet, very distant diesel train (other side of New Haven), wind in the pine branches. Dogwood buds fatten and open a little (purple edges of their tiny smile) preparing to open. The visitation closed today. Some of my eccentricities were complained of, but I am officially established in my present offbeat schedule (for instance instead of going to Vigils I take some traction to get the kinks out of my neck and then go, about 2:45, to novitiate chapel for an hour of mental prayer and then Lauds. As long as the back does not get in good shape, this would seem to be the thing to do).

Dom Columban wrote a good card fairly well clarifying the situation of the Brothers – in transit to the "unified status," etc. I think this will bring relative peace. But elsewhere in the Order there is so far only question of the *novices* (brothers) being in white.

[13] "The Climate of Mercy," published in *L'Évangile de la Miséricorde: Hommage au Dr. Schweitzer* (Paris, 1965): 311–29.

Trouble brewing with Farrar, Straus, I feel it coming – over the unfortunate situation with *Seeds of Destruction*. I will be glad and relieved to get away from them. Still have to get one more book to them. The manuscript of the Liturgy book[24] is typed and waiting for corrections. I am certainly going to write less, at least less in the way of formal essays and articles, less preaching, perhaps more creatively, though the *Collectanea* (Father Charles Dumont) wants me to do the *"Chronique"* of Hindu, Buddhist, Sufi, etc. monasticism (is there such a thing as Sufi *monasticism??*). That will be a chore, but profitable. In truth and above all it is good to do something on the home team. Meanwhile I am glad at the official approval – unsought – which steers me a little more in the direction of solitude here. Now it is a matter of taking better advantage of it. Less scattered "secular" reading, fewer curiosities, a deeper and more eschatological outlook. Who knows?

April 11, 1964

The time has probably come to go back on all that I have said about one's "real self," etc., etc. And show that there is after all no hidden mysterious "real self" *other than* or "hiding behind" the self that one is, but what all the thinking does is to observe what is there or to objectify it and thus falsify it. The "real self" is not an object, but I have betrayed it by seeming to promise a possibility of knowing it somewhere, sometimes as a reward for astuteness, fidelity, and a quick-witted ability to stay one jump ahead of reality. However, the empirical self is not to be taken as fully "real." Here is where the illusion begins.

April 13, 1964

This would be the fiftieth birthday of the Worker Priest Henri Perrin if he were alive. The publishers have sent me proofs of his autobiography (actually a collection of fragments of letters) [*Priest and Worker: Autobiography of Fr. Henri Perrin,* 1964]. The fact is that he was driven to despair by the stolid conservatism of the Church – her *refusal* to become detached from sterile commitment to a society that is finished. As a matter of fact the whole question is perhaps less complicated than it may seem. So much of the class consciousness – (left wing or right wing) – in France is just bourgeois anyway. The guilt at *not* being a worker is a bourgeois guilt. Henri Perrin very impressed by this solidarity of workers as a class, and everywhere the underlying

---

[24] *Seasons of Celebration*, published in 1965.

idea of the book is his need for a "real" solidarity (such as that of the workers, or what he believes to be that of the workers) as opposed to the largely fictitious solidarity of bourgeois Catholics. One gets the impression that he is less concerned with saving the worker by bringing him to the Church than with saving the Church by bringing her to the worker. But isn't this because he has to a great extent accepted a myth about "The Worker"? On the other hand there is no question that the Church cannot live in a hothouse of comfortable and inane prosperity.

Note exactly the same torment of conscience in Sartre's preface to *Aden Arabie*. A long querulous self-examination and confession, based on the fact that *Aden Arabie* (by Paul Nizan) is itself another version of the same confession. Finally I have received a book about a Jesuit who was brainwashed in China and I have no trouble in imagining what *he* confessed (or did not confess) – that he too was a bourgeois and still a worker. Meanwhile out of Detroit come some curious and lively documents, from Negro workers, with a whole new slant. That, with automation work is going to become an anachronism. Then the worker will have the joy of bourgeois confession too! All this does not alter the fact that Perrin was a brave and serious man, honest and frank about the difficulties of life and honest about the failings of the Church. And of course quite right.

April 17, 1964

This week – second week after Easter – Gospel of the Good Shepherd, bright warm days, productive work. On Tuesday I wrote seventeen pages about Gandhi (for the little New Directions book)[25] and then had a kind of hemorrhage in the throat. Which did not matter or mean anything and it was a beautiful day! Finished the Gandhi piece on Wednesday afternoon and went over it writing corrections and additions Thursday (yesterday).

Today Marie Tadié[26] called from Paris – it was the first time I had ever made a transatlantic phone call and one could hear better than on some of the calls from one department to another in the monastery. *The Black Revolution* [*La Révolution noire*, 1964] is out in France and is doing well, apparently, as people in Italy and Spain already want it.

Yesterday the relic of Benedict Joseph Labre was exposed (his feast!). Also there was a building committee meeting in which the front of the

[25] *Gandhi on Non-Violence*, 1965.
[26] Merton's French translator.

South wing was saved from the indignities that had been planned for it. The new abbatial suite is nearly finished but the machines in the kitchens are creating a problem of noise.

Reading [Vasilii] Rozanov – a new selection has come out in French. He is an important and dire voice, shocking and deeply convincing, completely opposed to the current optimisms and "humanisms," and one cannot help listening seriously to his warnings about structures which are *without reservation*. True, when he condemns the cosmic Joy of Dostoievsky's Zossima one need not entirely agree – and yet there is [a] point in what he says. Curious how convincing he is, how he compels assent – at least my assent – even though what he says is outrageous and exactly contrary to all the plans of Christians who have decided to convince the world that we are "nice people." Monks would go to the theater if only the plays were "a little better"?! He shows this to be completely ludicrous. There is real originality here and a deep religious Spirit – even though one does not accept all his perspectives, or all the consequences of what he says: do there have to be Inquisitions?

April 20, 1964

Tomorrow, St. Anselm. It is quite hot. The work on the infirmary sun porch is getting into its second stage – an elevator is being set up to raise the cement to the second and third floors and pour slabs there. Dogwood and redbud everywhere. Especially beautiful dogwoods among the dark pines in the grove by St. Edmund's field yesterday – a grey afternoon, with a few drops of rain now and again.

Tom Burns (of Burns and Oates)[27] was here and I had some talks with him. The Hammers had also been over Saturday and I was a bit tired of talking (though it was nice sitting among the stones and wildflowers with Victor and Carolyn, and talking about various things – a letter from Ernst Jünger's brother which Victor read in German and which I easily understood – reading Kittel has done me good).

Deeply impressed by Rozanov in the heat behind the woodshed. A magnificent piece of writing about [Mariano Cardinal] Rampola [del Tindaro] celebrating the offices of Good Friday in St. Peter's. But above all this: "With the birth of Christ and the spread of the Gospel, all the fruits of the earth have become bitter. . . . It is impossible not to notice that one can

---

[27] Merton's English publisher.

become enthusiastic for art, for family, for politics or science only on condition that one does not look at Christ with full attention. Gogol looked *attentively* at Christ and threw away his pen and died." How true and how heart-rending: yet with what art it is said. And it depends what you mean by politics. Tsarist careerism – perhaps, or any kind of Byzantine – or Washingtonian – officialism. Yet the great religious issues today turn out to be also political. To look attentively at Christ and not see Auschwitz? He would admit that with his shocking and altogether wrong *"le Christ est le prince des cercueils!!!"* ["Christ is the prince of coffins!!!"]. Yet his sense of the need to turn from the world to God is basically and perfectly right.

Letter of Dom [Jean] Leclercq about this today, too. Very good. He goes to Africa in May, meeting of representatives from all the monasteries.

April 21, 1964. St. Anselm

Considerable attention – too much in fact – is being given to the project of six monks of Achel who are planning to form a new kind of group to live as contemplatives in the world and as wage earners, on the ground that the well-established business life of the big monastery is contrary to the monastic ideal and creates too much pressure. What I regret most is that this has been made public before they have even been approved – and perhaps approval has been refused them. I do not know. The last thing they want is publicity anyway. It may in itself be a good idea. There is one ambiguity, if it is looked at in our American context. That now with automation the jobs are getting fewer and should a contemplative monk be taking a job that someone needs in order to support a family? The big question is – should a monk be a wage earner? In any event there has been a lot of discussion and Dom Ignace has certainly been more broad minded than Dom Gabriel would have been. The thing is out in the open in the Order (not *here* of course!!) and is freely discussed and there has been a meeting of Abbots, Bishops, etc.

I was talking to the novices and juniors on *"revision de vie"* ["revision of life"] which is not for us as we now are, I believe. Evidently these are people who have been in that sort of thing and are imitating the Little Brothers. There may be something there. But I think the real issue is this: the monk's sense of *his own reality*, his own authenticity. The hunger to have a clear, satisfying idea of *who* he is and *what* he is and where he stands, e.g. his "place in the world." But in the world the monk has no place. He is a stranger and wanderer on the earth. He cannot have the comfort of a clear and respectable identity. That is precisely the trouble and the joke of a place like Gethsemani. The best formula is still, I think, the small farm-community like Erlach.

April 23, 1964

Real Spring weather – these are the precise days when everything changes. All the trees are fast beginning to be in leaf and the first green freshness of a new summer is all over the hills. Irreplaceable purity of these few days chosen by God as His sign!

Mixture of heavenliness and anguish. Seeing "heavenliness" suddenly for instance in the pure, pure, white of the mature dogwood blossoms against the dark evergreens in the cloudy garden. "Heavenliness" too of the song of the unknown bird that is perhaps here only for these days, passing through, a lovely, deep, simple song. Pure – no pathos, no statement, no desire, pure heavenly sound. Seized by this "heavenliness" as if I were a child – a child mind I have never done anything to deserve to have and which is my own part in the heavenly spring. Not of this world, or of my making. Born partly of physical anguish (which is really not there, though. It goes quickly). Sense that the "heavenliness" is the real nature of things *not* their nature, not *en soi*, but the fact they are a gift of love, and of freedom.

April 24, 1964

Heavenliness – again. For instance, walking up into the woods yesterday afternoon – as if my feet acquired a heavenly lightness from contact with the earth of the path. As though the earth itself were filled with an indescribable spirituality and lightness as if the true nature of the earth were to be heavenly, or rather as if all things, in truth, had a heavenly existence. As if existence itself were heavenliness. The same – at Mass, obviously. But with a new earthy and yet pure heavenliness of bread. The ikons, particularly of St. Elias and his great red globe of light, and the desert gold, the bird red of the mountain: all transformed!

Even in Rozanov: description of a small store in Moscow where everyone used to buy onions, dried fish, mushrooms on the first Monday of Lent.

Other things, simple, earthly and not heavenly, roosters crowing at Andy Boone's in the middle of the afternoon. Large dogwood blossoms in the wood, too large, past their prime, like artificial flowers made out of linen.

The sharp, splendid, reasonable, human prose of Paul Nizan describing a man of action in *Aden*.

These things are good, but not heavenly.

• Less quality – [Bernard] Berenson's diary. I have only dipped into it. Diary of an old man for whom the world has made a kind of sense and who knows a lot of people. Barely earthly.

April 28, 1964

Bright, delightful day, washed clean of all smoke and dust by two days' rain, brilliant sky, bird song, hills clothed in their green sweaters (brightness of the days and hills all clean, at the cottage, and Lax's poem). There was a tanager singing like a drop of blood in the tall thin pines – against the dark pine foliage and the blue sky with the light green of the new leaves on the tulip poplar (brightness of the sunny hills between Marseilles and Cassis that February morning in 1933, when I strolled out to walk the coast. Thirty-one years ago!!).

The thought of traveling is perhaps going soon to be a real temptation, because soon it may happen that permission to travel may be given. (It could now, but Dom James is so afraid to let anyone out.) Hence I must decide and have decided against it. Instead of idly wishing, for instance, that I could visit the Cistercian sites in Wales. There are two serious invitations among others. (1) to Collegeville [St. John's Abbey] in 1965, from Father Godfrey Diekmann. Douglas Steere mentioned this in a letter from Rome the other day. He said he had been talking to Father Häring about how "important" it was for me to come to this conference on the interior life. (2) to Cuernavaca, where I am invited now by Msgr. [Ivan] Illich for a retreat (to be given by René Voillaume), and a conference on Latin America. How tempting!!

There seems to be trouble with another disk lower in my spine. Considerable pain early yesterday morning and most of the day, tapered off after I spent some time lying down flat on my back. I was afraid I might have to go back to the hospital.

Today I have the whole day in solitude with Dom James' permission.

One thing is certain. I am *sick, nauseated* with the purposelessness and futility and excess of my activity. It is my fault for accepting invitations to do and write things. Though in many cases the wasting turns out profitable. For instance the Schweitzer thing. Also last week I finished the long introduction to selections from Gandhi. Yet should I have written the notes on Father Perrin ["The Tragedy of a Worker-Priest"]? Glad I got the stuff on the *Deputy* ["The Trial of Pope Pius XII"] back from [Justus George] Lawler. He wants it but I am reconsidering. One thing is certain – I am simply sur-

feited with words and typescript and print, surfeited to the point of utter
nausea. Surfeited with letters, too. This is so bad that it amounts to a sickness, like the obsessive gluttony of the rich woman in Theodoret who was
eating thirty chickens a day until some hermit cured her. The only hermit
that can cure me is myself and so I have to become that solitary in order to
qualify as my own physician. But I also see that I am so sick that the cure is
going to take time and if by the end of the year it can be well begun I can
count myself fortunate. One plan to begin is perhaps in the area of letters –
and I am so sick I don't know where, except that when I respond to *another*
one asking for a blurb I feel like a drunk and incontinent man falling into bed
with another whore, in spite of himself. The awful thing is that I *can't* stop.

At least in the middle of this afternoon they came to find me in the hermitage and said the editor of a Catholic magazine was there to see me. So I
said I could not come. At least that much grace, that much sanity. I would
only have been involved in nonsense about some article or other, some
pseudo-serious crusade or even if the issue itself were serious (race for instance) how serious would it be when we all got through mouthing our
words? I am tired of retching up avant garde opinions to create the illusion
that we are all awake and "forging ahead."

This morning I wanted to do some work on the booklet [*Come to the
Mountain*] I promised to the monks of Snowmass [St. Benedict's Abbey,
Colorado] (on the monastic life) but unfortunately the typewriter broke
down. I took it in to the monastery at noon, and now I am better off. One
job I will surely try to stay with – that of doing the *"Chronique"* for Père
Charles and his *Collectanea*, on Oriental Spirituality. This makes sense.
How much else does not!

April 30, 1964

The feast of St. Robert was showery. The men were pouring the slab for the
infirmary porch. Portable typewriter in the hands of Father Peter to be
fixed. Borrowed Brother Clement's Hermes, a beautiful little machine but I
couldn't find anything. Tried to do a little work on the Snowmass pamphlet
in order to get it out of the way, and wrote very badly. Have to see the doctor today so I will miss a day's work, which is why I worked yesterday, but it
was not a good enough reason. Too impatient to get clear of the jobs to
which I am committed and be "free," but that is not the way.

In the evening of the feast, the dogwood still in full bloom stood out
against the dark, distant, horizontal clouds of a clearing sky.

May 1, 1964

It was a lovely cool dawn, with a half-moon behind thin clouds and a great smell of cow dung around the monastery. Later when the sun rose hot and brave the smell was tar, and Negroes worked on the roof of the garage (they were doing the roof of the juniorate chapel the other day). Now in the afternoon there is some red machine whacking into the hill in the middle of the horse pasture to make an air hole down into Brother Clement's cheese curing cave which, some aver, is also supposed to be a fallout shelter. This is never said or admitted.

I have not been able to finish the Snowmass pamphlet and am disgusted with it. It is the worst piece of writing I have done in years. But as soon as I forget it, everything is all right. Perhaps I will finish it and forget it tomorrow. Clearly I have no longer any business even thinking about writing such things.

May 8, 1964

Finished the Snowmass pamphlet last Saturday. Sunday was a good day of recollection – long afternoon outside, alone.

On Monday I had to go to the hospital for some tests and the best that can be said of it was that I got back quickly – on Wednesday. Hospitals bore and irritate me. Not only that I feel, and am, trapped when I am in one, not only the noise (if they had not given me pills I could not have slept through the traffic noise of Preston Street) but the sense of being in a totally alien country, a country of ceaseless movement, in which things are thought to be happening: where, if necessary, ingenious and complicated happenings are arranged, and engage the full-time attention of entire teams of people (e.g. the glucose tolerance test I had to take). The best thing about it all was the half day of fasting and the blood letting. I came back lighter by a couple of pounds (175) and found the monastery full of heat and noise (they were pouring the top of the infirmary porch). I have still not ceased to be tired, but quails whistle in the field, and everything is green for there was much rain yesterday (Ascension Day).

The archbishop [John A. Floersh] entered the hospital same day as I did, Monday – but he has cancer, and faces a grave operation – may not survive it. Poor man. It is fifteen years since he ordained me, and he is getting old – was old then. I wrote him a letter and sent him a copy of the Guigo booklet.

James Laughlin is pleased with the Gandhi book [*Gandhi on Non-Violence*, 1965] which I sent him a week or ten days ago. That introduction was easy writing! I don't know how the Snowmass pamphlet will look. It is being typed now.

Read José Coronel Urtecho's long, witty poem about his wife in *El Paz y la Serpiento*. Mark Van Doren would like it. Too long to translate. Coronel and Cardenal are thinking of an anthology of my work in Spanish. I am eager to read Carlos Martinez Rivas (just sampled him when Cardenal was here). Good poems by [Ernesto] Meija Sanchez who has for some reason been in Lincoln, Nebraska.

May 10, 1964

[28]Much as I want to let go of every "distraction" and live in the woods without a thought of "the world" a sentence like the above proves the futility of mere solitude and the necessity to have some of the blank austerity of Robbe-Grillet in one's meditation – or to go out into that particular desert which the Spirit has provided for our century!!

May 12, 1964

A new loud noise over in the direction of the dehydrator – mechanical snoring which will probably become in some way permanent (perhaps a new alfalfa chopper). It is very insistent. The same problem of machines here remains. As we get more used to them, the noise increases. Small wonder that Brother Basil was in last evening talking about becoming a hermit. I wish there were some way of making it "normal" for those who seemingly have such a vocation to live a completely solitary life here, but I do think it is becoming gradually possible – and certainly a *partial* solitude is already available, as I have it.

Sad story of the affairs at Berryville [Holy Cross Abbey, Virginia] that led up to the resignation of Dom Hugh. I am not too clear about it, except that apparently the community was split into two groups, conservatives led by the novice master and others, "progressives." The novice master following the old Directory to the letter, etc. Dom Hugh, thought to be one of the best American Abbots, is now at Vina [New Clairvaux Monastery, California].

Dom James home from visitation in the South is constantly talking about the "bad effect" of sending students to Monte Cistello, and gloating over the fact that a "case" is being made out of it and an increasing number of

---

[28] In the original journal, this paragraph is preceded by an indecipherable quotation from Robbe-Grillet in French.

abbots are refusing to send students there – which he himself refused for years until forced to by Superiors. The main tenor of his idea is – distrust and dislike of the exchange of ideas and the communication that takes place there, and the fact that men return to their monasteries with "new ideas." It is true that they come back with some bad ideas, but merely stopping all communication and keeping everyone in the dark about new developments is no use. Brother Basil said Dom James is like a man at a desk with wind blowing in through an open window, trying to hold down as many papers as possible with both hands.

Scripture conference in Chapter today. Impression of the whole group sinking deeper and deeper into boredom and resignation until finally, at the "discussion" when the same dutiful ones as always stood up to speak, the whole place was enveloped in dense spiritual and intellectual fog. Is this irremediable? Perhaps, all things considered, it really is. A community of men dedicated to the contemplative life without too much sense of spiritual things. Earnestness cannot compensate for such a lack. Virtue is putting up with despondency that results when they try to hide our collective failure!

May 17, 1964. Whitsunday

Yesterday, on the Vigil, a group of the Hibakusha[19] on the World Peace Mission Pilgrimage came out here. The grass was all cut, the hermitage all swept, a lovely bright day, everything ideal except that I had attempted to provide ice water by just providing ice, expecting it to be melted by the time we came to needing it. But it had not melted. It was moving and good to have them there. People signed and marked by the cruelty of the age, signs on their flesh because of the *thoughts* in the minds of other men. They are an important indication of what certain "civilized" thinking really means. When we speak of "freedom" we are also saying that others like these good, charming, sweet, innocent people will be burned, annihilated, if and when we think we are menaced. Does this make sense? Is it not an indication that our thinking is absurdly flawed?

True, our thinking is logical and makes war seem right and necessary when it is fitted into a certain context, starting from certain supposed "axioms." The trouble is with the context and the axioms, and the root trouble is the whole concept of man and indeed of reality itself with which man operates. The thinking has not changed because the "axioms" have not

---

[19] Survivors of the bombing of Hiroshima and Nagasaki.

changed. They are the axioms of sophistry and sophistry as Plato knew spells tyranny and moral anarchy. An illuminating experience, to read the last pages of *Gorgias* and to meet the Hibakusha on the same day. I spoke to them briefly, was not expecting an interpreter and was a bit put out – he translated and explained enthusiastically and I think we were in good rapport but there was not much discussion. Dr. Matsumoto, affable and kind, wanted to take pictures and leave or he would have to speak in the evening. The others were in no hurry.

Hiromu Morishita, with his burned chin and his immense shyness, gave me to read a poem he had written. I wish I had had a chance to ask him about calligraphy. Nobozu Yamada – saw the Sengai calendar and was telling me of the "spiritual principles" on which Idemitsu runs his oil company. Yamada is an old-style Buddhist, full of ineffable gentleness and tact. Dr. Namakura – I had little chance to talk to him, but he too was shy. The boy and girl interpreters were full of life and charm, and having grown up since the war gave a totally different impression. I thought they were American educated at least. Much closer to us. I think the one who impressed me most was the most silent, Mrs. Tayoshi. She was always thoughtful, said nothing, very much apart yet very warm and good. All she did was come up silently and with a little smile slip a folded crane on the table (I had read them a poem on Paper Cranes). After they had all gone, it was Mrs. Tayoshi's paper crane that remained silent and eloquent, the most valid statement of the whole afternoon.

I forgot the newspaper reporter, Matsui, a very alert and pleasant man. It was wonderful to meet all these people, and quite a few monks and brothers came up to meet them, too. They had to leave earlier than we all expected.

May 22, 1964

Last day of a Paschaltide that was gone too fast. Getting warm. Trinity Sunday tomorrow. A busy week, with a novice leaving after a psychotic breakdown, and a postulant leaving because I knew, and he knew, he could not make it here. A day at Loretto, busy, much talking, and then Archbishop [Thomas] Roberts was here yesterday. He does not impress one as either starry eyed or fanatical but as a very solid, radical, clear thinking person. Perhaps a bit combative, certainly frank, and in no sense an ecclesiastical politician!! I think there really was something great about him and he is one of the few, perhaps the *only* bishop in the Church who is an outspoken pacifist! He has got the whole English hierarchy up in arms about birth control by suggesting that the Council ought to reconsider the Church's rigid position on this question of "Natural Law."

"La vraie et seule histoire d'une personne humaine c'est l'émergence graduelle de son voeu secret à travers sa vie publique; en agissant, loin de la souille, elle le purifie." ["The true and only story of a human person is the gradual emergence of his secret wish in his public life; in acting, far from defilement, it purifies him."]

May 26, 1964

Anniversary of ordination (fifteen years already!). I was expecting Zalman Schachter and two other Rabbis in the morning. So far, (late afternoon) they have not come and I am just as pleased! Too many visits and too much talking and also I am convinced that I have been involved in the wrong kind of talking – a kind of untrue and in a personal sense unfaithful playing with modes and perspectives which I do not find as important or as relevant as I seem to when I am talking about them. This gets back again to my deep, unresolved suspicion of activism and activistic optimism in which there seems to me to be a very notable amount of illusion (though no one speaks intelligently *against* it) because I find in it no rest, no certainty, no real deep sense. This may be due to a lack in my own life and so I cannot feel sure of my misgivings. The fact remains that I feel myself in fact caught, and hesitant, indeed profoundly dubious between the two triumphalisms of the Council: that of the conservatives, the static kind, which is obviously absurd (note the interesting connection between this and a certain type of Marian dogmatism) and that of the progressives, the dynamic kind, which after all is in a kind of frenzy over accidentals to a great extent (nuns' habits) and is also somewhat naive in its estimates of the possible future. Behind this one senses serious possibilities for real intelligence and real concern. (Pope Paul's talk at the Brazilian College read today.)

May 29, 1964

Yesterday, Corpus Christi, was a day of cold, pouring, beating rain, crashing down uninterruptedly through the trees. For the first time, no complex, formal designs in the cloister, only a neat carpet of alfalfa, but the smell of alfalfa in the cloister and church is vile. Some of the seniors were furious about this, of course (furious about the end of the formal designs and all the hullabaloo that went with them).

A student from the Cistercians at Spring Bank is on retreat here and I spoke with him briefly. Things do not sound too wonderful up there, but

I wonder what they can possibly do. Got a note from Dom Leclercq in Africa. He read his excellent essay on *"l'érémitisme en occident"* in the Athos volume.

Am reading [R. M.] Enomiya Lasalle, in German, on Zen, and like it [*Zen, Weg zur Erleuchtung*, 1960]. Fascinating picture of *shiji*, a Zen nest among evergreens in the mountains!

June 2, 1964

More business visits. Yesterday afternoon a long council meeting (the first time there has been a serious discussion in the council of the problem of noise around here). In the middle of it a call came from Bob Giroux in New York. It appears that the problem of publishing *Seeds of Destruction* is being finally resolved. (Giroux wrote to the General and got a settlement. One essay on war may be printed if I will "transform" it. What the "transformation" requires I do not yet know.)

Bishop John Gran, the Norwegian Cistercian from Caldey who is now coadjutor of Oslo, is here after wild traveling. Had supper with him and Rev. Father and Father Eudes last evening. Mostly anecdotes about Cardinal [Richard] Cushing [of Boston], and some talk about monastic questions of friendship in the monastery.

Saturday I spent the afternoon (at Rev. Father's desire) with the wife of the head of Columbia Records [Goddard Lieberson]. She turned out to be [Vera] Zorina, who starred in Claudel's *Jeanne d'Arc* and also it was the feast of St. Joan. Very good, spiritual, a bit tormented and I like her. She is Norwegian too and knows the Bishop. It was nice to talk to someone with whom I instinctively felt I had a lot in common. Yet at the same time there is not much use getting terribly involved in direction, etc.

Morning mist clearing – a sweet dialogue of woodthrushes outside the window. Before the mist cleared I would have thought the window looked out perhaps on the sea, through the gap in the trees. Now the familiar fields and woods appear but not yet the hills on the other side of the valley.

Reading about Celtic monasticism, the hermits, lyric poets, travelers, etc. A new world that has waited until this time to open up.

I suppose that in some way I have been going through a small spiritual crisis. Nothing new, only the usual crisis and struggle, a little more intensified by the "fiftieth year." Still it is getting to be quite decisive because there are fewer evasions possible. As I go on, the ways of escape are progressively closed, renounced, or otherwise abandoned. I know now that I am really committed to stability here, and that even the thought of *temporary* travel is useless and vain. I know that my contacts with others of like mind by mail, etc. are relatively meaningless, though they may have some *raison d'être*. I know that my writing solves nothing for me personally and that it has created some problems which are still unresolved. I know there is nothing to be solved or settled by any special adjustment within the framework of the community. That my position is definitively ambiguous and my job is to accept this with the smallest possible amount of bad faith.

Today I have faced the fact that even if I could obtain permission to live permanently in the hermitage (I don't think under Dom James this is possible and under his successor I will be too old) it would not be the solution it once appeared to be but only "vanity and vexation of spirit." However, all this being true, it also remains true that the hermitage is there and I should make the best use of it, not as an evasion but as a real place of prayer and self-renunciation.

Reading the little book on Eberhard Arnold on the Bruderhof [Emmy Arnold, *Torches Together: The Beginning and Early Years of the Bruderhof Communities*, 1964]. I think this (from his statement on his fiftieth birthday) applies well enough to be almost a word of God to me. "Let us pledge to him that all our own power will remain dismantled and will keep on being dismantled among us. Let us pledge that the only thing that will count among us will be the power and authority of God in Jesus Christ through the Holy Spirit; that it will never again be us that count but that God above will rule and govern in Christ and the Holy Spirit."

June 12, 1964

Full summer heat. Blazing and stifling. Not cool anywhere, either at hermitage or in monastery. (The novitiate generally gets a cool breeze from the forest, to the N.W.)

A busy week. I finished the rewriting I was asked to for the peace section of *Seeds of Destruction*. Two new poems also.

After writing the above about travel – by surprise I got a letter Wednesday from Daisetz Teitaro Suzuki's secretary saying Suzuki was going to be in New York this month, could definitely not come here, but really wanted to meet me: so could I come there? I thought about it and since it is probably the only chance I will ever have to speak to him, I thought it important enough to ask Dom James' permission. I certainly did not think he would give it, but, somewhat reluctantly, he did, and a flight is booked for me next Monday 15th. Since this decision has been reached I am upset and distracted, certainly without much real joy at the thought of seeing Suzuki. I can think of nowhere I would less rather go than New York. I am to stay on the Columbia campus or at any rate uptown, out of the midtown section where I would meet friends, and that is all right.

The only way I can stomach the whole idea is that I think, in good faith, it was God's will for me to ask, and for some reason I should go, not only for my own benefit. I am not supposed to understand, but have to trust. There is more here than I know. I see how much I am attached to this place, these woods, this silence. That is as it should be. And if I am to be shaken up a bit, shaken "loose," that is good also.

June 13, 1964

Rain in the night, at bedtime. Rain this morning during my early Mass, Mass of Our Lady. At the last Gospel I could see the blue vineyard knob in the grey west with a scapular of mist on it, and then during thanksgiving those other knobs, the pointed one, the woods, of which I never tire. Is it really true that I have no "place"? The little poplar tree I planted on the west side of the chapel in 1957 or 58 is now up to the second floor windows, and I saw great drops of rain sitting on the fat leaves after the rain had stopped.

Where will I say Mass in New York? Corpus Christi probably. Last night I dreamt I had found a clean, cool convent of nuns on West 114th, near where I used to have my room. I seem to think less about Suzuki than about a million trifles: will I get to the Guggenheim museum: will I find *all* the Klees in the Guggenheim museum? Will I find Rajput painting and Zen drawings in the Metropolitan, and will I perhaps slyly get to some concert?

PART II

The Suzuki Visit

June 1964

June 15, 1964

All shaved and ready to go after I get Father Abbot's blessing and some money. But I can't say I look forward to the trip with pleasure or with joy. I have thought of all kinds of things that could be unpleasant (boring and talkative neighbor on the plane) and the mere thought of New York gives me stomach spasms. Seeing Suzuki is important, and this is in the hands of God.

Apart from this, New York is in a ferment with the race trouble, and I may witness a little of it, who knows? Columbia is right over Harlem. There has been violence on a small scale all around Harlem and near it. What can one do or think in the presence of blind and irrational forces, which are so inevitable and so understandable? Causes have effects, and the effects are long overdue. What else can one expect? If only people knew what to do. No one really does. Legislation is far behind the needs. If by chance I were to suffer something in and for this critical need, at least that might be offered. Suffering and silence are perhaps the greatest values – provided one has not hesitated to speak, even though uselessly, when speaking was demanded.

However, I have no intention of looking for trouble. I have one job to do: to see Suzuki and try if possible to keep my presence in New York unknown. And then perhaps to look up a few things in the libraries.

June 16, 1964

Extraordinary climb and lift of the jet (my first time on one) straight up into the clouds like a huge projectile, leaving over Louisville and the river, out of the dirty mist lying on the valley like a scum of water, fairly large wave of cumuli rising here and there out of the scum like something in a fair or dream.

After Columbus (long stay during which I read a John Cheever story in the *New Yorker*) terrific climb to get over storms, and then the usual thing,

as soon as you are 35,000 feet on top of piles of bright cloud in the absolutely pure sky, the girls start bringing you shrimps. Extraordinary –
when the girl came to ask my destination, and when New York came out as
the most obvious and natural thing in the world, I suddenly realized after all
that I was a New Yorker – and when people had asked my destination in the
past, it was New York, to which I was coming back.

Actually I thought I was going to hate the trip – but I loved it, and as
Sandy Hook came in sight I knew what it was, immediately. Then the long
string of beaches on the Jersey shore, and the twinkling water with boats in
it, and dark brown hot Brooklyn and Manhattan over there. Idlewild,
Kennedy Airport, enormous rumble of trucks and buildings, a vast con-
geries of airports, and then in the American Airlines Building fantastic beings, lovely humans, assured yet resigned, some extraordinarily beautiful,
all mature and sophisticated actual people, with whom I was in a profound
rapport of warmth and recognition – these are my people for God's sake! I
had forgotten – the tone of voice, the awareness, the weariness, the readiness to keep standing, an amazing existence, the realization of the fallible
condition of man, and of the fantastic complexity of modern life.

I loved being here, seeing familiar houses and places and unfamiliar huge
apartments yet knowing where I was (Forest Hills, e.g.). Then sure enough
the Fair, preposterous, just like the old one but tamer, no tower and ball,
but the same place, same Jewish cemetery that I used to look at with river-
dazed eyes. I tried to pick out Hillside Avenue (Elder Avenue) or whatever
the street was where I lived forty years ago.

Morning of the 16th bright clear sky and wind on Broadway, noble and
vast with lots of new trees. Mass at Corpus Christi all by myself at Our
Lady's altar before that lovely Italian Medieval triptych – no word for it.
Fortunately the priest whose alb I had grabbed and who was to say the 8
o'clock mass was late. Good morning in the library. Read the *Teaching of
Maelruain* (Rule of Tallaght) and some Irish poems. On FM in the afternoon Mozart's 21st Piano Concerto and a lot of the new jazz. Van Gogh exhibition at the Guggenheim. Some of his last things most moving, the vast
open sky over a field, a tree full of black calligraphy with a wonderful saf-
fron light around it and dark world. The Chateau of Anvier. I had never
seen this. One of his greatest. Also the yellow house at Arles and self-
portraits (better ones here).

My room in Butler Hall [at Columbia University] looks out over Harlem.
Out of Harlem – the noise of traffic and the uninterrupted cries of playing

children, cries of life and joy coming out of purgatory, loud and strong the voice of a great living organism. Shots too – and there is no rifle range! Frequent shots – at what? More frequent than in the Kentucky woods behind the hermitage in hunting season. And drums, bongos, and the chanting of songs, and dogs barking and traffic, buses like jet planes. Above all the morning light, then the afternoon light, and the flashing windows of the big new housing developments.

The campus is better, the old south field track is gone, dorms there now (the sundial is gone), flashy new buildings and lots of foreign students.

About Suzuki later. How impressive and what a warm and charming visit today! The tea, the joy.

[June 17, 1964]

Suzuki and his secretary Mihoko Okamura. This a.m. he was reading from the Blue Cliff Collection. How he liked the bits from Fernando Pessoa I read to him! His most enthusiastic response.

Yesterday – a little (very informal) tea ceremony – I liked the tea very much. Suzuki says [Paul] Tillich likes the tea ceremony, says it clears the head, and won't hear a word of [Meister] Eckhart, saying he is a heretic. That Zen is dying in Japan (and everywhere). On the poverty of translations of Zen texts into English.

Yesterday – his talk with Heidegger. "Thought Heidegger understood."

We could not get anywhere definite on the idea of "person." We are all different expressions (words) of the same emptiness (cf. Pessoa). Agreed on not encouraging novices to be "mystics." Mihoko Okamura told me how happy Suzuki was to see me and to be understood, and it was worthwhile to have written so many books, etc. Most of the Zen stories he told me I had heard before except for Hakuin's dream about his Mother and the mirrors. I asked him to write out the four ideographs of the tea ceremony. The thing he insisted on most – in Christianity and Buddhism – love more than enlightenment. He says he has written an essay on humor, based on Bespoir's *Le Rire*, which he considers very important. How much he likes Chuang Tzu – "he best philosophy in Asia."

June 20, 1964

The first thing about New York was that I was delighted to see it again, recognized Sandy Hook immediately from the air, and the new bridge over the Narrows. So much recognition, everywhere, right down to the two big gas tanks in Elmhurst, landmarks of all the family funerals, from mother, to

Aunt Elizabeth, to Pop's and Bonnemaman's! When the plane took off from Louisville and was climbing up above the clouds, the hostess came and asked my destination. I said New York and as soon as I said that, there was a great joy in my heart because after all, I was going *home!*

And staying in Butler Hall, on the thirteenth floor (I had 13A for two nights), watching sunset and sunrise over Harlem, and meditating, and looking out toward the Sound, when it was clear, and watching the red lights go on and off on top of the stacks of what must be the atomic reactor in Long Island City. There were shots in Harlem and I found out two gangs of Black Muslims were fighting. It was not at all secure and respectable around Butler Hall. There have been muggings and murders everywhere and the last day I was in New York a man was murdered in an elevator in an apartment house in the '90's.

Two good long talks with Suzuki. He is now ninety-four, bent, slow, deaf, but lively and very responsive. Much support from Mihoko Okamura, his secretary, very charming and lively. They were both *extremely* friendly. Apparently he had read several of my books, and it seems a lot of Zen people read *The Ascent to Truth*. That is somewhat consoling, though it is my wordiest and in some ways emptiest book. He was very pleased with the essay in *Continuum*,[1] thought it one of the best things on Zen to have been written in the West. Mihoko made the green tea and whisked it up in the dark brown bowl and I drank it in three and a half sips as prescribed: but found it wonderful. (J. Laughlin had said it was awful.)

So I sat with Suzuki on the sofa and we talked of all kinds of things to do with Zen and with life. He read to me from a Chinese text – familiar stories. I translated to him from Octavio Paz's Spanish version of Fernando Pessoa. There were some things he liked immensely. (Especially "Praise be to God that I am not good!" – "That is so important," said Suzuki with great feeling.) He likes Eckhart, as I already know from the book I got at the University of Kentucky several years ago. These talks were very pleasant, and profoundly important to me – to see and experience the fact that there really is a deep understanding between myself and this extraordinary and simple man whom I have been reading for about ten years with great attention. A sense of being "situated" in this world. This is a legitimate consideration, but must not be misunderstood. A story he told of Hakuin's dream of his mother was new to me. The mother with two mirrors, one in each sleeve,

---

[1] "The Zen Revival," *Continuum* (Winter 1964): 523–38.

the first one black, the second containing all things. Then on the first one Hakuin sees all things and Himself seeing them looking out.

I tried to explain things that perhaps did not need explaining, and we both agreed on the need to steer clear of movements and to avoid promoting Zen or anything else. Mihoko seemed very eager about this too and obviously knows her Zen. I felt she and I were in close sympathy too, in fact I like her very much. For once in a long time felt as if I had spent a moment in my own family. The only other person with whom I have felt so at home in recent years is Victor Hammer. And Carolyn. It was rather like one of their visits. (I hear Victor is to have an operation for cataracts.)

The evening before the flight home I moved downtown to a hotel close to the air terminal, listened to FM radio, went to La Moule for supper and had a very good one with a couple of glasses of wine and some Benedictine. That day, too, on the way down, saw the Van Gogh exhibit at the Guggenheim. The only thing I found really irrational about the place is that most of the pictures are not hung but in storage. Hence, no Klee, no Miró, etc. Alas.

Coming home. Taking off over the Atlantic, clouds over New Jersey, read a bit of [Auguste] Jundt on *Les Amis de Dieu* [*Les Amis de Dieu au quatorzième siècle*, 1879] which I had borrowed from the Columbia Library. Looked at the long thin edges of the Appalachians in West Virginia, bounced through thunderstorms over Eastern Kentucky, and then came down to Louisville in rain and muggy heat and went to say Mass at Carmel.

Perhaps Suzuki and Mihoko will come down to Gethsemani if they are in the U.S. next year. Suzuki said I must come to Japan – but I cannot. He said it with meaning, not in a polite formula. And I know I should go there. God will provide that just as He provided this extraordinary meeting.

Said Mass two mornings entirely by myself, without servers, deeply moved, at the altar of Our Lady before which I made my profession of faith in Corpus Christi Church twenty-six years ago! No one recognized me or discovered who I was. At least I think not.

PART III

The Joy and Absurdity of Increasing Solitude

June 1964–April 1965

June 23, 1964

Blazing hot, stuffy air, barely moved by a little breeze here in the woodshed. What a day it is going to be! Even the woods will be an airless furnace. It calls for one of those nature poems, a kerygma of heat such as the Celts never had. (Finished Kenneth Jackson's excellent book on *Early Celtic Nature Poetry* before Prime as the fierce sun began to burn my field.)

First real interest in the "Honest to God" question.[1] Is it really so new? I think the problem is real enough and even one which Christianity has faced since the beginning. But the solution tends to be a debacle?? A complete surrender to nonsense and desperation and confusion. Is it really true that man is now totally and complacently content with modern technological culture *as it is?* Is there a great distance from Bonhoeffer's acceptance to Eichmann's acquiescence? Certainly! One must not stop at appearances and at a few texts out of context.

June 26, 1964. Saints John and Paul

Said a Mass for John Paul [Merton, his brother] and included Sartre in it. Cooler. Two great pigeons have set up shop in the rafters of the woodshed, and with gurgling and cooing and beating of wings make the place more delightful. This morning they were playing some kind of serious game, flying around the gutters and looking at me through cracks between the gutter and the roof.

I finished the old Jundt book on *Les Amis de Dieu* which I borrowed from the Columbia Library. (Will not forget reading the chapter on the book of the mine rocks while flying over the Appalachians.) Must find out more about Rulman Merswin. This afternoon – wrote a note on Kabir [*One Hundred Poems of Kabir,* 1962] for the *Collectanea [Cisterciensia].*

[1] The "question" was prompted by the publication in 1963 of J. A. T. Robinson's *Honest to God* and later in 1963 by David L. Edwards's collection of essays, *The "Honest to God" Debate: Some Reactions to the Book* Honest to God.

June 30, 1964

Bob Giroux sent M. Serafian's *The Pilgrim*. I have read about twenty-five pages of it and find it great. So much finer than X. Rynne's gossip column. The most serious book about the Council I have read since Küng's book (the one before the Council [*The Council, Reform and Reunion*, 1961]; I have not read any others). Simply clarifies and confirms what is already obvious: the ghastly problem that all through the Church the "will of God" can and does resolve itself into "the will of an Italian Undersecretary in the Holy Office" and that in fact the conservative Vatican bureaucrats think they have the right to contradict the Pope himself – *they* are the ones who are infallible. Mystique of infallibility, conservatism, and power politics. This is leading to a colossal crisis in order and obedience throughout the Church. When will it really break? I don't know. The risks are great, and the promises – no one knows. In any event something is going to happen.

Curious similarities with the conservative pattern in the South – the defiance of law by those who are convinced that their own mystique of society is sacrosanct, leading to the collapse of law and to anarchy.

How badly we need a real spirit of liberty in the Church, it is vitally necessary and the whole Church depends on it. Thank God "Serafian" has had the courage and good sense to admit and state frankly that so far the Council has dealt in relative trivialities! The problems that are largely irrelevant to the world at large, problems that are generated by gratuitously adopted and formalistic attitudes of the Church herself – incrustations of her own history. "*The irrelevancy of the problems which Catholicism considers fundamental and over which it has consumed itself in two long, expensive sessions is an offshoot of the Church's attitude to humanity.*" Bull's eye! He traces this to the inner contradiction in the Post-Constantinian Church between a mystique of virginity and flight from the world on one hand and the pragmatic worldliness and political orientation, identification of the Church with post-Roman civilization.

I had not realized how completely Cardinal Bea had been defeated nor that Pope Paul had been led to withdraw his support from Bea in the last Session. I knew of course that the Pope had announced a complete reform of the Curia – and done nothing about it. Also of course the unscrupulous political acts of the curial party were to some extent well known. The appalling scandal is the way in which the whole idea of the Church's authority is brought into question by these politicians! It raises once again the serious question of my own "vocation" (frustrated (?) by a political deal between the Abbot and the Congregation?). Certainly I do not doubt Providence, but just as certainly I cannot let a strictly political, pragmatic and juridical answer be the final word. And of course I have never intended to. In any case, I am in a hermitage. The important thing is understanding, and resolution of doubts and misgivings.

Reading this book has been important for me. At one point it looked like a real hatchet job on Paul VI, but he takes it back to some extent. The ending is not conclusive. But I realize that here we are at the end of June and still nothing definite has been said about the next session. I certainly expect nothing from the new Secretariat for non-Christian religions. At best a political expedient – (in part to field the ball of the Jewish problem before it gets lost in the bushes).

After a series of really bizarre incidents our Father Bernard has gone off to the monastery of the Prairies. Dom Walter (of the Genesee) has vanished. I think he has gone to the Carthusians. Father Herbert has left. Father Marion is going to Weston Priory. (Then where?) Father Francis and Father Gerard going to Rome to study. My undermaster, Father Felix, is now Guestmaster. Brother Timothy (Kelly) is the new undermaster.

July 2, 1964

Meadowlark sitting quietly on a fence post in the dawn sun, his gold vest – bright in the light of the east, his black bib tidy, turning his head this way, that way. This is a Zen quietness without comment. Yesterday a very small, chic, black and white butterfly on the whitewashed wall of the house.

July 8, 1964

On Sunday, after Father Abbot had left for visitations in the West, some visitors from Nicaragua came. Alfonso Calleja, etc. For nearly ten years his family has been trying to give us a coffee plantation near Chinandega, Nicaragua, to form a monastic community there. I told him I was sure the Abbot would not accept it. Then he asked me to come and preach a retreat. I said permission would never be given. He insisted. I said that only if the Pope himself told me to go would I be able to go. He said he would get the Nuncio in Managua to ask the Pope.

There is some worry about President Johnson's policies in Asia. To make sure of votes, he has to threaten war and promise "results" against the Communists. Something very strange about a system where political power for a party demands the sacrifice of lives of poor people thousands of miles away who never heard of democrats and republicans! I am not talking about Communist power only, but that of Democrats or Republicans. Can I honestly vote for any one in this year's election? The possibility of a long, stupid, costly, disastrous and pointless war in Asia is no mere phantasm. It will certainly bring no good whatever to anyone. But because it does not involve a nuclear threat to the U.S., everyone shrugs and thinks about something else.

Card from [Wilbur Hugh] Ping Ferry who was here a couple of weeks ago, is now in Scotland – card of the West Coast near Iona. I am reading Adamnan's *Life of Columba* [1962], one of the great *Vitae*. Full of a very special character and spirit of its own: not the general aim of Latin hagiography. (For instance the two chapters about the whale, and those about men shouting across the strait for a boat to the Island.)

July 10, 1964

Rafael Squirru's "New Man" pamphlet is very provocative. How much this is needed. The little that is published on Latin America in this country is likely to be nonsense. There is no deep interest in the question – yet this is one of the deepest and most urgent questions. As for Antonio Cruz, a brilliant, violent book, but Cruz is still the Mexican stereotype, magnificently redrawn. But is that the way Latin America is to be forever – as U.S. wants it to be forever? There is much more to it, surely! And I must read, read, and read. It is my vocation. The risk is not in seeking and knowing these things, but in claiming to intend more than I am able to intend. They are looking for a Savior and will take *anyone* as one. And I suppose I am looking for a Savior or an Earth Mother. I still believe in the idea of the dark Ecuadorian Virgin I got Jaime Andrade to do for the novitiate. She is there, I do not talk of her, nobody prays to her, but such a presence nevertheless! (Dom Gabriel did not like her.)

Remembering so many things that come back from New York. Especially the raining streets around Columbia on the first evening, on Monday. Amsterdam Avenue, wet, empty, a few cars and buses speeding along, and a tall girl with long white bare legs and a little black jacket hurrying to Johnson Hall. The trees along 116th Street, the dark comfort of the rainy trees and of their shadow and half shelter. Foreign students everywhere, the comfort of foreign languages, French, German, Polish, Puerto Rican Spanish. The *New Asia* restaurant and the grey-haired Chinese waiter who had seen everything. Pork and fried rice and then tea, and egg drop soup. I was hot and wet. Ate gladly but there was too much. Too much the next day at lunch at the College Inn. Too much Japanese food at the Aki next to Butler Hall. (Bits of eels, bits of chicken, etc. floating in a nice broth. Rice in a wooden bowl. Then tea.) I was hot and wet in the Aki. Many Japanese faces. Earnest Japanese student talking to American student there by the window. Not much else. Hot and wet in the paperback book store. Too many books. Glad to get back to Butler Hall and have a bath. I sit in pajamas on the floor looking out over Harlem (lights, but not so many) and listening to all the sounds, and drinking that cheap wine. Lovely vacation!

The Wednesday – a lovely morning and noon. Riding down in the taxi to the Guggenheim Museum around one o'clock, through the park, under tunnels of light and foliage, and the driver talking of his problems, his nerves, his analysis and his divorce. The more I think of the museum the more I recognize it as a light and beautiful and airy and intelligent place. And the Van Goghs. Wheels of fire, cosmic, rich, full-bodied, honest, victories over desperation, permanent victory. Especially the last light and shadow calligraphic impastos. But the Metropolitan was zero. In and out. An old world, an old station. The people walking on Fifth Avenue were beautiful, and there were those towers! The street was broad and clean. A stately and grown-up city! A true city, life-size. A city with substance and scale, large and right. Well lighted by sun and sky, anything but soulless, and it is feminine. It is she, this city. I am faithful to her! I have not ceased to love her to the last page of this ballpoint pen, the gift of Nazionale Distributing Co. (distributors of Stroh's and of Schlitz) in Follansbee, West Virginia.

Down at the end of Park Avenue, shadows, darkness, noise, crowds, traffic, a building being destroyed. The mornings going to Corpus Christi; coming from Corpus Christi. Walking in the sun and wind of Broadway along the Barnard Fence or behind Earl Hall. (I remember the medical examinations!) The pleasant sunny plaza, near the library. Campus Corner and going to work at the catalogue, finding almost everything I looked for! What an experience to go to a library and find what you look for! It is not that way in Louisville, but I do enjoy mornings at the University of Louisville Library. Stroh's is dead. Schlitz is dead.

Some conclusions: literature, contemplation, solitude, Latin America – Asia, Zen, Islam, etc. All these things combine in my life. It would be madness to make a "monasticism" by simply excluding them. I would be less a monk. Others have their own way, I have mine. To write to Squirru. Follow Grinberg as he goes to San Francisco then to Argentina, with a letter when needed. To think with those new men. The opening to the South has not closed. One day to the monastic places in Western Ireland!

July 12, 1964

Deeply moved by Adamnan's extraordinary life of St. Columba. A poetic work, full of powerful symbols, indescribably rich. Through the Latin (which is deceptive – and strange too) appears a completely non-Latin genius, and the prophecies and miracles are not signs of *authority* but signs of *life*, i.e., not signs of power conferred on a designated representative (juridically) – a "delegated" power from outside of nature, but a sacramental power of a man of God who sees the divine in God's creation. Then the miracles etc. are words of life spoken in the midst of life, not words breaking into life and silencing it, making it irrelevant, by the decree of absolute authority (replacing the authority of life which life has from its Creator).

July 14, 1964

An amazing and fruitful evening yesterday: drove in with Father Prior (Flavian) to meet Abraham Heschel at the airport. A fine sunny afternoon, cool, the hills, all green and splendid, noise in the airport about the Republican Convention where Goldwater will obviously be nominated. (One of the first things Heschel said was that he was disturbed at this incredible thing – Heschel of course went through the Nazi persecution and escaped with his life.)

At least half a dozen Loretto nuns were around the airport meeting other Loretto nuns coming for their General Chapter which opens today – a fine day for it!

Riding back in the car, and at supper we talked of many things – of his new book *Who Is Man* (not *what* is man!), of the basic sin idolatry. Two Rabbis, Akiba and Ishmael (?) – argued as to what was the greatest commandment – Love of Brother or prohibition of idolatry. Both are right. I would be inclined to think the prohibition of idolatry was more fundamental, since when one has "an idol" (and any God that stands in the way of loving one's brother is an idol) one can permit himself to sacrifice everything to it – including truth, love, justice, etc. The function of the idol is to *permit everything*, provided the idol itself receives (unconditional) adoration. Heschel talking about Rabbinic commentary on the phrase "other Gods" – Gods that are always changing (always "others"). Gods made by others, etc. To have a God other than the Lord is to be alienated. Idol = principle of alienation.

Heschel is convinced that Serafian's *Pilgrim* is perfectly right. We both look at this book in the same way, as crucially important. Heschel thinks the Jewish Chapter will never be accepted in the Council. We spoke of how symbolic this fact was! In my opinion the acceptance of this chapter and the consequent at least implicit act of repentance is *necessary* for the Church and in reality the Church stands to benefit most by it. Heschel said, "Yes, but when I was a child I was beaten up often (by Catholic Poles) for being a Christ-killer, and I want to see that fewer Jewish children are beaten up for this reason." He thinks [Cardinal] Bea is really finished, that he suffered a crushing defeat in the Second Session (obvious). The envy aroused by his American trip brought him many enemies, and he had plenty before that. Heschel very impressed by Willebrands, now a bishop. Has much hope in him. Scorns Monella and the new Secretariat for Non-Christian Religions (in which I have no interest!).

Sat up until 10:30 talking with Heschel after a good supper fraught with dietary problems too great for Brother Edwin to solve, but Heschel did well on cheese, lettuce, etc. He enjoyed the wine and smoked a couple of long cigars.

This morning before High Mass Brother Simon [Patrick Hart] told me a letter from the Definitor, Dom Lawrence, had come, and the long section on peace for *Seeds of Destruction* had been passed without change by the General! Thus the real heart of the forbidden book, *Peace in the Post-Christian Era*, is to be published after all. Now this would never have happened if Dom Gabriel had not been so stringent with the other three articles, which would have been used in *Seeds of Destruction* if he had not forbidden their reprinting. Thus in effect the very thing he wanted to prevent most has happened *because* of his own authoritarianism! This is something to remember when we think of religious obedience. The Church is *not* entirely run by officials!! None of this was arrived at, in the end, by my initiative! Again, Dom Ignace's part – demanding the reworking of the one article the Publisher tried to insist on, led to this whole new approach! *How strange are the ways of God!*

Must write the preface to E[dward] D[eming] Andrews' new edition of *Shaker Furniture*. But first a short article for Père Hervé Chaigne, O.F.M. – a French Franciscan interested in non-violence. And I still have to proofread the typescript of *Seasons of Celebration* which has been lying around for several months. The job does not appeal! I have heard a rumor that E. D. Andrews is dead. Am not sure and have not dared to write to his wife [Faith Andrews] to find out.

Brother Alphonse, the Ecuadorian, has his arm in a cast (broken elbow). Brother Eugene, from Texas, drawls, goes about with his hands in his pockets and is for Goldwater because Goldwater "Knows where money comes from and is for the individual." These are our two postulants of the summer. Another, younger, is to come from a farm in Michigan, and it was decided yesterday that a Jesuit from the Detroit province did not have a vocation to our life. This afternoon I am to talk to one who was a postulant in the big group in 1957 and who left after an appendicitis operation. Perhaps wants to reenter. How many of those that entered then are still here? I can think only of ones that have gone. Perhaps Brother Methodius is the only one left, and Brother Paul of the Cross. And are *they* going to last? I really do not make a crisis out of these departures. But they are significant. Others would say ominous. For what? For the big institution, yes, but not simply for "monasticism."

July 18, 1964

Yesterday, which is the Feast of Our Lady of Carmel in our Order, I wrote that Shaker preface ["Religion in Wood"]. It still needs to be revised. Perhaps I brought too much of Blake into it. A fine quiet afternoon, with one long intermittent thundershower.

The *Navigatio S. Brendani* came yesterday from Boston College. I began it this morning, studying it as a Tract on the monastic life – the myth of *peregrinatio*, the quest for the impossible island, the earthly paradise the ultimate ideal. As a myth it is, however, filled with a deep truth of its own.

A Cuban exile who does not speak English is here to be a family brother but I do not think he will be able to settle down. He comes from Sancti Spiritus, a lovely plain little town which I remember.

Read an excellent piece by [Jorge] Carrera Andrade on Ruben Darío. Important, a key man for the *"consciencia americana"* – and the "new man." I must read him sometime, and also Martí. Vitier mentioned him in a letter recently.

July 19, 1964. Ninth Sunday after Pentecost

Sun rising in streaks of dirty mist. If I had seen a Japanese print I would probably have experienced it in a purely western way: seen one thing among many. A multitude of trees, enclosure wall, etc. in the foreground. *Sumie* [black-and-white drawing] makes the whole view *one*. One, or unity seen because the sun is in the center, a unity which is more than the sum of a number of parts. But in the infirmary kitchen – atrocious printed color photos from paper companies, to advertise the quality of their paper. Emphasis on bright color. Colored objects without composition, without sense, dolls, flowers, toys, food. Food. Food. Food. Enormous hamburgers. Gook for chocolate icing in a bowl, etc. Thrown at you! Total barbarity.

Last week Goldwater was nominated on the first ballot at the Republican convention, and made statements and a platform that were supposed to sound reasonable.

Father Baldwin [Skeehan] is back from Rome and spoke in Chapter, saying how much he hated Rome. But Assisi, Subiaco and Chartres were "inspirational." Just what Dom James likes best. He has taken a trip and suffered. He has not known enjoyment. He has a degree but has learned nothing dangerous. In fact he has learned a philosophy which, he avers, is useless for his spiritual life and cannot be meditated on ("being" is in his way of thinking an unreality). This is excellent! He has been away for two years and comes back without ideas and indeed with a repugnance for thought. This is just what Dom James likes best. If only they were all so! Should one then waste time thinking about what goes on in Rome?

July 21, 1964

It has been cool. Today will perhaps be hot, as the sun looks red and angry through early haze and one can barely discern the hills (which a novice the other day referred to as "the Appalachians") across the valley.

I sent the article on "Honest to God" to the *Commonweal* yesterday. Really Bonhoeffer is far deeper than Robinson would lead one to think. I am reading Bonhoeffer's prison letters [*Letters and Papers from Prison*, 1953], which are very "monastic" indeed – in fact I mean to make a collection of some of the "monastic texts" there. His "worldliness" can only be understood in the light of this "monastic" seriousness, which is however not Platonically "inward." It is not a withdrawal, a denial, it is a mode of presence. Paradoxically then Bonhoeffer's mode of unnoticed presence in the world is basically monastic – as opposed to the "clerical" presence which is official and draws attention to itself and has a "message." That is the trouble with the Bishop of Woolwich. He is concerned with "The Message" and in the end he seems still to be saying that he has discovered another sales pitch that will perhaps work. If that is so, he is wasting his time except that others like himself may feel comfort for a while. His whole problem boils down to that of *being needed in the world* even when he begins to admit he may be not needed.

Graham Greene's *A Burnt-Out Case* – takes this up a bit savagely and very well. The complete burning out of Christianity in the official, clerical sense, is the subject of the book. Not a great book, but still timely, urgent, convincing. Greene knows what he is saying. Burning out of the appetites of the bourgeois world, sexual, cultural, religious: the appetite for life: Pfft! (On the back of the paperback, the usual inane comments, about that same mythical "other" book which is the one the salesmen sell, not the one the author wrote. He was famous! She was lovely! Ra ta ta ta TA TA!!)

Finished first reading of the *Navigatio Brendani* this morning. Interesting monastic vocabulary. The geography – a liturgical mandala? I have to check back on the significance of directions. North is liturgical hell here too, and the Promised Land is West (except that in reference to the Paradise of the Birds it is east (liturgical)). Two traditions perhaps.

July 23, 1964

Jim Forest sent me clippings from Monday's *New York Times* about the big riots in Harlem last weekend. It all took place in the section immediately below Butler Hall, from 116th to 130th and between 8th and Lenox. I can imagine the houses, the rooms, the streets now. And the racket! The police shot thousands of rounds into the air but also quite a few people were hit, and one man on a roof was killed. In the middle of all the racket and chaos and violence a police captain was shouting "Go home! Go home!" A Negro yelled back "We *are* home, baby!"

The *Burnt-Out Case* is not much of a book, really. It is competent, but is itself a bit burned out and silly. Yet one reads it with interest. It is the same problem as in *Honest to God* but turned around. The priests who insist that Querry is not an atheist but is really in the Dark Night. All of a sudden one realizes that this approach has perhaps become usual. Indeed, it is Greene's own mainspring. I mean that of most of his novels. Here it is very tired but still works.

I am very impressed and deeply moved by Ramana Maharshi – not only his life (of which I know only the bare outline) but his doctrine – traditional Advaita – or rather his experience. Whatever may be the deficiencies of the doctrinal elaboration, and the misleading effect of some of the philosophical concepts, this is the basic experience: God as the ultimate "I" Who is the Self of every self! It is this that Christianity too expresses in and through the doctrines of grace, redemption, Incarnation, Trinity. Sons in the Son by grace, we recognize the father as Him with Whom we are one – not by nature but by His gift. But the impact of Maharshi's *experience* awakens in us the real depth of this truth, and the love that springs from it. How powerless most Christian writing and teaching is today, in this respect! How lost, how far off the *real* target! The words are there, the doctrine is there, but the *realization* is absent. Maharshi has an inadequate doctrine, perhaps, but the real realization.

July 28, 1964

It is very hot and damp. We are getting our hot weather now. Last night, storm and rain in the middle of the night. I was awakened by a mosquito, then a jet went roaring over, low down, in the rain, and through the shutters I could see the lights swinging rapidly away eastward. Probably one of the SAC planes, for one has been going over regularly at that time (about 1:20 a.m.). Another in the afternoon around 4 (?) on and off.

Interesting background to the *Navigatio Brendani* – its connection with the Lotharingian monastic reform in the tenth century. A few fine paragraphs from the life of Bruno, archbishop of Cologne, and his love of learning (Irish and Greek). The *Navigatio* is using Celtic myth as a hook on which to hang a manifesto of spiritual renewal in the monastic life, both eremitical and cenobitic.

Children from the Christian Church of Carrolton here yesterday. Good, simple children, open, unspoiled – not frightfully interesting but I felt a kind of compassion for the simplicity they will probably lose. I think of their little town on the Ohio. Think what? I don't know. Emptiness. These children are relevant only in emptiness. As soon as one begins to specify . . .

August

Letter in *Commonweal* by a crusty old man called Evelyn Waugh. I understand conservatism – he is one of the few genuine conservatives: he wishes to conserve not what might be lost but what is not even threatened because it vanished long ago . . . In supporting "conservatives" with Goldwater, one only lends a hand to the more rapid and efficacious destruction of what was sound and valid in the past.

August 2, 1964. Eleventh Sunday after Pentecost

Very hot, steamy, clammy. The tropics have nothing we don't have here in summer except thicker vines and more spectacular snakes. (We are friends of the King snakes around the novitiate and at the hermitage.)

The *Commonweal* intends to print my article on *Honest to God* – if the censors don't stop it. Sent my article on race to Hervé Chaigne in Bordeaux (new article ["Religion and Race in the United States"] – he asked for one). There have been riots in Rochester. I finished [William] Stringfellow's book on Harlem [*My People Is the Enemy: An Autobiographical Polemic*, 1964] and will write to Joe Cunneen about it. It is first rate – full especially of important information. How the rent system works, etc. It becomes clearer and clearer that this is an utterly sick system, but anonymous. If there were one sick King he would be deposed and replaced. Here "they" operate and get rich and it is not always clear who "they" are or how they get rich.

Finished a piece on "Pilgrimage and Crusade."[1] Still have to go over it.

Ulfert Wilke was out the other day and discussed some of the abstract drawings I have been doing; we talked about ways of mounting and framing them. I want to see his new paintings. He spoke a bit inarticulately of Ad Reinhardt, and of Japanese artists he knew.

August 3, 1964

Hottest day yet. Sweat all over everything. Difficult to get any work done. Someone has sent a book, *African Genesis* [by Robert Ardrey]. I had heard of discoveries of Leakey at Olduvai, prepared to accept hypothesis of Africa as the cradle of the human race. This book, however, takes scientific hypotheses and creates a myth of violence around them. Man's ancestor is the meateating club-carrying, sinister "killer-ape" who fought his way up from vegetarianism in order to become a cannibal and a nationalist. These, say the myth, are the facts. And when a myth says that it means, of course, *the only facts*. Man is by essence a predator, a killer, a property owner, a hater, a joiner, an agitator, perhaps even a Goldwaterite. This is the scientificmythology of proto-fascism. With all that, I am not as willing to accept Leakey, who is a different story, less "romantic" – of anthropoids that used tools and weapons?? Already man?

August 5, 1964

It is difficult to read or hear the story of Port Royal without having a great deal of sympathy for the Jansenists. Wrong as they may have been, there was a rightness that the heart knew and clung to. Dangerous, no doubt. But were the others much less so? Daniel Rops on this, in the refectory.

---

[1] Published under the title *Pilgrimage to Crusade*, Cithara 4 (November 1964): 3–21.

I have been sending out a mimeographed memorandum on monastic reform, and perhaps Dom James does not like it. He says nothing, but in his Chapter yesterday all was about heresy, intellectual pride, the downfall of "Dr. Martin Luther, Ph.D." Not to mention Judas Iscariot. If that was prompted by my paper – and letter to Dom Leclercq? – then it must be an indication that he fears I may be right. Yet does it matter so much? I am not going to get into controversies, and even the whole question of "monastic reform" seems to me to be full of illusions. The time of a real and serious reform is not, it seems, vows or not, here now. Doubtless something may begin elsewhere. There are places like Erlach. My article "Monk in Diaspora" is making more noise – and perhaps trouble – than I anticipated. I am not a reformer. I am glad that I have certain relaxations in diet, etc. I am disqualified from the start as an ascetic baroque, a new Rancé!!

I hear the bodies of the three civil rights workers murdered in Mississippi in June have been strangely found – in an earth dam which leaked because of them. Significant!

Today in Chapter Father Abbot announced that there was trouble with the Pacific fleet off Viet Nam. Those big bullies (Viet Nam) had attacked the Pacific fleet with PT boats which had to be destroyed. Now "the nests" from which the bullies are sending these boats to attack and persecute us, must also be destroyed. Mao Tse Tung is interested in this. In an election year, it almost seems inevitable that the politicians and generals will have the war they want! Sheer waste, nonsense, and criminal stupidity! What can one do about it?

August 9, 1964

I said Mass for Maritain this morning. J. H. Griffin wrote of being with him at Kolbsheim – and he was thin but in good spirits.

The trouble in the Gulf of Tonkin has blown over, so it seems. This is fortunate, and Johnson is the gainer. North Vietnam is missing a few PT boats and an oil dump, and the U.S. lost a couple of planes. All is settling down again to "normal" – guerrilla warfare, napalm bombs, helicopters, etc.

The other day in Louisville picked up [W. H.] Auden's "Enchafed Flood" at the library. It is good background for Brendan. I must finally reread Melville – but when does one get time for such things? It all depends upon how badly I want to read Melville, and how guilty I will feel about doing so. Actually, there is no need of guilt. *Moby Dick* has a lot to do with the spiritual life, perhaps a great deal more than some of the professedly "spiritual" books in the novitiate library.

Perhaps unwisely I have consented to do an article on "Art and Morality" for the *New Catholic Encyclopedia*. (I thought the work on that would have been done long ago.) One reason why I consented was that I thought the editor of the section was Ned O'Gorman's friend, the Benedictine artist [Ronan Verostico, O.S.B.] (but am not sure).

Yesterday morning I said Mass in the middle of a thunderstorm, and then it got cooler. The afternoon was bright and serene. Got back to meditation which had not been working well in the heat. I found that in an hour's meditation I am somnolent for the first twenty minutes or so, not asleep, but "out" – in a kind of total blackout – then after that everything is very clear. So yesterday. The blackout seems to be necessary as a passage from confusion to truth, as a recovery from pressure and motion, a return to balance. Before it I am not awake, only moving around.

The Aylesburg Review was in the University of Louisville periodical room. I was quite astonished. There was a good poem of Stevie Smith, also two dark and good ones by a girl whose name I don't remember. And an article on J. C. Powys. Henry Miller recommended reading him. Where can I ever read all the novels one is supposed to read? I am, however, finishing *La Peste* (Camus). It is a precise, well-built, inexorable piece of reflection. Picture of our society as it really is when undefended by distraction. I can accept Camus' ideas of nobility – and certainly agree with him about the Jesuit sermon. Yet the nobility of the Doctor is still not enough – though it may be enough for the doctor, and it may be all that most men can do. There is a nobility in the simplification of reasons in the renunciation of religious explanations. But to live without ideology is not to live without faith. The doctor would not be possible without the Gospel or without some cryptic compassion that is more than simply humanistic. Has Camus got far beyond Kant?

Raïssa Maritain in her book on [Marc] Chagall [*Chagall: Où l'orage enchante*, 1948] speaks of the light of New York (the best for seeing Chagall's paintings). I agree: I was struck by that light above all in June. So much clearer, braver, more uncompromising than Louisville: a vague town.

La Peste – understandable in the light of Bonhoeffer's admirable prison letters. In connection with Camus and people like him – see this line of Bonhoeffer: "I often ask myself why a Christian instinct frequently draws one more to the religionless than to the religious, by which I mean not with any intention of evangelizing them but rather, I might almost say, in 'brotherhood.'" (*p. 165*)

August 10, 1964

Sister Emmanuel [de Souza y Silva, O.S.B.], in one of her usual letters on twenty bits and scraps of thin paper, included two poems by that wonderful Dom Basilio Penido, the Abbot at Olinda. One was written to the Superior of the primitive reformed monastery at Serra Clara, and I was deeply moved to read it – it is about St. Brendan's isle – the monastic paradise! I was moved to see how spontaneously this Brendan theme came to one concerned with monastic reform – and aware of its limitations.

August 12, 1964

For St. Clare, after days of heat, a cool grey day, with a lovely wind blowing through the dark novitiate chapel before dawn and dark clouds most of the morning. It was almost cold in the garden. Instead of writing letters, began some conference notes on art for the novices, somewhat against my own better judgment. Yet they seem to be needed. Also I already have material and ideas for the *Catholic Encyclopedia* article but no time to write it. Maybe next week. (I wonder if the editor of that section will take seriously my plea to wait until October or November!)

Last night I dreamed that Dom James suddenly announced that we would have funeral and quasi-military "parades for the dead" along with every office of the dead now. Monks would march in spaced ranks, slowly, through the Church, for a long time. I saw this begin and saw that the sick were all forced to participate, and indeed even the dead were in it, for Father Alphonsus was there, albeit stumbling. The Abbot was absolutely insistent on this preposterous new observance, as a firm manifestation of his will. I tried to reason with him, on the grounds of "simplicity" and even tried to find a copy of the *Spirit of Simplicity* for him to read but could find none anywhere. I have a suspicion that this is more than a dream and that we are in for arbitrary measures – more and more as he gets older. For instance, although everyone is now tired of Daniel Rops, having finished one book of his we immediately take up another, and a third is waiting after that! No use asking for anything else. I tried to get some essays from [David] Knowles' *Historian and Character* read, but no use!!

My hands have been afflicted with poison ivy for two weeks, in the last week the little lumps have swollen into blisters and boils and have burst, and the skin has flaked off, then new blisters have begun again underneath. At High Mass I sit in the infirm benches, my hands covered with ointment. At that time I can dispense myself from touching anything.

Then the mass is over and I go for the mail and everything is confusion. Typing is difficult.

August 16, 1964. Thirteenth Sunday after Pentecost

Yesterday, Assumption, two postulants entered and little Brother Martin of Berryville came. The day before that spoke with two Moslems of the (heretical) Ahmadiyyah sect, one old and tough, the other young and eager (Dr. [Abdul] Aziz). They were from Pakistan and are "missionaries" here with headquarters in Dayton. And on Thursday Father Irenaeus [Herscher, O.F.M.] of St. Bonaventure [University] was here with a group of Franciscans and Capuchins. I had not seen him in twenty-three years.

On Friday I finished a first draft of the "Art and Morality" article. Yesterday (cloudy and cool, quiet afternoon) I went out to the little wood by St. Malachy's field (carefully avoiding poison ivy). Meditated a bit and read some Pessoa – whom I like less than I did at first. I think his "Zen" characteristics are genuine up to a point, but are they really a manifestation of his life, or only a *tour de force?* Hard to say.

Some question whether Brother Alcuin (Grimes) should leave. Last evening we talked of Peace Corps, Little Brothers of Jesus, etc. There is something lacking in this life here, not essentially perhaps, but the way we are living it in practice. Not that it is not strict, or fervent, but do the strictness and fervor have any meaning – beyond satisfying the religious compulsions of a certain type of person that thrives here? After twenty-three years I can say that I have never seen any serious evidence that the strictness of the life *as we interpret it* was anything to really deepen the spiritual life of the monks. It keeps them in line, but there is *no development.* The life is static, if you like it is safe, it gets nowhere, but in reaction against this there is now a lot of rather sterile and worried agitation over liturgical gimmicks, new ways of singing, conferences (mine!), etc. These are expected to produce life!!

August 17, 1964

Ecclesiam suam, Pope Paul's first Encyclical, is being read in the refectory. All encyclicals used to sound alike, one listened dutifully. There were no surprises. Pope John came along, *Mater et Magistra, Pacem in Terris,* so good, so open, one could hardly believe it. Now in this one we are back to the safe course, precise notes of condemnation (for existentialism), prime duty to "guard the deposit," the "structure" of the Church must be left untouched (the curia of course!), what matters now is reform in the sense of returning to what we have always had, etc. Danger of paying too much attention to "the world" – danger of rash experiments, dangers of placing false hope in a charismatic renewal. In a word the danger of change. Something has frightened him badly, so badly that he is now solidly and permanently (?) with the conservatives and we can all get back into our shelters. And watch what we say! Probably the affair of Father [William] DuBay had a great deal to do with it. And so many others like that. But when one has lived through the pontificate of a John XXIII, one cannot go back to the old positions again. One has to see things forever in a new light. I know now that there are forces awake in the Church that will refuse to go back to sleep. I don't know what will come, but there may be momentous stresses and pressures. Still, I expect little from the next Council session. Perhaps now that the Pope is behaving, the conservatives will let the Council go on for several more sessions.

I was prepared for this encyclical by a speech the other day (read the other day) on the importance of pomp and grandeur in St. Peter's, affirmation of Papal Primacy, etc. The old image of the See of Peter: Gregory VII, Pius V, etc. etc. *Tene quod habes.* [Hold on to what you have.] Don't let go at any price. They have seen the danger of letting go, even a little. The whole thing may get away from them if they relax their grip. For my part: well, under John XXIII I began to pay attention. I began to realize certain things. If doors are shut now, they are shut upon the way back, not upon the way forward.

August 18, 1964

"Vana sunt opera, et risu digna: in tempore visitationis suae peribunt. Non sicut haec pars Jacob: quia qui fecit omnia, ipse est, et Israel sceptrum hereditatis eius: Dominus exercituum nomen eius." ["They are worthless, a work of delusion; at the time of their punishment, they shall perish. Not like these is the Lord, the portion of Jacob, for he is the one who formed all things, and Israel is the tribe of his inheritance; the Lord of hosts is his name."] *Jeremiah 51:18–19*

The incomparable sound of the Vulgate. I have been reading about the Scriptorium of St. Gall. What a spiritual discipline must have been the copying of such texts. *"Ecce ego ad te mons pestifer, ait Dominus, qui corrumpis universam terram: et extendam manum meam super te, et evolvam te de petris, et dabo te in montem combustionis."* ["I am against you, O destroying mountain, says the Lord, that destroys the whole earth; I will stretch out my hand against you, and roll you down from the crags and make you a burned-out mountain."] *Jeremiah 51:18–19*

More here than comparison of Babylon and a volcano. More than prophecy of a moment of cataclysm. In the cataclysm is revealed the inner nature of the mountain of plagues and poisonous snakes. A valid replay? Only another poem and other symbols in the same tone. Meaning what? More than one knows. What "turning" from this morning's *lectio?* That if I will advance into these thickets of symbols which I think I know, I will find myself lost in what I do not know and that perhaps I will find myself different, and walking in a new way. But this must be dared, with patience and belief. (For after reading some of it once or twice one ceases to believe there is "more," and this is the danger.)

August 21, 1964

Father Abbot is back from the Abbatial blessing at Oka. The Encyclical was finished in the refectory yesterday. The last part, on dialogue, was the best, and made up for the compromising beginning to some extent. After a couple of hot days, now a windstorm, clouds, or little rain.

This morning I finished proofs of *Seeds of Destruction* which, after many delays, is scheduled for January. Bob Giroux is now a partner at Farrar, Straus and Giroux. I am happy for him.

Another nice letter from Nora K. Chadwick yesterday. Her sister was a Carmelite at Waterbeach for sixty years or so. Am finishing two excellent books Nora K.Chadwick recommended. [James Midley] Clark on St. Gall [*The Abbey of St. Gall as a Centre of Literature and Art*, 1926] and Dudley Simpson on the Celtic Church in Scotland (demythologizing St. Columba's mission – restoring others to importance). Have been reading about the Hebrides (G[eorge] Scott-Moncrieff [*The Scottish Islands*, 1952]) – would like to see them someday. Astonishing number of monastic settlements used to be there – exactly the place for small, eremitical communities! Many especially on Tiree. I wonder why? Will I ever see the place?

August 24, 1964

A wonderful sky all day beginning with the absent expressionist Jackson Pollack dawn – scores of streaks and tiny blue-grey clouds flung like blotches all over it. And before my conference (on Liturgy – a recent Reinhold article) deep, clear blue with astounding small luminous clouds, than which I never saw lighter and cleaner. Exhilarating coolness and airiness of these clouds. *New Directions 18* came in, and the "Early Legend" looked better than I expected. Laughed at the Russell Edson stories.

For our Abbots' meeting in October – I have to think up something about the ability or inability of modern (young) postulants to settle down in our life. It is a real problem. They come here often seeking their own identity and find themselves in a life that explicitly frustrates the quest of identity. Systematic fabrication of non-persons by this rule when it is understood and applied rigidly and without understanding. But when the spirit of our usages is precisely this – even the "new" usages which, though very slightly simplified, represent no serious improvement. A mature person can handle the situation fairly well. It seems to damage the young ones – sometimes quite badly. Perhaps it would not do so if they all came from a stable and secure Catholic environment. But their background is always ambiguous. As for the supposed security the Rule seems to promise – this promise cannot be kept if certain basic problems are left unresolved: the human and social problem of the insecure American teen-ager. And yet the new one just in from a farm in Michigan seems completely carefree and happy.

There is oak wilt in our forest, and a lot of it too, suddenly. Both in the white oaks and in the black. I have got Brother Aelred started on some of them this afternoon, the ones in the fine straight stand on the hillside, on the way up from the sheep barn to the hermitage. I hope we will not lose too many but six or eight are affected in that one acre.

August 29, 1964

This afternoon – worked on abstract calligraphies – perhaps too many. Some seemed good. I took a batch to the Frame House on Thursday with Ulfert Wilke, who was a big help in showing how they should be framed. Afterward we had lunch and went out to his studio in Pee Wee Valley, in a Garage next to a gambling club. Some fascinatingly calm, large abstractions which I cannot describe. A calligraphic economy of points and small white figures on large black or maroon backgrounds (some lively red and yellow ones but the somber were more serious and profound).

Have not done much writing except letters for the last two weeks. Have to get back to it next week. Am finishing off footnotes as an afterthought, for the "Pilgrimage to Crusade" article. Had to emend "Monk in Diaspora" for French translation (by Dom Leclercq). The General doesn't like it. Today for the first time in years seriously imagined a project for a novel. But I doubt if it is sound. And it would interfere with more important things.

Today a good letter (rare one too!) from Dom Damasus [Winzen]. About the monastic crisis in the Cistercians and big Benedictine houses. Certainly there is one. Five monks of Conyers were at the Liturgy Conference in St. Louis I hear (why not, after all?) and Father Bernard [Murray] came back suddenly from Notre Dame des Prairies.

September 1, 1964. St. Giles

I said his Mass in a lovely starlit pre-dawn, cool, silent. The old moon, and the liquid silent morning star. And now it is a clear September day, warm, bright, and one feels that the year has turned and is going toward the fall. There are moving passages and sentences in the [Meriol] Trevor biography of Newman that is being read in the refectory. Particularly prayers, and lines from his Journal. I feel closer and closer to him, yet with an even deeper respect for his religious depth.

It has been a busy day: after Vespers there was a Council meeting, and then I had to go and talk to a Cuban family brother who had become psychotic. Was shouting and breaking dishes and pounding on the walls, and said the wrath of God was coming down on this place because it was "too rich." And why all this *impieza* [cleaning] in the guest house? I suppose that long hours of work left to himself, and his inability to talk English, and his intense meditations – on the threats and promises of Fatima, on the Apocalypse, and on Castro – had finally cracked him. He tried to demonstrate how in Roman numerals the Apocalypse number 666 spelled out Fidel Castro Ruiz – which I was not able to see. He is supposed to leave for Cincinnati today – for a place in Covington where there are Cubans.

Then in the middle of the morning, just as I was getting down to type the footnotes for "Pilgrimage to Crusade," the Tiller family from Jackson, Mississippi, arrived. She is a convert who had been writing to me, he is an Episcopalian minister, and it is a lovely family. We talked for an hour or so, and I got some idea of the difficulty of the moderate Southerner who wants to do what is right and who is caught in the grip of totalism and prejudice, so that the slightest misstep puts him out of touch with his neighbors, and yet he does not know who to trust among the insiders. It is a very difficult position, and they really mean well, and have a lot of courage.

Yesterday J[ames] W[ygal] was out here with a problem in the afternoon. Several oaks are down, along the path up to the hermitage. (Cutting for oak-wilt.)

This morning I began [Hans Urs] Von Balthasar's *Herrlichkeit* – a long book to try to read in German, but the first pages are very promising and I respond to them completely. Perhaps this is the theology we have been waiting for. And I was reminded also of my studies on the School of Chartres two years ago (looked briefly again at my notes. I must write them up).

September 4, 1964

José the Cuban stayed a few more days, and today I spoke to Father Nieman who is taking him to his Boys Home in Covington. José is apparently better since we decided he must leave. Father Nieman said there were four days of race riots in Philadelphia – the worst ones yet, worse than Harlem and Rochester. I don't know any details. The situation in Viet Nam is "worse" in the sense that it may seem that the U.S. will be asked to get out. Whether that is worse for the prestige of the U.S. or for the people of Viet Nam I am not really certain! But they are in no position to solve any problems, with or without us.

Yesterday Father Abbot gave me several sheets of notes – proposals for the Abbots' and Novice Masters' Meeting in October: Notes extracted from Letters of the participants, indicating points they thought important. Theoretical (and rather useless) points attacking the Maritains' ideas on Liturgy of several years ago. Vehement pleas for the vernacular, a very testy demand for immediate action and an end of "gradualism" in dealing with the Brothers, as if the question of the Brothers were identical with that of civil rights. The one who wrote it (probably Dom Eusebius of Vina) insinuated that "certain Abbots" wanted to keep the Brothers as a reservoir of "slave labor." (Actually it was Dom Columban of Oregon.) In actual fact, at least here the Brothers want to keep their status as a guarantee of a certain amount of freedom, to be left to themselves and not herded into choir. I am rather depressed by all these notes which bear witness to a style of life and aspirations in which I have no interest – a form of monasticism in which solitude, contemplation, etc. are treated as irrelevant and all that matters is a lively and interesting choral service, well-organized work, a big lively booming community, etc.

Father Arnold was taken ill on Sunday and went to Bardstown hospital Monday or rather Tuesday. I hear he is having blood transfusions but do not know what the matter is. Perhaps hemorrhaging ulcers. He was in theology with me and is close to my time though I have never had much to do with him. He is one of those who are always "around" and regarded as "characters" – the kind that in the end are the backbones of monastic communities, though eccentric. (He cultivated with great energy a small unofficial flowerbed outside the professed Grand Parlor.)

September 5, 1964

Hot, bright, clear, quiet. I was going to burn some wastepaper, but it is too dry a day. Sent out to the girl [Donna Mae Miller] at the University of

Arizona the review of *African Genesis* ["Man Is a Gorilla with a Gun"] she asked for. I was not able to ignore this request. There is something good and special in this small, unprepossessing attempt at running a magazine (of all places in a Department of Physical Education for Women). I don't quite understand it, but there is something there. A sense of genuineness and humanity in spite of the clichés.

An afternoon to listen for a poem or just to be quiet (in fact, however, I will probably answer the letter I got the other day from Dom Damasus Winzen). Dom Emmanuel, Abbot of Bellefontaine, is supposed to be coming here tonight. Today – in conference – drawing primitive Celtic crosses on the blackboard. They seemed to enjoy it.

Poison ivy is eating my thumb again. Cannot get rid of it.

September 10, 1964

For the third time this summer poison ivy has taken the skin off my forefingers and thumbs and this time it seems to be spreading further. Had something akin to it on my face – some allergy.

Czeslaw Milosz was here yesterday. Same face as on the new French book (*Une Autre Europe*) but considerably aged. I am enthusiastic about the Polish poets that he has gathered into an anthology (Anne Freedgood is doing this for Doubleday). A great deal of irony, depth, sophistication, intelligence and compassion. This seems to me to be real and human. I react to it as I do to most Latin American verse: or to something belonging to *my* world. (I can hardly say this for most American or English poetry except Stevie Smith and Peter Levi.)

Abraham Heschel sent a memo on the new Jewish chapter. It is incredibly bad. All the sense has been taken out of it, all the originality, all the light, and it has become a stuffy and pointless piece of formalism, with the *incredibly* stupid addition that the Church is looking forward with hope to the union of the Jews with herself. As a humble theological and eschatological desire, yes, maybe: but that was not what was meant. It is this lack of spiritual and eschatological sense, this unawareness of the real need for *profound* change that makes such statements pitiable. Total lack of prophetic insight and even of elementary compunction.

It is precisely in prophetic and therefore deeply humiliated and humanly impoverished thirst for light that Christians and Jews can begin to find a kind of unity in seeking God's will together. For Rome simply to declare itself, as she now is, the mouthpiece of God and perfect interpreter of His will for Jews (with the implication that He in no way speaks to them directly) is simply monstrous. It is perfectly true that the Church in the highest sense can indeed speak a message of prophecy and salvation to the Jews. But to say that the few blind juridical niceties of curial officials and well-meaning Council Fathers are the *only* source of light for the Jews today – this is absurd misunderstanding of the Church's mission. Reflect that the Church in this rather imperfect sense (of Bishops, etc. speaking more or less humanly and politically) delivered the Jews over to Hitler without a murmur (here and there helping a few individuals to escape, to make it less intolerable to conscience).

September 12, 1964

Everything that a September day should be – brilliant blue sky, kind sun, cool wind in the pines. But I have to wear white gloves because I cannot go near the woods without getting more poison ivy. I seem to have become extraordinarily sensitive, and if I am within fifteen or twenty or thirty feet of it I seem to get more. On my face too, but I shall go with face bare. If necessary I shall make myself a mask out of a little bag with holes in it and come into solitude looking sinister like a Ku Kluxer. Tiny, delicate fishbones of clouds in the sky. Harps of sound in the sweet trees. Long shadows on the grass. The distant bottomland flat and level and brown, ploughed and harrowed. The hills.

Last night on Night Watch read about Olduvai, the discovery of Zinjanthropus in the *National Geographic*. Fabulously wonderful. I found this religiously stunning – 600,000 years ago was this man evolving and making tools out of pebbles. And was strong, bigger than I. Lived in great African rains (and there were glaciers in the north and south). And pigs as big as rhinos – most wonderful stories, more fabulous than the stories of the old days. Magic, tradition, racial memory. *Truth* in them. Dragons for instance!! I wonder how many of our stories, stories we heard as children go back all the way to Olduvai? That idiot Ardrey thinks Zinjanthropus was an ape and that Australopithecus, with his bone club, was a better and more progressive ape. Now I will revise an article on race riots.

Yesterday got a long letter from Dom Ignace, the Abbot General – "If you have such a lot of ideas, tell me what they are!" Well, I wrote at once, some three pages on monastic changes, and suggested a committee to study the formation of an American hermitage. This will probably meet all kinds of opposition, first of all from Dom James. I don't expect to get anywhere with it but why not at least bring it up? If he wants to know what I am thinking. All this started with "Monk in Diaspora" which turns out after all to have been a bit of a time bomb. Heard from Brother Pachomius at Erlach about it today (translating it into German). Books from Von Balthasar. Wonderful.

Censor at New Melleray (Shane Regan) says I am "written out," know no theology or philosophy, have nothing to say, etc., etc. but grants *nihil obstat* ["nothing stands in the way," approval by censor] to *Seasons of Celebration*.

Dom James in chapter today, has highest praise for those who simply "run with the herd" (his own words), do not think for themselves, conform (he regrets that "conformism" is regarded as a bad trait by those who seek only "liberty" to "do their own will"). And he wonders why he has problems with the monks leaving! And I am supposed to give a magic talk at the Abbots' meeting, to dissect the mind of youth, show where all their trouble comes from. I honestly think he expects me to say, in some way, that it all comes from radicals and self-will which is the only answer he is prepared to believe.

September 13, 1964

Last night before going to bed I was struck by a line of Job I had never noticed before: *"Lampas contempta apud cogitationes divitum, parata ad tempus statutum"* ["In the thought of one who is at ease there is contempt for misfortune. It is ready for those whose feet slip."] Job 12:5. Its mysteriousness intrigues me. What is it about? And this in Wisdom 5:7: *"Lassati sumus in via iniquitatis et perditionis: et ambulavimus vias difficiles, viam autem Domini ignoravimus"* ["We have left no path of lawlessness or ruin unexplored: we have crossed deserts where there was no track, but the way of the Lord is one we have never known"].

How true of all human life, especially now. Certainty and uncertainty of the *Viae Domini*, certain where one least expects (the certainty is then His gift) and uncertain where one imagines they should be clear. *"Ipse novit et decipientem, et eum qui decipitur"* ["The deceived and the deceiver are his"] Job 12:16.

"Qui revelat profunda de tenebris, et producit in lucem umbram mortis" ["He uncovers the deeps out of darkness, and brings out to light the shadow of death"] Job 12:22. There is still an incomparable poetry in the Vulgate text. Such substance, and so moving.

One of the most pertinent lines of the Bible for us, with our ready answer to everything: *"Numquid Deus indiget vestro mendacio?"* ["What need does God have of your lying?" Job 13:7] All is there!

Sunday morning, bright, windy, fresh. Brother Alcuin saw smoke to the north before Prime. He and I and Brother Colman drove up to see where it came from – on Andy Boone's land. Brush burning on a hillside in a little pine grove. He just set it alight and left it. A small pine tree was on fire, but it did not seem the fire would go anywhere. We went to the farmhouse, then to the barn (I had not been to the house before). A little orange-colored puppy came running out on the grass, in silence. Lovely Sunday silence and peace over everything. Vistas of the stunning and blessed hills, of the clear, quiet valley. Hills and woods. Small houses, looking wiser and safer for the Lord's Day. Andy shaved and at peace, after Mass, bringing in some fodder for his cows. It was his sixty-second birthday. I missed Chapter and was not downcast, for the Sunday Chapters are awful. *"Pro Deo iudicare nitimini?"* ["Will you contend for God?"]

"Quare lacero carnes meas dentibus meis, et animam meam porto in manibus meis?" ["Wherefore do I take my flesh in my teeth, and put my life in my hand?" Job 13:14]

This morning read the awful article of Dom [Odon] Lottin in RTAM [*Revue de théologie ancienne et médiévale*], 1959. That the vow of *conversatio morum* [conversion of manners] *cannot be* anything else but a vow to remain a cenobite and never to go into solitude – "exclusion" of eremitism. Arbitrary and iron-bound logic based on a quasi-mathematical analysis of Chapter 1 of the Rule in the light of the three vows. Repeated insistence "no other interpretation is possible." But indeed many others are not only possible, but far more likely in the light of history!

September 15, 1964

Hotter. Very bright. My hands are still skinned. I have medicines which Dan Walsh got from town. Father Eudes promised Rhulicream ten days ago but nothing happened.

Mother Luke [Tobin] from Loretto was here for a talk before going to Rome. The Third Session of the Council opened yesterday. She will consult with Cardinal Suenens and he is trying to arrange some way in which Nuns can be represented on the Sacred Congregations.

Writing some notes on Flannery O'Connor.

September 19, 1964

Yesterday, in rain (the first since August) I went to town to see old Dr. Simon the allergist, who said something about "fungus infection." Surely that cannot account for the state my hands were in for three weeks (they are somewhat better, but being in the woods affects them). Perhaps, however, I am mistaken about the poison ivy. Maybe I am affected by something that goes along with the oak wilt! Maybe I have the disease of some tree? It was pleasant driving to town in the rain, and getting there in rain, and sitting in the doctor's office stripped to the waist with the tests itching on my back, watching the rain on the bus station and the Courier Journal Building and the Post Office. I was there ten years ago, when I had worse sinus and more colds. He seemed old and prim and the room I was in was full of faded manila folders, shelves of them, records of patients probably going back thirty years or more. He gave me a good ointment and some wild hexagonal pills and a serum for shots.

It was fine driving back through Lyons and Younger's Creek, with the trees already beginning to turn yellow and red, and tobacco cut in the fields and hanging in the barns. An old rickety house was full of hay bales. Through the open door of the school room you could see the children sitting at their desks in the little hillside school outside Lyons.

September 22, 1964

More rain today and semi-tropical heat, dampness, haze, the kind of mist that sours and rasps in your throat. But a good day at the hermitage. Reading some notes Father Tarcisius [James Conner] brought back from Rome, etc. Father Prior wrote me a note yesterday with some ideas on the eremitical life. There is no question that this remains a live and urgent issue and no amount of official stifling will ever smother it. There are too many genuine vocations coming here, and ones who cannot be fully content merely with the formal and official pattern. And there is no question, once again, that I am only fully "normal" and human when I have plenty of solitude. Not that I "think" but that I "live" according to a different and more real tempo, live with the tempo of the sun and of the day, in harmony with what is around me. It would be infidelity to deny or evade the obvious truth that such a life is fully and completely right, and I cannot doubt it is the life I was meant for. Most of my troubles have come from tendencies to half believe those who may doubt it. But I have got to the point where I can no longer take them seriously. Though obviously I am still limited by my obedience.

Certainly the "problem" tends to resolve itself, and I am more and more alone, so that solitude just ceases to be a problem and becomes a *fact*. Whether it is a fact everyone likes or approves of really does not concern me much anymore – from the moment I have the permissions and approvals that are required – I have these and more besides.

On the opening (work) day of the Council, said the news report read today with incredible unction in the refectory, the Fathers "got off to a fast start." This resolved itself into a long school-marmish warning by Pericle Felici (the "Dean of Discipline") that the Fathers must not try to go to the coffee bar before eleven a.m. And if they go they will find it *closed* and it will be no good knocking on the door either! He then darkly threatened the theologians and others (Bishops) who might feel tempted to pass out hand-bills, etc. in the neighborhood of St. Peter's. There was a row about this last year and Felici was photographed snatching handbills from a Bishop on the steps of St. Peter's.

Brother Ephrem has fitted me out with a camera (Kodak Instamatic) to help take pictures for a picture book Dom James wants done. So far I have been photographing a fascinating old cedar root I have on the porch. I am not sure I know what this baby can do. The lens does not look like much – but it changes the film by itself and sets the aperture, etc. Very nice.

September 24, 1964

Our Lady of Ransom (but not here). Prayed at Mass for prisoners. Yesterday at the end of the morning work it cooled off and dried up and the afternoon was brilliant, fresh, distracted, active, seemed lost, yet great gain perhaps. After dinner I was distracted by the dream camera, and instead of seriously reading the Zen anthology I got from the Louisville Library, kept seeing curious things to shoot, especially a mad window in the old tool room of the woodshed. The whole place is full of fantastic and strange subjects – a mine of Zen photography. After that the dream camera suddenly misbehaved. This marvel of technology and design would not close. The back would not lock shut. Hardly a twentieth-century problem. Or is it? Rather typical to have a camera that calculates for you and corrects your mistakes, but then will not lock shut – and fogs the film. Even the number two Brownie used to close.

After None drove with Brother Nicholas into the hills behind New Hope, where Edelin has land he may leave to the monastery. A perfect, remote, silent, enclosed valley about two miles deep, wooded, watered by a spring and a creek, no roads; perfect solitude, where there were once two cabins for freed slaves a hundred years ago. Now it is all cattle, a herd of these hundred Herefords and Angus roaming loose in the pasture and the woods and at least two full grown thoroughbred Black Angus bulls, not to mention scores of bull calves. They were quiet though. The silence, the woods, the hills, were perfect. This would be an ideal place for a "desert" (I think it has been mentioned by someone before). One could run a road up through the woods bypassing New Hope and free from the county road, and have a house and chapel for people coming up for a few days. Then scatter five or six hermitages on the hillsides for permanent occupants. It would be marvelous. I am anxious to get this project studied, if Dom James will let his suspicion be allayed and his inertia be moved.

September 25, 1964

This ember week has been fantastic, alive, full of unexpected things, brilliant days, and surprises, and absurd hopes that yet seem astonishingly firm. It is suddenly seen to be a week of *Kairos*.

Yesterday I spoke to Reverend Father (after doubting whether I ought to) about the project of the "Desert" in Edelin's valley and found him remarkably interested and open. I was astonished. He seemed to take the project very seriously. He listened to everything I said, raised good questions, had constructive comments to offer and was thoroughly ready to get "in" it. This was marvelous. I actually think there is a very real possibility that this will go through. It is certainly something to work for. Now I look with astonishment across the valley at those hills. Trees hide the ridge behind which "the desert" is hidden. But I am aware of those silences with a new awareness. When will I get over there again?

Then yesterday morning I went to the mailbox and there was a letter from Father [Heinrich] Dumoulin saying I ought to come to Japan for a few months to get a first-hand knowledge of Zen. He thought it was very important and had spoken about it to the Bishop of Hokkaido and to the Trappist Superior [Our Lady of Pharo] – or at any rate a Trappist who was positive about it. Nothing else to do but propose this to Dom James, who was shocked. He does not seem at all disposed to let me go, but I asked only that he study the question objectively with the Abbot General. He agreed that was reasonable, but I can see he retains all his objections. Yet he seemed interested in what I said about Zen discipline, and I think even here there is some hope. It would be very worth while – the suggestion was surely providential. I will see what comes of it.

Camera had to go to town to get fixed. Marvelous sun today.

September 26, 1964

Camera back. Love affair with camera. Darling camera, so glad to have you back! Monarch! XXX. It will I think be a bright day again today.

Mother Luke (as I rather expected) is one of the women observers at the Council – the only American. Wonderful! This has great implications for the nuns, and it may lead to an opening and to considerable progress. Anyway I can hardly think of a better person for this. Cardinal Cushing's (first) speech the other day at the Council in favor of "Freedom of Conscience" must have been very stirring. This session is lively after all.

September 27, 1964

Slowly plugging at Von Balthasar's *Herrlichkeit*. Certainly this one central thing: all theology is a scientific doctrine and originates at the point where the act of faith (in God acting and revealing Himself in history) becomes understanding. This sounds trivial, but is extremely important. Here our theology actually contacts all the primitive revelations including Zen, though the contrary might seem true. (Wonderful article of Cardinal Suenens was read in refectory based on a principle laid down by John XXIII in Candlemas talk, 1963 – that in all religions there is trace of a "primitive revelation"). The true beauty of Theology is then in the wisdom and grace that apprehend salvation in the act of belief in an anticipation of the eschatological fulfillment promised by God – i.e., in Augustinian *fructio* [fruition].

September 28, 1964

Continuous rain, yesterday and today. Box scores of Council voting in the refectory. Collegiality of Bishops got through by an immense majority. The debating on whether Mary ought to be called Mother of the Church did not seem to be too relevant, at least from the news reports. Hostile editorials from papers in Israel, about the revised Jewish chapter, were quoted in a new article. The Jewish issue is not at all understood.

A good letter from Dan Berrigan, who is back in New York, came today.

I have not yet written out notes for the talk I am to give to the Abbots next Monday. I must also try to draw up a list of observances that seem to have become somewhat irrelevant. I wonder if this makes sense, however. One loses a sane perspective focusing on one little observance after another and saying "this is meaningful" (e.g., touching the floor when you make a mistake in choir). From a certain viewpoint it may retain a meaning. The end of the brothers is, monastically speaking, the most important. The brothers have an authentic and simple monastic life, one of the best forms in the Church. They are left pretty much on their own, with a lot of responsibility and good work to do. People want to take this from them and herd them into choir. Actually, as long as it is only question of "one category" of monks, there is no problem.

Other questions – concelebration, should priests say private masses or go to communion at High Mass? (Violent opposition to this on part of Dom James.) Personally I think it would be foolish to rush into these things here when people are *not* really prepared for them and perhaps have barely thought about them. On the other hand I have misgivings about a "preparation" that would be nothing but a propaganda barrage of special readings selected by zealots and imposed on the community. For one thing this would simply create a hard core of suspicion and indifference.

Looking through the *Usages* for things that might be dropped as "artificial" – noticed with alarm that they are all built into the very structure of the life. To take away these observances would be in fact to take away what practically constitutes the "Trappist Life" for many monks! This is very serious. It seems that there is no real "adaptation" possible?? That all that can be expected is to preserve what we have in a fairly reasonable and alert spirit – in community: and be at peace away from all this when one is free. It is a problem – probably more easily accepted in French monasteries.

October 2, 1964

Dark, wet, warm: continuous throbbing of guns at Fort Knox. Guardian Angels today, guides of hermits.

The last three days I have been working hard on material for the talk to the Abbots next Monday. (I dread that week of talking!) I must have written over 7000 words and set them aside, too long, too complex, and attacked it over again from another angle – about 2500 words perhaps, and all notes and not yet saying all I have to say. And perhaps it is not yet what ought to be said. Perhaps too my own feelings and frustrations are involved. I will try to be objective and peaceful in giving it all out. Meanwhile there is an inner tension, a deep and frantic and immobile anguish of helplessness, in the center of me somewhere, as if it were all futile.

Yesterday Dom James was very positive and very eager talking about the hermitage plan (I gave him a long memorandum on it Wednesday morning). He has been over to see the Valley, wants the plan to go through, says he is convinced it is "from God" and wants to talk of practical details. In fact we had a very good conversation. This is very encouraging and consoling, from a certain point of view, and yet there is anxiety in this also for me, as I don't relish being too closely associated with him. There is so much in him that I can't abide and accept peacefully – not in his reticences and suspicions so much as in his sweeping and at times almost inhuman bursts of idealism – that which he keeps most to himself, but he seems in a way to live by it. Yet it seems unreal, forced, according to the books, rather than according to reality. Actually the life he envisages would be extremely strict on some points. *No* contact with *anyone*, and so on. Absolutely sweeping. *No* letters. *No* visits. *No* talking. To do any kind of productive work "would spoil the purity of intention." No benefactors ("They would have a hold on you"). This is wise enough. I don't know to what extent he means all this.

He wants to keep the whole thing passionately and jealously secret even to the point of not consulting people who, I think, should be consulted (Dom Leclercq, Dom [Jacques] Winandy). The secrecy, however, is prudent, witness the Achel affair and how that was ruined by publicity. Actually any publicity would be really fatal. Nevertheless I do feel a bit insecure with Dom James taking everything completely into his own hands and consulting no one but the General. There may be some arbitrariness in his approach, but I think he is willing to be reasonable too. I will certainly go along with him, because this is the practical way to get a genuine hermitage going and one which will make the Carthusians and Camaldolese look silly, if only we are prudent and faithful, and follow grace! One thing is sure: When he gets his mind set on something like this – a foundation, a new project – he has his way. He knows how to handle the politics of it better than anyone.

Five big flickers playing and feeding beautifully on the lawn.

October 3, 1964

"It is not right that these eyes that belong to others should see in my own interest; it is not fitting that these hands that belong to others should move in my own interest. Being solely preoccupied with the self you cannot escape suffering. The unhappy are so because they have sought their own happiness; the happy are so because they have sought the happiness of others." *Shantideva*

Without this "Franciscanism" of Shantideva, no religious solitude makes sense. What would be the use of being a hermit merely for self-affirmation, even if one affirmed oneself in praise of God? What self?

October 8, 1964

We are in the middle of the meeting of Abbots and novice masters and I am exhausted. Have had to talk too much. It goes on all day. Yesterday I got to no office except None. Sessions began at 7 a.m. Went on practically until dinner; talking all during dinner; after dinner I got away and sat in the sun and tried to read but could hardly get my mind on it. The weather is beautiful. How nice it would be at the hermitage! Today I imagine we ought to propose that the Novice Masters have further meetings, but if I never go to any more it won't worry me!

Yesterday's meeting, about the future of the Brothers, was important and lively, and in spite of Dom Columban's crusading approach, it seems to be an earnest effort in the right direction. It is really wrong to speak of "abolishing the brothers" though the nature of their life will be to some extent changed, but so will the life of the choir monks be changed. Certainly it would be preposterous merely to move the Brothers bodily into the choir. At Spencer, as here, a great number of professed brothers are opposed to changes, not quite knowing what to expect.

The meetings of novice masters (we are apart from the Abbots after the coffee break) are more peaceful and more academic. Sessions on *conversatio morum*, stability – work – studies, etc.

Father Basil [Pennington], the canonist from Spencer, is a good mind and well trained. His ideas are the most valuable. Dom Thomas of Spencer seems the most articulate of the abbots. It is good to know Dom Emmanuel of Utah better, he is very capable. Dom Anthony of Mepkin is much aged, quiet, good to talk to him again. I like the little Abbot and Novice Master of Calvaire, but they are from a different world – an old-style small monastery of Acadian Trappists!

October 12, 1964

The meeting ended three days ago and I am still working with the trauma of it. Continual talk. I kept myself keyed up with black coffee, and kept having things to say and in the end talked too much. The worst days were the last. As to what was accomplished, I don't know. Certainly there were some "gains" of a sort. At least it was in some sense useful to get to know the various abbots, from the two amiable and open Canadians (Dom Alfonse of Calvaire, Dom Fulgence of the Prairies – who was here before) to the complex, aged, self-assured Dom Columban of Guadalupe who seems to have a "mission" and is causing all the trouble. (If there was antagonism it was between Guadalupe and Spencer.) Very friendly and open – Dom Augustine (Conyers), Dom Eusebius (Vina), Dom Joachim (Snowmass). Dom Emmanuel of Utah was capably "in charge" of the meetings. Dom James said little while we were there, and gave a general impression of rather frenzied politicking – for evidently to him this is a great and serious political event. But it is even more to Dom Columban. Dom Anthony (of Mepkin) and Dom Jerome (of Genesee) said practically nothing. In fact Dom Anthony said *absolutely* nothing in the meetings where we were but was benign and friendly outside, looks old, frail, holy. Dom Matthias, the new Abbot of New Melleray, had nothing to say. But when I had defended Latin in the liturgy he came up afterwards and said, "We ought to get some of these writers of hit-tunes" to do something. "That will get the young people back into the Church." He was serious.

I did indeed speak up to say at least one or two houses ought to keep the Latin liturgy and Gregorian, but met with no sympathy except from Dom Alfonse, who had been led to believe there was complete unanimity on this point. That *everyone* wanted vernacular. Actually, in Canada, where the houses tend to be bilingual, Latin is something of a blessing.

Though the Abbots in general seemed disposed to favor a little more solitude (days of recollection, perhaps week retreats) it seems unlikely that a full-scale hermitage project, such as Dom James was interested in two weeks ago, when I proposed it would be accepted. The General seems frightened of it.

October 13, 1964

One good result of the change in thinking, on the part of Dom James, is his desire for solitude. He gave me permission to sleep at the hermitage, without any special restriction, though not necessarily all the time. The understanding is that I can spend the night there once in a while, when I wish to. Last night I did this for the first time. (Brother Colman brought a bed up there Saturday evening) and it was most helpful. It finally helped me to get the noise and agitation of the Abbots' meeting out of my system.

Though it had been quite cold for several days, I got enough sun into the place in the afternoon to dry it out and warm it up. Got up there about nightfall. Wonderful silence, saying compline gently and slowly with a candle burning before the icon of Our Lady. A deep sense of peace and truth. That this was the way things are supposed to be, that I was in my right mind for a change (around the community I am seldom in my right mind). Total absence of care and agitation. Slept wonderfully well, even though there was a great pandemonium of dogs in the woods when I got up about 12:20 and went out to urinate off the edge of the porch.

I thought I would hear the bell for Vigils at the monastery and didn't. However, I woke up soon after that and lit the fire and said Lauds quietly, slowly, thoughtfully, sitting on the floor. I felt very much alive, and real, and awake, surrounded by silence and penetrated by truth. Wonderful smell of pre-dawn woods and fields in the cold night!

October 16, 1964

Yesterday afternoon news got all over the monastery that Krushchev was fired. I understand his pictures were all being taken down, nobody is quite sure where he is, and meanwhile the Chinese have, it seems, exploded an atom bomb (?). And though the papers say the two successors of Krushchev will carry on his policies, it is by no means sure that there will not be a reunion of Russia and China, a "hard line" in Asia, etc. Here we go again!

Also the Cardinals came up in a month from fourth place (I mean the St. Louis Cardinals) and won the World's Series. Disedifying news but it is known through the monastery. Rather, not that the news is "disedifying" but the fact that it is known may be so to some. Apparently it was a "great Series."

Today I was supposed to see Dr. [Randolph] Scheen about the skin on my hands, had an appointment, and had also arranged to say Mass in Carmel. But Reverend Father told me to meet Georgio La Pira at the airport instead. So I went there from Carmel. He was there with the head of his school board (a lady), a reporter and a young physicist – is on a quick official visit, full of strong statements ("The Council ought to canonize John XXIII by acclamation" – and I agree). There was a mix-up at the airport, but I found him and his companions, we talked volubly in French in the car coming out (on the Council, on his trips to Moscow, Africa, etc.). Less volubly during dinner with Dom James (at which Dubonnet was served as a wine) and after dinner my volubility was gone, but his was still in gear. I showed them the novitiate, the refectory, etc. I was left at last with a strong impression of the meaning and greatness of Florence, and his *"spes contra spem"* ["hope against hope"] and the reality of his convictions and of his mission. As I left him he was writing out a Telegram to Paul VI, hailing him from Gethsemani with the assurance of prayers. Yet when all is said, I don't think the "crusade of prayers" idea of contemplative monasteries tells the whole story.

Got on the phone to Dr. Scheen whom I will see next week. The hands are getting better anyway.

October 17, 1964

My scripture reading today (early morning – firelight and candle light – hermitage) was from Baruch, Chapter 5. I went to it with thirst and got this: *"Exue te, Jerusalem, stola luctus et vexationis tuae: et indue te decore, et honore eius, quae a Deo tibi est, sempiternae gloriae . . . Deus [enim] ostendet splendorem suum in te, omni qui sub caelo est. Nominabitur enim tibi nomen tuum a Deo in sempiternum: pax iustitiae et honor pietatis."* ["Jerusalem, take off your dress of sorrow and distress, put on the beauty of God's glory for evermore . . . for God means to show your splendor to every nation under heaven, and the name God gives you for evermore will be: Peace through Justice and Honor through Piety."]*(Baruch 5:1–4)*

A beautiful text. I don't remember having paid any attention to it before! The next line (5), yes, is an advent antiphon. Further on it echoes Isaias. And then this, above all: *"Obumbraverunt autem et silvae, et omne lignum suavitatis, Israel ex Mandato Dei. Abducet enim Deus Israel cum iucunditate in lumine maiestatis suae, [cum misericordia et iustitia] quae est ex ipso."* ["And the forests and every fragrant tree will provide shade for Israel, at God's command: for God will guide Israel in joy by the light of His glory, with the mercy and justice which comes from him."] *(Baruch 5:8–9)*

October 19, 1964

I am reading the very rich *Collectio Monastica* from Ethiopian manuscripts (CSCO #239). Late manuscripts but very traditional and full of meat. Von Balthasar's *Word and Revelation* excellent. One fine passage where he says substantially what Juliana of Norwich says about "all manner of things shall be well." Namely that Christ judges and separates good from evil in order to reveal the truth about man in this separation, but the "rejected" will turn out to have been those "chosen" with a greater and more mysterious mercy. Can there be a limit to the mercy of Christ, who has fully satisfied forever all God's justice, and now has the world in His hand to do with it according to His merciful Love?

With all this about love and mercy, yet yesterday I was angry as assistant priest, standing next to the abbot at the altar. Clearly it is my pride. It is a real distraction and a threat to faith. But when I think that he has power to be most unreasonable in my life, and has used this power so arbitrarily and still does, I am filled with frustration and resentment. Yet it is precisely this that I must accept, and it should be all the easier when in fact he has, perhaps unreasonably, given me much latitude in other matters. It is galling to have a hermitage as a political benefaction!

October 20, 1964

Yesterday afternoon Dom Thomas Aquinas Keating, the Abbot of Spencer, stopped here on his way back East from the new foundation of nuns he has just made in Iowa. There was some more discussion of the two points he will bring up at a meeting before the General Chapter. One regarding the laybrothers and the other regarding solitude in the Order. About this second question I also wrote to Dom Ignace on Sunday. Whether the Order will officially recognize the eremitical life as appropriate for Cistercians and permissible within the Order is not at all certain. But it is possible that a relative solitude (such as I already have) will be at least recognized in some form or other.

At the same time I am beginning to see that the question of solitude for me is finally getting to be no longer a question of *wish* but of *decision*. I still do not know what scope for decision may be given me, but I do know that I must prepare to face a serious decision, and one about which I had more or less given up thinking. It seems to be a real "encounter with the world" that I must not evade, and yet, as in all such things, I am not too sure just where the encounter is, except that my heart tells me that in this question of the solitary life there is for me a truth to be embraced which is not capable of a fully logical explanation, which is not rooted in my nature or my biography, but is something else, and it may also cut clean through the whole network of my own recent work, ideas, writings, experiences, etc., even those that in some way concern the solitary life, monastic renewal, etc.

For the moment, it seems to involve also cutting off a hundred contacts in the world and even legitimate and fruitful concerns with the events and needs of the time. I do not know or understand how far this needs to go, except that I am caught in all kinds of affairs that are no longer my business, and that they may prove to be great distractions and evasions. Yet I do not yet see where to begin. And it will also involve renouncing, definitively, some of the securities of the community.

Sleeping here has been a great grace. Last night, full moon. At midnight the whole valley was drenched in silence and dark clarity. Cold this morning. Going down to the monastery in the dark I could feel frost on the grass and the dry corn husks under my feet.

October 21, 1964

Lamplight! It is good, quiet. Many years since I have had a lamp to read by! Not since St. Antonin, forty years ago! The lamp came today. It was in a paper bag on my desk in the novitiate after High Mass.

Dom Leclercq's book on *Otia Monastica* came today too (the library copy). I had been waiting a long time for this. It is just what I have been needing.

October 25, 1964. Twenty-Third Sunday after Pentecost

On Thursday I was in town, saw the skin doctor (things are slowly improving but the trouble is a greater mystery of pollen and wave-lengths of light than I am capable of grasping).

I went to Catherine Spalding College with the twenty-six abstract drawings of mine that are to be exhibited in November. They are well framed, thanks to Ulfert Wilke's advice, and look good, at least to me. I gave them names and prices, not without guilt feelings (perpetuating a hoax?). But the drawings themselves I think are fairly good. As Wilke says, they "are real." But now Jim Wygal is annoyed that they are being exhibited at Catherine Spalding and not at Bellarmine [College]. I had to send him some others for Bellarmine, etc., etc.

Yesterday Marco Pallis was here. He is touring with his English Concert of Viols. I was glad to meet him. He spoke a lot of Frithjof Schuon who has a brother in our order at Chimay, who is also a disciple of Ahmad al'Alawi. Schuon has written a fine article on Monasticism for the *Collectanea*, being forthright about the necessity of not compromising with current fashion in spirituality, especially those which lead the monk to reformulate his life in terms influenced too deeply by Marxism "and the fatal Teilhard de Chardin." I would have liked to hear the Viols play some Orlando Gibbon but this is not possible.

We spoke of Zen and of Shiva, and Tibetan Buddhism (a little) and how if the Tibetans were to seek refuge outside of India it would probably be in

America rather than Japan, though Japan is Buddhist. And why? Because of the ease and simplicity with which they become totally infatuated with the West.

Dom Winandy has written an excellent pamphlet on the hermit life. (He is now on Vancouver Island.) Father [Peter] Minard's monastic notes, which I read some time ago, are very good. There are hermit groups springing up in several places. With Winandy are men from our monastery in Utah and from New Melleray and from Colorado (Snowmass). As well as from Benedictine houses.

October 29, 1964

Clouds running across the face of the waning moon. Distant flashes of lightning. I know what it is: a "warm front," etc. Clouds running over the face of the waning moon. And who cares what the weather may be? It is money that cares about weather and pays to predict it, perhaps someday to control it. And who wants a world in which weather is controlled by money?

Last night slept in the monastery because [spiritual] direction ran late and my shoulder also was hurting so that I wanted the traction which is fixed up on my bed in the novitiate dorm. Sleeping at the hermitage gives one a totally different sense of time – measured by the phases of the moon (whether or not one will need the flashlight, etc.). This in itself is important. The whole day has different dimensions. And so for office in choir, its artificiality impresses me more and more. Not that it is not a "good thing." Not that there is not a great will to do good and praise God there. But the whole decor of habits and stalls and stained glass seems unreal when you have been praying the psalms among pine trees. The thing I most appreciate about the monastery is the electric light. The lamplight of the hermitage is primitive and mysterious, but the lamp smokes and one cannot read well by it. Which is all right since it means more meditation. Yet I like and need to sit here with the book open and really read, take notes, study.

As to the brethren, it is good to be with them and to see them (even though I know them enough to recognize their tensions and troubles) but I can tell that a feeling of loneliness for them would probably be a deception – or a *reflex*. One can love them and still live apart from them without explanation.

Yesterday a small deer fell into the reservoir by the new waterworks and thrashed around trying to climb out, but the concrete wall was not negotiable. I was afraid it might drown. But it got through the joists of the foot-bridge and to the other end where there was foothold, and trotted off across the road into the woods looking beat and confused.[3]

Rewrote "Monastic Vocation and Modern Thought." Perhaps too much concerned with it. In the end I saw I was getting too complicated and trying to deepen it so as to avoid merely repeating platitudes about "identity crisis" and "authenticity." Not successful.

Trouble with Marie Tadié. A letter from a brother novice who left recently to try to join the Little Brothers of Jesus in Detroit. He is working on the docks, though rather small for a stevedore. [Ping] Ferry sent Jacques Ellul's book on Technology [*The Technological Society*, 1964], just out. Long telegram from Heschel asking me to join him in protest against Goldwater's hypocritical outcry about "morality" in the current campaign – criticizing a "morality charge" of some Democrats with not a word about the moral implications of slums, nuclear war, etc. Gnats and Camels!

Good news. Dom James has had a letter from the Abbot General saying that he is not opposed on principle to experiments in the hermit life within our Order and that such an experiment on the property of one of our monasteries is quite feasible. And that he thinks Gethsemani would be a reasonable place for such an experiment. He will discuss it at the December meeting of Abbots and it will be taken up at the General Chapter.

October 30, 1964

For three days they have been reading in refectory the Bulletin of the Liturgical Commission and the Congregation of Rites on the new changes to go into effect next Lent. The changes are good in the main, and are the ones that have been expected. But while the changes tend to simplicity, this document is itself complicated, tedious, a ponderous, grim effort to organize everything, leave nothing unforeseen, even that which seems to be a concession to initiative. How can we have "renewal" with such elaborate formalities as this?

Reading Jacques Ellul's book *The Technological Society*. Great, full of firecrackers. A fine provocative book and one that really makes sense. Good to read while the Council is busy with Schema 13 (as it is). One cannot see

---

[3] Soon after this incident Merton wrote the draft of a poem called "Merlin and the Deer" in his Working Notebook #14. Merton's whimsical comparison of himself with the sorcerer Merlin plays out the theme of solitude of this section of the journal. See *The Collected Poems of Thomas Merton* (1977), p. 736.

what is involved in the question of "The Church and the Modern World" without reading a book like this. I wonder if the Fathers are aware of all the implications of a technological society? Those who can only resist it may be wrong, but those who want to go along with all its intemperances are hardly right. Or do they know this might be what they were wanting?

Gentle whistles of a bluebird and in the mist a SAC plane swoops huge and low over the ridges where Edelin's valley is and where the final hermitages are to be. I wonder if it carries bombs? Most probably. They all do, I am told. The technological society! I will go out and split some logs and gather a basket of pine cones. Good for starting fires in my fireplace, in the small hours of the morning.

October 31, 1964

An impressive passage in Balthasar's *"Verbum Caro"* – a deep and poignant essay. I will use part of it perhaps in conferences to novices and juniors on poetry and human experience. But I cannot help seeing it rather in its reference to my own vocation at the hermitage. These nights I have spontaneously been remembering the days when I first came to Gethsemani twenty-three years ago: the stars, the cold, the smell of night, the wonder, the *Verlassenheit* [abandonment] (which is something else again than despondency) and above all the melody of the *Rorate coeli* [Drop down dew, heavens]. That entire first Advent bore in it all the stamp of my vocation's peculiar character. The solitude inhabited and pervaded by cold and mystery and woods and Latin liturgy. It is surprising how far we have got from the cold and the woods and the stars since those days.

My fiftieth year is ending and if I am not ripe now I never will be. It is the *Kairos*, say the stars, says Orion, says Aldebaran, says the sickle moon rising behind the dark tall cedar cross. And I remember the words I said to Father Philotheus, which may have been in part a cliché, but they were sincere and I know at the time that I really meant them. And they were unpremeditated: that "I want to give God everything." Until now I really have not, I think. Or perhaps in a way I have tried to. Certainly not too hard! I cannot say my life in the monastery has been useless, or a failure. Nor can I say where or how it has had a meaning. Nor will I probably find where and how the hermitage has a meaning. It is enough that there is the same mixture of anguish and certitude, the same sense of walking on water, as when I first came to the monastery.

November 2, 1964. All Saints

There was sunlight and haze for the procession in the cemetery and Brother Ephrem taking photographs over the wall with a ladder. And as the procession rounded the corners of the cloister I thought it looked spiritless, as if the monks were going through it all merely with resignation. They were tired from the longer office, and so on. Brother Canice, extremely introverted, left today.

I am going on with Ellul's prophetic and I think very sound diagnosis of the Technological Society. How few people really face the problem! It is the most portentous and apocalyptical thing of all, that we are caught in an automatic self-determining system in which man's choices have largely ceased to count. (The existentialist's freedom in a void seems to imply a despairing recognition of this plight, but it says and does nothing.)

A titmouse was swinging and playing in the dry weeds by the woodshed. A beautiful small, trim being! A quail was whistling in the field by the hermitage, in the afternoon. What a pure lovely sound! The sound of perfect innocence! A tiny shrew was clinging to the inside of the novitiate screen door, trapped. I took her up and she ran a little on to my sleeve and then stayed fixed, trembling. I put her down in the grass outside and she ran away. But what of the wasp in the hermitage that I killed with insecticide? I was shocked to find it an hour later in great agony. It would have been simpler to kill it with the flyswatter.

Last night in bed here (at the hermitage) I fell asleep thinking of the Avergnon valley at Bruniquel. There is no longer any train, now (I remember all those little stations!). Father Chrysogonus went to St. Antonin and wrote me a long letter about it – Father's house [The Villa Diane], etc.

Victor Hammer finally wrote. I had been worrying about his health. He tires easily but is working. The operations on his eyes were successful and he can see well, he says.

November 3, 1964

Four o'clock. I went out on the porch to see the starlight and the cocks were crowing, at Andy Boone's near at hand and then up the road and then off in the east and south where I did not know they were close enough to be heard. The bell for Lauds of St. Malachy had just rung briefly at the monastery. I had been reading Chapters 3 and 4 of Ezekiel. During meditation, looking at the fire, I suddenly remembered this was election day.

November 4, 1964

Yesterday, before dawn, wrote a four-line Latin poem at Victor Hammer's request – a thanksgiving for the return of his sight, so that he works again and he wants this for an inscription. One thing saddens and embarrasses me – that he will be shocked at my exhibition of drawings or calligraphies or what you will. There is no way to explain this to him, and in a way I am on his side, on principle. And yet they have a meaning, and there is a reason for them: an unreasoned reason perhaps. I feel like writing to him and saying: if you heard I had taken a mistress you would be sad but you would understand. These drawings are perhaps worse than that. But regard them as a human folly. Allow me at least, like everyone else, at least one abominable vice, etc.

Went over to vote with Matt Scott and George Reiter just when all the children were coming to school. No one at the polls. I ended up voting for Chelf when I didn't mean to – pulled the party lever by mistake and got the whole bunch of them!

In the afternoon, lots of pretty little myrtle warblers were playing and diving for insects in the low pine branches over my head, so close I could almost touch them. I was awed at their loveliness, their quick flight, their hissings and chirpings, the yellow spot on the back revealed in flight, etc. Sense of total kinship with them as if they and I were of the same nature, and as if that nature were nothing but love. And what else but love keeps us all together in being?

I am more and more convinced that Romans 9–11 (the chapters on the election of Israel) are the key to everything today. This is the point where we have to look, and press and search and listen to the word. From here we enter the understanding of Scripture, the wholeness of revelation and of the Church. Vatican II is still short of this awareness, it seems to me. The Chapter on the Jews has been woefully inadequate. It was naturally cautious, I will not say to the point of infidelity, but it was obtuse. It went nowhere. And in its inadequacy it is itself a providential sign, a "word." So we must look harder and further into this mystery. A "contemplation" that is wide of this is simply a waste of time, vanity and vexation of spirit.

November 6, 1964

The other morning before Prime there was a notice in the Little Cloister saying Johnson had won the presidential election in a landslide. After that I went to Louisville to see the skin doctor, and bought a Coleman lamp and stove. I got the stove filled and working yesterday, and the lamp this evening. It gives a brighter and better light to read by for long periods than the other one does.

Yesterday I was reading [Eugène] Ionesco's *Bald Soprano* and laughing myself silly behind the forage boxes packed in the woodshed.

I think Ellul is perhaps too pessimistic. Not *unreasonably* so – but one must still have hope. Perhaps the self-determining course of technology is not as inexorably headed for the end he imagines. And yet certainly it is logical. But more is involved, thank heaven, than logic. All will be brought into line to "serve the universal effort" (of continual technological development and expansion). There will be no place for the solitary! No man will be able to disengage himself from society! Should I complain of technology with this hissing, bright green light with its comforts and dangers? Or with the powerful flashlight I got at Sears that sends a bright hard pole of light probing deep into the forest?

Tonight the new moon was shining in the west. And really new! Although men have seen the same for more than a million years I suppose. That is one of the good things about being in the woods – this living by the sun, moon and stars, and using (gladly) the moonlight – which should now be available for some three weeks, on clear nights, at the beginning or at the end. But I am surprised how easy it is to follow a familiar path even by starlight.

November 7, 1964

The election campaign was hot and dirty. One of the disturbing things about it was the quasi-religious character of the zeal for Goldwater. I am surprised he did not get more votes. For many people apparently Goldwaterism was Christianity – or *is*. Because I don't think we have done with it!

Reading Ezekiel 6. This is about our idolatry as well as Israel's. Idolatry is the basic sin. Therefore that which is deepest in us, most closely related to our final sin, most likely to deceive us under the appearance of true worship, or integrity, or honesty, or loyalty, or idealism. Even Christianity is often idolatrous without realizing it. The sin of craving a God who is "other" than He who cannot be made an idol – i.e., an object.

November 8, 1964

Marie Tadié continues to write angry and demanding letters at the rate of one or two a week. After she began to sell books in Italy and Spain even though I asked her to stop, I began to think of dropping her entirely even as agent in France. Now, though I am willing in view of her past service, to let her continue to handle major books in France, she demands to have all my business in her hands, even down to the material I want to be free to dispose of to religious orders without a money transaction. This will have to stop, and I don't know a good, effective and humane way to reasonably settle it as she is entirely unreasonable. Very trying.

November 10, 1964

This morning I went down to the monastery earlier than usual because I had forgotten my glasses and could not read comfortably in the hermitage. But I was not unaware that it might have been better to meditate in the dark until six, rather than read. I settled the case because I "might be needed" in the novitiate. Nevertheless the question of using the darkness and limited light of the early hours in the hermitage is not to be ignored. Is this one of the limitations providentially intended for me? Why should I automatically suppose that because it is possible to have electricity and read more, it is therefore necessary to do so? Still there are other considerations. And it was certainly profitable to read Balthasar and Gordon Zahn's little book on the objector [Franz] Jägerstätter, which is surprisingly good [*In Solitary Witness*, 1964]. Also if I had not gone down I would not have corrected the letter to *Ramparts* (on their policy towards Cardinal McIntyre) and decided to send it.

Yesterday a large group of Baptists from Southern Baptist Seminary in Louisville were here. I enjoy talking to them, but I don't know if I will continue next year. It is obviously fruitful and meaningful. But you can't have everything.

The exhibition of drawings at Catherine Spalding College is to open next Sunday. A private showing will be held on Friday (Feast of All Saints of the Order). Already everyone seems very interested in it. Apparently there was something in *The Courier Journal* about it, which I did not see. Some excerpts from this Journal are in *Sewanee Review* (had proofs the other day).[4]

Finally, last Saturday, Msgr. Moore, who instructed and baptized me (twenty-eight years ago this Sunday), was here briefly with Jack Ford Saturday afternoon. It was good to see him again. Not much changed, fatter, in better health – has been chaplain at West Point twenty-five years.

---

4 Merton was reviewing "Barth's Dream and Other Conjectures." The excerpts mentioned were not taken from this journal, but from the one published as *Turning Toward the World: The Pivotal Years*, vol. 4 of *The Journals of Thomas Merton*, edited by Victor A. Kramer (HarperSanFrancisco, 1996).

A quotation that needs no comment. "The truth about the nature of risk of thermonuclear war is available. The reason why it is not embraced is that it is not acceptable. People cannot risk being overwhelmed by the anxiety which might accompany a full cognitive and affective grasp of the present world situation and its implications for the future. It serves a man no useful purpose to accept this truth if doing so leads only to very disquieting feelings which interfere with his capacity to be productive, to enjoy life, and to maintain his mental equilibrium." *LeGuinsporre*, Peace News, *November 6, 1964*

November 12, 1964

Reading proofs of Zahn's book on the Austrian peasant Jägerstätter, executed by Hitler for conscientious objection. It is an excellent job. Moving above all are the notes of Jägerstätter himself, his "commentaries" on the war. Their lucidity and accuracy are astounding, and so much greater than that of so many bishops and scholars, and commentators at the time. Here was a simple, barely educated man who saw things clearly and stated them as he saw them! One thing strikes me above all. The Catholic Church in Germany and Austria, having condemned Nazism before it came to power, and having afterwards collaborated with it when in power, was surely aware that Nazism was irreconcilably opposed to the Church – just as much as Communism. Why did the Church support Nazism and never compromise with Communism? Perhaps because the Nazis were more pragmatic in offering a means to compromise. But also, basically, because of property.

November 16, 1964

Twenty-sixth anniversary of my baptism. Warm and dark coming down from the hermitage. Warm wind and stars. Moon, nearly full, had set. They have harrowed the cornfield in the bottom by the sheep barn, and it will be rough to walk through when they shall have ploughed it.

Brother Antoninus [William Everson], tall, bowed, gentle, benevolent, given to quiet laughter was here from Friday to Sunday. We had some good talks and he spoke to the novices and juniors of the "poet's presence," his aura, tone, his ear, imagination, the sovereign intellect, the compaction of images. He reads poetry more attentively and intelligently than I do. Told me I [*Emblems of a Season of Fury*] was well reviewed by [Haydn] Carruth in the *Hudson Review*. I had vaguely heard of this but not seen it. Brother Antoninus did not like [Robert] Lowell's new book. Offended by its destructiveness, its desiccation, and Lowell's obsession with destroying that in himself that might save him. But for my part (less compassionate no doubt) I liked its hardness (*For the Union Dead*).

Technology. No! When it comes to taking sides, I am not with the *beati* [blessed ones] who are open mouthed in awe at the "new holiness" of a technological cosmos in which man condescends to be God's collaborator, and improve everything for Him. Not that technology is per se impious. It is simply neutral and there is no greater nonsense than taking it for an ultimate value. It is *there*, and our love and compassion for other men is now framed and scaffolded by it. Then what? We gain nothing by surrendering to technology as if it were a ritual, a worship, a liturgy (or talking of our liturgy as if it were an expression of the "sacred" supposedly now revealed in technological power). Where impiety is in the hypostatizing of mechanical power as something to do with the Incarnation, as its fulfillment, its epiphany. When it comes to taking sides I am with Ellul, and also with Massignon (not with the Teilhardians).

"*La bénignité des apôtres de ces techniques, qui asservissent le spirituel au temporel, souillent la vie à sa source, avec une saveur d'hypocrisie que nous ne pouvons pas ne pas dénoncer.*" ["The kindness of the proponents of this technology, which puts the spiritual in bondage to the temporal, taints life at its source, with a flavor of hypocrisy that we cannot fail to denounce."]

(Massignon, Opera Minora [1963], III, 802)

November 17, 1964

Abbé [Jules] Monchanin was convinced of the great importance of his prayer for "all the dead of India" as part of his mission to India, as part of the "convergence" of all mankind upon the Christ of the Day of Judgment.

Massignon and Foucauld – both converted to Christianity by the witness of Islam to the one living God. Someone wrote of Foucauld (and his devotion to the dead of Islam): "*Mais pour un mystique les âmes des morts comptent autant que celles des vivants; et sa vocation particulière était de sanctifier l'Islam éternel (car ce qui a été est pour l'éternité) en lui faisant donner un saint au Christianisme*" ["For a mystic the souls of the dead count as much as those of the living; and his particular vocation was to sanctify the eternal Islam – for that which has been is forever – in helping it to give a saint to Christianity"] (quoted by Massignon, *Opera Minora*, III, p. 775). "*L'ascèse n'est pas un luxe solitaire nous parant pour Dieu mais la plus profonde oeuvre de miséricorde: celle qui guérit les coeurs brisés par sa propre brisure et blessure*" ["Asceticism is not a solitary luxury preparing us for God but the most profound act of mercy:

that which heals broken hearts by its own breaks and wounds"] Massignon, *Opera Minora*, III, 804.

Today: FOR [Fellowship of Reconciliation] group coming for retreat. A. J. Muste, Jim Forest, J[ohn] H. Yoder, Dan and Phil Berrigan, John Olivier Nelson, etc. Paul Peachey can't come, had to fly to London at last moment to replace John Heidbrink, who is having an operation on his spine. Tom Cornell, editor of the *CW* [*Catholic Worker*], and Tony Walsh from Montreal also coming, and W. H. Ferry. Maybe also Bayard Rustin, I am not sure.

November 19, 1964

This FOR retreat has been remarkably lively and fruitful. Sessions in the gatehouse mostly (because of rain) but we got to the hermitage yesterday afternoon. Ping Ferry has been very helpful (he and I talked a lot at first about Ellul), then Yoder spoke well this afternoon on protest from the Mennonite viewpoint that is biblical. Revelation of technology to the "principalities and powers" of St. Paul (not at all akin to the mind of Ellul, whom he in fact quoted – a lecture of his). For personal intensity and sincerity I have also liked very much the remarks of Elbert Jean, a Methodist from the South – was a minister in Birmingham and was fired for his integrationist ideas ("Desegregation can be brought about by anyone, but integration only by the Holy Spirit"). A. J. Muste is impressive in real wisdom, modesty, gentleness. He is like Archbishop Floersh in a way, and yet much more mild and without cramps and compulsions.

Today as we were beginning our session Brother Simon [Patrick Hart] gave me twelve copies of *Seeds of Destruction*, for the retreatants. *Motive* also came with three of my letters in it.[5]

Dan Berrigan said a way-out Mass in the novitiate chapel yet it was beautiful too. We had two ministers (Nelson, Muste) read Gospel and Epistle. Dan's celebration of the sacrificial liturgy was simple and impressive. All in English and "uncanonical" even to the extreme point not only of Communion in both kinds but Communion to the Protestants!! I suppose it will be the same again tomorrow – in the old juniorate chapel, where the altar is better suited for standing around in a circle.

Last night – my dream of the Chinese "princess" has haunted me all day ("Proverb" again). This lovely and familiar archetypal person (no object! and how close and real, yet how elusive!) who comes in various mysterious

[5] Three letters were excerpted from *Seeds of Destruction* in *Motive* (November 1964): 4–8.

ways into my dreams! She was with her "brothers" and I felt overwhelmingly the freshness, the youth, the wonder, the truth of her – her complete *reality*, more real than any other, yet unattainable. Yet the sense of understanding, of her "knowing" and loving me, yet not merely in my individuality and everyday self, as if this self were utterly irrelevant to her – (not rejected, not accepted either).

Now – rainy night, I sit writing this in the green technological light of the Coleman lamp at the hermitage. They will leave tomorrow.

The material of medieval contemplatives on *"quies"* [literally, "rest"] seems so dated, so innocently complacent, so much part of a vanished social order. [Charles Pierre] Péguy's poem on Chartres, earthy and strong in the wonderful new Chartres book from La Pierre qui Vire. It moved me strangely in the small hours of the morning.

November 22, 1964

After the rain, yesterday, the Presentation (which we are still, to my surprise, celebrating as a Feast of Sermon), it got cold and bright. Very cold in fact. It must have been about twenty when I went up to the hermitage to sleep – and apparently it was down around five or ten this morning. And now though the sun has been up for hours the grass still shines with thick frost. I observed the whiskers of frost on the dead cornstalks and on the creosoted gateposts. I walked out to the little pond in the ravine that goes through the knobs to [Herman] Hanekamp's old place, and walked about praying psalms on the dry salty place on the rise, where small pines are coming back in. Wasted, perhaps, time and film photographing an old root with inexhaustibly interesting forms, constructions and textures, in the weak sun.

No matter how naive the medieval doctrine of *"quies"* may seem, it makes sense. It is part of a whole which we no longer have (Chartres!) but I am nevertheless not divorced from it. Realized it clearly singing with attention the Gregorian melodies of the Feast. They are simple, solid, incomparable (only the Common): perfectly satisfying without being the best in Gregorian. Always I have the sense that anything we may attempt will be less good – no adequate replacement. (How in my early days here the chant gave meaning and coherence to the whole life for me!)

Adam the Carthusian (Scotus) in a fine text on *quies claustralis* [quiet of the cloister] (published by Leclercq in *Otia Monastica*) sums it all up, simply and adequately, the need for *quies*, not bothering with concerns foreign to our life. I want to give up the retreats. Yet already a letter has come from the Baptist Seminary begging me not to stop my talks. I was touched by it. No one could be more sincere and less political than Glenn Hinson, who wrote it.

November 23, 1964

Péguy's prayer at Chartres – how close to my own feeling. The past cannot be restored and we do not seek for that.

> *Nous ne demandons pas que le grain sous la meule*
> *Soit jamais replacé dans le coeur de l'épi,*
> *Nous ne demandons pas que l'âme errante et seule*
> *Soit jamais reposée en jardin fleuri.*
>
> *. . .*
>
> *Nous ne demandons rien dans ces amendements,*
> *Reine, que de garder sous vos commandements*
> *Une fidelité plus forte que la mort.*[6]
> [We do not ask that the grain under the millstone
> Ever be replaced in the heart of the corn,
> We do not ask that the soul, wandering and alone,
> ever be relaid in a garden of flowers.
>
> . . .
>
> We ask nothing in these improvements,
> O Queen, than to keep under your commandments
> A faithfulness stronger than death.]

November 24, 1964. St. John of the Cross

In the Night, a rumpled thin skin of cloud over the sky, not totally darkening the moon. It has become thicker as the morning wears on. There is a feeling of snow in the air. Streaks of pale, lurid light over the dark hills in the south. The SAC plane sailed low over the valley just after the bell for consecration at the conventual Mass and an hour later another one went over even nearer, almost over the monastery. Enormous, perfect, ominous, great swooping weight, grey, full of Hiroshimas and the "key to peace."

This is my full day at the hermitage. No question whatever that this is the kind of schedule to live by. Went down to say Mass. Will go down again for

---

[6] Quotation from *"Les prières dans la Cathédral de Chartres. II. Prière de Demande."* In Charles Péguy, *Notre Dame* (Paris: Gallimard, 1941), pp. 48–50.

dinner. The rest of the time here does not begin to be enough! How full the days are, full of slow and quiet, ordered, occupied (sawing wood, sweeping, reading, taking notes, meditating, praying, tending the fire, or just looking at the valley). Only here do I feel that my life is fully *human*. And only what is authentically human is fit to be offered to God. There is no question in my mind that the artificiality of life in the community is, in its own small way, something quite atrocious (saved by the fact that the artificiality of life in the "world" is totally monstrous and irrational).

It is good to know how cold it is, and not by looking at a thermometer. And to wear heavy clothes, and cut logs for the fire. I like washing in the small basin with the warm water left over from making coffee. And then walking down in the moonlight to say Mass, with the leaves growling under my feet. Not pulled at, not tense, nor waiting for what is to descend on me next, but looking for a place quiet enough to read in . . . Life seems real, and in the community it is *mental*, forced. You can see some of them "thinking" (about what?) and others behind whose frowns there is no place for thought left, only the tension of being, and of forfeiture – all "offered up." God is doubtless pleased with them, or full of compassion for them. But what a system!

November 29, 1964

Good rains in the last few days. This morning, with rain pounding down all over everything, looked out from the novitiate porch over the shining wet roof of the sheep barn. Gave a conference on Péguy's Chartres poem.

The Council session ended last week. I have not yet read the full report, but the whole thing seems to have been decidedly ambiguous and disturbing. The Pope overruled a majority of the bishops at the last moment – not only on the question of liberty of conscience (which has been put off again!) but on various others [Merton crossed out: especially to do with the collegiality of Bishops]. I am not sure exactly what took place, but there is anger in the air. Since I do not know exactly what happened I shall say nothing of it at the moment. At best there are rumors going around.

Yesterday I was in Louisville. Skin on my hands is in bad shape. "Badly damaged" after the long siege of dermatitis. I was able to see the drawings as they now are on exhibit at Catherine Spalding. A very attractive exhibit. Also the Merton Room at Bellarmine is quite decent, quiet, pleasant (and overheated). All this is comforting in a way, but I don't know why I should attach importance to it. I am grateful to the people who have taken so much trouble with these things. Especially Jim Wygal.

November 30, 1964

Woke up in the hermitage and walked out to see snow on the ground, with the wind blowing snowflakes around my bare ankles. Lit the fire and said Lauds. No trouble seeing the way down in the dark with snow on the ground!

The Christian faith enables, or should enable, a man to stand back from society and its institutions and realize that they all stand under the inscrutable judgment of God and that therefore we can never give an unreserved assent to the policies, the programs and the organizations of men, or to "official" interpretations of the historic process. To do so is idolatry, the same kind of idolatry that was refused by the early martyrs who would not burn incense to the emperor. The apostles on the other hand (by reason of their renunciation and detachment from the world) could sit on twelve thrones (society, even sacred society, as they knew it). The Pharisees, identifying themselves with a secular order, carried out the judgment of God upon that order in the very acts by which they sought to defend it.

The policies of men contain within themselves the judgment and doom of God upon their society, and when the Church identifies her policies with theirs, she too is judged with them – for she has in this been unfaithful and is not truly "the Church." The *power* of "the Church" (who is not "the Church" if she is really rich and powerful) contains the judgment that "begins at the house of God."

Night. Zero cold. Frozen leaves crackling like glass under my feet on the path through the woods. The REA men must have been here today seeing about the electric line but I missed them, saw only their footprints in the snow. And so stay down in the monastery to see Father Matthew [Kelty] before None.

Need discipline, and need to get my solitary life more organized. I can see this is the big battle – to stay centered on something and not float out into space. The need for seriousness. Yet it *is* serious, and constantly so. Suddenly hit hard by the lesson and promise of Isaias on the Kingdom of Peace. Where is that peace?

The other day a letter from the General came to Dom James about the Japan project. "This is not from God." No capacity to understand the meaning of it. No matter. Perhaps I shall still go someday, in spite of everything.

The Constitution on the Church, promulgated at the end of the Third Session, is really beautiful and deeply moving. I think it is a great document. Now being read in the refectory.

December 1, 1964

"Θεγ ουν εν τη ΨυΧη σου αποΘανειν πρωτον η αποστηναι του ζωηφορου τουτου ζητηηατοζ." ("Resolve to die rather than abandon this lifegiving search.") Read slowly, in the lamplight, early cold morning, Simeon the New Theologian is a man of burning words indeed. In the comfort of the monastery it is easier to neglect him as an extremist. "To have no thought of oneself for any earthly end, but to have one's whole mind centered on Christ. What measure, think you, will this procure of heavenly good, and of angelic condition?" (Catechism, *II*)

How clearly I see and experience this morning, the difference and distance between my own inertia, weakness, sensitivity, stupidity, and the love of Christ which instantly pulls all things in me together so that there is no longer any uncertainty or misdirection or lassitude. What a shame and dishonor to Christ if I let my life be such a mess of trivialities and silly concerns (that are in reality only a mask for despair)!

Will not easily forget the thin sickle of the old moon rising this morning just before dawn, when I went down to say Mass. Cold sky, hard brightness of stars through the pines, snow and frost, exaltation on the bright darkness of morning. In the cold of Advent I recapture the lostness and wonder of the first days when I came here twenty-three years ago, abandoned to God, with everything left behind. I have not felt this for a long time here. The monastery is too warm, too busy, too sociable for that! But breaking off and living (to a great extent) in the woods brings me back face to face with the loneliness and poverty of the cold hills and the Kentucky winter – incomparable, and the reality of my own life!

Finished the Martin Marty book *Varieties of Unbelief* I am supposed to be reviewing for the *Commonweal*.

Now snow clouds are coming up in the west, and the bones of the hills in the south have snow on them and the trees are picked out sharply like iron bristles against a streak of pale, indifferent green sky. The alfalfa field in the bottoms is as green as watercress, streaked with snow. The evening is very silent. The bell for Vespers rang early – there must be office of the dead. I will go down and check the Ordo and say it before Collation. Then I see Dan Walsh (who is full of all the rumors that go around among the brothers, about hermits that are to live in trailers in Edelin's valley, etc.). Dan hears everything and, when he tells it, improves it beyond measure.

December 2, 1964

Hurray for Ionesco! He has some very good ideas, and here is one of them (against those obsessed with ideologies and with theories of history.)

"Nous sommes pris tous dans une sorte de complexe historique et nous appartenons à un certain moment de l'histoire – qui cependent est loin de nous absorber entièrement et qui au contraire n'exprime et ne contient que le part la moins essentielle de nous mêmes." ["We are all of us caught in a kind of historical complex and belong to one special moment in history – which is, however, far from absorbing us entirely but rather expresses and contains only the least essential part of us."] *(Notes et contre-notes [1962], p. 16)*

December 3, 1964

> Evening: The heart is deceitful above all things
> The heart is deep and full of windings.
> The old man is covered up in a thousand wrappings.
> *(Lancelot Andrewes, Preces)*

True sad words, and I would not have felt the truth of them so much if I had not had so much solitude, these days, with rain coming down on the roof, and hiding the valley. Rain in the night, the nuisance of water in the buckets. Or cutting wood behind the house, and a faint smell of hickory smoke from the chimney – while I taste and see that I am deceitful and that most of my troubles are rooted in my own bitterness. Is this what solitude is for? Then it is good, but I must pray for the strength to bear it! (The heart is deceitful and does not want this – But God is greater than my heart!)

> I will acknowledge my faults O Lord
> O who will give scourges to my mind
> That they spare not my sins?

December 4, 1964

It rained all night and is still raining.

How often in the last years I have thought of death. It has been present to me and I have "understood" it, and known that I must die. Yet last night, only for a moment, in passing, and so to speak without grimness or drama, I momentarily experienced the fact that I, this self, will soon simply not exist. A flash of the "not-thereness" of being dead. Without fear or grief, without anything. Just not there. And this I suppose is one of the first tastes of the fruits of solitude. So if the angel passed along thinking aloud, to himself, doing his business, and barely taking note of me. But taking note of me nevertheless. We recognized one another. And of course the other thing is that this "I" is not "I," and I am not this body, this "self," and I am not just my individual nature. But yet I might as well be, so firmly am I rooted in it and identified with it – with this which will cease utterly to exist, in its natural individuality.

In the hermitage – I see how quickly one can fall apart. I talk to myself, I dance around the hermitage, I sing. This is all very well, but it is not serious, it is a manifestation of weakness, of dizziness. And again I feel within this individual self the nearness of disintegration. (Yet I also realize that this exterior self can fall apart and be reintegrated too. This is like losing dry skin that peels off while the new skin forms underneath.)

And I suddenly remember absurd things: The song Pop had on the record forty-five years ago! "The Whistler and His Dog." Crazy! I went out to the jakes [outhouse] in the rain with this idiot song rocking my whole being. Its utterly inane confidence! Its gaiety. And it is in its own way joyful – the joy of people who had not seen World War II and Auschwitz and the Bomb. Silly as it was it had life and juice in it too. Confidence of people walking up and down Broadway in derbies in 1910! Kings of the earth! Sousa's whole mad band blasting out this idiot and confident song! The strong, shrill whistle of the whistler! (O fabulous day, calao, calay!) and the bark at the end (that I liked best). Brave whistler! Brave Dog! (As a child I had this Whistler confused with the one who painted his mother!)

December 5, 1964

Today we say the Mass of St. Francis Xavier, in whom I am much more interested than I used to be (more as a symbol of aspirations than as a model). I think of Father Dumoulin, Father Enomiya Lasalle, Father [William] Johnston at Sophia University. I wish I could have gone there, as they suggested, but perhaps someday I still may get to Japan and see a Zen monastery. Meanwhile a little book [*All Else Is Bondage: Non-Volitional Living*, 1964] by Terence Gray (Wei Wu Wei) is in the hermitage and I find it clear and right on target. Using a jumble of western terms, but o.k. One must improvise!

In the hermitage, one must pray or go to seed. The pretense of prayer will not suffice. Just sitting will not suffice. It has to be real – yet what can one do? Solitude puts you with your back to the wall (or your face to it!) and this is good. One prays to pray. And the reality of death. Donne's poems and Lancelot Andrewes.

Then it becomes very important to remember that the quality of one's night depends on the thoughts of the day. I had a somewhat fearsome night after reading *The Lord of the Flies*. This a hangover from my cenobitic after-dinner flight into light reading (which is all right, I do not despise it). So many good books around and in the woodshed after dinner. Pasternak once. Lately Ellul, and Felix Green's *Curtain of Ignorance* (good information on the bad reporting about China), Stevie Smith, Françoise Henri on Irish art, Auden "The Enchafed Flood," and last summer Kenneth Jackson's *Early Celtic Nature Poetry*. Also Nora Chadwick, etc., etc. (I got a charming letter from the Carmelites of Waterbeach, her friends). And of course recently Ionesco – *Rhinoceros, The Future Is in Eggs*, etc. I am still busy with his *Notes et contre-notes*.

Still, the quality of one's nights depends on the sanity of the day. I bring there the sins of the day into the light and darkness of truth to be adored without disguise – then I want to fly back to the disguises. Who ever said that the solitary life is one of pretense and deception? As if pretense were *easy* in solitude!!! It is easy in the community, for one can have the support of a common illusion or a common agreement in forms that take the place of truth. One can pretend in the solitude of an afternoon walk, but the night destroys all pretenses, one is reduced to nothing, and compelled to begin laboriously the long return to truth.

Evening: Yet after all that, this afternoon I made myself a cup of coffee (after dinner) strong enough to blow the roof off the hermitage, and then as a result got into an orgy of abstract drawings. Most of the drawings were awful – some were even disturbing. So that now I see that I cannot afford to play with this either, in solitude. But perhaps I will do some careful and sane drawings, based perhaps on Romanesque sculpture, until I get some better ideas. Not now, anyway. Went down to the monastery feeling confused and ashamed, but singing Vespers and the Advent hymn was a comfort. I will continue to need some Liturgy – certainly the Conventual Mass for a long time, and Vespers generally, and the other hours when I am in the monastery anyway.

Tonight it is cold again and as I came up in the dark, a few small snowflakes were flying in the beam of the flashlight. The end of an oak log was still burning with small flames in the fireplace. On the way up I had been thinking of the letter from ex-Brother Alcuin (Grimes) and how he visited the Little Sisters in Chicago, and thought maybe of sending them some cheese for Christmas. One of the sisters, he says, seems lonely for her home in Burgundy. Came up with candles, and sugar for coffee, and a jar to urinate in so that I won't have to go out in the snow in the middle of the night. What greater comforts could a man want? Well, of course I will be glad to get electric light. The question of light is an important one. Not that I have anything against Sister Lamp here – chaste and quiet and faithful. But a bit dim for serious reading. And yet for centuries, who had more than this? St. Thomas may have had much less good a light than my lamp here!

December 6, 1964. Second Sunday of Advent

Thank God I have been purged of Sartre by Ionesco. I don't think Ionesco is a great artist but he is healthy and alive and free. Sartre is not free, for all his academic mumblings about freedom and "engagement." Nor is his refusal of the Nobel Prize to me a convincing proof of anything except perhaps that he is clever enough to know how much he needs to fight his own bad faith. And so now, sure enough, he is in *Life* with a sly little smile – and essentially he is a clever, mild little bourgeois. An honest modest man. But he has to be a dragon and that is his trouble. Hence – "misguided direction," arrogance, pontifical ceremonies, declarations, etc. But who is without guilt? Ionesco carries it off better than Sartre. He is more truly a child, and independent.

December 7, 1964

In solitude everything has its weight for good or evil, and one must attend carefully to everything. If you apply yourself carefully to what you do, great springs of strength and truth are released in you. If you drift or go inattentively, automatic and obsessed, the strength is against you and becomes a storm of confusion, and dashes you on the rocks. And when the power, the energy of truth is well released, then everything becomes good and makes sense, and there is no contrast to be made between solitude and community or anything else, because all is good. It seems to me, though, that these springs do not get to run for me in the community, and that I simply go along in the heavy, secure, confused mentality of the community (though I know that for others the springs are running). And instead of everything being *one*, everything is merely confused. Though now, as a result of solitude, the psalms in choir and especially the hymns and antiphons (Advent!!) have all their old juice and much more too, a new mystery.

Guerric [of Igny]'s beautiful Fourth Advent sermon on the consecration of the desert, and the grace placed in it by Christ, "preparing a new place for the new life" and overcoming evil not for Himself "but for those who were to be future dwellers in the wilderness." Not just evil, the Evil One! The desert is given us to get the evil unnested from the crannies of our own hearts. Perhaps again my tendency to find this in solitude rather than community is simply subjective. After twenty-three years all the nests are well established. But in solitude and open air they are revealed and the wind blows on them and I know they must go!

December 8, 1964

A constant thumping and pummeling of guns at Fort Knox. It began last night when I was going to bed. Then there were big "whumps," unlike cannon, more like some kind of missile. Now, it sounds like a new kind of rapid-fire artillery, not the old rolling kind of the last war.

Undoubtedly there are many who are ready to go to war in the Congo, and once again repeat the madness of Viet Nam and bring in American power where the withdrawal of European colonialists seems to have left confusion and vacuum. Seems – because all are eager to have it that way, and make things be the way we need them to be. The horrible Mississippi story (recent arrest of the sheriffs, etc. who are thought to have murdered the civil rights workers last June –), the obsessions of Viet Nam, the madness of patriots all make this land seem possessed by a demonic illusion, driven to ruinous adventures by technological hubris.

2:15. Bumps and punches at Fort Knox faster and faster. I am reading [Stephane] Lupano in the hermitage [*Logique et contradiction*, 1947].

December 9, 1964

Last night after a prayer vigil in the novitiate chapel (didn't do a good job – was somewhat disorganized and distracted), went to bed late at the hermitage. All quiet. No lights at Boone's or Newton's. Cold. Lay in bed realizing that what I was, was *happy*. Said the strange word "happiness" and realized that it was there, not as an "it" or object. It simply was. And I was that. And this morning, coming down, seeing the multitude of stars above the bare branches of the wood, I was suddenly hit, as it were, with the whole package of meaning of everything: that the immense mercy of God was upon me, that the Lord in infinite kindness had looked down on me and given me this vocation out of love, and that he had always intended this, and how foolish and trivial had been all my fears and twistings and desperation. And no matter what anyone else might do or say about it, however they might judge or evaluate it, all is irrelevant in the reality of my vocation to solitude, even though I am not a typical hermit. Quite the contrary perhaps. It does not matter how I may or may not be classified. In the light of this simple fact of God's love and the form it has taken, in the mystery of my life, classifications are ludicrous, and I have no further need to occupy my mind with them (if I ever did) – at least in this connection.

The only response is to go out from yourself with all that one is, which is nothing, and pour out that nothingness in gratitude that God is who He is. All speech is impertinent, it destroys the simplicity of that nothingness before God by making it seem as if it had been "something."

December 10, 1964

"Les gens d'aujourd'hui ont une peur atroce de la liberté et de l'humour; ils ne savent pas qu'il n'y a pas de vie possible sans liberté et sans humour, que le moindre geste, le plus simple initiative, réclament le déploiement des forces imaginatives, qu'ils s'archarnent, bêtement, à vouloir enchaîner et empoisonner entre les murs aveugles du réalisme le plus étroit qui est la mort, et qu'ils appellent vie qui est la ténèbre et qu'ils appellent lumière." ["But nowadays people are scared stiff both of freedom and of humor; they do not realize that life is impossible without freedom and humor, that the simplest gesture and the slightest effort require the full deployment of our powers of imagination; and like brutish beasts, they want to enchain and corrupt themselves inside the blind walls of the narrowest kind of realism, which is death, and which they call life, and which is darkness, and that is what they call light."]

Ionesco, Notes et contre-notes, p. 178

Sister Luke came over from Loretto to talk to a dozen of us or so about the Council (she was the American woman auditor there this last session, one of the first group). Talking to her made the session very understandable, even the last couple of days, which were pretty ferocious. The great question is what was Pope Paul trying to do? Was he forcing the conservatives against the liberals? Is he proving himself a "transition pope" (whatever that means)? My guess is that he was simply trying, by means of curial politics, to keep things together as far as possible. But it also seems to me that he was much more acquiescent to the conservatives and their desires, than to the liberals.

Scribners sent Daniel Callahan's book *Honesty in the Church* in proof. I will not make a statement on it, as it would tend to mislead people if I did.

(That is to say a lot of readers who lack the maturity and sophistication to understand such a book might get in trouble reading it.) However, it is a very outspoken, even indignant, criticism of all the doubletalk, maneuverings and pretenses that are too characteristic of the Church's official acts sometimes.

Celebrating my twenty-third anniversary of arrival at Gethsemani. Came straight up to the hermitage after Sister Luke left. Cooked myself some oatmeal (first supper I have cooked here) and ate alone, looking at the hills, in great peace. Long quiet evening, rain falling, candle, silence: it is incomparable!

December 11, 1964

Sister Luke said that Archbishop Roberts was not allowed to give his intervention in the Council on conscientious objection! Can this be true? Perhaps only that he was one of several whose interventions on nuclear war had to be submitted in writing! But I hate that Bishop Hannan's intervention (the NATO line!) was not only permitted but received much publicity. His speech, and the similar one of Liverpool,[7] was one of the few reported in full by the NCWC.[8]

Heavy rain all night. Now the rain on the roof accentuates the silence, and surrounds the dryness and light of the hermitage as though with love and peace. The liberty and tranquillity of this place is indescribable – more than any merely bodily peace, this is a gift of God, marked with His simplicity and His purity. How one's heart opens, and what hope arises in the core of my being! It is as if I had not really hoped in God for years, as if I had been living all this time in despair. Now all things seem reasonable and possible. A greater self-denial seems obvious and easy. (Though perhaps it may not be!) A whole new discussion of life is no longer a desperate dream, but completely and simply credible.

December 16, 1964

Yesterday for the first time was able to live a complete day's schedule as it "ought to be" (at least in this transition period) at hermitage.[9] Came down

---

7 Merton here refers to the Archbishop of Liverpool, John Carmel Heenan.
8 National Catholic Welfare Conference, precursor of the National Conference of Catholic Bishops (NCCB).
9 Dom James (Abbot James Fox), now seemingly a supporter rather than an opponent of the hermit life, gave Merton permission to spend "full days" at the hermitage starting on December 16, 1964. There were signs – such as Dom James's order to have the hermitage wired for electricity – that Merton would be allowed to spend more and more time there, perhaps eventually to live permanently at the hermitage.

only for my own Mass and dinner. Cooked supper at the hermitage etc. In fact cooked too much rice, having miscalculated, and sat half an hour consuming it, with tea. But it was a splendid supper (looking out at the hills in the clear evening light). After that, washing dishes – the bowl, the pot, the cup, the knife (for oleo), the spoon – looked up and saw a jet like a small rapid jewel travelling north between the moon and the evening star – the moon being nearly full. Then I went for a little walk down to my gate (about 100 yards) and looked out over the valley. Incredibly beautiful and peaceful. Blue hills, blue sky, woods, empty fields, lights going on in the Abbey, to the right, through the screen of trees, hidden from the hermitage. And out there, lights on the three farms I can see. One at Newton's and two others out there in the hills behind Gethsemani station.

Everything the Fathers say about the solitary life is exactly true. The temptations and the joys, above all the tears and the ineffable peace and happiness. The happiness that is so pure because it is simply not one's own making, but sheer mercy and gift! And the sense of having arrived at last in the place destined for me by God, and for which I was brought here twenty-three years ago!

December 20, 1964. Fourth Sunday of Advent

This morning in Chapter Dom James finished a series of remarks (facts) about Scandinavia. He returned Wednesday from Norway and has been talking about it in the evening chapter. Was there for the consecration of Bishop John Gran. Everyone is wondering whether there will be a foundation – he says nothing definite about that, but presumably he is open to the idea.

I had permission to go and see Victor Hammer in Lexington Wednesday. He was thin and drawn, marked by sickness, is unable to go out, but works on his painting of the resurrection. It was a pleasure to be in the beautiful little house on Market Street, and to talk with him and Carolyn. Some very special Pedro Domecq brandy came out for the occasion with their excellent espresso coffee.

Two nights ago it turned very cold. Yesterday morning as I came down to the monastery in bright, frozen moonlight, with the hard diamonded leaves crackling under my feet, a deer sprang up in the deep bushes of the hollow. Perhaps two. I could see one in the moonlight. Finished article for *Holiday*[10]

---

[10] "Rain and the Rhinoceros," *Holiday* 37 (May 1965): 8, 10, 12, 15–16.

and sent it yesterday. Apparently the REA men have been around as I can see stakes for poles – but just where I don't want them!

Am working on Philoxenus and Ephrem. Yesterday I finished Ionesco's *Le Piéton de l'air* which is extraordinarily beautiful, though uneven. The basic idea is wonderful, and it is his best, deepest idea. Especially moved by Marthe.

December 22, 1964

Lax sent me from Greece (from his island, Kalymnos) a typewritten copy of the trial in Leningrad of the poet ("militant work-shy element") [Joseph] Brodsky. Finally as a scene from Ionesco: Brodsky . . . "belongs to a group where the word 'work' is greeted with Satanic laughter . . . Brodsky has been defended by coarse rascals, work shy elements, loudmouths and Beatles." In his diary Brodsky had called Marx "an old glutton framed by a wreath of pine cones." (Santa Claus?) The only thing is – who is laughing? It was published in *Encounter* and of course *Time*, etc. picked it up. The question I ask is this: in what significant way does the mentality of *Time* readers differ from that of the people who condemned Brodsky? They are perhaps a little less crude, but are they any less square? Do they have any better ideas about poets and poetry? Of the value of work? (The value of work measured by the money one makes and the status one gets, not by the work one does!)

Fortunately I am a success, have status, on thin blue paper, while eating breakfast in the hermitage.

Epiphany antiphons are already running through my head. Also at chant practice yesterday I realized how much I had grown to love the antiphons of Christmas Eve and of Christmas Vespers, eloquence of the melody, in its simplicity, saturated with the mystery of the Virgin birth and with *all* mystery. Yet plain as the afternoon.

Am finally reading Vladimir Lossky's fine book *La Vision de Dieu* which reminds me that the best thing that has come out of the Council is the Declaration on Ecumenism, particularly the part on oriental theology. If it were a matter of choosing between "contemplation" and "eschatology" there is no question that I am, and would always be, committed entirely to the latter. Here in the hermitage, returning necessarily to beginnings, I know where my beginning was, having the Name and Godhead of Christ preached in Corpus Christi Church. I heard and believed. And I believe that He has called me freely, out of pure mercy, to His love and salvation, and that at the end (to which all is directed by Him) I shall see Him after I have put off my body in death and have risen together with Him. And that at the last day "*videbit omnis caro saluteni Dei*" ["all flesh shall see the salvation of God"]. What this means is that my faith is an eschatological faith, not merely a means of penetrating the mystery of the divine presence resting in Him now. Yet because my faith is eschatological it is *also* contemplative, for I am even now in the Kingdom and I can even now "see" something of the glory of the Kingdom and praise Him who is King. I would be foolish then if I lived blindly, putting all "seeing" off until some imagined fulfillment (for my present seeing is the beginning of a real and unimaginable fulfillment!). Thus contemplation and eschatology are one, in Christian faith and in surrender to Christ. They complete each other and intensify each other. It is by contemplation and love that I can best prepare myself for the eschatological vision – and best help all the Church, and all men, to journey toward it.

The union of contemplation and eschatology is clear in the gift of the Holy Spirit. In Him we are awakened to know the Father because in Him we are refashioned in the likeness of the Son. And it is in this likeness that the Spirit will bring us at last to the clear vision of the invisible Father in the Son's glory, which will also be our glory. Meanwhile it is the Spirit who awakens in our heart the faith and hope in which we cry for the eschatological fulfillment and vision. And in this hope there is already a beginning, an "*arrha*" ["earnest"], of the fulfillment. This is our contemplation: the realization and "experience" of the lifegiving Spirit in Whom the Father is present to us through the Son, our way, truth, and life. The realization that we are on our way, that because we are on our way we are in that Truth which is the end and by which we are already fully and eternally alive. Contemplation is the loving sense of this life and this presence and this eternity.

In the afternoon (this is my whole day in the hermitage) the guns were pounding at Fort Knox while I was making my afternoon meditation, and I thought that after all this is no mere "distraction," and that I am here because they are there so that, indeed, I am supposed to hear them. They form part of an ever renewed "decision" and commitment for peace. But what peace? I am once again faced with the deepest ambiguities of political and social action. One thing clear is that there is a will and intention of God bearing upon me (and to let it bear fully on me is to be free!) and my life has no meaning except as a conscious and total self-dedication to the *fulfillment of His intention* (which in its details remains a complete mystery). As far as I know it, I must seek to be a man wholly given to prayer here in this place where I am, in which He has put me. But I am far from being "totally" a man of prayer. Obviously, even writing is not excluded.

My will, however, cannot simply lose itself in this or that, in meditation, or writing, or study, or "tranquillity" or work, but simply must surrender in all this to the mysterious and dominant intention of the Lord, the Master whom I have come here to _serve._ I am not here to be this or that, but to obey Him in everything, _Gleichheit_ [likeness] (Eckhart). And to learn slowly, patiently, the tempo of such obedience. If I had been a better cenobite I perhaps would be more familiar with it!

The REA men were here in the morning (cold and misty). The hermitage will tie in to a line that will eventually go to a sewage disposal plant to be built in the bottom, by the creek.

December 23, 1964

For Eusebius, the Roman empire had resolved the problem of the conflicting nations, and conflicting "angels" (of nations) against the one Lord. The angels and nations were subdued in one empire where the religion of the true God had taken over. Hence the _pax romana_ was in effect the peace of the messianic kingdom. Hence the emperor represented Christ on earth, the prince of peace, etc. We are still stuck with this ideology which put the power (angel) of the empire at the right hand of God (see Peterson in _Dieu vivant,_ 22).

For Origen a man's "adversary" is his bad angel deputed to keep him firmly in subjection to the angelic prince of his nation or tribe, so that he will not free himself and belong only to God, in Christ (who is above all nations and has vanquished all the powers). (_Hom_[ilies] _in Luc,_ 35.)

[Jean] Daniélou has said: "Material civilization in its demiurgic character seems to be one of the places where demonic action is most intense. Judeo-Christian tradition maintains the positive significance of political and cultural values. In this, it is opposed to the Gnostic doctrine of the _cosmocratores_ [worldly powers] but it recognizes that, in fact, these domains are invaded and dominated by demonic powers." _Daniélou,_ Dieu vivant, 22, pp. _102–103_

December 25, 1964

First Christmas at the hermitage, very peaceful, no trouble sleeping through. There was of all things a thunderstorm! For two days the weather had been damp, windy and warm as it sometimes is in spring and at one moment I even heard the frogs singing, Christmas Eve. The day before that the novices were cutting down poplars and cedars in the field, where the REA line needs to get through, and I finished some digging I thought I had to do to keep water from accumulating next to the cottage. I got up and said my night office in the hermitage (all that is said about night, silence, shepherds, etc. sounds much better here!), went down for midnight Mass. The novices were happy around the Christmas tree and I was happy with them over the "spiritual gifts." (Bible texts printed out and distributed blindly.) The midnight Mass was simpler than it has ever been.

St. Maximus [the Confessor] says that he who "has sanctified his senses by looking with purity at all things" becomes like God. This is, I think, what the Zen masters tried to do. A letter from John Wu spoke of running into Suzuki at Honolulu last summer. They talked of my meeting with him in New York. Suzuki was going to ask me a question but didn't. "If God created the world who created the Creator?" A good koan.

December 29, 1964. St. Thomas of Canterbury

On Christmas Day, in the afternoon, Brother Colman and I drove over into the hills behind New Hope, in the area where Edelin is giving the monastery land for hermitages. As there is no road near the west end of that land (or I think not) we got an idea of it from the next valley, where the old ridge road goes from New Hope to Howardstown. Then we explored other such valleys, following the back roads as far as they went. The hills that look like a solid mass from here are, of course, a labyrinth of deep, silent, wooded valleys, with farms in the bottom. A whole world of wonderful hidden places, some very lost and wild. I am planning to get over there some day and spend the day on foot exploring the area around Edelin's and seeing where his land goes (if I can get any idea of the boundaries!).

There was a little sun Christmas afternoon but the rest of the time has been grey and dark. I can't even remember what I did St. Stephen's afternoon, when it was raining. Yesterday, Holy Innocents, Brother Joachim was looking the hermitage over to plan the wiring for lights and an electric cooking stove. I finished Von Durkheim, *The Japanese Cult of Tranquillity*. The best and most revealing part is the appendix from a Japanese master of swordsmanship speaking of the "sword that kills and gives life" in the tradition of Takuan. Actually the pinnacle of swordsmanship is *not* violence and killing but simply a "truth" against which the opponent can ruin himself or by which he can be enlightened. A fascinating concept. Only "the animal man" seeks to "win" ("prevail"). But the spiritual man is simply true and the law of truth has to "win" in him.

"Love comes from prayer and prayer from remaining in seclusion" (Isaac of Syria). Certainly the break in my more solitary routine (going down to monastery earlier without the long meditation, spending most of the day there, ceremonies, lectures, etc.) has created a kind of confusion, disturbance and laxity. But in the trouble itself and in the confusion I have had to struggle for deeper conviction and commitment. Solitude is not something to play with from time to time. It is going to be difficult to remain divided next year between hermitage and community, two tempos and two ways of life. And yet of course I still need a good part of common life, and will always need to maintain very definite contacts. But it is hard and confusing to be uprooted from peace every time you begin barely to get into it – or rather, not to be able to sink completely into unity and simplicity. There is peace too in community, of course, but it has a different and more active rhythm.

Yet in this solitude there must be, with the fiery substance of the eternal prophets, also the terse anger and irony and humor of the Latin American poets with whom I am united in bonds of warmth and empathy, for instance the Peruvian Blanca Varela (I must translate her, a poem or two), or Jorge Eduard Eielson!

At last there is light again. First there were some stars here and there, when I first got up at 2:15. Then a surprise – in an unexpected corner of woods, the thin last slice of leftover moon, the last moon of 1964. The sun came up at 8:05 (our time here is unnatural, as we are on Eastern standard). Then there was the extraordinary purity and stillness and calm of that moment of surprise and renewal. Peace of the woods and the valley, but there somewhere a heifer salutes the morning with enthusiastic lowing.

January 1, 1965

I woke up this morning with the vague feeling that something was walking around the hermitage: it was the rain again. So begins the imagined new year. Yet it is too well imagined, and the date 1965 on the new ordo confounds me. My Mass was fine and so was the thanksgiving afterward, and the last thing I read before going to bed in the "old year" was a letter of Peter Damian to two hermits (recently republished by Dom Leclercq). They wanted to be buried, when they died, at their hermitage and nowhere else. I can agree with that!

I got a fine letter from John Wu and a chapter of his book (in progress) on Zen [*The Golden Age of Zen*, 1967] – a good chapter on Hui Neng. Also a letter from Webster College, where they will want the exhibit of drawings in April. A card from the Polish Marxist who was here with the group from

Indiana University – where was it? I had a long talk with Brother Basil (McMurry) who thinks he will leave here when his simple vows run out, and go to Mount Saviour. But on a special basis.

It seems to be a mistake to read in uninterrupted succession in the refectory one speech after another by Pope Paul, just as it was a mistake to try to read all the Council interventions. One becomes very oppressed with the jargon, the uniform tone of official optimism and "inspirationalism," etc. Yet the Pope said good things both at Bombay and in his Christmas message, on Peace and the need for disarmament. And against nationalism and the arms race and stockpiling "overkill" weapons.

January 4, 1965

Worse than Council speeches in refectory – Archbishop O'Boyle's "explanations" of the last two days of the Council. And then after that the *Time* story on the murder of hostages in Stanleyville (Congo) last November. A tragic thing but the true story, equally tragic, assumes fantastic perspective. No indication that anybody could possibly be wrong but the African rebels. And that the Tshombe-Belgian-American intervention is the only thing that could possibly be reasonable, human, etc. Were the hostages martyrs to a Red plot, or also to the greed of the people who want to hold on to the mines in Katanga? The trouble is that indignation and horror swept the community (and they should). But with them also a complete conviction that of course the implied judgment and interpretation of *Time* was completely satisfactory and final.

When you think that all over the country it is this way about Cuba, Viet Nam, the Congo etc. – what can possibly come of it but one dirty adventure on top of another. Use of torture in Viet Nam (by our side) is admitted without apology as something quite reasonable.

January 6, 1965

Yesterday was extraordinary. I had planned to take a whole day of recollection out in the knobs around Edelin's hollow, to explore the place and get some idea of where it goes and what is around it. Fortunately old Edelin came along with Brother Colman, who drove me out in the Scout, to show me where one could get into his property from the top of the knobs on the west. It is wonderful wild country and I had a marvelous day. We left the monastery about 8:15, started back into the knobs to the southwest of New Hope, and climbed the narrow road that clings to the steep hillside above

Old Coon Hollow. (Not to be confused, Edelin says, with Coon Hollow.) At the top of the rise we got onto a rolling table land of scrub oak and sassafras, with deep hollows biting into it. The old road runs along the watershed between the Rolling Fork valley and the other valley where Edelin's house is. It is a magnificent wild, scrubby, lost road. The sun was bright, and the air was not too cold.

I got off near where the woods slope down (about a mile) into Edelin's Hollow. At the top, amid the thick tangle of trees and wild grape is a collapsed house. In a half-cleared area there are still pear trees, and Edelin says the deer like to come and eat the pears. Here too, in a gully, is the spring which feeds the stream running through Edelin's pasture (actually one of several streams that join there). So they left me there, and I went down to the spring, found it without trouble. Wonderful clear water pouring strongly out of a cleft in the mossy rock. I drank from it in my cupped hands and suddenly realized it was years, perhaps twenty-five or thirty years, since I had tasted such water: absolutely pure and clear, and sweet with the freshness of untouched water, no chemicals!! I looked up at the clear sky and the tops of the leafless trees shining in the sun and it was a moment of angelic lucidity. Said Tierce with great joy, overflowing joy, as if the land and woods and spring were all praising God through me. Again their sense of angelic transparency of everything, and of pure, simple and total light. The word that comes closest to pointing to it is simple. It was all simple. But a simplicity to which one seems to aspire, only seldom to attain it. A simplicity that is, and has, and says everything just because it is simple.

After that I scrambled around a bit on the steep, rocky hillside, in the sun to get oriented, and then started through the thick sassafras out on a long wooded space which, I guessed, would overlook the Hollow, and it did. After about half a mile through very thick brush, with vines and creepers and brambles and much young growth (bigger trees damaged by fire), I came to the end, and could see the hollow in haze against the sun. I could see the part of the pasture on a hillside a mile or so away where three walnut trees grow. And of course the other side of the valley and the country road. Most of the view was of knobs and woods, a sea of sun and haze and silence and trees. Sat there a long time, said Sext, read a letter from Milosz (an important one) and had a marvelous box lunch which Leone Gannon at the Ladies' guest house got up for me. And as time went on I was more and more under the spell of the place until finally, about 12, the sky began to cloud over.

The SAC planes. I forgot to mention that while I was at the spring after Tierce, when I was about to go, the huge SAC plane announced its coming and immediately swooped exactly overhead not more than two or three hundred feet above the hilltops. It was fantastic, and sure enough I could see the trap door of the bomb bays. The whole thing was an awesome part of the "simplicity," a sign and an "of course," and it had a great deal to do with all the rest of the day. During the day, in fact, five SAC planes went over, not exactly over this particular hollow but all visible from it, i.e., very close, within a mile (otherwise one could not see them, flying so low, with so many hills around). Only the first and the last went directly over me. But directly so that I was looking right up at the H bomb!!! This was fantastic. Of course the mere concept of fear was utterly meaningless, out of the question. I felt only an intellectual and moral intuition, an "of course," which seemed to be part of the whole day and its experience.

Speaking perhaps unwisely, yet soberly, the thing that I was left with was the most overwhelming conviction that I was called by God simply to live the rest of my life totally alone in that hollow where I would be morally and symbolically "under the bomb" and where also a hundred years ago slaves were living. It would mean real poverty, real solitude, real interiority, real renunciation, a silence that would break ties of identification with *all movements* monastic or otherwise, pacifist or otherwise, and yet also the possibility of being shot by some drunken neighbor who finally discovered that I was not in full accord with the time-honored principles of the South.

Near the collapsed house is a clearing with rubbish lying around. Beer cans with bullet holes in them, a pair of shoes, chewing gum wrappers, etc., etc. It was, said Edelin, a "dance hall." A place where people from the hollows came up to get drunk and raise hell. It is near the spring but far from the hollow.

I went down a logging trail (many trees were cut this fall and winter), beautiful wet trail, into the hollow full of tall beech trees and other hardwoods (most of the mature oaks were cut), a lovely, silent walk, with streams full of clear water, and suddenly came out into Edelin's pasture, at the bottom. The place just took my breath away. I had seen it before in September, but without this "angelic light" (now the sun was hidden and the sky overcast, but there was a sense of blessed silence, and a joy, and again that "simplicity"). But also the sense that here was the place for "the house." I wandered up and down the hollow, in the empty pasture, tasting the silence and peace. Went up the hillside where the two knob hawks came out screaming and wheeled over to the other side of the valley. I found the old half burnt barn (belonging to one of Edelin's neighbors) in a branch of the hollow. I began the office of Epiphany in the open space where there are still stones from the foundation of the slaves' house (I could use them as foundation for "the house"). Went back to "my place." Sat on a felled white oak and looked down the hollow until I had to go. The last SAC plane went over again, right overhead, the bomb pointed to the chosen place.

I read a beautiful blessing over the valley (a *Benedictio Loci* in the Breviary – the long one). Never has a written prayer meant so much. I know one day there will be hermits here, or men living alone. But I think the hollow is already blessed because of the slaves that were there (perhaps one of them was very holy!). So I went back up the logging trail and met Brother Colman and Edelin in the Scout coming along the old road at the top. Never was there such a day. On the way down we stopped and looked at a new log cabin, and Brother Colman is anxious to build one.

January 8, 1965

When I got back and calmed down the other evening, I realized I was being enthusiastic and unreasonable. All day Epiphany I had a sort of emotional hangover from that day in the woods. Sat at the top of the field looking down at the hermitage, tried to meditate sanely in the sun, came out quieter. And cooked myself some supper – a thin potato soup made out of dust in an envelope.

Then as the sun was setting I looked up at the end of the field where I had sat in the afternoon, and suddenly realized that there were beings there – deer. In the evening light they were hard to descry against the tall brown grass, but I could pick out at least five. They stood still looking at me, and I stood looking at them, a lovely moment that stretched into ten minutes perhaps! They did not run (though kids could be heard shouting somewhere down by the waterworks) but eventually walked quietly into the tall grass and bushes and for all I know slept there. When they walked they seemed to multiply so that in the end I thought there must be at least ten of them.

Yesterday I spoke to Reverend Father about Edelin's valley and he said there could be no question of going there until the monastery had title to the land. And he is also thinking of buying other property next to Edelin's so that the place will be protected. He seems intent on eventually having hermitages there. It is clearly not yet time to be thinking of moving there, and I have this place now that I have just begun to really "live" in. Brother Joachim is slowly getting it wired up for electric light, etc. and there is an old beat-up electric stove to cook my soup on, when it has current to work on.

As for the SAC, it is perfectly impartial. Yesterday afternoon as I was saying office on the walk below the novitiate, before seeing Reverend Father, the SAC plane swooped by right over the hermitage. I would say it was hardly 150 feet above the tree tops.

January 9, 1965

Again, last night in the warm dark, before the plentiful rain, the plane again (though perhaps smaller than the SAC) came right over the hermitage in the dark, a cross of the four lights, a technological swan.

> *La espesa rueda de la tierra*
> *Su llanto húmedo de olvido*
> *Hace rodar, cortando el tiempo*
> *En mitades inaccesibles.*
> [Its wet complaint of forgetting
> Is what makes turn the world's thick wheel.
> Cutting time
> Into inaccessible halves.]
>
> *([Pablo] Neruda)*

Full of rice which I found a new good way of cooking. Peace. Silence.

Clayton Eshelman sent his translation of *Residencia en la Tierra* [by Pablo Neruda]. Some of it is very successful. On the whole a good translation.

January 10, 1965

Jaspers says (and this is analogous to a basic principle in Jacques Ellul also): "Once I envision world history or life's entirety as a kind of finite totality I can act only on the basis of sham knowledge, in distortion of actual possibilities, far from reality, vague about facts, achieving nothing but confusion and advancing in directions altogether different from those I wanted" (*Nietzsche and Christianity*, p. 58). And this applies also to monastic reform.

"Whenever my knowledge is chained to total concepts, whenever my actions are based on a specific world-view, I am distracted from what I am really able to do. I am cheated on the present . . . for the sake of something imagined (past or future) rather than real, which has not been actually lived and has never been realized" Ibid. p. 60. (Note that in "monastic ideals" this is precisely the problem. One assumes that the ideal was once fully real and actually lived, and then one has every "reason" for resentment at the unrealization of what cannot be, and never was real. In actual fact the true monks had a reality which was quite different, and accorded entirely and precisely with their own accepted circumstances.) "The man who keeps faith with reality wants to act truthfully in the here and now, not to derive a second hand here and now from a purpose" (p. 60).

Problem of false "Christian" historicism which sets up history as a unity that "can be comprehended." Nietzsche did and did not see this danger (he may have fallen into it himself). But he said that because of this change of focus centered on history, "God was dead" and His death was the fault of Christianity. Nietzsche also made his classic analysis of Christian morality and the Christian will to truth being in the end self-destructive. The ultimate end of the Christian will to truth was to destroy even itself by doubt, said Nietzsche. (This Christianity ends in nihilism.) We certainly see something of this in monasticism today – with the breakdown of confidence in authority and the insatiable thirst for an "authentic" ideal, monks are becoming incapable of accepting and resting in anything – yet they do not really seek God, they seek a "perfect monasticism."

All that Nietzsche said about Christianity immediately becomes true as soon as one puts anything else before God – whether it be history, or culture, or science, or contemplation, or liturgy, or reform, or "justice," etc., etc. But Jaspers has a brilliant insight into the real possibility of Nietzsche – if "all is permitted" there is an alternative to the nihilism of despair. The nihilism of strength "drawn from the darkness of the encompassing and able to do without ties to supposedly finite objectives, maxims and laws" (p. 84). Is not this Christianity? "It needs no such ties because from the depths of the encompassing it will always come upon what is true and what is to be done. It will know historically and with the tranquillity of eternity," etc.

Maybe. But it seems to me that the Gospel says this and that the Gospel remains necessary if men are to attain this freedom rightly and not fall into the fanaticism and arbitrariness rooted in despair. In any case Jaspers certainly shows the difference between the popular residue of Nietzsche's anti-Christianity and its really profound implications – and ends with Nietzsche's curse on his own admirers: "To this mankind of today I will not be light, nor be called light! Those I will blind!!" (p. 102).

Thank God that after interminable NCWC reports of this or that speech we are finally back to Meriol Trevor's biography of Newman in the refectory. I have missed it for three months!

January 11, 1965

I spoke too soon. The NCWC reports started again yesterday (Sunday).

A little Nietzsche is stimulating, but what I like is to read Isaac of Nineveh in the hermitage or Zen Masters in the fields. I like to say Lauds of the Little Office of Our Lady coming down through the woods by starlight, with everything *there:* starlight, frost and cold, ice and snow, trees, earth, hills, and cozy in the lighted monastery, the sons of men.

January 17, 1965

It is the Feast of St. Anthony, but because of Sunday (Second after Epiphany) there is nothing in the Office.

Brilliant night, deep snow, sparkling in the moon. Difficult to get this ballpoint to write. A good fire keeps the front room of the hermitage warm and I think it will be wonderful walking down to the monastery in an hour or so. The snow began in the early morning yesterday and by the time I started down to the monastery it was blowing in my eyes so that I had to keep them half closed. It blew and snowed all day.

In the monastery after dinner I played Brother Antoninus' record "The Tongs of Jeopardy" to the novices and some of the juniors. It is remarkably good – meditation on the Kennedy assassination. He was talking about his ideas on this when he was here and I was very struck by them then. They cannot be summed up simply as "Jungian." A remarkable and sensitive poetic insight into the state of the American mind – better than anything else I know (for instance how much deeper say than Paul Goodman's *Growing Up Absurd* which I have just recently read). More than Jungian, the "Tongs" meditation is deeply Buddhist, and the Cain idea, the drive to fratricide as the great weakness in the American psyche, is most impressive and I think accurate. Illtud Evans is coming to preach the retreat and I will talk to him about it. Am tempted to review it for *Blackfriars*.

Stunning how the Kennedy assassination moved people rightly or wrongly, sanely or otherwise. One of our Brothers did a drawing (nothing to do with the record) of a crucifixion: on the cross was Jacqueline Kennedy (!!). A failure of taste and full of curious implications: a concept that to me is unintelligible. She of course was central in the whole thing. Brother Antoninus had little to say of her in "Tongs." Perhaps the Irish keening at the end was meant to carry what could not be articulated. My feeling was that the relationship *to her* in which we all ended up was the most significant thing of all. As if *she* had redeemed us from all the evil. (Of course I suppose that was the

idea of the Brother who did the drawing.) She was a presence of love and nobility and truth who *chose* to be as she was and to forgive inexplicably, and to
be loved and admired. It was she, actually, who did the greatest thing of all,
and the noblest thing, disinterestedly and without strings (Brother Antoninus contrasted the funeral rites with the mendacity of conventions, etc.) and
gave America a sense of being true which we rarely get in public life.

When I step out on the porch the bristles in my nose instantly freeze up,
and the outdoor jakes is a grievous shock. The temperature must be zero or
below. Inside the house the thermometer by the door says 45 but it is unre-
liable. I am warm by the fire – but have plenty of clothes on! But the whole
valley is bright with moonlight and snow – and perfectly silent.

Last week I wrote the preface for Phil Berrigan's book [*No More
Strangers*, 1965] in which there are many fine ideas and some bad writing.

January 19, 1965

Very cold again. Snow still fairly deep, but a bright day. Father Illtud Evans
began our retreat last night. Sister Luke came over with him from Loretto
yesterday. She is now on a sub-committee working on Schema 13 for the
Council – one of the first women to be in such a position – and she wanted
to talk about it, I mean the work of the committee, and the Schema. So I
gave her what ideas I had. And I think that as long as they don't take account
of the real problems posed by technology, anything they say or do will be
beside the point.

January 20, 1965

"*Verumtamen audito Deo Pater, nullus tam auditus sit filius et non festinat ad
verigenitoris amplexus*" ["Truly having heard God the Father, there is no one
who having heard the Son who does not hasten to accept the Son's
source."], says Venantius Fortunatus in his commentary on the Pater which
I came upon by accident this morning (in [Migne's] *Patrologia Latina* 88,
looking for the "Irish" rule for nuns which is curious).

January 21, 1965

Another good day in Edelin's valley. Snow, sun, peace; this was yesterday. I
explored a little more, climbed back up the gullies to the spring and came
down again by the logging trail. All was undisturbed snow except for the
tracks of dogs and rabbits, though at the top of the ridge, on the old wagon
road to Howardstown, were the steps of a man who had been there probably the day before.

Reverend Father came out there with Brother Nicholas and I ran into him – which I did not particularly want to do. The talk got around to electric fences, boundary lines, snakes, etc. He is very interested in the place, and especially in acquiring the place. He is full of ideas and deals, and Edelin is dealing with somebody whose name sounds like Cruise, and getting ready to trade something for something else. The big trees have been cut off "Cruise's" land and the tops are lying around all over the place. Cruise, it is said, buys only in order to sell. And so on. "Cruise" owns the valley where the ruined barn is and this is right next to Edelin's so that if we wanted to be fully protected we would have to have it. Besides his valley would be good for hermitages. I saw it yesterday, and it goes back deep into the hills.

But when I think of all the dealing and organizing and planning and so on, and the "institution" that might finally result, the whole thing gives me pause. Would I be a fool to go along with all this? Would it not be much wiser and simpler to stay where I am and make the best of it, for at the moment I am really *on my own*, and need to make no more plans, and am arousing no comment, and am dependent on no one. And the hermitage behind the sheep barn is a very decent and beautiful solitude. All this is something to think about.

January 22, 1965

Vintila Horia sent me his novel about Plato and I find it extraordinarily beautiful, a sustained tone of wisdom, with all kinds of modern undertones. Very "actual." He says (Plato): "I saw the world rushing into stupidity with such natural self-assurance that it caused me to suffer keenly, as if I had been personally responsible for it, while the people around me saw the future as a new pleasure to be expected from a certain joy: as if by being born into the world they acquired a right to this." *(p. 101)*

Meanwhile an ex-novice (Brother Alcuin Grimes) sent a copy of the *Kiplinger Newsletter*, which wound up 1964 with the gift of prophecy – peering into the glad future of 1980. Millions more people but no nuclear war, no world war, but more, more, more of everything – more super highways, cities rebuilt, more suburbs, more money (ignores the question whether all these "more people" will have more jobs), more recreation, more fun, more college, and even, with all the money around, a boom in art, music and literature!! I just can't wait to be sixty-five (still not fully able to believe I will make it to fifty, in nine days' time!). Will I see this glorious future, in which he does hint at the possibility of "problems"?

What total lack of imagination – the prophecy is unimaginative enough to be perhaps even true! But how intolerable. Nothing to look forward to but more of the same inanities, falsities, clichés, pretenses. But there will surely be more frustration, therefore more madness, violence, degeneracy, addiction. The country will be one vast asylum. I have higher hopes. I dare to hope for change, not only quantitative, but even qualitative too. But through darkness and crisis. Perhaps I say that out of custom.

January 25, 1965

St. Paul's day, and nearly the end of the retreat. I have been making a good one, I think. An element of emptiness and anguish from the concentration of it, but not much. Actually I feel more sure than I ever have in my life that I am obeying the Lord and am on the way He wills for me, though at the same time I am struck and appalled (more than ever!) by the shoddiness, the laziness of my response. I am just beginning to awaken and to realize how much more awakening is to come. And how much to be faced. How much I must admit and renounce ambition and agitated self-seeking in my work and contacts (I am so tied up in all this that I don't know where to start getting free!). But God will take care of me, for in my confusion and helplessness I nevertheless feel (believe in) His closeness and strength. I don't have to know and see how it will all come out.

My intention is, in fact, simply to "die" to the past somehow. To take my fiftieth birthday as a turning point, and to live more abandoned to God's will, less concerned with projects and initiatives (which have, however, perhaps also been His will). More detached from work and events, more solitary. To be one of those who entirely practice contemplation simply in order to follow Christ. And who am I anyway?

Illtud Evans has been preaching a good retreat. We had a couple of walks and long conversations together on grey, windy afternoons, about Cambridge, and *Blackfriars*, and the new colleges, and the Hebrides (on Rum now they allow no one to live except those protecting the wildlife and trying to restore the original ecology. This is wonderful!). And California. (He is not impressed with Ed Keating or even with Antoninus!) And the *Times Literary Supplement*, etc., etc. He says the manager of the Beatles said on a TV program that he had read *Elected Silence* five times, that it was one of his favorite books. He described it as "a novel about Roman Catholicism."

January 27, 1965

The retreat ended yesterday, Father Illtud tired, with a cold. John Howard Griffin came (because of Illtud) and I saw him briefly. He spoke of a bombing in Youngstown, Ohio (house of some Negroes who moved into a white neighborhood). So now it all moves North. He said my stuff on the race issue was by no means too pessimistic (some reviewers are indignantly stating that it is).

There was a concelebrated Mass (the first here) (after some difficulties with the Bishop – not exactly obstruction, but meticulous observation). It was solemn and impressive and I think a very great grace for the community and a fine ending for the retreat. I was not one of the concelebrants as I preferred to watch it, this time, and also wanted to be sure not to exclude someone else who is more keen on Liturgy than I am. I am near the top of the list, so I might exclude one of the Junior priests if I signed up for it. Actually, only three priests senior to me got in it, Fathers Joseph, Raymond and Amandus. But it was a great festival, but over long due to great slowness and delay, for instance purifying patens, chalices, etc. at the end. The Communion of the concelebrants went extremely slowly. Still, it was impressive.

After the Mass I came out into a high wind and a strange massive fog, a dust storm from somewhere. The infirm[ary] refectory was full of dust at dinner. A swinging window was smashed and fell in the elevator shaft (put in where there are still windows). The fire alarm went off, and everything was in confusion. And I was buried under the avalanche of mail they had obligingly saved up over the retreat.

Best thing in the mail: two books from Nicanor Parra. I would love to translate some of it. Maybe a book of translations from Parra and Pessoa, and call it "Two Antipoets." Maybe write Laughlin about this! And not to neglect Chuang Tzu either.

January 30, 1965

A cold night. Woke up to find the night filled with the depth and silence of snow. Stayed up here for supper last night, but having cooked soup and cut up a pear and a banana for dessert, and made toast, finally came to the conclusion that it was all much too elaborate. If there were no better reason for fasting, the mere fact of saving time would be a good enough reason. For the bowl and saucepan have to be washed, and I have only a bucket of rainwater for washing, etc., etc. Taking only coffee for breakfast makes a lot of sense, because I can read quietly and sip my two mugs of coffee at leisure, and it really suffices for the morning.

There is a great need for discipline in meditation. Reading helps. The early morning hours are good, though in the morning meditation (one hour) I am easily distracted by the fire. An hour is not much, but I can be more meditative in the hour of reading which follows (and which goes much too fast). (This can be two hours if I go down later to the monastery, which on some days I do.) The presence of Our Lady is important to me. Elusive but I think a reality in this hermitage. Here, though I do not agree with the medieval idea of *Mediatrix apud Mediatorem* [the Mediatrix with the Mediator] (without prejudice to her motherhood which is a much better statement and truth). Her influence is a demand of love, and no amount of talking will explain it. I need her and she is there. I should perhaps think of it more explicitly more often.

In the afternoon, work takes up so much time, and there can be so much. Just keeping the place clean is already a big task. Then there is wood to be chopped, etc. The fire is voracious – but pleasant company.

Sent off to *Holiday* a revised version of "Rain and Rhinoceros" which is also being censored. Telegram (yesterday) from New Orleans that the drawings had not arrived. (Frame House however said they had sent some by Air Express. Catherine Spalding College is supposed to have sent the others ten days ago.)

Vigil of my fiftieth birthday. A bright, snowy afternoon, delicate blue clouds of snow blowing down off the frozen trees. Forcibly restrained myself from much work around the hermitage, made sure of my hour's meditation and will do more later. How badly I need it. I realize how great is the tempo and pressure of work I have been in down in the community – with many irons in the fire. True I have there gained the knack of dropping everything and completely relaxing my attention and forgetting the work of going out and looking at the hills. Good the novitiate work is not exceedingly absorbing. (Biggest trouble now is letter writing.)

More then of my vigil: Shall I look at the past as if it were something to analyze and think about? Rather I thank God for the present, not for myself in the present but for the present which is His and in Him. The past: I am inarticulate about it now. I remember irrelevant moments of embarrassment, and my joys are seen to have been largely meaningless. Yet as I sit here in this wintry and lonely and quiet place I suppose I am the same person as the eighteen year old riding back alone into Bournemouth on a bus out of the New Forest, where I had camped a couple of days and nights. I suppose I regret most my lack of love, my selfishness and glibness (covering a deep shyness and need of love) with girls who, after all, did love me I think, for a time. My great fault was my inability really to believe it, and my efforts to get complete assurance and perfect fulfillment.

So one thing on my mind is sex, as something I did not use maturely and well, something I gave up without having come to terms with it. That is hardly worth thinking about now – twenty-five years nearly since my last adultery, in the blinding, demoralizing summer heat of Virginia. And that heat, that confusion and moral helplessness of those summer days made me know what is in the weather of the south: what madness and what futility. I remember walking on the beach with her the next day and not wanting to talk to her, talking only with difficulty, and not wanting to share *ideas*, or things I really loved. Yet being attacked with something in my solar plexus.

I suppose I am the person that lived for a while at 71 Bridge Street, Cambridge, had Sabberton for my tailor (he made me that strange Alphonse Daudet coat, and the tails I wore perhaps twice – once to the boat race ball where I was very selfish and unkind to Joan). And Clare was my College, and I was a damned fool, sitting on the steps of the boat house late at night with Sylvia, when the two fairies came down expecting to get in the boat house, saw us there, turned and hurried away. . . . All things like that. Adventures.

What I find most in my whole life is *illusion*. Wanting to be something of which I had formed a concept. I hope I will get free of that now, because that is going to be the struggle. And yet I have to be something that I ought to be – I have to meet a certain demand for order and inner light and tranquillity. God's demand, that is, that I remove obstacles to His giving me these.

Snow, silence, the talking fire, the watch on the table. Sorrow. What would be the use of going into all this? I will get cleaned up (my hands are dirty). I will say the psalms of my birthday.

"*Quoniam tu es, qui extraxisti me de ventre: spes mea ab uberibus matris meae. In te projectus sum ex utero: de ventre matris meae Deus meus es tu. Ne discesseris a me.*" ["Yet it was you who took me from the womb; you kept me safe on my mother's breast. On you I was cast from my birth, and since my mother bore me you have been my God. Do not be not far from me."]

(Psalm 21 [22]: 9–11)

No matter what mistakes and illusions have marked my life, most of it I think has been happiness and, as far as I can tell, truth. There were whole seasons of insincerity, largely when I was under twenty-one, and followed friends who were not my own kind. But after my senior year at Columbia things got straight. I can remember many happy and illumined days and whole blocks of time. There were a few nightmare times in childhood. But at Saint Antonin life was a revelation. Then again at so many various times and places, in Sussex (at Rye and in the country), at Oakham, at Strasbourg, at Rome above all, in New York, especially upstate Olean and St. Bona's [Bonaventure University]. I remember one wonderful winter morning arriving at Olean to spend Christmas with Lax. Arrivals and departures on the Erie were generally great. The cottage on the hill, too – then Cuba: wonderful days there. All this I have said before and the whole world knows it.

Here? The profoundest and happiest times of my life have been in and around Gethsemani – and also some of the most terrible. But mostly the happy moments were in the woods and fields, alone, with the sky and the sun – and up here at the hermitage. And with the novices (afternoons at work). But good moments too with Protestants coming here, especially with the Hammers of course (and one or two visits to Lexington), good visits with J. Laughlin, Ping Ferry – Good days in Louisville with Jim Wygal – lunch at Cunningham's, etc. But the deepest happiness has always been when I was alone, either here in the hermitage (best of all) or in the Novice Master's room (that wonderful summer of the gardenias and Plato!) or simply out in the fields. Of course there was the old vault, too, and I must mention many happy moments with the students when I was their Father Master. Also a couple of good days in the hospital when I was well enough to go out and walk about near the grotto.

I could fill another page just with names of people I have loved to be with and love to hear from – Lax above all, and Mark Van Doren and all the old friends, and Reinhardt and so on, and Naomi [Burton Stone], and Bob Giroux, and all my Latin American friends like Ernesto Cardenal and Pablo Antonio [Cuadra]. . . . So many students and novices, especially for some reason the group that came in 1960–61. (Brothers Cuthbert, Denis, Basil, etc.) And so many that have left – Father John of the Cross! . . . Why go on? *Deo gratias* [thank God] for all of them.

January 31, 1965

"*Intrans in domum meam, conquiescam cum illa: non enim habet amaritudinem conversatio illius, nec taedium convictus illus, sed laetitiam et gaudium.*" ["When I go home I shall take my ease with her, for nothing is bitter in her company, when life is shared with her there is no pain, nothing but pleasure and joy."]

(Sapientia [Wisdom] 8:16)

On this day I could set these words to very sweet music if I really knew how! I can imagine no greater cause for gratitude on my fiftieth birthday, than that on it I woke up in a hermitage!

Fierce cold all night, certainly down to zero (I have no outdoor thermometer) and inside the house almost to freezing, though embers still glowed under the ashes in the fireplace. The cold woke me up at one point but I adjusted the blankets and went back to sleep.

But what more do I seek than this silence, this simplicity, this "living together with wisdom"? For me there is nothing else. *C'est le comble!* [It is the pinnacle!] And to think I have had the grace to taste a little of what all men really seek without realizing it. All the more obligation to have compassion and love and pray for them. Last night, before going to bed, realized momentarily what solitude really means: When the ropes are cast off and the skiff is no longer tied to land, but heads out to sea without ties, without restraints! Not the sea of passion, on the contrary, the sea of purity and love that is without care. That loves God alone immediately and directly in Himself as the All (and the seeming Nothing that is all). The unutterable confusion of those who think that God is a mental object and that to love "God alone" is to exclude all other objects to concentrate on this one! Fatal. Yet that is why so many misunderstand the meaning of contemplation and solitude, and condemn it. But I see too that I no longer have the slightest need to argue with them. I have nothing to justify and nothing to defend: I need only defend this vast simple emptiness from my own self, and the rest is clear. (Through the cold and darkness I hear the angelus ringing at the monastery.) The beautiful jeweled shining of honey in the lamplight. Festival!

A thought that came to me during meditation: The error of racism is the logical consequence of an essentialist style of thought. Finding out what a man is and then nailing him to a definition so that there can be no change. A White Man is a White Man, and that is it. A Negro, even though he is three parts white is "A Negro" with all that our rigid definition predicates of a Negro. And so the logical machine can devour him because of his essence. Do you think that in an era of existentialism this will get better? On the contrary: definitions, more and more schematic, are fed into computers. The machines are meditating on the most arbitrary and rudimentary of essences, punched into IBM cards, and defining you and me forever without appeal. "A priest," "A Negro," "A Jew," "A Socialist," etc.

(Problem of the Mexican intellectual and editor Garcia Torres, and his passport trouble because some idiot in an embassy office punched his card as "Red.")

February 2, 1965

Again very cold. On the 31st it was about four below, this morning it is almost down to zero. Yesterday it was warmer (about twenty-eight) and there was more snow. A great deal of the wood I have for the fire is wet or not sufficiently seasoned to burn well – though finally this morning I got a pretty hot fire going with a big cedar log on top of it. This is some of the coldest weather we have had in the twenty-three years I have been here. But sleeping was O.K. No worse than anywhere else. In fact very snug, with a lot of blankets.

It is hard but good to live according to nature with a primitive technology of wood chopping and fires, rather than according to the mature technology which has supplanted nature, creating its own weather, etc., etc. Yet there are advantages too, in a warmed house and a self-stoking furnace. No need to pledge allegiance to either one. Get warm in any way you can, and love God and pray.

I see more and more that now I must desire nothing else than to be "poured out as a libation," to give and surrender my being without concern. The cold woods make this more real. And the loneliness, coming up last night at the time of a very cold sunset, with two little birds still picking at crumbs I had thrown for them on the frozen porch. Everywhere else, snow. In the morning, coming down: all tracks covered by snow blown over the path by the wind except tracks of the cat that hunts around the old sheepbarn. Solitude = being aware that you are one man in this snow where there has been no one but one cat.

February 4, 1965

The cold weather finally let up a bit today – the first time in about a week that it had been above freezing. Zero nights, or ten above. Very cold, sometimes even cold in bed. Had the night watch last night and came back through the frozen woods to a very cold cottage. But today the snow melted, in fact, and ran loquaciously – the bucket I had collected last time was nearly finished. I am burning in the fireplace shelves from the old library. Not the chestnut shelves but the sides – (poplar?) – They are dry and quickly make a good hot blaze. Quickly cut the cold early this morning.

The new library officially opened in the former brothers' novitiate building – on Sunday, my birthday. I was very happy with it. The stacks are well lighted, a big pleasant room with desks (formerly a dormitory) and the reading room upstairs is pleasant. It is too far for me to go often, but I am glad of the change.

Last night I had a curious and moving dream about a "Black Mother." I was in a place (where? somewhere I had been as a child, but also there seemed to be some connection with the valley over at Edelin's) and I realized that I had come there for a reunion with a Negro foster mother whom I had loved in my childhood. Indeed, I owed, it seemed, my life to her love so that it was she really and not my natural mother, who had given me life. As if from her had come a new *life* and there she was. Her face was ugly and severe, and yet a great warmth came from her to me, and we embraced with great love (and I with much gratitude) and what I recognized was not her face but the warmth of her embrace and of her heart so to speak. We danced a little together, I and my Black Mother, and then I had to continue the journey I was on. I cannot remember more about this journey and many incidents connected with it. Comings and goings, and turning back, etc.

Today, besides a good letter from Gordon Zahn and other pleasant things in the mail, came a fantastic present from Suzuki – a scroll with his calligraphy: superbly done. And the scroll too, in its perfect little box, the whole thing was utterly splendid, I never saw anything so excellent. It will be wonderful in the hermitage – but no clue as to what the characters say!! Also, there was a letter from John Pick saying he wanted my drawings for exhibit at Marquette [University] (they are now at Xavier University in New Orleans).

February 9, 1965

I must admit I am much moved by Horace – as for instance a quote from the *Second Epode* which I ran across by chance when leafing through the *Liber Comfortatorius* of Goscelin (11th century letter to a Recluse). The structure and clarity and music of Horace are great and he is *not* trite. There is, it seems to me, real depth there, and this is shown by the sustained purity and strength of his *tone* and this is I think really untranslatable.

Rereading the issue of _La Vie spirituelle_ on solitude (in 1952) I am struck by the evident progress that has been made. In those days the tone was not one of real hope – simply a statement of the deplorable fact that the hermit life had practically ceased to exist. And that religious superiors could not be brought to see its meaning and relevance. Now on the contrary it is once again a fact and we are moving beyond the stage where it was thought necessary for a monk to get exclaustrated in order to be a solitary (in order to fulfill his monastic vocation!!). I am working on a paper about this for a meeting of canonists (to which I will certainly not be going) at New Melleray this spring.

February 11, 1965

Depressing news from Viet Nam. Because of the successful guerrilla attacks of the Viet Cong on American bases in South Viet Nam, there has been bombing of towns and bases in North Viet Nam and signs today are going around the monastery that there was a "big bombing," evidently of a city, by "our" planes. Perhaps Hanoi has been bombed. All I can feel is disgust and hopelessness. Have people no understanding left and not even a memory? Haven't they enough imagination to see how totally useless and absurd the whole thing is, even if they lack the moral sense to see the injustice of it? The whole effect of this will be to make America more hated, just as the Russians were hated after the Hungary business in 1956. There is no better way than this to promote Communism in Asia. We are driving people to it, instead of "liberating" them.

Today I finished the first draft of the paper on eremitism.[11] Rain all day. Did not get back to the hermitage until after supper. It seems that everything looks favorable for my moving up here when Father Callistus gets back from Rome. But now there is doubt about Father Flavian taking the novice master's job, he wants to go to the Camaldolese, of all things, which sounds foolish to me. If he is in that kind of mood, he may not even be stable in the hermitage here, which he will certainly be able to be in if he wants it.

Nightfall. Wind from the west. The porch shines with rain and low dark rags of cloud blow over the valley. The rain becomes more furious and the air is filled with voices, and with what might sound like confused radio music in another building, but there is no other building. And the song seems to be coming to a brassy crescendo and ending, but it does not end.

[11] "For a Renewal of Eremitism in the Monastic State," _Collectanea Cisterciensia_ 27 (1965): 121–49.

Also the jet planes. High in the storm are jet planes. Today I got the censor's approval for "Rain and the Rhinoceros" (written in December). The rain is different this time, more serious, less peaceful, more talkative. A very great deal of talk.

February 12, 1965

Whatever is actually happening in Viet Nam I don't know except that the American policy there is proving itself to be a very stupid failure and they are now perhaps seeking a solution by "escalation" of the war in North Viet Nam. My guess is there is a real possibility that the military are doing this on their own because they are afraid that Johnson means to pull out of there altogether as soon as he gracefully can. They may succeed in making this impossible.

In Viet Nam as in China and Latin America, the same mistake has been made.

1. We send in people who have no understanding whatever of the people, the country, the culture, etc.

2. In order to get along they deal with "operators" who give them a falsified or distorted picture of things. These westernized Asians see their way to power and wealth, establish themselves in a strong and lucrative position, convince the Americans that everyone else is a communist, and try to "keep order" by force. And they get rich on American aid.

3. Instead of encouraging real political reform and genuine democracy, the Americans simply support these operators, pay them to "keep things quiet." Every attempt at protest, at reform, is labeled "communist revolution." Those who really want liberty are driven to unite with the Communists, or are treated as Communists (v.g., the Viet Nam Buddhists).

4. Against these people, military force is useless. But coercion and force provide guerrilla resistance which is all the more effective when the force marshalled against it is useless and unwieldy. However, the only answer the westerners know is bigger and more destructive weapons . . . a spiral.

The cruel and ruthless – and pointless – destruction of towns in North Viet Nam can become a potent argument for Communism, and Asia will despair of getting America to make sense . . . a dismal prospect: yet it could have been foreseen with a little intelligence. But no . . . our mass media take up the story given out by the "operators" we favor, and the whole country imagines we are Galahads engaged in a crusade against Communism. Actually, we are doing more than anyone else, China included, to make Asia effectively Communist.

February 14, 1965. Septuagesima

The other day a letter came from Godfrey Diekmann asking me to participate in an ecumenical meeting, together with Father Häring, Dom Leclercq, Father Barnabas Ahern, etc. and on the other side Douglas Steere and nine others. Asked Father Abbot, and this permission which, in the circumstances I think any other Superior would have granted, was refused. It is not that I had my heart set on going. About that I can be indifferent. I would have liked to go, and think it would have done me good. I would have learned a bit, would have the grace of having done something for the Church, participated in a dialogue that would be evidently blessed, etc.

There was no discussion of why I should not go: just emotion on the part of the Abbot; that look compounded of suffering and stubbornness, interpretable in many ways, but which on this occasion made him look as if he thought I was stealing something from him – the key to his office for example. In a word a look of vulnerability and defiance: a man threatened in his belly or somewhere. With the determination that I should never get away with it. Thus the confused motives ("it is not our vocation to travel and attend meetings") become clear in ways other than by words (after all, Father Chrysogonus is traveling all over the place, attending all kinds of things, and his stay in Europe has already been prolonged twice). Dom James regards this as a personal threat to himself, to his prestige, to his very existence as Father – image and ikon. (If *he* were invited he would certainly attend! After refusing the Japanese permission he took off himself for Norway!)

I am sure he is not aware of this himself. It appears to him only in the most acceptable terms: that my humility would be deflowered by this meeting with Dom Leclercq, etc. (He detests Leclercq, Winandy, Damasus Winzen, all of them.) But I have to learn to accept this without resentment. Certainly not easy to do! So far I have hardly tried and to tell the truth it angers and distracts me. So that is the vow of obedience: you submit yourself also to somebody else's prejudices, and to his myths, and to the worship of his fetishes!! Well, I have made the vow, and will keep it, and will see why I keep it, and will try at the same time not to let myself be involved in the real harm that can come from a wrong kind of submission (and there are several wrong kinds, and the right kind is hard to find!).

February 16, 1965

I must admit that over Sunday I was troubled by the whole business of that refused permission. Reverend Father preached a long impassioned sermon on vanity, ambition, using one's gifts for one's glory, etc., etc. on Sunday morning, and I could see he was upset in it – there was emotion, his voice was trembling in the beginning, his breathing was not altogether under control and so on. I could only infer that it had something to do with my request, and I thought it was quite unfair if it was, but anyway I was troubled and irritated – and finally depressed. Feeling of powerlessness and frustration, and most of all, humiliation over the fact that I should feel it so much and be forced by my feeling to think about it all day! How absurd. And yet the efforts I made to see it rationally as something trifling and laughable would not come off. Nor did the religious arguments and the repeated acceptance of it as a cross and humiliation. Nothing seemed to make any difference and finally I lay awake half the night – the first time this has happened in the hermitage.

At last I wrote a note to Reverend Father saying I was sorry I had offended him and that his sermon had made me miserable, but that my writing, etc. was not pure ambition and vanity, though obviously there was some vanity involved in it. And that I wished he would accept me realistically and not expect me to be something I cannot be. He replied that the sermon had had nothing to do with me, that he had no intention of hurting me, was most concerned, etc. So maybe it was all an illusion, but anyway, there it was. I was relieved that it was all settled. A tantrum. I am surely old enough to be beyond that!!

Yesterday in the morning when I went out for a breath of air before my novice conference I saw men working on the hillside beyond the sheepbarn. At last the electric line is coming! All day they were working on holes, digging and blasting the rock with small charges, young men in yellow helmets, good, eager hard-working guys with machines. I was glad of them and of American technology pitching in to bring me light as they would for any farmer in the district. It was good to feel part of this, which is not to be despised, but admirable. (Which does not mean that I hold any brief for the excess of useless developments in technology.)

Galley proofs of the little Gandhi book for New Directions came and I finished them in a couple of hours. They were pretty clean. It was nice reading them in the fairly warm sun. A good letter from Morcelliana[12] – a small book of bits and pieces will be called *Fede e Violenza* – and an architect in Madrid who will use two essays on art from *Disputed Questions*, etc., etc. Drawings from Lax. And a couple of the usual letters from crazy people. It

[12] Publishers in Brescia, Italy.

is good to be part of all that too! Alas! Vanity. But that is the thing about solitude. To *realize* how desperately we depend on the "existence" that recognition gives us, and how hopeless we are without it until God gives us feet to stand alone on. I have those feet sometimes, but once again, let me realize that there is no absolute "standing alone" – only awful poverty and insecurity and clinging to God in one's *need* of others, and greater appreciation of the smallest and most insignificant of communal verities!!

(Afternoon) Landscape of stylites! REA men all over the hillside, one on top of each pole, brand new copper wire swinging and shining, yellow hats all over the place. The light is coming. *Venit lumen tuum Jerusalem!* [Your light comes, Jerusalem!] (This at 1:30 p.m.) They came in the morning and the first pole was already up by 9. I hope it may be finished by tonight. I was talking to some of them, and they are real nice guys. Open and friendly and without guile.

A moving letter from a woman in Texas, Mrs. [Elizabeth Land] Kaderli – who had written here and whom I had answered in 1962. (I remember being touched by her letter, which was about the fact of death, her daughter's awakening to that fact.) Now it turns out she also wrote to Mark Van Doren, Katherine Ann Porter, Aldous Huxley, Leonard Bernstein and a lot of people like that (Graham Greene too) and got good letters from all of them. Now the letters are to be in a book. Curious thing! At first sight one might think it was a trick, but it is so typical of the time and place – this country now – ! That it turns out to have been a charismatic act and probably quite fruitful.

A nice little card came from Hiromu Morishita, the poet, in Hiroshima (who was here with the group last summer).

Evening. About 2:45 the red-faced foreman (a very good simple man) came and set up the meter, and I put on the switch and had light. I was in the middle of translating some Pessoa poems for Suzuki in return for his calligraphy. The light is a great blessing. I thought I would dislike the fluorescents in the front room but actually they are perfect and fit in with the milieu. There are enough shadows in the corners, and the stone fireplace shows up well and the concrete blocks too – there is enough roughness so that it looks like anything but a factory, thank God. In fact the modulation provided by the latticework blocks is really impressive! And the New Mexican mask at the end of the lattices – Suzuki's black ink shows up wonderfully – better than by daylight. The ikons look presentable – (much better in ordinary daylight when the light is outside and they are in the shade of the room).

I celebrated the great event with a good supper of potato soup, cooked on the old beat-up electric stove which nevertheless works well. So it is an evening of alleluia.

February 17, 1965

Early morning. The light is a great help, a simplifier. Makes prayer simpler. No fussing with matches, candles, flashlights. The electric heater is sufficient for a morning that is not freezing, and there is no distraction of logs and pokers. Also the fact that the light comes from other people, a collectivity, a rural cooperative – "Salt River RECC" – this is to me a significant and consoling thing. I am united by it to the people of the countryside who share the same source of light as I. (Incidentally not the monastery, which is on K.U. – I am with the poor farmers on REA!)

Reading the remarkable notes of (Abbé Saintanlieu) in *La Vie spirituelle* of 1952 on solitude. One thing I know now that I could not realize then: it is not enough to be a part-time hermit living mostly in community. *"Quand il faut composer entre les deux esprits, on partage ses forces entre deux tiédeurs."* ["When one has to compromise between the two spirits, one divides one's forces between two mediocrities."] Perfectly true! I must keep working toward the day of genuine solitude, perhaps even without conventual Mass. (But I think that it makes sense to take dinner down there to avoid the fuss of cooking.) As long as I have the novices I am tied, however. And (as Father Flavian my confessor says) it remains a duty of charity to be present with the community for some things.

After dinner Brother Timothy (the undermaster) said there had been news of an attempt on Pope Paul's life by a bomb in his Vatican apartments.[13] The bomb was nowhere near the Pope! No one apparently was hurt. One wonders who was behind this. Poor Pope Paul VI! I do not envy his job. He has tried to do well in a diplomatic way, and his sincerity and friendliness, his desire to be open, certainly make him a good Pope. I would be very sorry to see anything happen to him!

One of the things I liked about the REA foreman yesterday was that after asking whether I saw any deer around, he said "I don't think I could ever kill a deer." And he seemed to think deer came around here "because they know they would be safe." That was nice! But I told him I had to chase

---

[13] Merton wrote the following note in the margin: "I leave this as it stands. All through this book are such 'rumors,' all exaggerated. I leave them as they were when they came to me."

hunters out of here all the time even though it is supposed to be a wild-life refuge.

Translated some more Pessoa today.

February 24, 1965

I have to go in to Dr. Scheen again today. The skin of my hands erupted again, leafed and cracked, deep holes in the skin are quite painful. It interferes with work. Even tying shoes is painful. Wore gloves to make my bed. Mess!

Brother Joachim was up yesterday to put some finishing touches on his electrical work, and Brother Clement bought me a big glossy refrigerator which came Saturday – or was installed here that day. It immediately became a big distraction and in many ways I wish I did not have to have it, but in summer it will be necessary. The first couple of nights I was annoyed by the noise it makes when it wakes up to cool itself, and each time it did this I woke up too, but I set myself to learn sleeping again and by the grace of God it worked. And I might as well forget about being guilty. The thing is splendid. But – local farmers have such, and they have TV too. Really I am glad of the lights, even the fluorescent.

Everything about this hermitage simply fills me with joy. There are lots of things that could have been far more perfect one way or the other – ascetically, or "domestically." But it is the place God has given me after so much prayer and longing – but without my deserving it – and it is a delight. I can imagine no other joy on earth than to have such a place and to be at peace in, to live in silence, to think and write, to listen to the wind and to all the voices of the wood, to live in the shadow of the big cedar cross, to prepare for my death and my exodus to the heavenly country, to love my brothers and all people, and to pray for the whole world and for peace and good sense among men. So it is "my place" in the scheme of things, and that is sufficient!

Reading some studies on St. Leonard of Port Maurice and his *Retiro* [retirement house] and hermitage of the Incontro. How clearly Vatican II has brought into question all the attitudes he and his companions took completely for granted: the dramatic barefoot procession from Florence to the Incontro in the snow – the daily half-hour discipline in common – etc. This used to be admired, if prudently avoided, by all in the Church. This was "the real thing" even if one could not do it. Now we have come to be openly doubtful of the intrinsic value of such things. The sincerity was there, and it meant something to them. Depth psychology, etc. have made these things forever questionable – they belong to another age. And yet there has to be hardness and rigor in the solitary life. The hardness is there by itself. The cold, the solitude, the labor, the need for poverty to keep everything simple and manageable, the need for the discipline of long meditation in silence. But not drama, not collective exercises of self-chastisement, into which there can come so much that is spurious and questionable.

I also question Pessoa. He has some good intuitions, but lacks real depth and his pretenses are also quite dubious. Yet what is valuable is beyond question – the Zen-like view of things – his phenomenology.

Yesterday had a session with Brother Ephrem and Brother Pius about the photo book[14] we are supposed to do. Went over contact sheets, and there is much good stuff!

(Evening.) It has been a strange day. I end it writing with dermal gloves as the rain pelts down on the cottage. I was supposed to go to town with Bernard Fox but he had left when I arrived at the Gatehouse at 8:03. As a result, while I was waiting for another ride, the Brothers in the store were making signs: "Good thing that fellow that wanted to kill you has gone away!" Apparently some nut in the Guesthouse (from New York) was breathing fire and brimstone on my account. In the mail too there are some letters from fanatics – varying degrees.

Then I rode in with Bobby Gill who is afraid to drive in city traffic and who in fact had never driven in Louisville before. He got me to the Medical Arts building all right and slept peacefully in the parking lot while I was in Dr. Scheen's office. Read a "Party of One" in *Holiday* by Kingsley Ames, on Science Fiction. Dr. Scheen simply does not know what is causing this dermatitis. He took bits of skin for lab tests. I wear dermal gloves. My hands hurt. Riding back (about 12) we made good time. If I had been with Bernard and the others it would have meant lunch in Louisville. As it was Bobby Gill wanted only the sandwiches he had left on his job with Brother Christopher. I got some food at Kroger's in Bardstown, and ate lunch at the hermitage.

Had a couple of direction sessions in the novitiate. Went to infirm[ary] kitchen to stock up on sugar. Over the public address from Chapter – reproof of hermit life in a Benedictine's book. Father Amandus was standing there, told me Brother Gerard had been anointed at 6 p.m., and was very low.

---

[14] *Gethsemani, A Life of Praise*, 1966.

Coming up in the rain, thought peacefully of death and accepted the fact that very possibly some madman will come up there one night and do me in. And if that is the way it is to be I am glad to accept it from God's hand if He will give me the grace to die in a manner pleasing to him.

Bobby Gill is now living at the entrance to the back road that leads to Edelin's place (Bell Hollow is its proper name. Keith Hollow branches north east from it). So that if I go to live in Bell Hollow, Bobby Gill will probably be my contact man with the monastery.

In the papers – much acrimony over Viet Nam: rightists clamoring for war. Others for negotiations. Malcolm X, the Negro racist, has been murdered (I am sorry because now there is bitter fighting between two Muslim factions).

February 26, 1965

I see more and more that solitude is not something to play with. It is deadly serious. And much as I have wanted it, I have not been serious enough. It is not enough to "like solitude," or love it even. Even if you "like" it, it can wreck you, I believe, if you desire it only for your own sake. So I go forward (I don't believe I would go back. Even interiorly I have reached at least relatively a point of no return), but I go in fear and trembling, and often with a sense of lostness, and trying to be careful what I do because I am beginning to see that every false step is paid for dearly. Hence I fall back on prayer, or try to. Yet no matter, there is great beauty and peace in this life of silence and emptiness. But to fool around with it brings awful desolation. When one is trifling, even the beauty of the life suddenly becomes implacable. Solitude is a stern mother who brooks no nonsense. The question arises: am I so full of nonsense that she will cast me out? I pray not, and think it is going to take much prayer.

I must admit that I like my own cooking. Rice and Pinto beans today, for instance, with applesauce from the monastery and some peanuts. A nice meal! Read an excellent Pendle Hill pamphlet Douglas Steere sent, by Edward Brooke. Three letters on the situation in South Africa. They are "hopeful" in a Christian sense. But I wonder if that hope will, in fact, be realized in history. Certainly it is important to understand South Africa if we want to get a real perspective on our own South.

February 27, 1965

Certainly the solitary life makes sense only when it is centered on one thing: The perfect love of God. Without this, everything is triviality. Love of God in Himself, for Himself, sought only in His will, in total surrender. Anything but this, in solitude, is nausea and absurdity. But outside of solitude, one can be occupied in many things that seem to have and do have a meaning of their own. And their meaning can be and is accepted, at least provisionally, as something that must be reckoned with *until* such time as one can come to love God alone perfectly, etc. This is all right in a way, except that while doing things theoretically "for the love of God" one falls in practice into complete forgetfulness and ignorance and torpor. This happens in solitude too, of course, but in solitude, while distraction is evidently vain, forgetfulness brings nausea. But in society, forgetfulness brings comfort of a kind.

It is therefore a great thing to be completely vulnerable and to feel at once, with every weakening of faith, a total loss. Things that in community are legitimate concerns are seen in solitude to be also temptations, tests, questionings: for instance the skin trouble on my hands.

March 2, 1965. Shrove Tuesday

Light rain. Forty hours. Pleasant vigil last night with the novices in Church. But it took a long time for the place to calm down. Sacristan running around until 7:30.

I am reading a good biography of Simone Weil, which I have to review for *Peace News*.[15] I am finally getting to know her, and have a great sympathy for her, though I cannot agree with a lot of her attitudes and ideas. Basically – I wonder what disturbs me about her. Something does. In her experience of Christ, for example. "Gnostic" rather than "mystical." But one had to admit, she seems to have seen this herself and she did not cling to it. "The attic" was a place she had to leave behind. Her mystique of action and "the world" is her true climate – now familiar – and I think more authentic (though the other was not inauthentic). For a time I think Catholics were running to Simone Weil to learn this but now they have forgotten her and Teilhard de Chardin is the prophet of this cosmic Christianity (and yet what about St. Francis?).

Yet one thing the hermitage is making me see – that the universe is my home and I am nothing if not part of it. Destruction of the self that seems to stand outside the universe only as part of its fabric and dynamism. Can I find true being in God, who has willed me to exist in the world. This I dis-

[15] Merton reviewed Jacques Cabaud's *Simone Weil: A Fellowship in Love* (1964) in *Peace News*, (April 2, 1965): 5, 8.

cover here not mentally only but in depth. Especially for example in the ability to sleep. Frogs kept me awake at the monastery, not here – they are comfort, an extension of my own being – and now also the hum of the electric meter near my bed is nothing (though at the monastery it would have been intolerable). Acceptance of nature and even technology as my true habitat.

March 3, 1965. Ash Wednesday

Though I am uncomfortable with Simone Weil's imaginative descriptions of her experience of Christ I think her mysticism is basically authentic. Though I cannot accept her dogmatic ambiguities, I think her reasons (personal reasons) for not joining the Church are sincere, profound, and also challenging. Furthermore I can also see that they might be "from God" and therefore have a special reference to the Church (an accusation if you will). What does impress me in her is her *malheureux* [ill-temper] of the unbeliever, the realization that God's love must break the human heart, and this, finally: "Blessed are they who suffer in the flesh the suffering of the world itself in their epoch. They have the possibility and function of knowing its truth, contemplating in its reality the suffering of the world. . . . But unfortunate are they who, having this function, do not fulfill it" (Cabaud, p. 251, Letter to Bousquet). "We have to discard the illusion of being in possession of time." Simone Weil – this implies consenting to be "human material" moulded by time, under eye of God.

March 4, 1965

I must admit that I am fascinated by a great deal of Simone Weil, but the thing is that she must be taken as a whole and in her context. Individual and independent as she was, the whole meaning of her thought is to be found not by isolating it but by situating it in her dialogue with her contemporaries. The way to dispose of her uncomfortable intuitions is to set her apart and look at her as if she were a totally isolated phenomenon. Her nonconformism and mysticism are on the contrary an essential element in our time and without her contribution we remain not human. Especial importance for instance of her critique of shallow personalism. Her remarks (prophetic) on the Americanization of Europe after the war deadening the "Oriental roots" of contact with East in Europe – of America being purely non-Oriental (and rootless). World threatened with rootlessness through Americanization. This is a thought! Symbolism of the Viet Nam conflict, the burning Buddhists! South America (this is my addition) is more "Oriental" as well as more European than North America and is perhaps the hope of the world (bridge). Remedy – she thought France should substitute cultural exchange for colonial domination. Exposure of America to shock of misfortune may make them see need for roots, she says. No sign of it so far.

(Evening.) Lots of wet snow. Had to spend the whole day in the monastery, as I had a conference, direction, etc. and then in the afternoon a long meeting of the Building Committee (from which I wish I could decently resign) about the project for the new Church. Came briefly up to the hermitage after dinner to sweep, get the water bottle to fill, and also read a few pages of a new book, Nishida Kitaro's *Study of the Good* which Suzuki sent and which is just what I am looking for at the moment. Magnificent! But the rest of the day was dreary enough – a test of patience and resignation, and really I don't care too much. But it was wonderful to get back to the hermitage and silence, and see the trees full of snow outside the bedroom window.

This morning I said a Requiem Mass for Simone Weil, and also spoke of her in the conference to the novices and juniors ([George] Herbert's poem on love, etc.). *Holiday* paid a thousand dollars for "Rain and the Rhinoceros" which they have changed into "The Art of Solitude" (only in proof, however). But otherwise no editing except my own. Though maybe they edited out the SAC plane. I must look again when it comes. Galleys were here a few days ago.

March 5, 1965

Nishida Kitaro – just what I am looking for. For example I see my objection to the cliché about "meaningful experience" (as if it was "meaninglessness" that made experience somehow real and worth while. "Experience" is made "meaningful" by being referred to something else, a system, or perhaps a report of someone else's experiences, and therefore its quality is *diminished*. So the ambiguity of meaningfulness is exposed. When experience is "meaningful" in this sense it is *unreal* – or *less* real. To live always outside of experience as if this were a fullness of experience: this is one of the basic ambiguities of written thought).

Curious thing finishing Cabaud's book on Simone Weil, I find it was Tom Bennett, my godfather and guardian, who tried to treat her in the Middlesex Hospital and had her transferred to Ashford because she refused to eat! Funny that she and I have this in common: we were both problems to this good man.

March 9, 1965

Several days of rain, mist, damp, cold. It is flu weather, and there is flu in the monastery. A postulant left, another one came – he has been a Carthusian for a few months at Parkminster, which does not mean that this is the best place for him. We had a meeting about him yesterday and decided to give him a try. Father Timothy is on retreat for diaconate so I spend more time in the novitiate and it was pleasant being there yesterday for Lenten reading. The place is very quiet and peaceful, almost a hermitage itself. It seems to me that since I have been more often in the hermitage the novices themselves have become much quieter and more serious. I have never done less work with them and never had them so good. My conclusion is that there is much too much anxiety on the part of superiors to interfere with and "direct" their subjects.

Yesterday I sent off the review of the Simone Weil book to *Peace News*, finished some translations of a few poems of Nicanor Parra (who is excellent, sharp, hard, solid irony) one of the best South American poets, a no nonsense anti-poet, with a deep sense of the futility and corruption of social life – a sense which has now been taken over entirely by poets and writers since the Church has abandoned everything but optimism for the technological future. I sent the Pessoa poems to Suzuki. Dan [Walsh] said he had read some of them to his class at Bellarmine. He came back with a terrific black eye and a cut on his eyebrow, from falling in the icy street.

The new Mass began Sunday and there are good things about it but it is obviously transitional. I will miss the Prologue of St. John, but am saying it in my thanksgiving (after all, that is what it was for anyway). Actually I did not realize how much this "Last Gospel" had drawn to itself and soaked up all the associations of all the joys of fourteen years of the Mass and of priesthood. All those simple, quiet masses – nine years and more of them in the novitiate chapel – summer mornings, saying the Last Gospel with the open window looking out toward the green woods of Vineyard Knob! The text itself is one of the most wonderful in the Bible – certainly ideal for contemplation.

March 10, 1965

There is no question now that Mass ends too abruptly, and one has to go more slowly and deliberately, perhaps with a few discreet pauses, or one is suddenly unvesting, as it were, in the middle of communion. Of course a whole new attitude toward the "shape" of the Mass is now required. This is contrived in the new rite, but one must feel it and bring it out. One needs to see the Mass celebrated by priests who have thought out the new implications and experienced their meaning. So far (after all, it is only four days!!) we here seem to be dutifully setting out the fragments in a new arrangement, without having grasped the organic significance of what is going on.

After four or five grim wet days, cold and dark, suddenly bright spring – cold, clear blue sky with a few very clean, well-washed clouds. Thin and full of light. The wet earth is springy, green moss shows in the short grass under the pines. The frogs sang for a moment (but it is still cold). The buds are beginning to swell. A flycatcher was playing in the woods near the stile as I came up, and the pileated woodpecker, bright combed, darted out, swinging up and down over the field to the east.

All day I have been uncomfortably aware of the wrong that is in me. The useless burden of pride I condemn myself to carry – and all that comes with carrying it. I know I deceive myself, as a monk and as a writer. But I do not see exactly where. Trying to do things that are beyond me, no doubt. Trying to have something to say about everything. Not enough mistrust of my own opinion. And beyond that, a rebellious and nasty dissatisfaction with things, with the country, the Church. (Not so much the monastery now – I am accepting it more peacefully, and see the silliness of rebelling against what is after all human and to be expected.) Impatience with the uniformly benign public pronouncements of Paul VI – as if he could be anything else, and he is certainly trying earnestly to do something about Viet Nam. Impatience with biographies of new cardinals in the refectory – at the root it is all a mean and childish impatience with myself and there is no way of dignifying it as a valid "protest." It is just idiotic and self-seeking nonsense.

March 14, 1965. Second Sunday of Lent

The sense of wrong stays with me. I now see the negative and weak side of my intentions in writing *Seeds of Destruction* – the element that was invisible to me before – the thing that others have seen first – that it is a kind of cry for recognition, as if I wanted to make sure that I too was part of the human race, and concerned in its concerns. And I am. There is nothing wrong with that. But for various reasons I do not understand, and because of all the usual ambiguities, I am too anguished and excited about it – especially being out of touch with what goes on. Because of this the book, or the part on race, fails to really make complete sense and is not useful in the current situation. The part on war has, I think, greater value. The letters may in some cases be all right but they show the foolishness and futility I have got into with all my mail. Yet I cannot honestly say I have wished this all on myself. The letters that come in impose a certain obligation by themselves. I have not asked for them!

Yesterday Bishop Maloney[16] was here to ordain Fathers Timothy and Barnabas to the diaconate. In his usual silly little talk at the end of the cloister afterward, he was lamenting the vagaries of the new liturgy. "But," he said, "I always look at the bright side." He did not say precisely what the bright side was for him, except that it was all "the will of God" or something. He is probably quite representative of a large part of the clergy and people in this country. Not too able to understand the issue.

March 15, 1965

Yesterday afternoon it was cold and rainy. Read a little of Eric Colledge's essay on Mechtilde of Magdeburg under the tall pine trees behind the hermitage before going down to shave, give conference (last on Ephrem and first on Philoxenus) and sing Vespers. I love the Lenten hymns. What a loss it will be if they are thrown out!

In the evening it cleared, was cold. I came up, sun setting, moon out. I looked out the bedroom window and saw two deer grazing quietly in the field, in dim dusk and moonlight, barely twenty yards from the cottage. Once in a while they would look up at the house with their big ears extended, and even a little movement would make them do this but eventually I walked quietly out on the porch and stayed there and they stayed peacefully until finally I began moving about and they lifted up the white flags of their tails and started off in a wonderful, silent, bounding flight down the field, only to stop a hundred yards away. I don't know what became of them after that, for it was bed time and I had not read my bit of Genesis (Jacob's dream).

March 16, 1965

On Sunday there was in Louisville a demonstration in protest of the murder of the Christian minister at Selma, Alabama, which has been the center of the biggest conflict since Birmingham – marches, police brutality, etc. Dan Walsh was in the demonstrations and so were many priests and nuns, and lots of ministers. Bishop Maloney spoke. About 3500 participated I

[16] Charles Maloney, Auxiliary Bishop of Louisville.

understand. The issue of voter registration is coming to a head, a new law is being drafted, etc. [George] Wallace of Alabama was in Washington to confer with President Johnson and some sour looking pictures of him were on the bulletin board in the cloister.

Sister Luke was here yesterday and Sister Mary of Lourdes, General of a Congregation of Ursulines (motherhouse at Tours), discussing problems. They both feel that the lid is off and there is going to be quite a lot of unrest, trouble and confusion in religious life especially in America. I do too though I think that in this house the worst is over (unless Dom James dies suddenly and we have an abbatial election now – no one really being ready for such a job).

March 19, 1965. St. Joseph

Bright full moon, cold night. The moonlight is wonderful in the tall pines. Absolute silence of the moonlit valley. It is the twenty-first anniversary of my simple profession (eighteenth of my solemn profession) – today I am to concelebrate for the first time. (The second time concelebration has been held here).

Last evening I was called over to the guest house for a conversation with Father Coffield, on his way back from Selma to Chicago. He is the one who left Los Angeles in protest against Cardinal McIntyre. Told of the tensions and excitements of Selma, and being "on the line" facing the police at 3 a.m. There was a legal and official march in Montgomery, though everything is not yet over – there seems to have been a breakthrough, and the violence of the police and posse men seems to have had a great deal to do with bringing it about. The protest is national and articulate, and Congress is intent on getting something done. This is due in great part to the fact that everyone (except monks) sees everything on TV. From now on I will be more careful of what I say against TV! He spoke of John Griffin who has been very ill – and is in the hospital again.

March 21, 1965. Third Sunday of Lent

St. Benedict is put off until tomorrow – which gives me an extra day to prepare a sermon. Was busy last week, especially with finishing the paper on "The Council and Monasticism" for the Bellarmine Studies.[17] Then on the afternoon of St. Joseph I went over to Edelin's Knobs with some novices, and went to explore on my own a couple of thickly wooded hollows over the

[17] *The Impact of Vatican II*, ed. Jude P. Dougherty, 1966.

ridges south of Bell Hollow. They are both excellent snake pits and I would not want to go there in summer! Coming back over the ridge into Bell Hollow, in very thick brush, I got hit in the eye by a branch of a sapling, wounding the cornea, and for two days I have not been able to see properly out of that eye. It is only a little better today, though it hurts less (what with ointment and dark glasses). Could do very little work yesterday – except cooking, gathering wood, etc. Said office, tried to read a bit with the left eye, and wrote a letter to Nicanor Parra.

March 23, 1965

Hausherr remarks that in Patristic times the theology of Baptism – especially in Catechesis – was the theology also of Christian perfection – ("Spiritual Theology"). This is more profound than it seems at first sight. By Baptism a man becomes another Christ, and his life must be that of another Christ. The Theology of Baptism teaches him *who he is*. The consequences are easy to deduce. The *Hagios* [holy] is the one who is sanctified in the sense of sacrificed (John 17:19). (Martyrdom is the perfect response to the Baptismal vocation!!) At the same time Origen (in the true spirit of nonviolence) warns against the impure motive of self-love that leads one to court death without consideration of the sin of those who would destroy us. More properly: importance of considering the spiritual welfare of the persecutor himself. It has also to be taken into account. The experience of the Deep South shows that the death of the "martyr" does not automatically redeem and convert the persecutor.

In any case – martyrdom is no improvisation: *"Qui ne s'improvise pas martyr du Christ?"* ["Who ever improvises on being a martyr for Christ?"] (In *Laics et vie chrétienne parfaite*, Rome 1963, p. 60). The only "preparation for martyrdom" is not some special training but – the Christian life itself. Thus eventually a truly Christian life, waiting to be consummated in martyrdom, is treated as almost equivalent to it, and you get the ideal of the confessor (and the monk). This is simply the life of their discipleship. The mark of such discipleship is perfect love of the Savior and of the Father's will. He who does not live according to his baptism and discipleship is living as a potential renegade (from martyrdom).

My eye gets better only slowly. Ointments, even a black patch, have been necessary for a couple of days. Am only today able to read with it again, and that makes it burn. But it has been a grace. I have been sobered by it. What was I doing charging through the woods on that God-forsaken knob? Trying to see if I would come out where I did. All right. But it was still useless.

I would have been better off quietly praying (as I did yesterday afternoon in that lovely, mossy glen where I used to go twelve years ago). Preparing the sermon on St. Benedict (which people seem to have liked yesterday) I was much struck by the idea of the *judicia Dei* (judgments of God), and the thought took a deep hold on me that what matters in our life is not abstract ideals but profound love and surrender to the concrete "judgments of God." They are our life and our light, inexhaustible sources of purity and strength. But we can ignore them. And that is the saddest thing of all.

(Evening.) My eye is slightly better, not healed. High wind all day. It is my day to be at the hermitage all day. In the middle of the afternoon a knock came on the door and it was my neighbor Andy Boone. Wanted to talk about the fence line he is working on and the deal about the three big white oaks he wants to cut down, offered me $25 a month for two months to pasture his cows in the field next to the hermitage, and I said no, on account of the locust seedlings we put in there last spring. And so on. But one very good thing came out of it. He told me there was an excellent spring that had got filled in and buried some years ago, and it is only fifty yards or so behind the hermitage, through thick brush. I know the place and did not realize there was a spring there, though water is running there now. We will have to clear it and pump it perhaps to the hermitage. Anyway clear it. Then also I saw a dozen places in the thick brush where deer had been sleeping. They are my nearest dormitory neighbors – thirty or forty yards from my own bed, or even less! How wonderful!

Andy was full of all kinds of information and stories.

The water from all these springs comes from the Lake Knob a geologist told him. (He had a geologist here looking for uranium.)

How he chased out people from E'town [Elizabethtown] who came to have wild parties at night by the old lake.

How hunters who were too lazy to get out of their cars sat in them by the roadside shooting woodchucks in the field, and how he was going one day to sit in the window of his house and smash up their motor with a bullet, just to show them. He showed me a wicked-looking bullet that goes three miles.

Story of how Brother Pius found there the last rock they needed to build the old bridge by the mill (now gone). And how Brother Pius threw the rock over the fence to them – and it took two mules for them to move it.

How Daniel Boone first came to Kentucky and spread his people all around wherever there was water, then went himself to Indiana. In Indiana he had a hole he hid in when the Indians were after him. He withdrew into it and pulled a stone over it and they never found it. The hole was eight miles long and twelve feet high and nine feet wide and had a stream in it. And when some powder plant was being built, on which Andy worked before World War II, a bulldozer disappeared into this hole and so it was discovered.

March 26, 1965

Vile rain and fog. Came up last night in very heavy rain with a cold beginning. As long as I stay in the hermitage and keep the fire going the cold is not too bad. It was a *bit* bothersome in the community where there is 'flu, where the choir is overheated, where you sweat and then get chilled, etc., etc. I wish I could simply stay up here and say Mass here! I have grapefruit juice in the icebox and that is a big help. Decided to take some bread with coffee this morning instead of fasting (on coffee only) until dinner. The rye bread was good, so was the coffee. And I read Ruysbroeck, thinking of him in terms of Zen. His "essential union" is quite like *Prajna* [wisdom], and "Suchness." Theological differences great – but the phenomenology is close.

Dan Walsh is giving his momentous talk at Catholic University today and I promised I would say a Mass of the Holy Spirit for the canonization of Duns Scotus. His talk is ostensibly about Scotus and Anselm but also and above all consists in the development of his own ideas on the metaphysic of faith. I shall be very interested to hear it when he gets back.

Buchanan, the postulant from the Polaris submarine, arrived yesterday lugging a huge bag. I saw him when I was in with Reverend Father. Buchanan has certainly planned a long time to come – even since before his graduation from Annapolis.

(Evening.) The weather continued to be very foul all day. Plague weather. Have not been able to see across the valley all day long. My cold is a little worse but not much. On the whole I do better at the hermitage. Came up after dinner, and a morning's work in the novitiate. Sat out the Conventual Mass alone in the back of the Brothers' choir, and could see a few look back disapprovingly from the choir – as if there were a divine commandment to sit in the transepts when you have a cold. Actually it was quite impressive to follow the Mass from back there – a thing I had never done. Chiefly I was there to be completely alone.

After I got back to the hermitage Andy Boone came by with a check for $125 dollars for the trees he cut down on the fence line. And he talked some more – am I going to be in perpetual conversations with him? About the connection of Dogwoods with the Passion of Christ, the sex of cedar trees (one of his favorite topics; "only the she-trees make good Christmas trees"), and the fact that our planting loblolly seedlings brought in the beetles which are killing cedars and Virginia Pine. This I believe!

This morning I wrote a short, perhaps ill-considered preface to Ludovico Silva's poem on the Bomb[18] (for publication in Caracas). In the afternoon began to get together some material from this Journal which Illtud Evans has asked for several times for *Blackfriars*.

March 27, 1965

The moon is out, and the sky is clearing at last. The air is drier and fresher. There is a very thin film of ice on the water buckets. Last end of the old moon. The next moon will be that of Easter!

March 29, 1965

The hope of better, dryer weather, died quickly yesterday. The sky darkened, and at night there was thunder, lightning, heavy rain beating down, and half awake I remembered I had left my rubber boots down at the house and thought of my cold which gets no better. Fortunately I had a raincoat up at the hermitage. A fire alarm went off about 5:30 and the rain abated, so I went down (false alarm – water got into the warning system!). Yet it kept on raining all morning.

Then an anonymous letter from Alabama from a reader who desired to prove her sincerity by saying she was a mother and a grandmother, and who said my book *Seeds of Destruction* was "appalling" (sic). Some clippings from the Alabama papers were enclosed – nothing but righteous indignation and outrage! In fact, the same irrationality, the same ferocity that one saw in the Nazi press. One theme only. That some degraded and entirely despicable people ("outside agitators") were simply defiling, insulting and gratuitously provoking the good people of Alabama. That such things were simply beyond comprehension and beyond pardon. That the thought of considering any apparent *reason* behind them was totally unacceptable. That Alabama had done and could do no wrong, etc., etc. Complete failure to face reality. Another murder took place last week after the Montgomery march.[19]

---

18 *Boom!!!* (Caracas: Esta Edicion, 1965): 3.
19 Merton refers to the death of Viola Liuzzo.

March 31, 1965

Better weather yesterday. My big distraction these days is Andy Boone, who extracted from me a vague agreement that he ought to cut down and sell some oaks at the top of the field east of the hermitage and whose sons have been out there with chainsaws making a frightful racket and sending the biggest white oaks (naturally) crashing down one on top of the other. By last evening the woods were in a fine mess with one big tree hung up in another and a third hanging on the one that is hung up. I persuaded him yesterday to direct his attention elsewhere and clean up the dead trees around the spring so that we can get in there and open it up. But my cold is better and I am trying to get back into some serious meditation. *Serious* – not part hanging around quietly. Here too there is a spring to be cleared, and I am not going deep enough these days!

A collection of poems [*Poemas Nuevos*] by Alfonso Cortes came, sent by his sister. It looks very interesting. With all his insanity there remains a great wholeness and real penetration in his work, and sometimes a really startling picture of intuition. I do not find much mere incoherence and posturing or mere vociferation – indeed I find less in him than in many who are "sane." Strange to find this sense of economy preserved, as it is in his verse. Yesterday morning finished Nishida Kitaro's *Study of Good* except for the appendix. One of the most remarkably helpful things I have read in a long time – and apart from his pantheistic concept of God, very close to home.

April 3, 1965

This morning I finished the appendix which gives some idea of the full scope of Nishida's thought. It is most satisfying. Happily there is at least one other of his books in English. *The Study of Good* is his first. The development from here is not linear but a spiral deepening of his basic intuition of pure experience which becomes "absolute nothingness as the place of existence," and "eschatological everyday life" in which the person, as a focus of absolute contradiction (our very existence opening on to death is a contradiction), can say with Rinzai "wherever I stand is all the truth." This hit me with great force. My meditation had been building up to this (awareness for instance that "doubt" arises from projection of the self into the future, or from retrospection, and not grasping the present. He who grasps the present does not doubt). To be open to the nothingness which I am is to grasp the all, in whom I am! I have already written my review of Nishida.[20]

[20] "Nishida: A Zen Philosopher," Zen + the Birds of Appetite (New York: New Directions, 1968): 67–70.

Some copies of the (early) *Conjectures of a Guilty Bystander* have been run off. Only a few. There is some nonsense in it. What I said about political life is belied by the very authentic political life displayed in the civil rights movement.

Yesterday, on orders from Brother Clement and Reverend Father, marked the trees Andy Boone is to cut, down in the hollow behind the hermitage, where the spring is. What a tangle of brush, saplings, vines, fallen trees, honey suckle, etc.! Marks of deer everywhere. A fire in there would be awful. I hope we can get a space of an acre or so good and clear between here and the spring, and keep it clear. And I can use the spring, for I *need* it. All this is the geographical unconscious of my hermitage. Out in front the "conscious mind," the ordered fields, the wide valley, tame woods. Behind, the "unconscious" – this lush tangle of life and death, full of danger, yet where beautiful beings move, the deer, and where there is a spring of sweet, pure water – buried!

April 4, 1965. Passion Sunday

Light rain all night. The need to keep working at meditation – going to the root. Mere passivity won't do at this point. But activism won't do either. A time of wordless deepening, to grasp the inner reality of my nothingness in Him who is. Talking about it in these terms is absurd. Nothing to do with the concrete reality that is to be grasped. My prayer is peace and struggle in silence, to be aware and true, beyond myself. To go outside the door of myself, not because I will it but because I am called and must respond.

Joy in the Masses of the past week, especially some of the second tone melodies – the introit *"Laetitur cor quaerentium Dominum"* ["Let the heart of those who seek the Lord rejoice"] – seriousness, humility and hope. Will these things ever be equalled? And of course I was again deeply moved by the *Vexilla Regis* at Vespers last night. Everything that I love about the world I grew up in came back: Romanesque churches, the landscape of Raverque, Languedoc, etc., etc. Useless to cling to all that, but I am humanly rooted in it.

April 6, 1965. Tuesday in Passion Week

A rainy, humid, stuffy day, as warm as summer. Had to go to town to see the eye doctor. My eye is still injured by the blow I got from the branch in the woods on St. Joseph's day. Saw Dr. [Jeremiah] Flowers – the first time I have been in the new Medical Tower, near all those new hospitals which have so transformed Gray Street from the lazy southern street it was ten years ago. The windows of the Presbyterian seminary are boarded up. They have moved out of the old false-Gothic building (South-Victorian-Tudor, or something!). So I sweated, and read copies of *Life* magazine, one more tedious than the other. There is great emphasis on the farce in Viet Nam, trying to make it look good, honest, reasonable, etc., which it is not. Senator Cooper gave a good speech in the Senate against extending the war and I got a letter from him in reply to one I had written about it. He seems serious and sane about it. Meanwhile, according to the papers, air raids against North Viet Nam bases have been constant in the last few weeks, in spite of the protests in this country. But the majority of people are apathetic.

Had lunch with Jim Wygal, who is tired and out of sorts (with the bug that everyone has, I suppose) and I bought a loaf of fine Bohemian rye bread at Linker's in Market Street – which I enjoyed for supper in the hermitage. So good to return to the silence. With eye drops and ointments and pills.

April 7, 1965

The other day was brought up short by a line in my poem "The Captives" (it has been set to music by R. Feliciano, a composer in Detroit and I read it in his program). "Blessed is the army that will one day crush you, city/ Like a golden spider. . . ." It is a bitter and uncomprehending thought about the world – Babylon – yet still it must be said that the Bible does not have too many kind thoughts in it about "Babylon." I still have to rethink a lot of things about "the world." The poem belongs to a superficial and arrogant period – my early years in the monastery (up to ordination, when deeper suffering began and a different outlook came with it). In the days when I kept all the rules without exception and fasted mightily and was an energy in the choir, I had this simple *contemptus mundi* [contempt for the world] (no doubt traditional!!). The world was bad, the monastery was good: The world was Babylon, the monastery Jerusalem, etc. (though in "The Captives" the division was more subtle and there was Babylon in the monastery too!).

This kind of view ends in pharisaism: I am good, they are bad. And of course any such view of the world is intolerable. My present view – provisionally –

A. "The world," in the sense of collective myths and aspirations of contemporary society, is not to be unconditionally accepted or rejected, because whether we like it or not we are all part of it and there is a sense in which it has to be accepted.

B. But I refuse an optimism which blesses *all* these myths and aspirations as "temporal values" and accepts *all* the projects of man's society as good, progressive and laudable efforts in which all are to cooperate. Here one certainly has to distinguish. War in Viet Nam no, civil rights yes, and a huge area of uncertainties, official projects dressed up in approved inanities = Alliance for Progress – in which there are a few good ideas and perhaps many bad applications of them.

C. I am convinced of the sickness of American affluent society. To bless that sickness as a "temporal value" is something I absolutely refuse. Love of "the world" in this case means understanding and love of the millions of people *afflicted by* the sickness and suffering from it in various ways: compassion for them, desire to liberate them from their obsessions (how can anyone do it? We are all afflicted) to give them some measure of sanity and authenticity –

D. The error is in rejecting the sick and condemning them along with the sickness.

E. The only right way – to love and serve the man of the modern world, but not simply to succumb, with him, to all his illusions about his world.

April 9, 1965. Feast of Our Lady of Sorrows. Friday in Passion Week

Dawn is beginning (5:30) on a mild spring morning. Holy Week is about to begin and I was never more conscious of its solemnity and its importance. I am a Christian, and a member of a Christian community. I and my brothers are to put aside everything else and recognize that we belong not to ourselves but to God in Christ. That we have vowed obedience that is intended to unite us to Christ "obedient unto death – even the death of the cross." That without our listening and attention and submission, in total self-renunciation and love for the Father's will, in union with Christ, our life is false and without meaning. But in so far as we desire, with Christ, that the Father's will may be done in us as it is in heaven and in Christ, then even the smallest and most ordinary things are made holy and great. And then in all things the love of God opens and flowers, and our lives are transformed. This transformation is a manifestation and advent of God in the world.

It is unfortunate that so much of monastic obedience has become formal and trivial. No use in lamenting it, but nevertheless renewal in this area must mean above all a recovery of the sense of *obedience to God* in all things, and not just – obedience to rules and Superiors where demanded, and after that go woolgathering where you may! A sad thing: that formal obedience or non-disobedience is an expedient which, in practice, justifies us in self-will in harmless and futile matters. (Thus our lives in fact become totally absorbed in the futilities which are "licit" and which are not subject to formal control.) Instead of "imitating" Christ, we are content to parody Him.

One of the fruits of the solitary life is a sense of the absolute importance of *obeying God* – a sense of the need to obey and to seek His will, to choose freely to see and accept what comes from Him, not as a last resort, but as one's "daily superstantial bread." Liberation from automatic obedience into the seriousness and gravity of free choice to submit. But it is not easy to see always where and how!

April 13, 1965. Tuesday in Holy Week

On Palm Sunday – everything was going well and I was getting into the chants of the Mass when suddenly the Passion, instead of being solemnly sung on the ancient tone in Latin, was read in the extremely trite and pedestrian English version that has been approved by the American bishops. The effect was, to my mind, disastrous. Total lack of nobility, solemnity, or even of any style whatever. A trivial act – liturgical vaudeville. I could not get away from the impression of a blasphemous comedy. Not that English is not capable of serious liturgical use – but the total lack of imagination, of creativity, of a sense of worship! Yet many in the community were delighted, including Father Felix, the professor of liturgy who, I must confess, is not famous for imagination!

In the evening I talked foolishly of Angela of Foligno, then back to Philoxenus of Mabbugh. After supper and direction (Brother Eric has just got out of infirmary) I went up to bed in the hermitage feeling unwell. Woke up after an hour's sleep, with violent diarrhea and vomiting which went on for most of the night. Fortunately the night was warm and moonlit. It is a flu bug that has been attacking the community. Weak and nauseated all yesterday, I began to feel better in the evening and took a little supper. Slept last night in the infirmary and slept well too! Had a good breakfast, fried eggs and coffee!! Felt a little weak this morning but on the whole I seem to have got off easy unless it starts again which I suppose it might! While it lasted it was a miserable experience.

April 15, 1965. Holy Thursday

Obedient unto death ... Perhaps the most crucial aspect of Christian obedience to God today concerns the responsibility of the Christian in technological society toward God's creation and God's will for His creation. Obedience to God's will for nature and for man – respect for nature and love for man – in the awareness of our power to frustrate God's designs for nature and for man – to radically corrupt and destroy natural goods by misuse and blind exploitation, especially by criminal waste. The problem of nuclear war is only one facet of an immense, complex and unified problem.

K. V. Truhlar, a disciple of [Karl] Rahner, writes: "It is the duty of the Christian to lead the world of nature to its natural perfection" and this is true in a sense, but it is written with a tone and implications that are perhaps quite misleading: the assumption that technology is obviously doing something to *perfect* nature (instead of squandering it in the most irresponsible and criminal fashion!). There are then very grave problems in the implications of certain kinds of Christian outlook on "the world." The crux of the matter seems to be to what extent a Christian thinker can preserve his independence from obsessive modes of thought about secular progress. (Behind which always is the anxiety for us and for the Church to be "acceptable" in a society that is leaving us behind in a cloud of dust.) In other words, where is our hope? If in fact our hope is in a temporal and secular humanism of technological and political progress, we will find ourselves, in the name of Christ, joining in the stupidity and barbarism of those who are despoiling His creation in order to make money or get power for themselves. But our hope must be in God. And he who hopes in God will find himself sooner or later making apparently hopeless and useless protests against this barbarism of power.

Is there not a false eschatology of the "new heaven and new earth" which places its hope in the power of science to transform earth and heaven into places of happiness and bliss? (With God or without Him for that matter.) Is the true prospect rather that the stupidity and pride of man will ruin the earth, and that God will restore it through the charity and tears of the poor, the "remnant" and the saints? I am not saying this false eschatology is in Truklar's article, which has excellent things in it – but theologians occupied with the Christian and the world are not sufficiently aware of what technology is doing to the world and in failing to make distinctions, they tend to embrace all manifestations of progress without question in "turning to the world" and "in Christian temporal action." Hence inevitably we get Christians in the U.S. supporting a criminally stupid military adventure in Viet Nam.

Yesterday I got out of the infirmary at my own request, perhaps too soon, but I felt better and I wanted to get back to the hermitage, though it tires me to come out here. Last night I was restless and feverish, sweating a lot, and had to change my shirt three or four times. At the end of the night I had some rather beautiful dreams and got up at 3. My meditation wasn't much good as I was feeling sick, but some superb tea Jack Ford gave me (Twining's Lapsang Souchong!) made me feel much better. It is the most effective medicine I have taken in all this – and is a marvelous tea. That with a little slice of lemon and a couple of pieces of rye toast (the last of the Bohemian loaf) made a fine frustulum and after reading a bit I am very alert and alive. But as heavy rain began about 4:30 I did not go down to the monastery for Chapter and mandatum of the poor. The rain is slowing down now (7:15). The valley is dark and beautifully wet and you can almost see the grass growing and the leaves pushing out of the poplars. There are small flowers on my redbuds and the dogwood buds are beginning to swell.

There is no question for me that my one job as monk is to live the hermit life in simple direct contact with nature, primitively, quietly, doing some writing, maintaining such contacts as are willed by God, and bearing witness to the value and goodness of simple things and ways, and loving God in it all. I am more convinced of this than of anything contingent on my life and I am sure it is what He asks of me. Yet I do not always respond with simplicity.

April 16, 1965. Good Friday

Today God disputes with His people. One of the rare times when He argues with Man, enters the court and pleads His own cause. "O my People, what have I done to you . . . ?" Man blames God for evil. But it turns out that all the evil in the world has been done, through man, by the mysterious Adversary of God. And all the evil has been done to God. He who need not have taken it upon Himself has done so, in order to save man from evil and from the Adversary. The Adversary (and man allied with him) makes himself "be" by declaring himself to be real and God less real, or unreal. Reducing Him to Nothing on the Cross. But God, the Abyss of Being, beyond the dichotomy of Being and Nothingness, can neither be made to be nor reduced to nothing. The Judgment: those who have turned their hate against God have in reality destroyed themselves in striving, in this manner, to assert themselves. The way to being is then the way of non-assertion, which is God's way (not that He has a "way" in Himself, but it is the Way He has revealed); revealing Himself as the way, "I am the Way" said Christ last night, and we went out of the Chapter into the Church for concelebration.

Marco Pallis had Lord [Walter] Northbourne send me his really excellent book *Religion in the Modern World*. Among many fine things he says this about tradition in art, religion, politics, sport, etc. The traditional constraints impose a vital unity, a hierarchical order of like with unlike, so that there is a final universality and wholeness in society and in the expression of man's spirit. Where this traditional principle is discarded, everything becomes individualized. But there has to be a semblance of unity nevertheless. This is sought by *collectivization* which, however, is not an order of like and unlike elements, but simply a grouping together of like with like. Or a seduction to superficial sameness, uniformity not unity. Within the superficial uniformity, civilization is segmented into "departments" out of contact with each other, but officially "interconnected."

April 17, 1965. Holy Saturday

The great sin, the source of all other sins, is idolatry. And never has it been greater, more prevalent than now. It is almost completely unrecognized – precisely because it is so overwhelmingly total. It takes in everything. There is nothing else left. Fetishism of power, machines, possessions, medicine, sports, clothes, etc. all kept going by greed for money and power: the bomb is only one accidental aspect of the cult. Indeed, the bomb is not the worst. We should be thankful for it as a sign, a revelation of what all the rest of our civilization points to: the self-immolation of man to his own greed and his own despair. And behind it all are the principalities and powers whom man serves in his idolatry. Christians are as deeply involved in this as everyone else.

Northbourne sees very well that the profane point of view is at the same time necessarily, in principle both agnostic and idolatrous to the highest degree. This combination is what makes it impossible for us to see what we are doing, and able to go to the limit in doing what we do not see: for we imagine that unbelief is also, first of all, a protection against idolatry. (We are unbelievers in the higher religions, *a fortiori* in the more primitive ones . . . .) No, on the contrary: unbelief and idolatry are inseparable. Faith is the principle of liberation, and the only such principle. The other thing: idolatry has consequences. And the most terrible possible consequences. Man must take these consequences unless he renounces his idols.

This is clearly one of the most important and inescapable messages of the Bible: that unless man turns from his idols to God, he will destroy himself, or rather his idolatry will prove itself to be his destruction. (The idolater is already self-destroyed.) The other thing: man as a whole will not change. He will destroy himself. The Bible sees no other end to the story. But Christ has come to save from this destruction all who seek to be saved. In and through them He will recreate the world. By no means are we to interpret this to mean that enlightened ethics and polite good intentions are going to make technological society safe for man, and that the new creation will be in fact the technological paradise (plus a renewed liturgy).

The last pages of Northbourne's book are remarkably good, and make clear the confusions that had given me trouble with the Schuon-Guinan line of thought. Northbourne is most insistent on not mixing up traditions, on *not* being syncretistic. On the great danger of pseudo-religious "nothingness" using a mélange of Eastern and Western elements – worse still, disciplines. "The effectiveness of any single religion as a means of grace and a way of salvation is impaired or neutralized by its supplementation or dilution with anything that is alien to it" p. 101. He sees clearly that these pseudo-religious, pseudo-mystical movements, while claiming to be a reaction against materialism, are in fact only the last convolution of the profane spiral, and complete the whole work. "Anything that purports to be initiation and spiritual disciplines that have authentic spiritual roots and thus retain some of their power." Case of poor Joel Orent and his guru. Northbourne's last chapter is invaluable.

Viet Nam: all one's thinking on this depends on the acceptation or rejection of this premise. "That America has a divine mission to destroy communism in Asia and everywhere else, or, failing that, at least to prevent its further spread." Those who accept this (on faith!) are the ones convinced that we have now reached the point where we must fight. I do not accept this premise. It is too much like the basic principle behind Hitler's thinking, that led to World War II. And as World War II led to the spread of Communism in Eastern Europe and above all in Asia, World War III will doubtless (if anyone survives at all) complete the job.

Warm bright spring day. Saw a palm warbler in the small ash tree behind the hermitage, with his red-brown cap and bobbing tail. He is on his way to the North of Canada! Why do they call him palm warbler?

April 18, 1965. Easter Sunday

Peace and beauty of Easter morning: sunrise, deep green grass, soft winds, the woods turning green on the hills across the valley (and here too). I got up and said the old office of Lauds, and there was a wood thrush singing fourth-tone mysteries in the deep ringing pine wood (the "unconscious" wood) behind the hermitage. (The "unconscious" wood has a long moment of perfect clarity at dawn, and from being dark and confused, lit from the east it is all clarity, all distinct, seen to be a place of silence and peace with its own order in disorder – the fallen trees don't matter, they are all part of it!)

Last night went down to the offices of the Easter Vigil by full moonlight and came back also by full moonlight, the woods being perfectly silent, and the moon so strong one could hardly see any stars. I sat on the porch to make my thanksgiving, after communion. (I did not concelebrate.)

I wonder if I have not said ill-considered things about Christian tradition – things that will only add to the present confusion, and motivated by some obscure desire to protect my own heart against wounds by inflicting them myself – (i.e. the wounds of loss and separation: as if I were saying since the Middle Ages are no longer relevant to us I may as well be the first to admit it and get it over. But *are* the Middle Ages irrelevant? Of course not, and I have not begun to believe it! And it is part of my vocation to make observations that preserve a living continuity with the past, and with what is good in the past!).

I think now is the time finally to read Sartre's *Erigena*.

April 19, 1965. Easter Monday

"*Fiducia Christianorum resurrectio mortuorum – illam credentes hoc sumus.*" ["The confidence of Christians is in the resurrection of the dead – we are those who believe this to be so."] (*Tertullian*, De Res, *1.1*)

(Study of Medieval exegesis – is a way of entering into the Christian experience of that age, an experience most relevant to us, for if we neglect it we neglect part of our own totality in De Lubac, Von Balthasar, etc.). But it must not be studied from the outside. Same idea in Nishida on Japanese culture and the Japanese view of life. I have a real sense this Easter, that my own vocation demands a deepened and experiential study, *from within* (by connaturality) of the Medieval tradition as well as of, to some extent, Asian tradition and experiences, particularly Japanese, particularly Zen: i.e., in an awareness of a common need and aspiration with these past generations.

April 23, 1965. Friday in Easter week

It is already hot as summer. Everything is breaking into leaf and the pine saw fly worms are all over the young pines. There is no visitation this year (Dom Columban [from the Motherhouse at Melleray in France] usually comes on Easter Friday) because the General Chapter opens next week and Dom James is to leave Sunday after Brother Dunstan's profession.

This morning I sat in the dentist's chair having my teeth cleaned and ex-rayed while the students banged and walloped next door demolishing the old library.

Early mornings are now completely beautiful – with the Easter moon in its last quarter high in the blue sky, and the light of dawn spreading triumphantly over the wide, cool, green valley. It is the paradise season!

And I was deeply moved by Tertullian. What magnificent Latin and what a concept of the dignity of man and of the body (*De Resurrectione*, esp. 6, 7).

Then yesterday Flannery O'Connor's new book [*Everything That Rises Must Converge*, 1965] arrived and I am already well into it, grueling and powerful! A relentlessly perfect writer, full of tragedy and irony. But what a writer! And she knows every aspect of the American meanness, and violence, and frustration. And the Southern struggle of will against inertia.

A pine warbler was caught in the novitiate scriptorium, beating against the window and I got a good look at him, letting him out. A couple of Towhees are all around the hermitage.

April 24, 1965

Tertullian. Certainly I am reading in perfect circumstances (viz., chapter 12 *De Resurrectione* at the time of this spring dawn!!) but I have to admit that his prose is more powerful and more captivating than any other I have ever read. I know no one who has such authority, by the beauty and strength of his language, to command *complete* attention. Everything becomes delightful, admirable and absorbing, and there is a real excitement in the compression and charge of his syntax, the precision and personal signature of his vocabulary. You feel that here is a man who is fully and expertly working in language making prose!

April 25, 1965. Low Sunday

I wonder if the singular power of Flannery O'Connor's work, the horror and fascination of it, is not basically religious in a completely tacit way. There is *no* positive and overt expression of Catholicism (with optimism, hope, etc.) but perhaps a negative, direct, brutal confrontation with God in the terrible, the cruel. (The bull in "Greenleaf" [short story] as the lover and destroyer.) This is an affirmation of what popular Christianity always struggles to avoid: the dark face of God. But now, and above all in the South, it is the dark and terrible face of God that looks at America (the crazy religious characters are to be taken seriously precisely because their religion is inadequate).

Yesterday Clayton Eshelman and his wife came over from Indiana University in a borrowed Volkswagen. It was nice to meet them, good, alive young people. He spoke of his translations of Vallejo, and how the widow Vallejo will not let anybody publish anything of Vallejo's. (She is a terror!) Talked of Japan, and of poets: v.g., Corman, Jonathan Williams, Creely, and many I do not know. And of the difficulties of *El Corno Emplumado*. One of the things that impresses me about this generation of poets and artists is their gentleness, their goodness. I felt they were far more gentle than I could ever be, and felt too that I was rather a violent and angry person as compared with them. We had sandwiches and beer together in the evening at the lake by the Bardstown road, and it came on to rain, with lightning behind Vineyard Knob, and I sheltered in the sheep barn while they drove off in the Volkswagen. The rain soon stopped but at night there was a long downpour with much lightning. While waiting in the car for them to get the sandwiches at the Blue Jay, I read Sartre's statements in the *Nation* about why he cannot come to this country, when it is doing what it is doing in Viet Nam.

5:40 a.m. Thunder over the valley, forked lightning and very black rain out there beyond the monastery, and all the birds sing, especially a woodthrush in the cedar tree. And rain begins to come down on the hermitage.

April 27, 1965

Father Abbot took off for the General Chapter early Sunday. Brother Clement will meet him in Paris after the Chapter and they will go to Norway and select one of three properties that have been offered by the Foundation. Meanwhile I have been thinking about the ideas which Dom James may or may not have about Edelin's Valley. He refuses to say anything explicit. I know he wants to start something there, but more and more I feel repugnance and misgivings about the way it seems to be planned. Living in trailers, for instance, with compact comforts and modern conveniences. Certainly this is practical and he is thinking of his own desire to live there himself. But that is simply not what I need or seek, and all in all I become more and more convinced I am much better off at St. Mary of Carmel where I am.

Today for the first time since Passion week – i.e., for exactly three weeks, I have news of what has been going on in and about Vietnam. Things are incomparably worse. Though there was a big demonstration of students in Washington on Holy Saturday; though the State Department, evidently at Johnson's request, wrote a conciliatory note to the Fellowship of Reconciliation about their big protest ad, though the South Vietnamese and especially the Buddhists are desperately trying to get a government that will be independent of the Pentagon and work for peace, and though the anti-aircraft defenses of North Vietnam are being much strengthened, not only does the bombing get heavier, but all kinds of indications show that thousands of American troops are to be sent in for a land invasion of North Vietnam. Not only is this disastrously absurd – (and with it goes the absurd demand for unconditional cessation of all resistance!!) but it makes one suddenly see in a ghastly light the moral picture of this country.

What with the South (picture of the fat grinning sheriffs of Philadelphia, Mississippi, *known* to be the murderers of the civil rights workers), what with the grave doubts about the Kennedy murder (still as grave as ever because of certain vital questions about the Warren report!), what with the Klan and the Birchites and all the Kooks and right wingers and all the self-deluded well-meaning liberals – this whole country suddenly appears as a moral landscape of damnation! And there seems to be nothing on earth that anyone can do about it.

I received a copy of Jacques Maritain's *Notebooks*, from Paris, and have already read the interesting (and sometimes funny) chapter on La Salette and his attempts to get his manuscript on it approved in Rome in 1918. Some very fine pages on the nature of prophetic language, the language of heavenly revelations. What comes out most of all of course is the simplicity and probity of Jacques himself and his evident loyalty to the Church. It is very edifying. I love the pictures of Raïssa and Vera [Oumansoff]. Though I never actually met them, I know they are two people who loved me – and whom I have loved – through our writings and the warmth and closeness that has somehow bound me to Jacques and to them. It is really a kind of family affection, which also reaches out to good Dom Pierre (Van der Meer) who wrote (through Dame Christine [Van der Meer]) about the article concerning [Georgio] La Pira's visit to America – and his (somewhat over enthusiastic account of Gethsemani).

PART IV

Day of a Stranger

Sometime in May 1965

The hills are blue and hot.[1] There is a brown, dusty field in the bottom of the valley. I hear a machine, a bird, a clock. The clouds are high and enormous. In them, the inevitable jet plane passes: this time probably full of fat passengers from Miami to Chicago, but presently it will be a plane with the bomb in it. I have seen the plane with the bomb in it fly low over me and I have looked up out of the woods directly at the closed bay. Like everyone else I live under the bomb. But unlike most people I live in the woods. Do not ask me to explain this. I am embarrassed to describe it. I live in the woods out of necessity. I am both a prisoner and an escaped prisoner. I cannot tell you why, born in France, my journey ended here. I have tried to go further but I cannot. It makes no difference. When you are beginning to be old, and I am beginning to be old, for I am fifty, both times and places no longer take on the same meaning. Do I have a "day"? Do I spend my "day" in a "place"? I know there are trees here. I know there are birds here. I know the birds in fact very well, for there are exactly fifteen pairs of birds living in the immediate area of my cabin and I share this particular place with them: we form an ecological balance. This harmony gives "place" a different configuration.

As to crows, they form part of a different pattern. They are vociferous and self-justifying, like humans.

But there is a mental ecology too, a living balance of spirits in this corner of woods. There is a place for many other songs besides those of birds. Of Vallejo for instance. Or the dry, disconcerting voice of Nicanor Parra (who certainly does not waste his time justifying anything). Sometimes at four o'clock on a very dark cold morning I have sat alone in the house with the

[1] Merton was asked by his friend Miguel Grinberg in Buenos Aires for some journal passages that would describe a "typical day" in his life and that could be published in the periodical he edited, *Eco Contemporaneo*. Merton responded by writing a "journal-like" essay, which he called "Day of a Stranger." This is the first draft of "Day of a Stranger"; Merton later revised and expanded the essay.

rain beating down on it, with a big cup of hot black coffee, translating some poems of Nicanor Parra. Or there is also Chuang Tzu, whose climate is perhaps most the climate of this hot corner of the woods. A climate in which there is no need for explanations. There is also a Syrian hermit called Philoxenus. There is the clanging prose of Tertullian. There is the deep vegetation of that more ancient forest than mine: the deep forest in which the great birds Isaias and Jeremias sing. When I am most sickened by the things that are done by the country that surrounds this place I will take out the prophets and sing them in loud Latin across the hills and send their fiery words sailing south over the mountains to the place where they split atoms for the bombs in Tennessee.

There is also the non-ecology, the destructive unbalance of nature, poisoned and unsettled by bombs, by fallout, by exploitation: the land ruined, the waters contaminated, the soil charged with chemicals, ravaged with machinery, the houses of farmers falling apart because everybody goes to the city and stays there . . . There is no poverty so great as that of the prosperous, no wretchedness so dismal as affluence. Wealth is poison. There is no misery to compare with that which exists where technology has been a total success. I know these are hard sayings, and that they are unbearable when they are said in other countries where so many lack everything. But do you imagine that if you become as prosperous as the United States you will no longer have needs? Here the needs are even greater. Full bellies have not brought peace and satisfaction but dementia, and in any case not all the bellies are full either. But the dementia is the same for all.

I live in the woods out of necessity. I get out of bed in the middle of the night because it is imperative that I hear the silence of the night, alone, and, with my face on the floor, say psalms, alone, in the silence of the night.

It is necessary for me to live here alone without a woman, for the silence of the forest is my bride and the sweet dark warmth of the whole world is my love, and out of the heart of that dark warmth comes the secret that is heard only in silence, but it is the root of all the secrets that are whispered by all the lovers in their beds all over the world. I have an obligation to preserve the stillness, the silence, the poverty, the virginal point of pure nothingness which is at the center of all other loves. I cultivate this plant silently in the middle of the night and water it with psalms and prophecies in silence. It becomes the most beautiful of all the trees in the garden, at once the primordial paradise tree, the *axis mundi*, the cosmic axle, and the Cross. *Nulla silva talem profert*. [No tree brings forth such.]

It is necessary for me to see the first point of light which begins to be dawn. It is necessary to be present alone at the resurrection of Day, in the solemn silence at which the sun appears, for at this moment all the affairs of cities, of governments, of war departments, are seen to be the bickerings of mice. I receive from the Eastern woods, the tall oaks, the one word DAY, which is never the same. It is always in a totally new language.

After dawn I go down into the valley, first under the pines, then under tall oaks, then down a sharp incline, past an old barn, out into the field where they are now planting corn. Later in the summer the corn will be tall and sacred and the wind will whisper through the thousands of leaves and stalks as if all the spirits of the Maya were there. I weep in the corn for what was done in past ages, in the carnage that brought America the dignity of having a "history." I live alone with the blood of Indians on my head.

The long yellow side of the monastery faces the sun on a sharp rise with fruit trees and beehives. I climb sweating into the novitiate, put down my water bottle on the cement floor. The bell is ringing. I have some duties in the monastery. When I have accomplished these, I return to the woods. In the choir are the young monks, patient, serene, with very clear eyes, thin, reflective, gentle. For fifteen years I have given them classes, these young ones who come, and grow thin, become more reflective, more silent. But many of them become concerned with questions. Questions of liturgy, questions of psychology, questions of history. Are they the right questions? In the woods there are other questions and other answers, for in the woods the whole world is naked and directly present, with no monastery to veil it.

Chanting the *alleluia* in the second mode: strength and solidity of the Latin, seriousness of the second mode, built on the *Re* as though on a sacrament, a presence. One keeps returning to the *Re* as to an inevitable center. *Sol-Re, Fa-Re, Sol-Re, Do-Re*. Many other notes in between, but suddenly one hears only the one note. *Consonantia* [harmony]: all notes, in their perfect distinctness, are yet blended in one.

In the refectory is read a message of the Pope, a strong one, denouncing war, denouncing the bombing of civilians, reprisals on civilians, killing of hostages, torturing of prisoners (all in Vietnam). Do the people of this country realize who the Pope is talking about? They have by now become so solidly convinced that the Pope never denounces anybody but Communists that they have long since ceased to listen. The monks seem to know. The voice of the reader trembles.

In the heat of noon I return through the cornfield, past the barn under the oaks, up the hill, under the pines, to the hot cabin. Larks rise out of the long grass singing. A bumblebee hums under the wide shady eaves.

I sit in the cool back room, where words cease to resound, where all meanings are absorbed in the *consonantia* of heat, fragrant pine, quiet wind, bird song and one central tonic note that is unheard and unuttered. Not the meditation of books, or of pieties, or of systematic trifles. In the silence of the afternoon all is present and all is inscrutable. One central tonic note to which every other sound ascends or descends, to which every other meaning aspires, in order to find its true fulfillment. To ask when the note will sound is to lose the afternoon: it has sounded and all things now hum with resonance of its sounding.

I sweep. I spread a blanket out in the sun. I cut grass behind the cabin. Soon I will bring the blanket in again and make the bed. The sun is overclouded. Perhaps there will be rain. A bell rings in the monastery. A tractor growls in the valley. Soon I will cut bread, eat supper, say psalms, sit in the back room as the sun sets, as the birds sing outside the window, as silence descends on the valley, as night descends. As night descends on a nation intent upon ruin, upon destruction, blind, deaf to protest, crafty, powerful, unintelligent. It is necessary to be alone, to be not part of this, to be in the exile of silence, to be in a manner of speaking a political prisoner. No matter where in the world he may be, no matter what may be his power of protest, or his means of expression, the poet finds himself ultimately where I am. Alone, silent, with the obligation of being very careful not to say what he does not mean, not to let himself be persuaded to say merely what another wants him to say, not to say what his own past work has led others to expect him to say.

The poet has to be free from everyone else, and first of all from himself, because it is through this "self" that he is captured by others. Freedom is found under the dark tree that springs up in the center of the night and of silence, the paradise tree, the *axis mundi*, which is also the Cross.

PART V

"Hermit in the Water of Life"

May 1965–December 1965

May 1, 1965

Perfectly beautiful spring weather – sky utterly cloudless all day – birds singing all around the hermitage – deep green grass. When I am here, all the time the towhees and tanagers are at peace, not worried, and with their constant singing I always know where they are. It is a wonderful companionship to have them constantly within the very small circle of woods which is their area and mine – where they have their nests and I have mine. Sometimes the woodthrush comes, but only on special occasions – like the evening of St. Robert's day. Last evening I interrupted my meditation to watch half a dozen savannah sparrows outside my bedroom window.

Today I finished a first draft of an article on "Contemplation and Ecumenism" for the Dominicans in California. A copy of the *Black Revolution* in Catalan came in. This has appeared in the following languages and in this order: (1) French; (2) English; (3) German; (4) Catalan!!

Rumors are going around the monastery about Johnson claiming to have discovered Communist missile bases in Santo Domingo and having sent in the Marines. I wonder to what extent this is deliberately trumped up to foment more excitement and favor his "escalation" policy in Asia. Today I read a xerox copy of Hermann Kahn's article on "Escalation" from a recent issue of *Fortune*. It is fantastic. His peculiar vocabulary makes it, in the first place, extremely comical. A parody of this technological doubletalk could hardly be more incredible. Yet it is all very serious because he is close to being the official spokesman for the government and the Pentagon.

It is all in the dispassionate language of the game theory of nuclear war. At no point does he suggest that the possible millions of victims are people. The main point is that he explicitly treats various "reasonable" ways in which all kinds of "conventional" acts of war and harassment, and also nuclear weapons, can and may be used "for bargaining" – including the mass evacuation of cities (to make "the adversary" convinced that we intend to bomb *his* cities) – in spite of an official "no cities" strategy "which is neither clearly understood nor firmly held even here." Where it gets really interesting is "slow motion counter property war," "constrained force reduction salvo," "constrained disarming attack," then of course "slow motion countercity war" in which the game becomes "city trading" – a nice "test of nerves." As long as it is "controlled" and does not become "spasm or insensate war" he conceives it as "thinkable," i.e., practicable. And here the word *control* will be enough to convince a number of Catholic theologians and bishops that this is a perfectly legitimate application of double effect. The moral theology of hell!! What bastards!

The more one considers all this the more there appears to be only one drastic solution. But as for me, all I can do is sit here in the country and think about it and pray and wait to see what happens, and hope that I will know what to do. His plea is that one "has to have an alternative between cataclysm and surrender." Has he ever heard of making peace? Evidently the real meaning of this article is that Washington plans climbing on to some of the rungs of Hermann's ladder quite soon in Asia, confident that Russia will join in and play according to rule. And I have no doubt this issue of *Fortune* was carefully read in the Kremlin. I wonder if there are really intelligent human beings, maybe, in Peking?

May 10, 1965

Already a most beautiful week of May has gone by. For part of it I was ill again, with the same bug that had me in the infirmary at the beginning of Holy Week. It was a good thing, for this time Father Eudes gave me an antibiotic which seems to have cleared it up properly. Last time it really stayed with me (my stomach remained quite upset even though I was "well"). So for a couple of days I lay around in the warm green shade of the end room, with no desire for any food, and read Martin Ling's book which he sent me (*Ancient Beliefs and Modern Superstitions*), a good chunk of De Lubac's *Exégèse médiévale* (Vol. I) and the early part of Herbert Read's *Green Child*. The most exciting for me was De Lubac.

J. Laughlin came last Monday (May 3) and on the Tuesday we went to see Victor Hammer (a pleasant drive), taking a few pictures of barns on the way. J. likes the parts of the Chuang Tzu book that have now been typed for him and I must get at the rest of it. It was he who lent me the *Green Child*, in case I could think up a photograph for the cover of the new paperback edition he is doing.

Yesterday, Third Sunday after Easter (already!) is my favorite, or one of them. The Introit and the Alleluias especially. The afternoon was warm and glorious with the new summer, the brand new summer, the wheat already tall and waving in the wind, the great cumulus clouds. And all the things one cannot begin to say about it – the new awareness that I am not the "object" that "they" think or even that I think, and that the I which is not-I is All and in everyone, and that the outer I must not assert itself anymore but must be glad to vanish, and yet there is no division between them, as there is no division between the surface of the pond and the rest of it. It is the reflection on the surface that seems to give it another being – and its flatness, etc.

What the whip-poor-will (actually rather an owl I think) really says is "Where's the widow! Where's the widow!" And he says it very peremptorily.

"Tam dictis quam factis praedicator resurrectio" ["The resurrection was predicted through the word as deed"], says Tertullian and proceeds to speak of things in Exodus which seem to have very little to do with resurrection except remotely (Moses' leprous hand, etc.). This is, however, the way typology speaks: all the Bible is preaching, announcing truths and events, not scientifically proving them, not formally "predicting" them (except in certain cases). Understanding of this depends on one's capacity to understand prophecy as witness to a central truth, rather than as linear prediction. If you say "Because God first said this would happen, then made it happen, and because I can prove this from Scriptures, I am convinced," you may have the whole thing backwards, and you may start either falsifying Scripture or emptying it in order to prove what you need to prove. On the other hand: "This is what happened, and it is what God everywhere pointed to, it is the central event and all others gain their true meaning when this is seen," then you have an access to the Scriptures in peace and contemplation – without the need to *prove* anything, which does not mean that proofs may not have their place. But the place is not central, just as reasoning is not central, but understanding, seeing.

May 11, 1965

Tomorrow Sts. Nereus and Achilleus: I said their office in anticipation in the fresh green woods after work clearing brush, where the fire still smoked. I will always remember their little empty church in Rome, half in the country, on a spring afternoon in 1933.

"Radices gentium superborum arefecit Deus, et plantavit humiles ex ipsis gentibus" ["The Lord has plucked up proud men by their roots, and planted the lowly from the peoples"] Eccli. 10:18[15].[1] (cf. the Magnificat – "He hath put down the mighty . . .")

If I were more fully attentive to the word of God I would be much less troubled and disturbed by the events of our time: not that I would be indifferent or passive, but I could gain the strength of union with the deepest currents in history, the sacred currents which run opposite to those on the surface, a great deal of the time!

"De ea re quae te non molestat ne certeris; et in iudicio peccantium ne consistas" ["Do not quarrel about a matter that does not concern you; and when sinners judge, do not sit in council with them"] Eccli. 11:9.

This, especially, strikes me: *"Cave tibi, et attende diligenter auditui tuo, quoniam cum subversione tua ambulas; audiens vero illa, quasi in somnis vide, et vigilabis"* ["Be wary, take very great care, because you are walking with your own downfall; when you hear such things, wake up and be vigilant."] Eccli. 13:16[13]. It seems to me that at the moment I very much need this kind of "attention" and "listening," for I have come to the most serious moments of my life.

May 15, 1965

A busy week. Yesterday Father Xavier Carroll and Edward Noonan, a Chicago architect, were here – the Poor Clare Abbess in Chicago wanted them to discuss with me the plans for their new monastery, which in fact looks very attractive and which involves some big changes in their approach to the contemplative life.

Thursday Sister Luke was here and we talked about the revised Schema for Religious (which as Council Observer, she had obtained from Bishop Huyghe of Arras – *not* from any American bishop).

Wednesday a short visit with Dom Philip, Benedictine Prior of Vallyermo in California. He had good things to say about monasticism in Africa – and about the group on the Island in Lake Kivu – from Père Erwin's place in the Landes. Sounds fine.

Brother Edmund (Buchanan), postulant from the Navy (officer on a Polaris submarine), left. Brother Ignatius (Ortwein) is in guest house trying to reenter.

---

[1] Merton quotes here from the Old Testament book Ecclesiasticus, not Ecclesiastes. Ecclesiasticus is often subtitled "The Wisdom of Jesus Ben Sirach." It is not included in the Jewish or Protestant scriptural canons.

May 20, 1965

Paschal Time is going by fast. We are in the fourth week already. There was more rain the other evening (as I came back from Louisville) and everything is very green. It is spoiled by the number of people who want to visit here all of a sudden. I would not mind seeing them far apart, but they all want to come at once. I can't very well say no to Zalman Schachter, and then Dan Berrigan wants to come and I think I should see him. And another one, charity seems to demand it, etc. But if I see everybody where is the famous "solitary vocation"? For once the contradictions in my life (which usually do not bother me) are suddenly painful and I see I must really do something about them. And there is no question I must stop the visits – all except a few that will remain really necessary, and far apart!

Working on Chuang Tzu I see how far I am from the kind of suddenness he talks about! Really the problem is there: in uniting a "hidden life" that is not after all hidden but famous or notorious. I do not want both, but I want one in such a way that the other goes with it and this is serious. I cannot shrug it off, and I almost seem to be helpless to really negotiate it, since it is so much my nature (as a writer) to get into this dilemma. Yet I see no need to get anguished about it. It will work itself out. I am certainly getting sick of the contradiction.

May 22, 1965

Grey dawn. A blood red sun, furious among the pines (it will soon be hidden in clouds). That darn black hound is baying in the hollow after some rabbit he will never catch. Deep grass in the field, dark green English woods (for we have had good rains). The bombing goes on in Viet Nam. The whole thinking of this country is awry on war: basic conviction that force is the only thing that is effective. That doubtless it is in many ways not "nice" but one must be realistic and use it, with moral justification, so as not to be just gangsters as "they" are (the enemy). Thus there is determination to settle everything by force and this being taken for granted, to make sure one's use of force is verbally justified. Hence a huge war effort with no sane reason, except that war is the only thing these people can believe in. Can a war with China be avoided? Only if China is determined to avoid it at a humiliating cost. Washington is certainly not working hard to avoid it, though suitable gestures of consultation and consideration are occasionally made for the benefit of the (unimpressed) public. What we need now is another Pearl Harbor: at present we are doing our best to provide *them* with one.

At this point it is not altogether easy to make an act of faith that all of history is in God's hands. At this point, and on the level where I have just been standing, the level of current opinion, where history is thought to be made by President Johnson and McNamara and Bundy and the Pentagon. But history is in the hands of God and the decisions of men lead infallibly to the full expression of what is really hidden in them and in their society. The actions of the U.S. in Asia are God's judgment on the U.S. We have decided that we will police the world – by the same tactics as used by the police in Alabama: beating "colored people" over the head because we believe they are "inferior." In the end, an accounting will be demanded.

We have to see history as a book that is sealed and opened by the Passion of Christ. But we still read it from the viewpoint of the Beast. Passion of Christ = passion of the poor, the underprivileged, etc. Viewpoint of the Beast: self-righteousness and cruelty of power. Hubris of human might and technological efficiency. But the same cruelty is bred by this hubris in the weak who grow strong by resisting and overcoming it – to be proud in their turn. Christ remains in agony until the end of time, and in His agony triumphs over all power.

May 23, 1965. Fifth Sunday after Easter

One lovely dawn after another. Such peace! Meditation with fireflies, mist in the valley, last quarter of the moon, distant owls – gradual inner awakening and centering in peace and harmony of love and gratitude. Yesterday I wrote to the man at McGill [University] who thought all contemplation was a manifestation of narcissistic regression! That is just what it is not. A complete awakening of identity and of rapport! It implies an awareness and acceptance of one's place in the whole, first the whole of creation, then the whole plan of Redemption – to find oneself in the great mystery of fulfillment which is the Mystery of Christ. *Consonantia* [harmony] and not *confusio* [confusion].

May 25, 1965

Whole day at the hermitage. I have come to see that only these days in solitude are really full and "whole" for me. The others are partly wasted. And yet I have "done" almost nothing, though it is true I worked an hour in the morning and another hour in the late afternoon on Book 23 of Chuang Tzu, one of the very best, and most rewarding. So I got some good material for my own Chuang Tzu book.[2] Also I went out in the afternoon and burnt

---

[2] *The Way of Chuang Tzu*, published by New Directions, 1965.

a couple of brush piles and cut down a few wild grape vines and some brush in the woods, actually accomplished very little but got very hot and tired doing it. I will need to keep this work up, at least moderately, to get back in shape for it. But I have been at it all spring two or three days a week. This is not enough, but there are other things to do!

Was down in the monastery for my own Mass only, and came back up. Did not go to vote in the County elections. Why should I? I don't know any of these people. And probably would be confirmed in my intention not to vote for them if I did! (Though really I like the county people in this county, and there is no more wonderful old farmer than Aidan Nally!)

Jack Ford brought me a couple of loaves of pumpernickel from a Jewish delicatessen in Louisville Monday, and he also gave me some excellent tea, which I iced for myself at supper tonight. Twining's Earl Grey. It was superb! And that was about all I had for supper with a can of mandarin oranges. Cool and pleasant. But it is still hot. The sky is cloudy. The birds still sing. Maybe there will be rain tonight.

For Meditation – part of the morning on the Sapiential books (Vulgate) and in the evening some of the time I spend on the Apocalypse in Greek. Have a good little book on Camus for light reading, finished Volume I of De Lubac's *Exégèse médiévale* (and enjoyed it immensely). Still haven't finished Tertullian on the Resurrection.

Tomorrow, Vigil of the Ascension and sixteenth anniversary of my ordination. At Mass I shall pray especially for the Buddhist, Vo Tanh Minh, who has been fasting since March in Brooklyn in protest against the fighting in Viet Nam. He will probably die, as there is little likelihood of a cease fire. His calm and peace are completely admirable.

May 28, 1965

A cool and lovely morning, clear sky, everchanging freshness of woods and valley! One has to be in the same place everyday, watch the dawn from the same house, hear the same birds wake each morning to realize how inexhaustibly rich and different is "sameness." This is the blessing of stability, and I think it is not evident until you enjoy it alone in a hermitage. The common life distracts you from life in its fullness. But one must be able to share this fullness, and I am not for a complete and absolute solitude without communication (except temporarily).

Yesterday, Ascension, was also St. Bede's day (he died on Ascension Day, 735). He is one of the saints I most love, and the simple story of his life and death fill me with love and joy. The afternoon was peaceful and marvelous – a nice walk and meditation at St. Malachy's field, then came back and gave a conference on Philoxenus. The simplicity and innocence of the monks is a real joy, a shining joy, so evident one does not notice it. Yet I must say that the concelebration in the morning did nothing to express the reality of love and oneness in Christ that is actually here. The singing was timid and depressing, and I must say that we are not anywhere near properly realizing and manifesting what it is all about.

May 30, 1965. Sunday within Octave of Ascension

Wonderful days. Bright cool weather. Clear skies and green hills, and I have this Sunday's Mass. Today I have finished Chuang Tzu "poems" (if one can call them that). More exactly, finished them yesterday afternoon and went over them all around dawn. I was exhilarated by the effect of all of them. They make a good group, and I never would have thought it possible for the result to be so (relatively) satisfactory. I am glad John Wu kept insisting that I do it. It has taken time, but most of the time was spent in getting to do it. At first I was very slow and hesitant, and progress was painful, but lately it has been fun.

Also the flycatchers, tamer and tamer, play about on the chairs and baskets on my porch, right in front of this window, and they are enthralling. Wrens come too, less frequently.

Father Felix gave a good talk on Cassian in chapter. And I spent a couple of hours in the morning with Father Robert McDole, who came up from Oklahoma: sorrows of a priest in civil rights and peace movement. Not easy! From what he says, I am quite right in thinking our military are looking for a pretext, any pretext, to smash China with bombs. This is atrocious as well as stupid, but I do think that in spite of all protests it has a good chance of happening. If it does, there will be great trouble for this country. Not that China could hit us back – and Russia would not – but there will be revolution all over the world, and perhaps even here. In any case much turmoil and chaos. The whole thing leaves me sick, mostly the unfairness and crass stupidity of it, and the needless, brutal violence that in the end will bring down *certain* punishment on its perpetrators.

My stomach is still upset – it has not been the same since the intestinal flu I had in April. Next Friday I have to go to Lexington for ex-rays, etc.

They continue the Trevor life of Newman in refectory and I do not get tired of it. My admiration for the man grows constantly, the more I know of the details of his life and all the nonsense he had to suffer from almost everyone. And with what good sense and patience, after all!

June 3, 1965

Finished the introduction to *Chuang Tzu* this afternoon. It is hot and misty, there is thunder in the distance. A cardinal sings loud in the quiet of evening.

Dan Berrigan was here Monday with Jim Douglass and Bob McDole. We talked a bit about Schema 13 and the alterations that have been made in the article on war. It really seems that they want to approve the bomb after all. In a way it is funny, though I should not say that! But behind it all I wonder if there is not an apocalyptic irony. But we must do what we can to prevent a disgrace and scandal of such magnitude.

June 6, 1965. Pentecost

On Friday I went to Lexington for some examinations at the clinic (Dr. Fortune) and was supposed to return that afternoon but stayed overnight in the hospital for more tests yesterday morning. What with enemas, proctoscopes, barium enemas, etc. I had a miserable time. When I began these examinations ten or fifteen years ago they were unpleasant but bearable. Since then, my insides have become so sensitive that they are a real torment. However, there is no cancer, there are no ulcers, just a great deal of inflammation and sensitivity, etc. The results of all the tests are not yet in. However, on Friday I had lunch with the Hammers, and borrowed from them the *Tao of Painting* [by Mai Mai Sze, 1963] to take to the hospital. I had some very enjoyable moments reading it. A very exciting first chapter. Also read [Samuel Nathaniel] Behrman's life of "Duveen" which is very funny [*A Biography of Joseph Duveen, Baron Duveen, 1869–1939*, 1952].

Apart from that – the usual hospital images and confusion. I am glad I got out so soon. In the clinic I seemed to be able to get hold of nothing but *Life* to read and it was full of helicopters in Viet Nam, white mercenaries in the Congo, Marines in Santo Domingo. The whole picture is one of an enormously equipped and self-complacent white civilization in combat with a huge, sprawling, colored and mestizo world (a majority!) armed with anything they can lay hands on. And the implicit assumption behind it all, as far as *Life* and apparently everyone else is concerned, is that "we" are the injured ones, we are trying to keep peace and order, and "they" (abetted by communist demons) are simply causing confusion and chaos, with no reasonable motives whatever. Hence "we," being attacked (God and justice are also attacked in us), have to defend ourselves, God, justice, etc. Dealing with these "inferior" people becomes a technical problem something like pest-extermination. In a word, the psychology of the Alabama police becomes in fact the psychology of America as world policeman. In one word – there is a world revolution going on, in which now whole nations (a minority of nations) are "the rich" and the "aristocrats," and all the rest are "the poor." Russia is in a very ambiguous position as a "rich" nation that still claims to be on the "poor" side but isn't. America is oversimplifying all the questions – reducing them to terms which make sense to us only and to no one else, and expecting others to see things our way, since our way is by definition the only reasonable one. Hence the fatal breakdown of communication.

Wives of astronauts talk by radio with their husbands in outer space; a priest of St. Meinrad's in Peru can call Jim Wygal and talk to him on the phone he has in his car, while he is driving around Louisville. And what do they have to say? "Hi! It's a nice day! Hope you are feeling good, I am feeling good, the kids are feeling good, the dog is feeling good, etc., etc."

Coming home – through Shakertown, Harrodsburg, Perryville and Lebanon. Beautiful June countryside – deep grass and hay, flowering weeds, tall cumulus clouds, corn a foot high and beautifully green tobacco struggling to begin. The old road between Perryville and Lebanon – winding between small farms and old barns, with wooded knobs nearby, is one I like. After Lebanon, thundershowers, heavy rain and black sky over the fields to the north, with much lightning. Country people in the streets of Lebanon (Saturday afternoon). It was a nice ride. Coming through Pleasant Hill without stopping, saw new aspects of the wonderful Shaker houses – inexhaustible variety and dignity in sameness.

June 8, 1965. Whit Tuesday

The great joy of the solitary life is not found simply in quiet, in the beauty and peace of nature, song of birds etc., nor in the peace of one's own heart, but in the awakening and attuning of the heart to the voice of God – to the inexplicable, quite definite inner certitude of one's call to obey Him, to hear Him, to worship Him here, now, today, in silence and alone, and that this is the whole reason for one's existence, this makes one's existence fruitful and gives fruitfulness to all one's other (good) acts, and is the ransom and purification of one's heart that has been dead in sin.

It is not simply a question of "existing" alone, but of doing, with joy and understanding "the work of the cell" which is done in silence and not according to one's own choice or the pressure of necessity but in obedience to God. But the voice of God is not "heard" at every moment, and part of the "work of the cell" is attention so that one may not miss any sound of that Voice. When we see how little we listen, and how stubborn and gross our hearts are, we realize how important the work is and how badly prepared we are to do it.

June 11, 1965. Friday in Ember Week

Tomorrow Fathers Timothy and Barnabas are to be ordained priests. I shall concelebrate with Timothy on Trinity Sunday (the most competent and reliable of all my undermasters). Already Reverend Father is sending them to Rome this year and getting them ready quickly for Norway. We are to vote on the Norway foundation this morning in chapter. There is a certain amount of misgivings in the community about it, naturally. It is a risk, and Dom James is so obviously enthused that he is pushing ahead fast with the delight of the operator who has got a good thing going. (It *is* a good thing in many ways – possible support in Norway from Bishop John [Gran] and his friends, etc., etc.). But more men are leaving here and we are short handed, few novices come, Spencer is going to have to close down at least one recent foundation (ought to close the one in Chile. I hope they don't close Snowmass).

I take delight in Mai Mai Sze's *Tao of Painting*, a deep and contemplative book. I am reading it slowly with great profit. She is becoming (with Nora Chadwick, Eleanor Duckett) one of my secret loves. Nora Chadwick writes charming letters and Eleanor Duckett sent me a beautiful spontaneous note written in the Cambridge library on Ascension Day, with a splendid quote on the monastic life from a ninth-century text.

Am discovering Ambrosian chant. Maybe the various lesson tones of the Ambrosian rite may turn out to be very great aids to *lectio divina* (e.g., marvelous proper tone for Genesis). I will try this. Noticed that after practicing the Genesis tone (itself quite oriental), I turned to read a bit of Youssef Yousnaya on Humility (Syrian – ninth century). It had extraordinary depth and resonance. Chanting gets those things from the head down to the heart and center. Makes one's inmost center resound with the truth conveyed (not merely registering this in the reason).

June 12, 1965. Ember Saturday

Early mist. Trees of St. Ann's wood barely visible across the valley. A fly-catcher, on a fencepost, appears in momentary flight, describes a sudden, indecipherable ideogram against the void of mist, and vanishes. On both sides of the house, the gossip of tanagers. The tow lizards that operate on the porch scuttle away when I arrive on the porch, however quietly, from outside. But when I come from inside the house, even though I may move brusquely, they are not afraid and stay where they are. To be conscious of both extremes in my solitary life. Consolation and desolation; understanding, obscurity; obedience and protest; freedom and imprisonment.

In one sense I am transcending the community, in another banned from it. In one sense I am "rewarded," in another punished, kept under restraint. For instance, I cannot go to Asia, to seek at their sources some of the things I see to be so vitally important (all the discussions of expression and mystery in brushwork of Chinese calligraphy, painting, poetry, etc.). An "imprisonment" which I accept with total freedom (what I need could be brought to me here!) but nonetheless a confinement. A perfecting of monastic life and a final disillusionment with monastic life! Renunciation of meaningful action and protest in contemporary affairs, awareness that the action itself may be ambiguous, the renunciation of it more clear, better defined protest, etc.

I have no doubts and no hesitations about *not* being any part of the Norway project (passed yesterday with very few black votes), yet I can see where in other circumstances I could get totally and fruitfully involved. Much better not to, however. (Ambiguity of famous convert making friends with Bishop John's artistic crowd in Oslo, etc.)

I protest by obeying, and protest most effectively by obeying in an obedience in which I am not subject to arbitrary fantasies on the part of authority, but in which both I and the abbot are aware (or think we are aware) of a higher obligation, and a demand of God. That my situation has reached this point is a great grace. Some will say it has come to this perversely, through my fault. To say this is to see only those "reasons" one chooses to see. That is not hard to do, and it is done all the time.

Last evening, during a heavy rainstorm, learned and sang the marvelous *"Requiem Tuam Domine"* from the Ambrosian Vesperale. This will be, for a while, a short dawn office (with the *Benedictus es* and oration). It is one of the most beautiful things I have ever run across.

June 14, 1965

Two concelebrations: one for Father Timothy's first Mass yesterday, another for Father Barnabas today. Probably the best concelebrations we have had so far. Very spirited and joyful. One felt that all the celebrants were really in it with their hearts! And I certainly was. Bright fine weather. I cleared out the closet where I keep typewriter and paper. Typed the Origen poem (written some time ago). Found a fine Ambrosian *Sanctus*. Dr. Fortune said tests showed a staphylococcus infection in my intestines and I have been taking an antibiotic for three days. It seems to be helping quite a bit.

June 18, 1965

Corpus Christi was yesterday. I did not concelebrate. It was a good cool day. Wrote to Marco Pallis in answer to a good letter of his (he liked my letter to Northbourne). John Wu wrote and sent some chapters of his book on Zen. I corrected proof of the Eremitism article which is coming out in the *Collectanea* (though I would have preferred otherwise. I don't want to appear to publicize solitude in the Order, or to be crusading for it! Quite the contrary, it is best that people in the order do not become excited about this issue and make another "problem" out of it).

Brother Basil (McMurry) left to try hermit life at Mount Saviour. I think he is too young and unprepared, but they have (surprisingly) given him a chance and I hope he makes it. But he has a lot to learn (precisely because he is very bright).

"Solitude" becomes for me less and less of a specialty, and simply "life" itself. I do not seek to "be a solitary" or anything else, for "being anything" is a distraction. It is enough to be, in an ordinary human mode, with only hunger and sleep, one's cold and warmth, rising and going to bed. Putting on blankets and taking them off (two last night. It is cold for June!). Making coffee and then drinking it. Defrosting the refrigerator, reading, meditating, working (ought to get on to the article on symbolism[3] today), praying. I live as my fathers have lived on this earth, until eventually I die. Amen. There is no need to make an assertion of my life, especially to assert it as MINE, though it is doubtless not somebody else's. I must learn to gradually forget program and artifice. I know this at least in my mind and want it in my heart, but my other habits of awareness remain strong.

June 22, 1965

Will say the Mass of St. Alban when I go down today (Day of recollection). Misty morning. Lots of noise from Boone's cows. Yesterday Father Matthew with his crazy little tractor cut the long grass in the field next [to]

[3] "Symbolism: Communication or Communion?" *Mountain Path* 3 (October 1966): 339–48.

the hermitage, and in order to do work that would not require too much concentration, did some texts of St. Maximus on non-violence, perhaps for *Catholic Worker*. May finish these today.

Father Timothy (and Barnabas) going to Rome, perhaps first of September. This means a change of undermasters and I am trying to persuade Dom James to get a new novice master at the same time, but he is reluctant, for no very solid reason. Insists that I wait till January 1. "Better psychology!" etc.

The Mass of St. Alban (*Laetabitur justus*) was fine, especially the Epistle.

There is a fantastic picture of McDevitt in space over the curve of the earth and the North American continent, with the Gulf of Mexico under him. There is no denying the greatness of their excitement, and though it is useless, perhaps it is the uselessness of great art. Who knows? In any event I see there is no sense in remaining blind to this: to be aware of all this "Space age" business is to realize the tremendous symbolic importance of it, whether for good or evil I don't know and maybe it is not for me to judge. There is the *fact* of these happenings and of all that goes into making them. Hugely impressed, too, by the enormous gantries of Cape Kennedy, and the astounding room where the instruments show where the spaceflight is. NO question of the greatness of all this: and does it have to be necessarily the greatness of "the Beast"? I don't know, whether or not it is, there is no sense in screaming about it. So perhaps I too will become cool.

June 23, 1965. Vigil of St. John Baptist

The monks had haircutting and it was announced that the choir professed could get rid of their crowns [the tonsure] if they wanted to and just have their heads completely shaved. The only ones who kept the crown were Dom Vital, Fathers Idesbald, Arnold, Raymond, Bernard, Vianney, Bede, David, Paul of the Cross and myself. Ten out of about fifty. I did not keep it for sentimental reasons, but because the community, including the brothers, was supposed to vote on it – and this decides the issue before it can be voted on.

Ernesto Cardenal sent his new booklet of poems ("*Oración for Marilyn Monroe,*" etc.), and they are very fine, simple, direct, with an extraordinary poetic sense of modern life seen with great innocence and clarity. Also some pages he wrote on my anti-bomb essays reprinted from *Papeles de son Armedans*. The Chuang Tzu manuscript goes off to New Directions today.

June 26, 1965

Yesterday, Feast of the Sacred Heart, was very cool and clear – in the early morning (as also today) it was more like September than June. Father Lawrence, my undermaster when I was in the novitiate twenty-three years ago, returned from the monastery in Georgia for a while. I could not recognize him – he is much fatter (was very gaunt then). The Feast of the Sacred Heart was for me a day of grace and seriousness. Twenty years ago I was uncomfortable with this concept. Now I see the real meaning of it (quite apart from the externals). It is the *center*, the "heart" of the whole Christian mystery.

There is one thing more – I may be interested in Oriental religions, etc., but there can be no obscuring the essential difference – this personal communion with Christ at the center and heart of all reality, as a source of grace and life. "God is love" may perhaps be clarified if one says that "God is void" and if in the void one finds absolute indetermination and hence absolute freedom. (With freedom, the void becomes fullness and o = ∞). All that is "interesting" but none of it touches on the mystery of personality in God, and His personal love for me. Again, I am void too – and I have freedom, or *am* a kind of freedom, meaningless unless oriented to Him.

The other day (St. John Baptist perhaps) after my Mass I suddenly thought of Ann Winser, Andrew's little sister. She was about twelve or thirteen when I used to visit him on the Isle of Wight, in that quiet rectory at Brooke. She was the quietest thing on it, dark and secret child. One does not fall in love with a child of thirteen, and I hardly remember even thinking of her. Yet the other day I realized that I had never forgotten her and with a sort of Burnt Norton feeling about the part of the garden I never went to, and that if I had taken another turn in the road I might have ended up married to Ann. Actually, I think she is a symbol of the true (quiet) woman I never really came to terms [with] in the world, and because of this there remains an incompleteness that cannot be remedied. The years in which I chased whores or made whores out of my girlfriends (no, that is too strong and also silly, besides there were plenty that I was too shy to sleep with) did nothing to make sense of my life on the contrary. When I came to the monastery, Ginny Burton was the symbol of the girl I ought to have fallen in love with but didn't (and she remains the image of one I really did love with a love of companionship not of passion).

There is now more of a possibility that the change in the novitiate may be made in September, and I move entirely to the hermitage then.

Reading Karl Stern's *Flight from Woman*. Some fascinating material (loaded word – *mater!*) especially in the chapter on Descartes. Back to the picture of McDevitt in space (now in color on our cloister board). Space flights are after all a rather expensive way of convincing oneself that one is free from mother. I see the beauty of the uselessness, and its *uselessness*. This space business will certainly never get anywhere, or not to any "where" that they may be thinking of. It will have momentous results, but how and in what – ? I don't think anyone yet really knows. But for me, precisely I see what matters is not space but earth. The Bible spoke of *Paradise* in the beginning (harmony of Heaven and Earth, Father, Mother) not of man coming down from a heaven of ideas in outer space. What are we trying to find? What number? Who are we trying to contact out there?

Real importance of Teilhard – his affirmation of the "holiness of matter." And this is the real reason for the deepest opposition to him. (My own opposition is to naive Teilhard*ism* – not to Teilhard de Chardin because I have not studied him enough. I like the *Divine Milieu* and find him personally a very sympathetic figure.)

June 27, 1965. Vigil of Saints Peter and Paul

Visit of Alexander Peloquin Saturday to talk about composing the Freedom Songs for a concert in the Fall. His ideas (as yet not very well defined) sound good. I was irritated with Dom James yesterday. In preparation for the vote on "the crowns" next Sunday, he seemed to be intent on making sure everyone, or the majority, went his way. Last week at the haircutting time he got himself an ambiguous crown, one that was barely visible, the rest of the hair being cropped fairly long, not close shaved. Friday or Saturday he had the lot shaved off and Sunday he declared that having not even a crown symbolized "the renunciation of everything" – it now being obvious that most of the community want no crown. Thus he (who previously was *for* the crown) now has the distinction of leading everyone in the direction in which they have in fact led him.

The whole thing is a bit comical, and I am foolish to let it make me feel annoyed by it. But since I kept the crown (in order to try to keep *some* meaning for the vote, which now can have none whatever), I think he was implicitly criticizing me and trying to cut me (and the minority) down to size. What size? As if we had any importance at all in the first place! It is the pettiness of it that irks me.

Gnats in the jakes. Distractions at prayer. Brother Job has made some "wine" which is not bad (but certainly not as strong as he claims). Brother

Clement is still in Europe. The *Critic* has asked for an article on Existentialism and I think I will do it.

June 29, 1965. Saints Peter and Paul

Yesterday after my Mass I was distracted (as I am more and more, lately) by the fear that in the next abbatial election I might be elected abbot. I certainly do not think this fear is entirely irrational, though perhaps it distracts me too deeply. It is certain that I am very much respected by the majority of the community. The fact that they should continue to listen to my conferences with real interest after so long, and go out of their way (sometimes) to hear them does mean something. The brothers are especially interested, though I think they are to some extent under an illusion. Illusion or not, they now have a vote and will vote for the next abbot. When this was announced (read at refectory) my neighbor Father Amandus was making signs to me: "You've had it!!"

On the other hand, more than ten years ago, providentially, I made a vow never to accept an abbatial election. The vow was approved by Dom James and Dom Gabriel, and Dom James immediately used it in the Genesee elections where the voting was going my way (I am glad he did, seeing the trouble Dom Walter had!). If I were elected I would certainly refuse. But the distraction begins – supposing for some reason I could not refuse? Suppose it was forced on me. In the first place, I don't think it can be. But anyway, suppose it is? At this point I get overwhelmed with depression and despair. I can hardly imagine a more impossible situation (among those that are likely to happen in my life as it is). I am profoundly disillusioned with the Cistercian life as it is now going. I am certainly willing to obey those who are running it, but to run a community myself would be inconceivable. I have no interest in the aims that would have to be mine. I would not want to let the monks down, but how could I possibly do anything for them? And how could I handle all the misfits and malcontents (except by throwing them all out!)? It seems to me that if I took the job, within three years the monastery would be in a state of collapse. But I think I would probably collapse myself in three months. And so the distraction goes – much anguish.

Finally at the conventual Mass, I was moved by the Gospel and introit ("When you are old they will bind you and lead you where you do not want to go") – and I was able at least to accept the idea in peace – supposing the job *were* really obviously God's will. I would try to take it in a spirit of trust and faith and forget myself. But in any case I think my vow would be respected and I have no real fears. The surrender brought me real peace.

What matters is not the job or the refusal, but simply God's will and His ways. His love is enough.

Another painful situation is coming up with Dom James. The *Collectanea* board of editors is supposed to meet in Belgium in September. I am on the board and they want me there since the magazine is in crisis. (Well might it be! It is awful.) So though I have told the editor (Father Charles Dumont) the situation, he is intent on getting me there. Dom James will undoubtedly do everything he can to prevent it, by fair means or . . . He is not always scrupulously fair in such matters! And the emotionalism, the illuminist arguments! I dread it! However, I may not even be involved in the mess – he may just squash the whole thing in a five-page letter to the General and there will not even be any discussion on my part which is fine with me. One simply can't talk rationally to the man on such an issue. There is no communication. Meanwhile Brother Clement has been over there for two months and he finished his business in Norway a month ago. Father Chrysogonus' leave has been extended once again, and so on.

Slight difficulty with a novice – the business man type – who does not take correction easily. Sunday on my walk I had to be in a place where of all things I saw him sauntering across the field with his shirt off and his pink belly in the sun. Told him not to, as nicely as I could, but he pouted about it. Should I try to explain all this to him? Is it any use? Once again, a problem of communication. If you try to tell him something like this he just goes into a silent sulk, and does not want to discuss anything. Think of having to run a whole monastery with dozens like that in it! (Actually this may have been unjust. He is more sensible and moderate than this would indicate. One must be careful of appearances!! They mislead.)

Got down to the monastery to find a vituperative letter of a postulant whom we rejected in December. Unfair treatment, we gave him the bum's rush, etc. Considering this letter I am very glad we *did* reject him! Also the other day – a letter from a paranoid who writes frequently. Now all are "cruelly taunting" her because she is compelled to scratch her secret parts. Poor thing!!

I was glad to get back to the healing silence of the hermitage, the tall pines, in the hollow where Brother Colman and the novices have been cleaning out the pine tops left by Andy Boone after his messy logging operation last Lent. Not all was bad in the monastery: a good letter from Donald Allchin at Pusey House, and a good sermon on the missions by Father Romanus. And a letter from Dame Christine [Van der Meer] at Oosterhout.

June 30, 1965

Hot damp weather – as befits this season! Yesterday, Saints Peter and Paul, was hot and great and there was a succession of thundershowers, one at dinner time, one in the early afternoon, one toward supper time. The second was longest and best, many clouds and heavy downpour, it filled all my buckets with washing water. During part of the time Andy Boone was here, trying to get leave to cut some more pine trees, and telling all sorts of tall stories about the old days about water witches and gold diviners (a gold diviner here could seem to divine nothing but Fort Knox), civil war guerrillas, Brother Pius' great strength, the monks getting iron from Gap Hill to make the bolts for the first building, etc.

After supper I went down to the monastery and took my turn on night watch, came back in dark summer woods (a few fireflies). At night there was another storm but I barely heard it.

July 2, 1965. Visitation

This morning I had a long morning at the hermitage. I did not go down to the monastery until 10 for concelebration. The early hours were cool, I did some reading on Bultmann, then decided to write an open letter to the American Bishops, about Schema 13 and the chapter under way.[4] The main event of the morning: Mother Angela [Collins], my friend in the Louisville Carmel (whom I have not seen much of since she was Prioress), wrote the other day that she was going South to Savannah to be Prioress of the Carmel there, to try to keep it from collapsing. I was expecting her plane, for the southbound planes out of Louisville – at least the ones to Atlanta and Florida, go right over here fairly low. (The ones from Chicago are very high.) I walked under the pines and soon the plane appeared on time and went over, very fast, a beautiful big new jet with wings almost as far back as the tail. It was really a beautiful sight, and as I had told her to look out for us, I suppose she saw the monastery and perhaps even picked out the hermitage, as I told her where to look. I was happy for her up there in the sky and was even moved. I was always quite fond of her. She was one of the few people I could talk to absolutely freely about my ideas and hopes for the solitary life, which to a great extent she shares, and which she completely understands. She is very frank about some things I needed to know (about Dom James) and very much of a support. I felt she was very much of a sister

---

[4] "An Open Letter to the American Hierarchy (Schema XIII and the Modern Church)," *Worldview* 8 (September 1965): 4–7.

to me, and am grateful for her. Will miss her, and hope she will write. One thing about Mother Angela – in the light of Karl Stern's book – is that she is perfectly *feminine* and not one of those male nuns!! But with plenty of feminine character and courage.

July 5, 1965

Yesterday, Fourth Sunday after Pentecost, a vote was taken in chapter on the tonsure and concelebration. All the professed brothers voted, which made it an historic occasion. There were ninety-eight votes for getting rid of the (medieval) monastic corona, twenty-nine for keeping it – I conclude that more brothers and juniors voted *for* it than choir professed who still had it. (The purpose of the vote was to determine what *all* the professed would have. Answer: shaved heads, no "crown"). This is all right with me because it is simpler and less pretentious. But because of the ambiguous way in which the vote was approached I technically "abstained" from voting by putting in both the white and the black balls. Concelebration every Sunday was accepted, but over forty were against it. Actually I think this too is a good idea and we will come to appreciate it. I have signed up for the first Sunday Concelebration, next Sunday.

Does my solitude meet the standard set by my approaching death? No. I am afraid it does not. That possibility which is most intimate, isolated, my own, cannot be shared or described. I cannot look forward to it as an experience I can analyze and share. It is not something to be understood and enjoyed. (To "understand" and "contemplate" it beforehand is a kind of imposture.) But the solitary life should partake of the seriousness and incommunicability of death. Or should it? Is that too rigid and absolute an ideal? The two go together. Solitude is not death, it is life. It aims not at living death but at a certain fullness of life. But a fullness that comes from honestly and authentically facing death and accepting it without care, i.e., with faith and trust in God. *Not* with any social justification: not with the reliance on an achievement which is approved or at least understood by others. Unfortunately, even in solitude, though I try not to (and sometimes claim not to) I still depend too much, emotionally, on being accepted and approved.

Now it is true that in my life, the witness of solitude may perhaps be significant. But there is a great danger here, and it is one of the points where I see my defenselessness, my weakness, my capacity to pretend, and to be untrue. To face my untruth in solitude in preparation for the awful experience of facing it irrevocably in death with no more hope in anything earthly, only in God (totally unseen!). To do this without appealing to others for reassurance that I am not so untrue after all. How do they know, one way or the other? Certainly enough is evident merely in this Journal to destroy me forever after I am dead. But that is the point: not to live as one who can be so "destroyed." This means, not ingeniously discovering infallible ways of being "true" in the eyes of others and of posterity (if any!) but of accepting my untruth in the untransferrable anguish that is characteristic of death and leaving all "justification" to God. Everything else is only wrath, flame, torment, and judgment.

The greatest "comfort" (and a legitimate one, not an evasion) is to be sought precisely in the Psalms which face death as it is, under the eye of God, and teach us how we may face it – and bring us at the same time into contact, rather communion, with all those who have so seen death and accepted it. Most of all the Lord Himself who prayed from Psalm 21 on the Cross.

July 9, 1965

Today is the Feast of Saints Thomas More and John Fisher. I will say their Mass (from the common, anyway). Am supposed to go to Louisville, and am to ride in with the Abbot from New Zealand [Southern Star Abbey], a big, earnest, modest Irishman, Dom Joachim [Joseph] Murphy, who is very intently seeking answers, and is still on his way home from the General Chapter. Difficulties of the New Zealand foundation – earthquakes, drought, etc. And all the usual difficulties of Cistercian communities – tensions, etc. He has a "hermit problem." I suppose everyone will have a "hermit problem" soon. That is, every community. He seems willing to have a hermitage. I told him, assured him, that I was not pushing the hermit idea for many and believed few in our Order would really want it. He spoke considerately of Parkminster and of Cistercians who had gone there. Spoke well of the Carmelites in Christchurch.

From the way Dom James talks, it seems he will probably be willing to make the change of novice masters when Father Timothy goes to Rome in September. In which case I will finally be up here for good, and will begin the real adaptation to solitude. Even sleeping here, etc. is still only a halfway solution. To finally cut the tie, no job, no "place" in the community. This will be momentous. And then the whole question of mail, of publication, etc. arises, but I think this will solve itself.

My one real difficulty with faith is in really accepting the truth that the Church is a *redeemed community* not only juridically, but so that in fact to follow the mind of the Church is to be free from the mentality of the fallen society. Ideally I see this. But in fact there is so much that is *not* redeemed, and that seems to get into the thinking of those who represent the Church. To my mind the idea of officially approving the bomb in Schema 13 is not exactly a convincing demonstration of holiness and guidance by the Spirit. I wonder what they will really do. Actually I must do much more praying and thinking about this question of the Church and see it more in depth than I do. Certainly I cannot accept a merely individualistic Christianity (authenticity for individuals, not for the Christian community); on the other hand, too external a view of the Church would be wrong. Who really is she, this Spouse of Christ, "so bright and clear"? I know she is the Catholic Church. But then . . . ? The life of Newman, which still goes on in the refectory is to me inexhaustibly important and full of meaning. The whole thing is there, existentially not explicit, but there for the grasping. The reality is on his kind of obedience and his kind of refusal. Complete obedience to the Church and complete, albeit humble, refusal of the pride and chicanery of Churchmen.

Evening – the sun is going down on what was evidently a day of peace. Rode in to Louisville with Bernard Fox and Dom Joachim Murphy, after saying the Mass of St. Thomas More, etc. (Common – *Sapientiam*) at the memento of the living, besides offering the Mass for my friends and particularly Jim Wygal. I also suddenly got the idea of including "anyone I may meet by surprise today." In the bookstore at the University of Louisville, I had been there about five minutes, I heard someone talking French. Turned around. They were three students from France who had just that moment arrived, having walked all the way from the Greyhound Station. What they were doing in the bookstore neither they nor I knew. They had been sent over on some exchange, had come a week early, no one had been notified, no arrangements were made for them, they knew no one, etc., etc. They had seen the man in charge of the project, and something was being done, however.

They were from Montpellier – students at the university. One from Agen in fact. We went and had some coffee and talked. It was very enjoyable, interesting, intelligent talk, people from home!! I invited them out to the Abbey, and perhaps they will come. There are some nineteen others whom I did not see. (They were wandering around and these three did not know where to begin looking for them.) The thing about the encounter was whether or not they got anything out of it, it was a revelation of Christ to *me* – just because they were human, open, frank, sincere, interested in ideas, and in a situation where they were fully exposed to risk and possibility. A meeting of possibilities resulting in new ideas, new directions for all of us (in a small way at least). The theology of "encounter" is not just a phrase. What else is the Acts of the Apostles? The whole life of the Christian is "The Acts of the Apostles."

From this has come the answer to the question about the Church as a "redeemed society." Socially in what sense? Merely organization? The scene of encounter, the peace of openness, where possibilities are kept free and clear, where the word can be spoken (not according to a predetermined pattern or clever manipulation, but simply *spoken*). And where it is spoken, there is the eschatological event, the freedom of grace, a freedom that breaks through all the artificialities of predetermination and prejudice and in fact acts right across all the accepted patterns of society. Yet not without some help from society (language, common aspirations, shared experience, etc.).

Tonight, reading Bultmann in the hermitage, was quite luminous. I see now, clearly, that a "gnostic" approach is inauthentic because not existentialist – it simply presupposes a cosmic presence and a substantial ground which one contacts or not by awareness (it makes not much difference). No! It is word and event. And mere "sitting" and "recollection" are not enough (though they have their place) – by themselves they lead to no decision, no overturning, no renunciation of one's precious "wisdom" in exchange for the foolishness of the Cross, in which is pure light. I would not have seen this now if I had not seen it before, but now much more conclusively. And the effect is conclusive too, for the hermitage. Meanwhile I realize how good and simple a friend Jim Wygal is too, after all, and I have been interiorly, to some extent, foolishly intolerant of some of his limitations – as if such things were of any importance whatever, especially since he is aware of them and humbled by them!

If I had thought less of wrath in those days, I would perhaps be less aware of this blessing. And all is blessing, even wrath!

July 11, 1965

Yesterday the new anthology by Paris Leary and Robert Kelly arrived. *Controversy of Poets.* Ambiguous title, good anthology, in fact it strikes me as one of the best and I am certainly glad to be in it.[5] Found a lot of new people I

---

5   Seven poems by Merton appeared in this volume, published by Doubleday (Anchor) in 1965.

had never heard of but like. Especially a fine long poem by Galway Kinnell about the Lower East Side. A good one on Kennedy's funeral by Georgia Lee McElhaney. (How would you pronounce it?) I like the abstract dances of Jackson Mac Low, and Jack Spicer's poem on the death of Billy the Kid. Diane Wakoski, O.K. Gary Snyder I had heard of but not read. Like his poems, they are more substantial because of Zen, not just poured out. Reading [Allen] Ginsberg's long ether-sniffing poem from Lima, have concluded *for* Ginsberg, it is a good poem and one must take Ginsberg on his own terms. I defy the cowards who bully Ginsberg. Jonathan Williams I knew before. Liked "Blues for Lonnie Johnson" and great atomic stuff in the Blake-like poem ["In England's Green and (A Garland and a Clyster)"]. Maybe Jonathan Williams best in the book. I'll get to know later. Denise Levertov always good. And [Lawrence] Ferlinghetti also. I liked the underwear poem and the Castro ["One Thousand Fearful Words for Fidel Castro"] I saw before.

July 12, 1965

Yesterday the regular Sunday concelebrations began. It makes sense to concelebrate on the Lord's Day and though in many ways I do not "like" it I see that this is best, and will sign up for it. There is no question that this makes far more sense than the old way (private Mass, then High Mass) for here the community *all* assembles, and most go to communion, and guests are there, etc. My difficulties are not with the principle or the idea, but still with the way we do it, and our apparent attitude. But this is of no real importance. Yet yesterday I was miserable over something, hard to say what. I concelebrated, but could not get any conviction that it was real. I suppose the real root is my deep distrust of Dom James (who is of course principal celebrant) and my profound disagreement with him, my inability to believe him. To stand up and affirm my "unity" with him seems like a damned lie, to say it frankly. And yet I suppose that is precisely why we should concelebrate. Because I *am* united with my Abbot in will and obedience, though not in agreement. Yet the situation is *not* healthy, and for that reason I still have a doubt about habitual concelebration.

To concelebrate in such circumstances is to be "under judgment" and "under wrath" (yet mercy, for accepting the wrath). Should I simply accept the wrath and contradiction? The question is – where is the wrong? Am I being untrue to God by affirming something I should not try to affirm? I think not. I think the unity of the Church comes first and that my affirmation of unity with a Superior by whom I feel myself exploited and harmed (though he has been very "kind" in God knows how many ways!) is an affirmation of unity with the Church, of willingness to be under the wrath which I see, not merely to criticize it and complain of it. I am part of it. I cannot stand outside and say "I am not like this Dom James, an operator, complex, inauthentic." It is good that concelebration should bring this out. I can see there is need for more! I am shamed by the evident faith and joy of the others!

Concelebration again, a theological ambiguity (existentially). Can I say that by this affirmation of unity I am delivered from the "powers of this world," the "elements" of Paul! When in fact for many in the community concelebration has a "political" cast, being an expression of "political" progress in community affairs and is the result of charity, yes, but also of an implicit "deal" an adjustment between abbot and members, in line with a "political" propaganda theme discernible in the Church (and in presence of the world) as a symbol of the Church's will to survive as a definite power and influence in the modern world. Is it an affirmation that "we count" (or want to) in the eyes of, and in the context of, a political universe?

This is probably neurotic hairsplitting, but the question presents itself.

July 14, 1965

A very busy day (after a quiet, long day at the hermitage yesterday). In the morning Father Peter came in (without formal permission) to talk of a vocation problem (sixty-seven years old, twenty-seven years in the monastery!) and it is a sad problem, not so much because there is not something that can be done, as because they insist on treating him as an infant and as a nuisance, for whom there is but one remedy: keep him locked up here, and let him do the best he can to keep himself from going nuts by any expedient he pleases (lately – taming birds). In a way it is sad and cruel. He has gone all the way to Rome (by letter) to get another impersonal and unconcerned "no," which should not have been necessary. Dom James with all his best intentions *cannot* deal directly and frankly with such a case and there is really no way of doing so, in the framework we have here. What Peter needs is simply a vacation. But that would hurt the precious reputation of Gethsemani. So he can rot here instead, incidentally disturbing a lot of other people in the process. I feel very sorry for him. I also think Dom James does what he can – but that is no solution. Is there a solution?

In the afternoon: Jim Douglass and his wife, Sally, and Father John Loftus came out. We went up to Dom Frederic's lake and sat under the young loblolly pines and drank cokes. Some local kids were swimming in the lake.

It was cloudy, but did not rain until supper time. There is still much talk of Pope Paul coming to the United Nations in September. I gave Jim the copies of La Pira's letters to Robert Kennedy. La Pira is working earnestly for disarmament – not much sign of this country disarming. The Vietnam war has shown the complete stupidity of Johnson in a way that everyone can see except the average American! Jim says the polls are running 70% in favor of the war, and that is all that matters! A fiction of self-generating public opinion, which justifies everything.

Came back to the hermitage, not feeling like going to bed. Mist over the field after rain. Diffuse sound of crickets in the dusk. I sat on the porch and the strange owl-like cry of a frightened deer came from the field. I saw the white tail bounding away in the mist. Nine o'clock rings. I had better think of going to bed.

July 17, 1965. Our Lady of Carmel

This is the patronal feast of the hermitage. The alarm clock worked for a change. I had a good meditation, the morning is quiet, high clouds in the south slowly parading Eastward with their faintly sunlit peaks (sun hidden by clouds still low in the east). Yesterday (which is Carmel's feast elsewhere) I did not get in the concelebration but took the day in the hermitage and woods, and must admit I feel saner and more peaceful for it. This is not to be taken as a statement of principle – only a fact, in my present circumstances.

Bultmann's inadequate notions of the Church. Good to see clearly where his existentialism falls short of genuine Christianity. This is of course a danger for me too. There is no question I think individualistically, to a great extent. But I also realize the insufficiency of this. At the same time a superficial inadequate communal spirit will only make things worse for me, not better. There is no question of the deep inauthenticity of the common life in this monastery, in most religious communities, and in the Church. It is due in part to the way authority is conceived and exercised (to the great psychological and spiritual harm of many) and to the fact that this can hardly be remedied as matters stand (at least here). The "new" approach, however, seems to me to be equally inauthentic, for reasons that are more obscure. I think the relationships set up are based more on insecurities and superficial needs than on the Spirit and on faith. They do not spell authenticity. In Ellul's *Propagandes* there are good reasons why. What is happening is not unity in the Spirit so much as a "propaganda for integration," and the participation of which all are so proud tends to be really a concerted and determined complicity in mutual persuasion – a kind of liberal triumphalism making itself come true.

I finished the article on Zen Monasticism[6] yesterday (really the day before – edited the long quote from Sekiso yesterday early). It seems to me to be a fairly good article – and it meant much to me when I was writing it. Father Charles English, one of the censors of *Chuang Tzu*, wrote that he liked the manuscript so much that he wants to keep it and use it for a while. I was consoled by this, for I had been tempted to think all this was useless for any but myself and a few oddballs like me. But perhaps it can reach many more. Father Charles of course is an intellectual too, so I suppose his reaction is not too surprising or representative. But from the reactions of novices, etc. I realize there is a great need for this element of recalling men to their selves, and they are not finding this easily in Catholic writings today, at least not in this particular form. Letters from Etta Gullick, about the same thing in England. The Catholics she (an Anglican) reaches with her ideas on prayer.

"An important part of the witness of the Church, or in other words an important way of proclaiming the Word must be simply a manifestation within the Christian community of a spirit of fellowship and love which cannot be found outside it," writes McQuarrie in his critique of Bultmann (*Existential Theology*, p. 221). He recognizes organization as a "problem." Love is least in evidence when the Church is most organized, perhaps most in evidence when Christians were driven into deserts or catacombs. (This is a concession he makes.) He also admits the Church can usurp what rightly belongs to the person and make all his decisions for him (or try to). (Why the question of the bomb is an "exposed nerve" in the whole problem of renewal.) Here is where the Bishops (especially American) want to decide the whole question of war, etc. beforehand, instead of letting the faithful come to their own conclusions as the situation develops.

July 18, 1965. Sixth Sunday after Pentecost
There is a special peace and sense of blessing on Sunday morning, though all mornings are equally quiet here (at hermitage) and the same birds always sing. This special peace is sensible even when there are no signs of Sunday – such as the faint Mass bell from the village church in New Hope, across the valley! Today the peace is even greater because of the storm and

[6] "Zen Buddhist Monasticism," *Mystics and Zen Masters* (New York: Farrar, Straus & Giroux, 1969): 215–34.

cleansing in the night. A very violent thunderstorm broke about 1, with continual lightning and uninterrupted thunder for about an hour. I slept through one of these a few weeks ago but not this one. Lightning touched the riser of my electrical system and was grounded, but I felt the click of it through the whole house, and even felt as if electricity were coming out of my feet (in bed).

Seeing more and more that my understanding of myself and of my life has always been most inadequate. Now that I want more than ever to see, I realize how difficult it is. Though there is danger, doubtless, in solitude, I realize more than ever that here, for me, is confrontation with the word, and with God, and with the only possibilities that are fully real, or with those that are most real. (There is something real after all in community, but more and more, as I go down there, I have the sense that reality is smothered there and words are substituted for it.) Yet my job and that of the Church remains this: to awaken in myself and in others the sense of real possibility, of truth, of obedience to Him who is Holy, of refusal of pretenses and servitudes – without arrogance and hubris and specious idealism. The terrible thing is that our society that pretends to be Christian is in fact rejecting the word of God, enabled to do so by the all-pervading suffocating noise of its own propaganda, able to make itself believe whatever it wants. This is a deluding, fanatical, stupid society. It is under judgment – and what can one say to it? It would be useless to pretend to be perfect, for no one, as far as I can see, is "sent" with any prophetic message. Least of all I – best I can do is the feeble attempt of the notes on Schema 13, etc. to the *Commonweal*, Bishop Wright, Archbishop Flahiff and others.

July 19, 1965

Big jet liner coming down toward Louisville in the dawn sky, beautiful great fish with an enormous tail fin and a long body which (at one moment only) caught under itself the clear bronze gold glint of sunrise. Then it slid on down behind my black pines.

Yesterday I went to talk to Father Abbot about Father Peter, who is getting through his crisis by suddenly doing everything in the community he has not done for years. Reader this week, hebdomadary next, etc. He is coming to choir in his rank and this turn[s] out to be next to me – a quivering, sensitive, tormented presence. Another disturbed monk, Brother B., was also very upset in infirm[ary] refectory at dinner, making signs to me about too much mockery. He would not stand for it. (Nobody ever mocks him.)

I will have to see the proctologist this week. Painful, unpleasant business, quite sore. I suppose this is part of being fifty.

However, when I went to Father Abbot after chapter about these things, he ended by saying that on August 20, Feast of St. Bernard, he would make the change in the novitiate and I would be free to be in the hermitage all the time, with no further responsibility except to give *one* conference a week in the novitiate (Sunday). Father Baldwin is to be the new novice master. Father Timothy will go to Rome soon after that. This was a very pleasant surprise and I was jubilant about it and very moved and grateful. Things like this make me ashamed of my fears and worries and my decision, as this, after all, is really remarkable and shows that he is not merely a politician. It is a most unusual step in the order and one he could not possibly have taken two years ago. Hence he is certainly not guided merely by his own likes and dislikes, his own preferences and fears, and he does really pay attention more than many others, to objective indications of what God wants for His Church. Easy to say this when he gives me something I want. But it has been the same with the new liturgy, etc. Here he has given up stronger repugnancies than he might have had to solitude in the Cistercian life (to which he is personally attracted). Concelebration after that was a moving, humbling and consoling experience, and I think I will have no more of my foolish feelings about it. Thank God for enough light to see my childishness.

Afternoon in the very quiet hollow behind the hermitage. A few apothegmata. Thinking seriously about the change that is to come, and is so momentous for me. One of the greatest mercies of God in my whole life! And the answer to so many prayers, yet one sees here that everything has really been leading directly to this even when it appeared to be hopeless. How happy I am that I stayed on the path where I was all along, and did not succeed in getting off it. (Though by God's grace my efforts to get off the path were just what kept me most truly on it, and if I had not tried to go elsewhere I would certainly not be in this hermitage now! I do not propose this as a working formula for everyone!)

In the evening began a perpetual Psalter – a necessity – not to say a given quantity any period of time, but just to keep the Psalter going from now on until I die (or can no longer do it). Need for the continuity the Psalter offers – continuity with my own past and with the past of eremitism. The Latin psalter is for me! It is a deep communion with the Lord and His saints, of my Latin Church. To be in communion with the Saints of *my* tradition is by that fact to be more authentically in communion with those of the Greek, Syriac, etc. traditions, who reach me through my own Fathers.

Important note from Ellul on Propaganda. A Mass-man is an individualist who has broken away from the small group and is in direct confrontation with Mass-society. The Mass-man is an individualist alone in the Mass. If one simply breaks away from a religious community and then remains in contact with the world through Mass Media – e.g. TV, radio – one can be a Mass-man in thinking oneself a hermit, i.e., one's solitude is not in the presence of God, or even in the Church, but in Mass society. No danger of this for me here, I think. But it is something to consider. More important, though – this type of mentality in the community itself, the alienated monks, not in full contact with his brothers, is "alone" in the abstract "community" which makes his decisions for him. An awful and empty solitude that has little meaning, but it is what some of them encourage! In such a situation, the uprooted individual is supposed to assume all the obligations of a mature, well-rooted spiritual freedom, and this is impossible. Why so many leave.

July 20, 1965

St. Elias today. He has something to do with it! He is in it!

Great peace for the last couple of days, since the decision. Any day one could write "great peace" but this is a very special and new dimension of peace: a tranquillity that is not got by cultivation. It is given, and "not as the world gives do I give unto you." The peace is not "it" but confrontation with Thou. Here Buber is certainly right. Confrontation with "Thee" in this word of solitude. All because this one word, yesterday. All unified in this. One will, one command, one gift. A new creation of heavenly simplicity. I will write little about this, surely. Enough.

"If a man hears Tao in the morning and dies in the evening, his life has not been wasted." I think now I really see what this means.

July 21, 1965

Went in to see Dr. Ryan. Actually things had already begun to get a little better, and he relieved the discomfort considerably. I had a certain amount of free time, read a good article on Ecology in *Daedalus*. Had an excellent lunch at the Old House (since Dr. Ryan gave me a Mass stipend!). The day and the drive were pleasant. As usual, the only darkening came from the news magazines in the doctor's office, including an appalling rape case in *Newsweek*, some weeks ago, in Los Angeles. The Vietnam war is taken for granted though there is vocal opposition (misguided liberals, "communist inspired," etc.). Tragic in Vietnam itself, and here nonsensical, complacent, vulgar, morally illiterate. Actually much of the news, most of it, was no news at all – fabricated. (A dialogue between McNamara and a Marine Colonel in Vietnam, etc.) Or else the usual scoresheet. So many of ours dead, so many of "theirs" estimated dead – estimated because our side drops tons of bombs on wide areas of people and hopes someone will get hit. Or else bombs cities in North Vietnam. Not yet cities as such, but targets which may be in or near them. The turn of cities as cities will eventually come. The news reports read now like those in the first nine months of World War II.

July 25, 1965

Very hot Friday and Saturday (the first really oppressive summer weather we have had in this extraordinary season). Last evening I was too torpid to pray seriously but hung around trying. Made orangeade for supper and put it in the freezer thereby accidentally discovering how to make rather good sherbet. Storm all night after 11. Slept through most of it. They still continue half-heartedly now in the morning 7:15. Since it rains I do not go down to Prime, will go later for concelebration.

Reading [Søren] Kierkegaard – selections from *The Present Age*. Very fine and completely prophetic. One of the best and in some sense most hopeful treatments of the individual in mass-society. "It is in fact through error that the individual is given access to the highest if he courageously drinks it . . ." The communication of the "cosmic" in the naked exposure of the individual, without mediation, to "pure humanity." (Can lead to liberation in naked exposure to word of God.) With regard to myself I seek only to pay this high price (far from doing it, we are trained in this!!). And for others – not to "help" them to escape it.

July 27, 1965

Today I tried out the schedule that I hope to follow when I am in the hermitage all day: that is, only going down to the monastery to say Mass and have dinner. I had at first thought of going down for Mass after Prime and then going to the conventual Mass, coming up and going down again for dinner. But I see this is really not practical.

Today I went down late, about 11, and said Mass at 11:30, came back up again after dinner, and that was it. It was a perfect day. Not to run back and forth to the monastery is certainly a blessing. I felt as if a great load had been lifted off me, and in the late afternoon, saying office before supper, I realized that a complete, total and solid peace had settled completely upon me – a happiness without afterthought and without reflection. "All things are yours and you are Christ's – and Christ is God's. If we live, we live unto God, if we die, we die unto God – whether we live or die, we are God's possession." What more could anyone ask? But I don't think for me such things could be fully experienced short of this solitude!

Fine letter from John Wu who is very pleased with the introduction to *Chuang Tzu*. Finished first draft of the existentialism article[7] for the *Critic* – thank God I have that out of the way. Now I have nothing to do but set things in order, clear out a lot of books and get ready to move entirely out of the novitiate, at the end of August.

July 28, 1965

Some schedule. With this one had time to know the meaning of freedom! And to taste, with all certainty, that free is what one is intended to be. For this one was created and redeemed. This particular form, solitude, is that for which I am "intended." Or perhaps if that is not an accurate way to speak, it certainly contains within itself the possibilities to which I am open.

How men fear freedom! And how I have learned to fear it myself! I know that in fact, without faith, this would be a different matter, this living alone. But with faith it becomes an eschatological gift. I have never before really seen what it means to live in the new creation and in the Kingdom. Impossible to explain it. If I tried I would be unfaithful to the grace of it – for I would be setting limits to it. It is *limitless*, without determination, without definition. It is what you make of it each day, in response to the Holy Spirit!

I am not even disturbed at the thought that when I call Dr. Ryan today (according to instructions) he may want me in the hospital for a few days. Who cares? It is God's will and His call. The same freedom is everywhere. It is not limited to places. Yet solitude, these pines, this mist, are the chosen locus of freedom in my own life.

August 6, 1965

Returned to hermitage today after a week in St. Anthony's hospital. In a way it was trying, at least a test of patience. Had to rest, take medicine and sit in a room with machinery going outside – and with an air conditioner on day and night. At least the even noise of the air conditioner neutralized the

---

[7] "The Other Side of Despair: Notes on Christian Existentialism," *The Critic* 24 (October-November 1965): 13–23.

heavy traffic on Barret Avenue and I was astounded to find myself sleeping nine hours a night!! Evidently it was something I needed, that and the diet, because my stomach calmed down. And I suppose I enjoyed it in a way – saying the new Mass (we don't have English at Gethsemani yet except for the Brothers), reading a lot. (Finished the Tom Wolfe *Kandy Kolored*, etc. book, a Herman Wouk novel, some Bultmann on New Testament, a book on Buddhism, Nietzsche's *Birth of Tragedy*, a couple of pages of Aeschylus, and Euripides' *Iphigenia in Tauris*.) Got some work done – finished the galleys of *Seasons of Celebration* and made a few additions. Revised the bit on Schema 13. About this I got a good letter from Archbishop Flahiff who sent the new texts of the Articles on war.

Sister Colleen lovely and friendly and Sister Franciscana the Superior super kind and very sweet, bringing in newspapers and even a box of candy. The sisters and nurses were lovely, through and through, so I enjoyed so much "tender love and care." I admit it! Tried to keep my presence quiet but Dr. Bizot was lector at my Sunday Mass, Jack Ford came in, Dr. Roser, etc.

Today drove home with Jim Wygal through winding county roads, Taylorsville, Bloomfield, etc. after a good dinner at the Old Stone Inn out beyond Anchorage (Simpsonville or some such name). It was awfully good to get back to the silence of the monastery and especially of the hermitage (freshly painted by Brother John of the Cross to fill in all the cracks).

Two weeks until the big change!

August 10, 1965. St. Laurence

The days since returning from hospital have been difficult. My stomach continued to be upset for a couple of nights. Had trouble readjusting to normal after a week of strong medicine and sleeping pills. Letters to write. Awareness that I cannot catch up with the backlog of mail. Proofs of *Chuang Tzu* suddenly came (an absurd accumulation of books this Fall, this must be straightened out). Because *Gandhi* was delayed, three books are scheduled for publication in four months. Farrar, Straus and Giroux wants to bring out *Seasons of Celebrations* early in December. I think *Chuang Tzu* ought to wait until spring!

The solitary life: now that I really confront it it is awesome, wonderful, and I see I have no strength of my own for it. Deep sense of my own poverty, and above all, awareness of the wrongs I have allowed in myself together with this good desire. This is all good. I am glad to be shocked by grace and to wake up in time to see the great seriousness of it. I have been merely playing at this, and the solitary life does not admit of mere play. Contrary to all that is said about it, I do not see how the really solitary life can tolerate illusion and self-deception. It seems to me that solitude rips off all the masks and all the disguises. It does not tolerate lies. Everything but straight and direct affirmation is marked and judged by the silence of the forest. "Let your speech be Yea! Yea!"

(I am frightened by the awful clarity of Anselm's argument in *De Casu Diaboli*. A view of liberty that is essentially monastic, i.e., framed in the perspective of an entirely personal vocation and grace.) The need to *pray* – the need for solid theological food, for the Bible, for monastic tradition. Not experimentation or philosophical dilettantism. The need to be entirely defined by a relationship with and orientation to God my Father, i.e., a life of sonship in which all that distracts from this relationship is seen as fatuous and absurd. How *real* this is! A reality I must constantly measure up to, it cannot be simply taken for granted. It cannot be lost in distraction. Distractedness here is fatal – it brings one inexorably to the abyss. But no concentration is required, only *being present*. And also working seriously at all that is to be done – the care of the garden of paradise! By reading, meditation, study, psalmody, manual work, including also some fasting, etc. Above all the work of *hope*, not the stupid, relaxed, self-pity of *acedia* [sloth].

The great need to honor God by personal truth, and trust, in the personal grace of solitude. ". . . *iustitia sive rectitudo voluntatis. . . . Hic est solus et totus honor, quem debemus Deo et haec est satisfactio, quam omnis peccator Deo debet facere.*" [". . . justice or the rightness of the will. . . . This is the sole and complete honor which we owe to God . . . that is satisfaction which every sinner ought to make to God."]

(Anselm, Cur Deus Homo? [Schmitt II, pp. 68–69])

In John Wu's Zen manuscript – this beautiful poem of Tung Shan.

> For whom have you stripped yourself of your gorgeous dress?
> The cuckoo's call is urging all wanderers to return home.
> Even after all the flowers have fallen it will continue its call
> In the thicket of the wood, among the jagged peaks.

August 11, 1965

"When you are serving others you are apt to be a hypocrite; but when you are serving heaven it is difficult to be a hypocrite." This is Suzuki paraphrasing a line of Chuang Tzu. It applies perfectly to the solitary life.

However, I have been completing this kind of view with others, the clear, reasonable, logical yet mystical little tract of Catherine of Siena, *Dialogo Breve sulla Consumata Perfezione* (which actually comes to the same thing – seeking nothing but to do God's will in everything, to please Him alone, to be perfectly united to Him in love by the renunciation of our own will). And Anselm's *rectitudo – stare in veritate* [standing in the truth]. It all comes to the same, but the approach is different, and I am still strongly devoted to medieval reason and wisdom.

August 12, 1965. St. Clare

The one point on which I most profoundly disagree with the Barthians is that of "natural theology." Our very creation itself is a beginning of revelation. Making us in His image, God reveals Himself to us, we are already His words to ourselves! Our very creation itself is a vocation to union with Him and our life, and in the world around us, if we persist in honesty and simplicity, cannot help speaking of Him and of our calling. But the trouble is that there are no "pure" natural traditions and everything gets overlaid with error. Still, there is truth there for those who are still able to seek it, even if they are few. Ought it to be called "theology"? That is a technical question. Certainly it implies – and can develop – a definite personal relationship to God in faith (of the *Proslogion*). Barth's interest in Anselm is very revealing.

Yesterday, Father [William] Johnston, a Jesuit from Sophia University, Tokyo, was here, talking of Zen, Father Dumoulin, Father Enomiya Lasalle, etc. He brought a new book on Zen with a lot of rich new material in it ([Philip] Kapleau's *Three Pillars of Zen*). I am slowly moving the mountain of books from the novice master's room to the library (novices do the carrying).

August 13, 1965

The joy that I am *man!* This fact, that I am a man, is a theological truth and mystery. God became man in Christ. In the becoming what I am He united me to Himself and made me His epiphany, so that now I am meant to reveal Him, and my very existence as true man depends on this, that by my freedom I obey His light, thus enabling Him to reveal Himself in me. And the first to see this revelation is my own self. I am His mission to myself and through myself to all men. How can I see Him or receive Him if I despise or fear what I am – man? How can I love what I am – man – if I hate man in others?

The mere fact of my manness should be an everlasting joy and delight. To take joy in that which I am made to be by my Creator, is to open my heart to restoration by my Redeemer. And it is to taste the first fruits of redemption and restoration. So pure is the joy of being man that those whose Christian understanding is weak may even take this to be the joy of being something other than man – an angel or something. But God did not become an angel. He became *man*.

August 14, 1965. *Vigil of the Assumption*

Yesterday I was busy most of the day trying to clean out novice master's office, sort out what to keep and what to throw away, etc. And when I did get up to the hermitage for part of the afternoon, Brother Clement showed up, and stayed about an hour talking about his European trip (interesting! The Irish Derby – driving a Mercedes through Germany, traveling around Norway, etc.). The insane accumulation of books, notes, manuscripts, letters, papers in the novice master's room simply appalls me. Trying to sort it out upsets my stomach. This is really a symptom of something – certainly of a kind of alienation. It is true most of it is stuff I receive gratis without having asked for it, and set it aside to read "sometime later" – and of course forget about it. Yet there is much I have asked for impulsively and got by pull from the publishers – and never read yet. This and the anxiety which tears my gut, and the writing of letters, etc., etc. is certainly a type of a real deep conflict, one I have not yet fully faced – a fear of being without support, substituting papers and books for personal relations, etc.

Certainly I must expect this to come out in the hermitage (and I must not accumulate so much junk up here!!). But I know more and more, "in silence and hope shall my strength be" if I can only develop a silence of printed words, or words possessed and accumulated (mere shit). But the first step in this is to *read seriously* the good things that are there and when I do this there is an immediate change for the better, a sense of presence, a recovering of reality, etc. I shall not forget the awful, automatic worried routine of piling up books, sorting papers, tearing some up, mailing them out, etc. It is not finished yet.

August 17, 1965

Yesterday, finally, I practically finished cleaning out, sorting, throwing away, sending to library, etc., etc. I wonder how many wastepaper baskets I have filled in the last week? And with this absurd ritual of wastepaper has gone a rending of the intestines, diarrhea at night, angst, etc. The revelation of futility and interminable self-contradiction. What a poor being I am. If I try to conceive myself as, on top of all this, "being a hermit" absurdity reaches its culmination. Yet I am convinced that I am on the right way. That to turn back is infidelity and sin (there simply *is* no turning back) and that in all this is hidden joy. Nor is it always hidden because I experience it, and powerfully. Not only in the silence of the early morning but also in the hot, muggy afternoon which in these days is tropical.

"Knowledge of the Spirit as Comforter adorns only the supreme points of affliction," says Norossky. My supreme affliction is to see my unbelief, my distrust of the Lord, my refusal to let myself go in hope. But to see this at last is also a joy. And I can begin to hope He will cure and transform me. I got a very fine letter from Naomi [Burton Stone] in answer to one of mine admitting my own confusion and self-contradiction. Full of mature realistic understanding, and feminine comfort – the warmth that cannot come from a man, and that is so essential. Psychologically, my doubt is based in this giant, stupid rift in my life, the *refusal* of woman which is a fault in my chastity (and in the chastity of so many religious!). But I am learning to accept this love (of Naomi, for instance) even if it means admitting a certain loss. (Chastity is in fact my most radical poverty, and my un-poverty in accumulating things is a desperate and useless expedient to cover this irreparable loss which I have not fully accepted. – I can learn to accept it in the Spirit and in love, and it will no longer be "irreparable." The Cross repairs it and transforms it.)

The tragic chastity which suddenly realizes itself to be mere loss and fears that death has won – that one is sterile, useless, hateful. I do not say this is my lot, but in my vow I can see this as an ever present possibility. To make a vow is to be exposed to this possibility. It is the risk one must run in seeking the other possibility, the revelation of the Paraclete to the pure heart!

August 18, 1965

Yesterday morning there was a meeting of the private council, to vote to approve of Father Baldwin as the new novice master. Then I left and they voted (favorably) on my retirement to the hermitage. The first time such a decision has been taken in the house! At least as far as I know.

In the evening at Vespers I realized again how much I will miss the sung office and the Gregorian psalmody, hymns and antiphons. Yet one must face the fact that the traditional office is over with, and will soon go, to be replaced by a new vernacular office. They may doubtless succeed in keeping a somewhat Gregorian spirit. I have an antiphoner in the hermitage, and can occasionally sing things that mean so much to me – for instance yesterday afternoon and evening I had the 1st-tone Magnificat antiphon for Easter Monday running through my head. Today, the Magnificat antiphon for Christmas Eve and the Christmas Invitatory.

August 20, 1965. St. Bernard

In Hebrews XI, after speaking of all the faith and suffering of former saints, the writer concludes: "All these having borne witness to the faith, did not receive what was promised, because God foresaw something better for us, that apart from us they should not be made perfect" (11:[39–]40). Entering upon the new way, I think especially of this: that from part of the promise and fulfillment for which others have suffered and hoped: and in turn I will suffer and prepare the way for others. In leaving immediate contact with people and society I enter into this other close-knit society of witnesses. I am very aware of their presence.

I go down to chapter for the last time (normally) and Father Timothy will preach his first sermon (then leave for Rome Wednesday). Brother Martin (Casagram) will make his stability. Dom James will announce the change of novice masters which is news to no one at all, and will make some remarks supposedly jocular and in some way political, to explain why a nut like me is allowed to live alone in the woods – but explain it in such a way that too many others will *not* be encouraged to follow suit. Meanwhile last evening he suddenly unloaded a rush job on me – writing a new postulants' guide, and he wants to have finished copies from the printer "in time to send out as Christmas presents." This presumably must be done without going to town or having reasonable contact with any printer except by mail??

August 21, 1965

The Chapter yesterday was not so bad. The day was a joyful one. A lot of gladness in the community, and most people seem pleased that I am going to live in the woods – for the right reason, I think – namely that it shows an opening up to the Spirit, an awareness of new possibilities and not just the evasion that condemned everyone to uniform and rigid adherence to one set of practices for all, meaningful or not. I gave my final official conference as Novice Master – but will continue the Sunday talks on monasticism.

The day was cool and peaceful, but still there were things to be done at the last minute, transferring to Chapel in library, etc. for Mass, getting a hook in the washroom in that building, writing and receiving notes, arrangements about clothes (will wear the old robes that have been discarded in community. I don't wear rags, but the robes that were replaced four years ago at Easter).

This morning – grey, cool, peace. The unquestionable realization of the rightness of this, because it is from God and it is His work. So much could be said! What is immediately perceptible is the _immense_ relief, the burden of ambiguity is lifted, and I am without care – no anxiety about being pulled between my job and my vocation . . . I feel as if my whole being were an act of thankfulness – even the gut is relaxed and at peace after good meditation and long study of Irenaeus (Wingren's book!) [G. Wingren, _Man and the Incarnation_, 1959]. The woods all around crackle with guerrilla warfare – the hunters are out for squirrel season (as if there were a squirrel left!). Even this idiot ritual does not make me impatient. In their mad way they love the woods too: but I wish their way were less destructive and less of a lie.

"Ego enim sum Dominus Deus tuus, qui eduxi te de terra Aegypti: dilata os tuum, et implebo illud" ["I am the Lord thy God, which brought you out of the land of Egypt: open thy mouth wide, and I will fill it"] Psalm 80 [81]. 80 is where I am in the Psalter, and there is no question that solitude gives a different horizon to the Psalter, precisely because [of] the light and nourishment one specially needs.

August 25, 1965. Feast of St. Louis

The five days I have had in real solitude have been a revelation, and whatever questions I may have had about it are answered. Over and over again I see that this life is what I have always hoped it would be and always sought. A life of peace, silence, purpose, meaning. It is not always easy, but calls for a blessed and salutary effort – and a little of this goes a long way. Everything about it is rewarding.

My stomach trouble has cleared up (except that it may flare up again when I go down to the monastery for Mass and dinner, e.g. yesterday). Everything is falling nicely into place. One can live at a good, quiet, productive tempo – manual labor in the morning, writing in the afternoon. There is time for reading and meditation and I notice that the reading schedule simplifies itself and I want to spend more time on one thing. The dispersion and agitation of "those days" are settling of their own accord. Already the novitiate is becoming incredible (these last months there have not been reasonable, and the change is welcome). (I remember the novitiate of two – five – eight years ago as more "real" – the first year was a strain, as if I were playing some role I did not really want to play.)

Getting down to the business of meditation and total silence. Realizing how little I really desire or need to simply "talk to someone" – certainly not for talking's sake. It is good to go whole days without speaking, at last – without really seeing anyone except a Mass server and a few monks encountered on the way to Mass or in the infirm[ary] refectory. Yet I had a good talk with Dan [Walsh] yesterday (though for some reason Dom James has been engaging in some kind of political operation to determine whether this should continue. It seems he wants it to).

Last week (the 20th, my first day here for keeps) I threw out some squirrel hunters. Thought there were probably no squirrels left anyway. This morning a beautiful, bushy tailed red-squirrel appeared on the porch and darted about before leaving. It was a delight to see him! How can they kill such beautiful live things!

But Dan says that the war situation in Asia gets more serious all the time. I have seen or heard no news, but apparently the war with Red China gets closer and more sure, and one begins to feel the way one felt in 1939, about this time. So Dan says, anyway. I can believe it. This is a "safe" war – it involves no massive, sudden, nuclear exchange. On the contrary, perhaps China can be provoked into dropping an A bomb on a concentration of our troops – and then we can let go and give them all we have. What a monstrosity! All we need is this excuse, and we are clever enough to manage it, surely! I regret ever having voted for Johnson. I wonder what a man can *do* in such a society? Signing petitions and printing them as ads in the paper surely has outlived whatever usefulness it may have had!

The blessing of prime under the tall pines, in the cool of early morning, behind the hermitage. The blessing of sawing wood, cutting grass, cleaning house, washing dishes. The blessing of a quiet, alert, concentrated, fully "present" meditation. The blessing of God's presence and guidance . . . I am very aware of the meaning of faith and fidelity, and of the implications of the relationship they establish. This place is marked with the blessed sign of my covenant with Him who has redeemed me. May I never fail this goodness, this mercy!

August 26, 1965

There was a great deal of traffic in the air last evening and in the very early pre-dawn hours, mostly military (i.e., east-west. The commercial planes are north-south, here). Now before dawn it is quiet again, only a cricket sings innocently in the weeds. A great blue cloud stood for a while in the dimly lighted East, a cloud with a hole in it like an eye. Dark pines stood still and silent, outlined against the dim light. The mornings are wonderful. But when I go down to the monastery for Mass and dinner, everything is broken up and in the afternoon it is hard to get back into the charm and peace. Also it is hot, stuffy. Only late in the afternoon with psalms in the shade, does the full beauty of the place come back. Yet Mass in the Library chapel is good too. A bit disconcerted by Brother Lavrans' ikon – the leaning figures – I miss Victor Hammer's crucifix in the novitiate chapel. Already I think of a chapel up here, and think of spots where it might reasonably stand. But that is premature.

Superb passage from Irenaeus (*Adversus Haereses*, IV. XXXIX.2. col. 1110):

"Si ergo opera Dei es, manum artificis tui exspecta opportune omnia facientem. . . . Praesta autem ei cor tuum molle et tractabile et custodi figuram qua te figuravit artifex . . . ne induratus amittas vestigia digitorum ejus. Custodiens autem compaginationem ascendes ad perfectum. . . . Facere enim proprium est benignitatis Dei, fieri autem proprium est hominis naturae. Si igitur tradideris ei quod est tuum, hoc est fidem in eum et subjectionem, percipies artem ejus et eris perfectum opus Dei." ["If you are the work of God wait patiently for the hand of your artist who makes all things at an opportune time. . . . Give to Him a pure and supple heart and watch over the form which the artist shapes in you . . . lest, in hardness, you lose the traces of his fingers. By guarding this conformity you will ascend to perfection. . . . To do this is proper to the kindness of God; to have it done is becoming to human nature. If, therefore, you hand over to Him what is yours, namely, faith in Him and submission, you will see his skill and be a perfect work of God."]

The reification of faith. Real meaning of the phrase we are saved by faith = we are saved by Christ, whom we encounter in faith. But constant disputation about faith has made Christians become obsessed with faith almost as an object, at least as an experience, a "thing" and in concentrating upon it they lose sight of Christ. Whereas faith without the encounter with Christ and without His presence is less than nothing. It is the deadest of dead works, an act elicited in a moral and existential void. To seek to believe that one believes, and arbitrarily to decree that one believes, and then to conclude that this gymnastic has been blessed by Christ – this is pathological Christianity. And a Christianity of works. One *has* this mental gymnastic in which to trust. One is safe, one possesses the psychic key to salvation. Only Christ is the key, the way, and salvation itself.

August 28, 1965. St. Augustine

The days go by and I am beginning to experience the meaning of *real* solitude. It is certainly real enough now. I go down at 10:45, to say Mass, do necessary errands, have dinner, and come back. Most days speak to no one, see very few members of the community – and of course no one else. So I am beginning to feel the lightness, the strangeness, the desertedness of being really alone. It was far different when the ties had not been cut and when the hermitage was only *part* of my life. Now that everything is here, the work of loneliness really begins, and I feel it. I glory in it (giving thanks to God) and I fear it. This is not something lightly to be chosen, and unless I were convinced God had chosen it for me, I would not stay in it. There is an inner psychic strength and "fatness," a good comfortable complacency of being, that comes with the presence and support of other people. Without it, one becomes innerly wasted. It is this "wasting" that I feel beginning, ever so little, and it is what I will have to bear.

Yet I feel closely united to my brothers in this above all. It is as if I had taken *their* loneliness upon me, for some mysterious purpose, and I think I have assurance that many understand this and feel themselves concerned in it. Father Prior told me in confession yesterday that many were praying for me. Well, I must go ahead sensibly and quietly, without nonsense!

A hard day, two days ago – clearing brush I ran into a hornet's nest and was badly stung. Very painful, very "wasting" – ran to the house with hornets all over me, fortunately I pulled my blue denim work shirt up over my head or it would have been worse. The acrid smell of attacking hornets! One or two continued to hang around the house all day. It was very sobering! Reflected that this was due to the delusive impetuosity with which I work. This has to be changed! I must *really* be meek and nonviolent, but I see the roots of this are deep.

Yesterday when I went down to say Mass, all the community, or a large group rather, were out gathering in the potato harvest under a blue, late summer sky, and I remembered the communal beauty of work in this season – the sense of brotherhood and joy when I used to go over with the students to cut tobacco twelve years ago! Or cutting corn in my novitiate, or the general corn husking that went on all through October when I was a student (and late into November even). Now that is all done by machine and there is little really common work outdoors. Anyway, I felt lonely, seeing them out there.

Today – finished Wingren's book on Irenaeus, which Brother Cuthbert had passed on to me. Some misleading theological statements in it, but the material from Irenaeus and its interpretation are in general magnificent. This is *theology!!*

In the evening: this turned into a beautiful, clear, cool afternoon and evening. In the afternoon I finished a first draft for the *Bible Today* article (for their December issue)[8] and had less trouble with it than I expected. I had been dreading it because I am no Bible scholar. But if they wanted technical competency they would not have asked me. After supper I walked outside the gate to the hermitage enclosure and said some Psalms, read and meditated a bit looking out over the bottoms and across at the green cool line of hills. It all came alive (as it all should be) and I realized then that I had been running the risk, these past few days, of tying myself down with a mental delusion – taking the hermitage too seriously, and myself with it – identifying myself with this stupid little cottage as if my whole life was bound up with it. What total absurdity! Looking at the hills and recovering the freedom of true prayer (of which incidentally I have had so much in the hermitage too), I realized that what is important is not the house, not the hermit image, but my own self and my sonship as a child of God. It is good to see that things which are supposed to be media between ourselves and Him so easily get in the way and become obstacles. I am determined not to fool myself with any such nonsense. My first obligation is to be myself and follow God's grace and not allow myself to become the captive of some idiot idea, whether of hermit life or anything else. What matters is not spirituality, not religion, not perfection, not success or failure at this or that, but simply God, and freedom in His Spirit. All the rest is pure stupidity. How often I saw this last year and before, just coming up for the afternoons – because then I was non-attached, non-identified, and the hermitage was a kind of nowhere. Now the terrible thing is that it has become a very definite home. But since I am a homeless body, being tied to a home disturbs me. But I am sure with God's grace this will all settle itself, and I can treat the place as any other hole in the wall that is "not mine." Though I must admit that it is full of a lot of books and nonsense. Here is where I think fasting will be important. Simplifying the meals I take here has already been quite a help. All that cooking of rice and cream of wheat, etc. which I won't scruple to use in cold weather.

Meanwhile, I am impatient of all desires. May the Holy Ghost bring me to *true* freedom!!

---

[8] "The Good News of the Nativity," *Bible Today* (December 1965).

September 1, 1965

September has come in a great downpour of rain. It began about supper time last evening, and has continued on and off all night, especially heavy around 4:15, when I went out and looked at it and listened to it. Rain creates a double isolation and peace in the hermitage. The noise of it and the thickness of it walls you off from the rest of the world. You know that no one is going to walk up through the woods with all this coming down! Sunday evening Brother Clement, the cellerar, showed up and brought a six-pack of beer. An act in the noblest tradition of monastic cellerars. (It was left over from the visit of Dom Vital's brother from Germany.) I think Brother Clement is quite fascinated by the hermitage; kept talking about the woods, the quiet, the stars, etc. Actually he came to talk about the monastery and its problems. I had previously decided there was to be no beer up here, but it was better to accept his gift. Did not drink with him as his ulcer prevents him from drinking. So I take one can each evening at supper. The first was delightful – I ate supper, drank Falstaff, and read the introduction to John of Salisbury's letters. Last night the same, except I read Jean Leclercq's offprint from the second Athos Volume on relations between Oriental and Occidental monasticism in the High Middle Ages. It is fascinating, but it reminds me of my resentment concerning Dom James' phobia against my traveling. As a matter of fact I am now pretty sure that the chief reason why I got in the hermitage so soon is that it was his best excuse to keep me from going to the meeting of the *Collectanea* board of editors at Chimay, to which I had been rather urgently summoned (end of September).

One would think an Abbot would have a little breadth of view in such matters as this. But there are all sorts of reasons why he has to be this way with me (again, the absurd attitude he took about the novice masters meeting: would not let me attend one anywhere but here). He is probably not aware of them all! Certainly one of them is a form of unconscious jealousy. I did not arrive at such a judgment myself – more than one other has expressed it to me. However, it is precisely for this kind of situation that I have a vow of obedience, and intend to keep it. But the irrationality remains. He does not see that it is because of his narrowness and wrong-headedness that he loses so many good monks. For instance Brother Sean, who left a couple of weeks ago. One of the best monks in the place, in simple vows (they expired). He simply could not put up with the spirit of the house under Dom James – or it boiled down to that, so I am told.

I don't know what news comes from Asia – certainly the war goes on and will go on. Johnson is listening to the Pentagon crowd, and his stubbornness and vanity will harden him against criticism or differences of opinion. I deeply regret having voted for him; but the landslide was significant. We got the president we deserved – and, I suppose, wanted. He is doing what Goldwater would have done, but in a manner that most people can accept: without moralizing too much, acting as a shrewd operator, vulgar, self-indulgent, an American Khrushchev.

A big synthetic rubber plant blew up in Louisville – that was a week ago. Saw pictures on the little Cloister board yesterday.

I am trying to write the new edition of the Postulants' guide for which Dom James asked when he sent me up here. I am afraid I don't have much taste for it, and the work goes slowly and hard. It will probably be awful. Fine letter from Cardenal about his ordination and first Masses and all the joy. His "project" (of a contemplative monastery) is bound to go slow and will meet more opposition than he expects. He hopes to come here.

The saddest thing about our monastery – Dom James is an efficient administrator and I see no one who is likely to equal him now in the community in this respect. But his organization is uncreative and restrictive, and he has done nothing, *nothing*, to foster a real spiritual life, even though he has tried earnestly to do this and speaks of it all the time, makes a definite ideal of it. But the whole thing is negative and his (strong) positive incitements to "personal love of Jesus" are in fact totally unconvincing and uninspiring, though he himself seems to be convinced and inspired by them. Actually, the only way in which he effectively communicates in spiritual matters is by restriction, and discouragement and suppression. In fact, his whole approach to the hermitage has been characterized by this. All the things I should *not* do! Yet he has been hesitant and has not dared to put upon me *all* the restrictions he would have liked. Because of a certain sado-masochism in his character, he associates love with negation and suppression, with "captivity." His mind circles around the idea of power and authority, the capacity to possess and be possessed. As Abbot he cannot believe in himself unless he feels that in some sense he *owns* the hearts of the monks. But they do not love him. His efforts to gain love and to show it are pitiful and embarrassing (those awful letters he writes when away on visitation!). He is a complex extraordinary man, not one of great character, but a kind of sign of the times and a mystery of judgment, as we have in politics today: one who comes to the top because what is mysterious and perhaps false in everyone is somehow embodied in him. But he has *force*, this one has to admit. A perplexity, smooth and unbending will, more a passion than a volition. A passion for a certain kind of disguised self-affirmation-in-restriction.

All this having been said – and I suppose on examination it would be found substantially true (with inevitable errors of perspective!!) – it proves nothing but my own lack of liberty, my own vulnerability, my own weakness. That I should still let myself be interiorly defeated to the point of having to justify myself is a sign of my own dread of the necessary loss of self: and if I dread it, there is good reason, for since I am weak I still see that in this situation, with this kind of abbot, I am likely to allow myself to be merely suppressed and destroyed (which is his unconscious but serious aim, I feel) rather than doing as I ought – making it a death and resurrection. But I *can*. I have the strength in Christ and solitude has been given me so that I may face this, get used to it, and live up to it!

Evening: this afternoon I finished the postulants' guide, after having discarded all that I wrote yesterday, but utilizing about half the old one, which seems satisfactory. It was written in 1957, the best time for it, when we had most vocations (during my time as novice master). The work upset my stomach. It was a relief to get it over with, go out and say psalms and look across the valley at the hills.

September 2, 1965

The sun rose in mist like a Turner painting over the reservoir as I went down early (6:30) this morning to say Mass at 7 and go to the Dentist in Lebanon. Fortunately there was not much to be done but a priest from St. Mary's had an awful time there with a wisdom tooth. Poor man! The ride back was beautiful – bright September day – and we got home for dinner. I came in just as Newman was dying, or had died, and the second volume of the Trevor biography ended. It was one of the best books we have had and I did not get tired of it. They then began H. Fesquet's *Wit and Wisdom of [Good] Pope John*.

In the paper I saw that Pakistan and India were nearly at war, which would certainly be tragic. But surely it is avoidable!! Another matter, perhaps more significant: on the back page of the first section – a report that an Indian in Arizona or New Mexico had died of bubonic plague, and that there were other cases! I thought immediately of Camus' novels. It is just possible that something like this might unexpectedly get out of control (that is the irony of the novel), and it would be so appropriate as an expression of the sickness of the country's spirit. But am I looking at it like Camus, or like his Jesuit, Paneloux? If the plague should sweep India, it would be a plague. But if it swept this country it would surely be an Apocalyptic judgment!

Judgments of mine, however, are fruitless. The plain fact is that these things are unthinkable, and the unthinkable is what sometimes has to happen.

September 6, 1965

Magenta mist outside the windows. A cock crows over at Boone's. Last evening when the moon was rising saw the warm burning soft red of a doe in the field. It was still light enough so I got the field glasses and watched her. Presently a stag came out, and then I saw a second doe and, briefly, another stag. They were not afraid. Looked at me from time to time. I watched their beautiful running, grazing. Everything, every movement was completely lovely, but there is a kind of gaucheness about them sometimes that makes them even lovelier. The thing that struck me most: one sees, looking at them directly in movement, just what the cave painters saw – something that I have never seen in a photograph. It is an awe-inspiring thing – the *Muntu* or "spirit" shown in the running of the deer, the "deerness" that sums up everything and is saved and marvelous. A contemplative intuition! Yet perfectly ordinary, everyday seeing. The deer reveals to me something essential in myself! Something beyond the trivialities of my everyday being, and my individuality. The stags much darker, mouse-grey, or rather a warm grey brown like a flying squirrel. I could sense the softness of their coat and longed to touch them.

I am reading Beryl Smalley's *Study of the Bible in the Middle Ages*. A very delightful book – in which for the first time I have managed to get a little information on Anselm of Laon. He emerges as a rather attractive scholar type with a very important circle of disciples, and doubtless had a considerable impact on the first Cistercians, his contemporaries.

All of Pope Paul's weekly allocutions to general audiences are read in refectory, along with some of his other more popular statements. He has occasionally had excellent things to say *elsewhere*, but in these one gets an impression of an official cheerfulness in issuing useful directives and the total result is: a mediocre job of public relations. The Pope has become the number-one propaganda medium of the Church as organization and institution. But because his ideology is not linked with sufficiently cataclysmic actions (he does not create international crises and then resolve them) it ends by being a more or less otiose exercise – almost an irritant and no more. It is true that the air of crisis has been somewhat successfully maintained by the conflict of liberals and conservatives in the Council, and that makes everyone still expect something dramatic from the Pope – (Pope

John *was* at times given to dramatic interventions, and not at all as a means of adding excitement to propaganda!). Hence there is some excitement about the Fourth Session which everyone expects to be "dramatic," and this has been brought about by the fact that it is the last chance of all the Bishops and no one quite knows what will happen. No doubt a lot of important questions will be simply unresolved.

September 10, 1965

Last night, at moonrise (the moon is full) a doe was out in the field again. She has become quite used to me. I walked about saying Compline in front of the hermitage and she was not disturbed, even came down the field *towards me!* Yet this is heartbreaking, because soon the hunters will be out after them (I don't know when deer season begins). I only hope this tameness is wisely confined to one association – with the white hermitage and the monk in white and black, without a rifle.

The other day Will Campbell and Jim Holloway, of the Committee of Southern Churchmen, were here. There has been much more trouble (race riots) in many cities I had heard nothing about. Consciously or unconsciously I think the riots are in some sense being provoked by the police. Not as a deliberate plot, but as a self-fulfilling prophecy. Violence is so constantly expected by them that their tenseness, aggressivity and "brutality" provoke it in the end. And doubtless they feel so menaced that they think they are not being brutal at all.

The peace of the hermitage: after three weeks I am settling completely into it, and far from missing the community I find the artificiality of the community life almost incredible, from the perspective of my solitude. Sunday, Day of Recollection, I went down to pray before the Blessed Sacrament and stayed in the Brothers' choir for vespers – it was really a bit sad, almost embarrassing. No wonder people are having as much trouble. Not that the community life as such is unreal, or that the men in it are not excellent (the young especially!) but the mentality, the rigidity and suppression of all freedom, which is the conservative policy and that of Dom James, simply stifles genuine life. There is little sense of the reality of Christ in all this, only discipline and observance for their own sakes and a formal, monumental "front" of liturgy and witness – which, I am afraid, are not convincing. We are trying to be much "more" than we really are, or at any rate other than we are.

There is no question that I really feel I am living a saner and better life. I would not exchange this for anything even though for four days a snake was living in the jakes – (I finally persuaded him to go elsewhere I hope!). In spite of the hornets, the noise of machines in the fields, the dogs and hunters, etc. All this is plain ordinary reality without any need of ideology or explanation. It *is*. That is enough. In the monastery everything has to be justified because everything is very seriously under question. Here only *I* am under question, and it is right for me to face the doubt which is my own empirical self, myself as question, knowing that in myself I also have Christ as answer.

For the rest – I love the night silence, the early meditation and the moon, the reading and breakfast coffee (or good tea!), sawing wood after sunrise, washing up, tired, as the sun begins to grow warm and the Atlanta plane goes over. Mass in the library chapel is fine, dinner in the infirm[ary] refectory is sometimes a trial and the heat of the day, coming up after dinner, is oppressive. Afternoon meditation slow – then work on the book (*Conjectures*) – office in the late afternoon, quiet supper, reading, walking, looking at the hills, the silence, the moon, the does, darkness, prayer, bed.

Father Prior told me India and Pakistan were officially at war. It is absurd!

September 11, 1965

In a sense, a very true and solitary sense, coming to the hermitage has been a "return to the world," not a return to the cities, but a return to direct and humble contact with God's world, His creation, and the world of poor men who work. Andy Boone is, physically, more my neighbor than the monastery. It is his sawmill I hear, not the monastery machines. His rooster crows in my morning, his cows low in the evening, and I just heard him give a guttural yell at some animal (again, another one, while the first bell for Prime rings at the monastery and a flycatcher squeals happily in the poplar tree).

I do not have the official "space" – sanctified, juridically defined, hedged in with elaborate customs – of the monastery as my milieu. To be out of that is a great blessing. It is a space rich with delusions and with the tyranny of willful fabrication. My space is the world created and redeemed by God, and God is in this true world, not "only" and restrictively a prisoner in the monastery. It is most important to see this, and I think that what those who are leaving see, often, is this. It is crucially important for the monastery to abandon the myth of itself as a purely sacred space – it is a disaster for its real "sacredness." Curiously, the thing is getting out in rumors, and though the situation is partly understood and partly not, it is interpreted with shock as "leaving the monastery." And this is true. The general reproach is then that I am not clinging, in spite of reason, grace, and everything else, to something God no longer wills for me: clinging to it just because society expects me to do so! My life is a salutary scandal, and that is another proof of the reality of my vocation, I believe. Here I see my task is to get rid of the last vestiges of a pharisaical division between the sacred and secular, and to see that the *whole* world is reconciled to God in Christ, not just the monastery, nor only the convents, the churches, and the good Catholic schools.

Late afternoon – a good rainstorm began before supper and it is going on now as darkness falls. A moment ago there was a hawk up there flying against the wind in the dark and in the rain, with big black clouds flying and the pines bending. A beautiful storm, and it has filled my buckets with water for washing, and the house with cool winds. It is good and comforting to sit in a storm with all the winds in the woods outside and rain on the roof, and sit in a little circle of light and read and hear the clock tick on the table. And tomorrow's Gospel is the one about not serving two Masters, and letting the Lord provide. That is what I must do.

"They have a good foundation," saith Love, "and high edification that resteth them of the things. Such creatures they can no more speak of God, no more than they can say where God is. For whatsoever it be that speaketh of God, when he will, and to whom he will, and where he will, he may doubt." The Mirror of Simple Souls, *III, 220*

September 14, 1965. Exaltation of the Holy Cross
The Fourth and last Session of the Council is opening today.

A very funny satire on our choir observances came in yesterday from Father Anselm at Conyers – sent to me as a member of the editorial board of *Collectanea* (as if I edited anything!). It is very hep, very American, very outspoken and would give all the abbots, and especially the people at Monte Cistello, apoplexy. The thing is, though, that it is very representative of the way people feel and think in our monasteries in this country. And the result is very extremely negative, as far as the present shape of our life is concerned. I know Dom James is very scared by this (especially as regards Conyers) but there is nothing he can do about it – he has neither the imagination nor the understanding that it takes. The other abbots, too, are "open" (more than Dom James for the most part) but helpless.

The problem is simply this: American vocations have been to our Order, eager, volatile, vulnerable, impatient. They have come with obvious possibilities. They have found an elaborate structure of usages and more or less of a spiritual void. When I came, you had people who still knew to take all the usages and all the hard work and make something out of it at least for themselves. Hence you had a few people who obviously had attained *something*, though God alone knew what. (No question about the old brothers, most of whom had come from Europe before entering.) Now all that anyone seems to have is an infinite number of doubts and questions. This is in a way a great pity, in so far as one *has to* have strong personal motives before this kind of life can make any sense. On the other hand it is inevitable, because when they get into a monastery their motives tend to be undermined by the sense that much of what is considered officially most important is in fact largely a matter of keeping up a front, provisionally hiding the void while, one hopes, some substance creeps back into the life somewhere. The ironies of this, Father Anselm [knows], are alive, significant and not hopeful. And they certainly show impatience with all that one has traditionally regarded as "the religious spirit."

September 15, 1965

In the refectory the other day articles on the Council were being read and a lot was said about St. Thomas – he is no longer on an official pedestal – he is no longer to be considered the one to be followed as chief authority in seminary teaching. This is the best thing that could happen to St. Thomas and to Catholic Truth, if we consider that he himself would never have consented to be the kind of authority the text books have made of him (and as a matter of fact the Church did not really constitute him an authority – but rather a *model*).

For a couple of days I was a bit disturbed about one of the problems of life here at Gethsemani. Dom James takes a completely negative and absolutist view of all "contact with the world." He goes to any length to prevent me from responding to any invitation to participate in anything, even in another monastery. I am sure for instance that the invitation to go to Chimay to the meeting of the board of editors of the *Collectanea* was what prompted him to move me into the hermitage in August rather than at the end of the year. Then the other day a letter came from Douglas Steere about the ecumenical meeting at Collegeville, to which I was forbidden to go. I have good reason to think some people in Latin America even tried to reach him through the Congregation of Religious so that I could be sent to Nicaragua to give a retreat. All this is not "returning to the world." Yet he will have none of it. And I don't think he realizes that such contacts could and would be *good for* one's Christian and monastic life. He has a negative and I think rather narcissistic idea of the contemplative life – and can get away with it because he is extremely active himself and travels a great deal. To justify his own activity and traveling he imposes his distorted ideal on *me*. I have been angry and bitter about this, but in the end, especially yesterday, I was able finally to see not only that obedience is the only practical thing, but it is really best for me. This expression of God's will may be in its own way irrational and even unfair but it *is* God's will. And what, in fact, could be better than that? I am much better off in a life of simple solitude, not compromising or playing around. And this also is much better for the Church. Certainly I will be criticized and called selfish, negative, passive, etc. I know well enough that I am not – at least not negative or passive, though I am selfish, I am afraid. But my solitude is not selfish. I don't think I could stay in it if it really were. I would be too guilty.

And now today I got a letter from old [Serge] Bolshakoff who, at times, is a bit of a bore. Yet there is something extraordinary about the man nevertheless. He knows monasticism and monks, and he loves the monastic life. He said he had heard I was going to the hermitage and approved it. He said it was the best thing for me, that he thought I was ready for it etc. He added: "I should say you should follow the way of the great Russian mystic of the last century, Bishop Theophane the Recluse. He felt an irresistible attraction to solitude. He resigned his see being fifty-one years old and a monk for over 20 years. He lived afterward twenty-eight years in solitude. For six years he went to the Abbey Church of Vysha for all services and received people who wanted to see him. He gradually accustomed himself to solitary living and only after Easter Vespers of 1872, being fifty-seven years old, he retired altogether with a house built for him and received none except the Abbot, his confessor, and a brother who served him, and only when he called them. He said his Mass alone as well as the offices. He practiced the prayer of Jesus, read copiously, wrote a great many books and conducted a vast correspondence on spiritual subjects, etc. You may very well go the same way. Like Theophane go into solitude slowly and gradually. Within five–seven years you will be accustomed to it. But even in complete solitude write books and letters at least for a time." And then he goes on to speak of Father Michael, recluse at Unsi Valamo, etc. Then he spoke of a group of Sobesedniks he is forming – including a Dom Alfred Spenser who has become a hermit at Prinknash, etc., etc. I know Bolshakoff is a bit of an actor and likes to cast himself in the role of Staretz, and I know it is flattering to be even remotely compared to a saint like Theophane the Recluse, but nevertheless the thing does seem to represent something of God's will for me.

In the long run, I have to face the fact that if I am here in such circumstances it is because the way leads to the real solitary life and this is God's will for me. It is not my natural inclination, and I would gladly compromise with a little apostolic work outside. But I think that is just not God's will for me. So I must sacrifice it and be content with writing and prayer. This decision gives me deep peace, and I trust in Him to lead me along this way He has decided for me.

September 16, 1965

A fine storm about Prime. Then I went down early (about 8:30) to the monastery to meet a Printer (Mr. Mill) and Peter Geist, a designer, from St. Louis. This in connection with the picture book which is to replace S[hirley] Burden's *God Is My Life*. (Brother Pius, Brother Ephrem and I have been on this for some time.) Also the new *Guide*, which I had to write recently. We got through our work quickly and I can see that Peter Geist is a first-class designer and that it is going to turn out well, or should. As usual, I am happy when there is prospect of turning out something that has a little quality and character to it. And one "worldly" pleasure I will never renounce is that of helping something to take shape with a good designer and an understanding printer. In the end I don't call this "worldly" at all because it implies a liberation from mendacious routines, not subjection to them. I think of the books I have given to Victor Hammer, for example. But Peter Geist is modern. All the better. I like what I saw of his work.

This afternoon, while I was working on *Conjectures*, there was a queer, tense electric storm. Very black, very low clouds, extreme stuffiness, a wind that cooled nothing, and repeated bolts of lightning and crashes of thunder without any rain. At one point, in the space of two or three minutes, lightning struck three times within a hundred yards of the hermitage, besides hitting all over valley. Three times the clap of lightning, then the crash of thunder – once I could see leaves flying off the poplar in the field that was evidently struck but not injured. Very exciting! Then the clouds went, and it was cooler. But the absence of rain was curious and disquieting, with all that lightning!

September 20, 1965

I have been working on *Conjectures* in the afternoon – at moments it gets to be like Cantares Hopscotch – criss-cross itinerary of the various pieces taken out of time sequence and fitted into what? An indefinite half-conscious pattern of associations which is never consistent, often purely fortuitous, often not there (and not sought in any case). A lot of rewriting. For instance rewrote an experience of March 18, 1958 (entry of March 19) in light of a very good meditation of Saturday afternoon, developed and changed. A lot of telescoping, etc. In a word, transforming a Journal into "meditations" or *"Pensées."*

A splendid pre-dawn, with a big thin light slab of cloud in the south red in the east, light mist over the field, last quarter of the moon high up, and a quail whistling in the field to my deep chagrin because the place was alive with hunters yesterday – kids only, I suspect, as one was firing a twenty-two. Raging about them disrupted my morning. They were not close enough for me to go after them and throw them out.

September 21, 1965

A brilliant September day – cool wind everywhere but in the hermitage. One of those winds the cottage does not catch directly because of the rise to the southwest. Fasting. Heavy work splitting logs in the morning and very good for me. My back feels it a bit but I think I can get along if I work carefully and steadily.

Sister Penelope has sent translations of Isaac of Stella which seem to me very good indeed. I have not read them carefully. (She is an Anglican nun at Wantage.) A good letter from Sor Emmanuel after a long silence. They have finally got rid of a Superior who, I guessed, was being rather nasty and would not let Sor Emmanuel write me annual letters though she is handling all my Portuguese translations. Dom Timoteo [Amoroso Anastacio] is elected abbot at Bahia. Dom Basilio Penido's monastery at Olinda is doing very well.

It is said that the war in Kashmir is due in part to some machinations of the CIA. This is a very strange outfit from what I hear, and in some ways typical of what is ill about America. It appears to be monumentally stupid in the first place! What this country has to suffer from fools in government! But since it is the most powerful country in the world, the whole world is endangered by the folly of these idiots.

September 23, 1965

Rain most of the day. Dom James is back from visitations in New York and the West looking well. I hear there is a truce in the Kashmir war. Pope Paul's visit to the United Nations next month is a hopeful sign and should do something for peace, at least by giving his support to the U.N., which has been made more or less ridiculous by the U.S.A. in these past months.

September 25, 1965

It got cold during the night and on getting up this morning I sprayed one of the two big hornets nests that are within a hundred feet or so of the hermitage. The second is less easy to get at. The sun came up in mist and as I was finishing my wood chopping the house was steaming like a big contented beast. The sun was warm but tonight promises to be cold again. Maybe I shall build a fire in the early morning. Enjoyed the Ember Saturday Mass. Last evening began again reading parts of Maritain's *Carnets de notes* – good things on the layman and a plea to be left unorganized!

This afternoon Father Chrysogonus and Father Prior (Flavian) came up for a visit. Father Chrysogonus is just back from Europe. He brought a bottle of white Gaillac sent by the man who owns our old house in St. Antonin and so we drank it. Very pleasant. He had a lot to say – does not think much of Dom Ignace, the General, though he is liked by the students. Some good stories about Père Charles Dumont, my friend, editor of *Collectanea*. The picture of the Order I get from Father Chrysogonus and from everybody else, always, is quite depressing!

After they left I leafed through a book about St. Antonin he brought. It was sent by Mme. Fonsagrives, wife of the Doctor (whom I have frankly forgotten). I learn that Dr. Fonsagrives "saved my life," i.e., diagnosed me as having TB or being disposed to it in 1926 or 7. That was why I had to go to Murat and also why I had special food in infirmary at the Lycée, etc. I was never told. But my health as a child was always quite poor. I know that all right. I remember spending most of my time at the lycée in the infirmary. My health picked up when I went to school in England and was excellent until about my senior year at Columbia. Has never been too good since, but is as good now as I can remember, though I have chronic trouble with the stomach. My hands have broken out again.

So many things I did not know about Saint Antonin. They have found bone weapons, etc. and also engraved stones from stone age (reindeer, horse, bison). The town was under the special protection of St. Louis – that was its best period, from the mid-thirteenth century to the Hundred Years War. Albigensianism was strong. Protestantism also. The part where I lived, across the Bonnette, used to be in Guercy. The town itself was in Rouesque. Louis XIII besieged the place and watched the siege from the Calvaire, above the site of our house. He had a good view!! A lot of old houses were destroyed in a flood in 1930, so there is a big square that I never knew, right by the bridge before the Place de la Condamine.

September 30, 1965

The month began in rain and is ending in it – though there were a couple of long dry periods. A fine rainstorm with lots of southeast wind began just as I was finishing my afternoon work (and finishing the selections from this Journal to be used in the book for Doubleday. Took it up to end of 1963). It went on during supper, at which I was reading Harrington's *The Other America* – the shocking chapter on the aged! Time goes fast in the hermitage. September already over. I do not regret the monastery for a moment. I have plenty to do – have split practically all the wood that was piled up behind the cottage – there is writing to be done, there is the main business of all which is prayer.

After a bitter debate the Religious Liberty declaration was voted on and accepted in principle in the Council – but there will be changes still. It sounded good to me. Cardinal [Josef] Beran of Prague, after years of imprisonment, made one of the most moving speeches in its favor and so did the Ukrainian, Archbishop [Joseph] Slipyj, so long a prisoner in Siberia. The fighting in Kashmir has not stopped.

Rain keeps blowing up out of the dark valley. The trees continue full of wind and the storm will probably continue all night. I have been walking up and down on the porch for an hour and am full of the joy of it. Somehow I seem happiest here when rain encloses my solitude. Perhaps I will need a fire in the morning (did not light one the other day) but some of the wood on the porch is wet.

October 5, 1965

Finally built the first fire of the season, though it is not freezing outside. 40 or 45 I should judge. It was about 55 in the house, before I built the fire on getting up. Sunday, the third, was bored with the liturgy as we have it, but concelebration, etc. is I feel something I must go to out of faith. I need this contact with the expressed mystery of the community, however poorly expressed. But it is heavy and tedious. A good bright afternoon. Went up to the end of the long field next to [the] hermitage and walked in the sun reading [Mathieu Richard Auguste] Henrion on St. John of the Cross. Good letter from Maritain the other day. He had been to see Pope Paul and found him with a "great firmness" that lifted him above the struggles and conflicts around him. That is something to be grateful for.

Yesterday, Feast of St. Francis, I made a holiday of it. In the morning (bright and cold) walked through the hollow then to the long field and in and out the wood where the deer sleep. In the afternoon took a long walk to

Dom Frederic's Lake and around by St. Edmund's field to the shallow lake, etc. Stopped at the monastery on the way back to get a few pieces of bread. The only difficulty in the day was another letter from Marie Tadié, who is getting excited again. She is a very troublesome and demanding person and under pretext of doing me favors and helping me she is causing more trouble than all my publishers and agents put together. Now she insists she must be my agent for Italy as well as France and Spain and is very strong about it. I have no need whatever of all this "help" and she is trying simply to badger me into it. It is very insulting to undergo such exploitation, and I don't know how to handle it in the first place because I have never kept up with business and anyway business information has been kept from me. (For instance I have no idea if she has sent in any royalties at all in the last four or five years.)

October 6, 1965

There was frost yesterday after all (became evident when the sun rose) and probably today too. Brilliant October sun yesterday – more today, so it seems. Pope Paul's speech at U.N. Monday was a magnificent appeal for peace and seems to have had a great effect (some of it was read in refectory yesterday).

I see more and more the fruitfulness of this life here with its struggles, its long hours of silence, the sun, the woods, the presence of invisible grace and help. It has to be a creative and humiliating life, a life of search and obedience, simple, direct, requiring strength (I don't have it but it is "given"). There are moments of frightening disruption, then recovery. I am only just beginning to know what life really is – away from all the veils, cushions and evasions of common life. Yet see my great need of common life. Seriously, last night at supper, a deep awareness that I need the saints and angels with me in my loneliness. (Cf. Maritain on the Heavenly Church.) Read Maritain's beautiful biographical note on Vera [Oumansoff]. This is the real dimension of Christian community. What could be more beautiful or more real? There is much of this in the monastery, in spite of everything.

Picture of Galla Placidia in H[erbert] Read's book [*Icon and Idea*, 1964]. Byzantine Medallion of her, her son and her daughter. A most lovely and fascinating picture. The children are beautiful but dull. She is full of life and character. A fascinating face. How is it that this face is so contemporary to me, so ready to speak to me? As if she were someone I had always known. I can imagine it is mother, perhaps, I see in her; there is some resemblance, the same kind of features. Anyway I am moved by the picture.

October 11, 1965

Dawn. Cold. Mist in the valley. The rampart line of hills is always new every day.

There has been much self-searching, some futile, some disquieting. It may be excessive, but there is something in the core of my being that needs to be revealed. I wonder if I can face it. Is it futile even to try? "Let sleeping dogs lie, leave things as they are, etc. . . ." I will try to do whatever God wills. Jeremias XX.14–18. (Cursed be the day on which I was born . . . etc.) Lines I do not experience or understand. I hope to God I do not have to experience them. Reading them is enough. I have the Vulgate and Luther's German (which is much more graphic and concrete). Importance of obedient meditation. God will take care of the rest.

Dom Leclercq was here for three days. Very ebullient. We had some good talks.

October 13, 1965

Frost again. Yesterday – beautiful October weather. I burned some rotten logs that were behind the house, cleaned up around the woodpile. Father Arnold and Brother Stanislaus (of Mepkin) brought up a couple of loads of branches that Brother Wenceslaus has pruned off the sweetgums in the Front Avenue of the monastery. The Governor is apparently coming tomorrow but I am not concerned with that, thank heaven.

Secular workmen are now putting in the elevator (monks did the shaft) in the refectory wing. I finished Read's *Icon and Idea* – Monday finished [Josef] Pieper *In Tune with the World: [A Theory of Festivity,* 1965] and wrote a review. Brother Dunstan is typing the last of *Conjectures*. The problem of Marie Tadié is still unsolved. She is very demanding and unreasonable. Have not heard from Naomi Burton, who is on vacation. Have not heard what happened in the Council last week when they debated the war question.

Saturday with Dom Leclercq and Father Prior [Flavian] – drove over the Ridge Road (Cecil Ridge) on the wilds above Edelin's Valley and went all the way to Howardstown. It is *very* cold and the road easily gets lost. So did we at one point. Parts of the woods were beautiful. Much of it is just scrub. There is only one house on the whole ridge – his pigs were running loose, his two boys were operating a big chain saw. All the rest, wild thicket for five miles and more. That is how they traveled in the Middle Ages. This is one of the oldest "highways" in this part of the state. It goes back to revolutionary times.

Reading Isaac of Stella. Disappointed in Eric Gill's book on clothes [*Clothes: An Essay upon the Nature and Significance of the Natural and Artificial Integuments Worn by Men and Women*, 1931]. Can't carry on with it (I was struck by it that Christmas at Fronti in Exeter thirty-three years ago). Will return it to the Hammers.

Sun up. Say Prime and cut wood!

October 14, 1965

"When he comes toward the end he will suddenly perceive a beauty of wondrous nature . . . not fair in the likeness of face or hands or any other part of the bodily frame . . . but beauty absolute, separate, simple and everlasting . . . are you not certain that it will then be given him to become a friend of God?" Plato – *Symposium*. How little we think of the beauty of the Divine Light – and how drab life is in consequence. We do not let the beauty of earth remind us where we are to go. As a consequence, not even the earth is beautiful to us, or as beautiful as it might be.

I am not going to be bitter about Dom James, it is useless and silly, and besides shows lack of charity and of perspective in me. But – another typical instance of how he operates. To me it means something as I am sensitive to *all* the implications and suggestions. Today the Governor came "with his suite." That old routine, which always used to bore me blue in the community. Delighted now that I don't have to be anywhere near it. I have never been involved in the business of meeting the people and entertaining them. O.K. Today, I could see Reverend Father was hinting in a very confused and clumsy way that he wanted me to be there, and meet everyone or, to be exact, he wanted to provoke me to *ask* to be there. He kept hinting and suggesting, "the President of the University of Kentucky" is coming, etc., etc. Since I have that LL.D. from the University of Kentucky the implication is obvious. He presented this as a problem and a come on. I didn't come on at all. If he wanted me there, he could have invited me. No, he wanted me to invite myself, get him off the hook he was on, and also give him an opportunity to play it both ways, joke with others about the hermit who wanted to get in on the Governor's party, meet the old girls, etc. I was fed up with the whole thing. In the end he was issuing ambiguous, but of course good-humored, suggestions that because I had failed to please him I might be held to account for it in some way – (v.g., perhaps by being forbidden to see someone I wanted to see, on some other occasion). All of this completely devious. Nothing explicit. If he had simply said he wanted me there I would have gone, no doubt with a certain amount of grumbling and ire, but this refusal of frankness is in a way much more insulting.

October 16, 1965

A warm day. Everything is bronze. But too warm for fall. Art Fillmore was here taking pictures for the picture book Reverend Father has had us working on. I took Fillmore around in the woods and by a couple of lakes and up behind Nally's. He shot a lot of film. And told me about the high new steel arch they are putting up in St. Louis, over 600 feet high and more than that. It sounds fantastic – a pleasant insanity. But something I don't begrudge them, if they want to be extravagant! Symbolic and purposeless. I am glad they can be purposeless at such cost and with such frenzy – for it has been quite a stunt to get it all up in the air.

[François] Mauriac, reminiscing on his eightieth birthday, said of the Maritains at Meudon: *"Je me demande si à l'époque actuelle il y a rien qui ressemble de près ou de loin à ce qu'il fut cette maison de J. et R. Maritain à Meudon, un foyer spirituel . . . etc."* ["I wonder if at the present time there is any place, near or far, that resembles this house of J. and R. Maritain at Meudon, a spiritual center . . . etc."] An even more moving statement of Mauriac, on discovering Mozart in his old age: *"Mozart a été – il demeure pour moi – un témoin de Dieu. . . . Pour moi Mozart est de tous les musiciens celui qui possède cette valeur de témoignage, d'autant plus que l'on trouve chez lui cette pureté originelle l'enfance non pas de Freud mais du Christ. Mozart si frivole, son destin, cette mort. . . . Dans ses toutes dernières oeuvres dans ce Concerto pour Clarinette, on unit comme un reproche à Dieu, comme une plainte d'enfant"* ["Mozart has been – he remains for me – a witness of God. . . . For me Mozart is of all the musicians the one who has this value of a witness, all the more so because we find in his childhood that original purity, not so with Freud, but with Christ. Mozart (was) so frivolous that death (was) his destiny. . . . In all his last works, in the Concerto for Clarinet, they join like a reproach to God, like the complaint of a child"]. He also said Colette was like a "great bee" getting in everybody's business but that she was also in a strange way very *"spirituelle"* ["spiritual"].

A good long letter from [Clayton] Eshelman in Peru. Doesn't like [Alejandro] Vignati, was disappointed in Nicaragua, didn't click with Cardenal but liked Coronel.

October 18, 1965

[Jakob] Boehme – [Rainer Maria] Rilke. A new climate. Two people I have met in passing for years and never really talked with. Now I begin first Boehme because I have a book [J. J. Stoudt, *Sunrise to Eternity: A Study in J. Boehme's Life and Thought,* 1957] that treats of his life and work and gives all the most relevant passages of his work in clear English, so that I finally have some inkling of what he is really saying – and respond to it. How much I respond to it.

At the same time I begin also to respond to a quite different quality in Rilke. This is something I had been resisting, suspicious of it, as if to be open to Rilke were a weakness. As if it were something one could not safely admit – for example his loneliness ("merely neurotic of course") might turn out to have something to do with my own solitude and this would be a discredit to me, etc. Well, it is true. Certainly the "poetic" element in my solitude is like Rilke's to some extent. Neurotic? So what. So I am scolded then by some Gorgon-like Hilda Graef! (Reviled incidentally by a Right-wing type called Molnar for my open letter to the Bishops. He accused me of being a communist.) So I share some of Rilke's fear and vulnerability, and it is true. *"Der Nachbar"* is certainly part of my own experience of "the others" – this is the worst possible admission to make in the current enthusiasm for togetherness. But there is a deep truth in *"Der Nachbar."* And those who simply rush together will only debase friendship if they never sense one another as "alien violins." It is a very deep poem. The programs of *"Klage"* – a typical modern experience, trite even this experience. But under it the modern lostness, at least one star has not gone out – perhaps. One stands firm like a white city stud where the beam begins. I read Rilke, then sing the poems aloud, making up *Lieder.* They are very moving. I keep notes on them. The world of spiritual senses in Rilke! How did I get this book? Yesterday after the High Mass I went to the library and was "told" to go to the poetry shelf and look. I came up with this and Peter Levi (whose stuff I greatly admired already two years ago). This has been very healing. I needed it.

I discovered yesterday that the Postulant Brother John of the Cross (Williams) had left. He had been here about four months. I rather liked him, he was a good man – sailor, carpenter, etc. He did a very good job painting the hermitage, putting up a shelf in the closet, filling in the cracks in the closet wall, etc. I will remember him gratefully. A good guy and a good workman.

What a difference from Rilke in Boehme, starting like this a vision of wrath and mercy. "When I was at Jericho there my beloved companion opened my eyes for me ... etc." Here is no weakness, and wrath is accounted for, and Jesus is no violin.

Evening. It was a little cooler late this afternoon – wind – cirrus clouds – maybe we will get cold weather again tonight. I finished revisions and additions to *Climate of Monastic Prayer* and am glad to get it done. It has been hanging over me for a long time. This morning there was concelebration (Dom James' anniversary of Abbatial blessing) and afterwards as I made my thanksgiving in the Brothers choir it suddenly came to me to think, again, about what I am going to do – which is nothing. But that I should not even *think* of moving to another hermitage (Edelin's for example – starting out from scratch!). This one has many inconveniences (one hears a lot of machinery and Andy Boone's horses), but it is where God has put me. I thought – suppose after all in five or six years I die or my health gives out! I would want to have made the best of *this* chance. I have been thinking of this all evening. The first two months here have been a bit slack, I think. Fasted for one week (Ember week), no real vigils, prayer has been mediocre and I have concentrated too much on reading and work – with a kind of intellectual gluttony. So now I have got to emphasize prayer more: what else is there? And what could be better? I know this when I am in my right mind. Some of the offices have been fine – some meditations, etc. But here I must do better, and really get *into* it. I did not come here just to write – quite the contrary. (St. Francis' Day, when I compelled myself *not* to do manual work in the morning or write in the afternoon, was one of the best days here!)

"*Ecce ego obducam eis cicatricem et sanitatem, et curabo eos: et revelabo illis deprecationem pacis et veritatis.*" ["Behold, I will bring it health and cure, and I will cure them, and will reveal unto them the abundance of peace and truth."] *Jeremias 33:6*

October 19, 1965

Last night I took an hour out of my sleep and made a two-hour meditation before retiring instead of one. As a consequence this morning's meditation was much more serious and my reading has been more sober and fruitful. It was a good inspiration, and I will do it again once in a while. (Not habitually, for it would be just another routine.) During the night I dreamt I was in a strange city with some other monk (?), and we had to go to some place at the center and begin a journey. A waitress in a lunch-room left to come with us and show us the way. I remember the warmth of her presence sitting in the car with me. I spoke of streets like "Page" and "Sky" which I found on a map, but she had another and shorter way. All along, it was a case of her *knowing* the way and my not knowing it.

> *Wer jetzt kein Haus hat, baut sich keines mehr,*
> *Wer jetzt allein ist, wird es lange bleiben,*
> *wird wachen, lesen, lange Briefe schreiben*
> *und wird in den Alleen hin und her*
> *unruhig wandern, wenn die Blätter treiben.*
> [Whose house is not built now shall build no more,
> who now is lonely long shall be alone,
> shall lie awake, and read, long letters write,
> and restlessly, among the drifting leaves
> of avenues shall wander, to and fro.]

Rilke's autumn poem ["Autumn Day"]. Beautiful and close to home.

October 20, 1965

Late yesterday afternoon Brother Dunstan came up with typed copies of the book *Barth's Dream* (*Conjectures*) – much bigger than I expected. Then it rained (quietly) most of the night and today it is cooler. I said Mass (of St. Anselm) for all my friends in England and Anglican friends everywhere. There is a woodchuck which has dug a new hole outside my jakes, and I watch him furnishing it with dead leaves for the winter.

October 23, 1965

Two remarkable days. Thursday, after Mass, I found in the refectory a note that Ernesto Cardenal was here and wanted to see me. Father Abbot had said nothing of it, though I had permission to see him (since last summer sometime). Had a very good visit. He spoke of his project for the Solentiname community (small, isolated island in Lake of Nicaragua, truly *remote!*) and wants me very much to come as spiritual father. Pablo Antonio [Cuadra], etc. all join in telling me to come. They are willing to go direct to the Pope with a petition signed by scores of Nicaraguan intellectuals, etc. and even the President. Certainly this much is from God, and I can only consent. I am sure even Rome will be very favorable. I am also sure that once again Dom James will do everything to block it. In the end I think the answer will rest with Paul Philippe. There is a year to wait anyway. Ernesto Cardenal and a delegation from Nicaragua plan to go to Rome in September, 1966. I have taken no initiatives, I only accept what

God obviously asks of *me*, and give my consent – and will await the decision of superiors.

Yesterday, as planned, Hildegard Goss-Mayr who is giving talks in this country, came out for the afternoon with Jim Douglass. Rain. Talked with Cardenal while waiting (the plane was late). The visit was a real manifestation, in simplicity, of the mystery of the Church. Hildegard, from Austria, talking of her work for non-violence in Brazil. Jim who has worked so hard to get something said on peace in the Council. Ernesto from Nicaragua with his economically slanted project. Jean [Goss-Mayr] had sent Hildegard a small packet of clippings from *Le Monde* on the Council to await her arrival here. I had a chance to glance over them – Ottaviani's great speech, very strong. Liénart, Léger, Dom Butler, Bishop from England, a strong stand in favor of conscientious objection, etc. All fine! Hildegard Goss-Mayr made an extraordinary impression. A warm, fine, lovely person radiating the spirit of Christ, simplicity, love, peace. One felt one was meeting a true person in all the meaning of the word. It was a real joy to sit and talk with her. Her visit was a blessing, and I think she also enjoyed and appreciated it. Also she represents all I have obscurely and confusedly tried to say in *Barth's Dream* (the whole book I mean) about Christian civilization, etc. She represents all that – Vienna, her father, the Fellowship of Reconciliation, etc. I forgot to ask her about Father Metzger. She spoke of a Father Journet (not the cardinal), an O.P. who died. Wonderful things about Brazil. Urged me, from Jean and herself, to write more on non-violence.

I gave Ernesto three letters – one for himself as a statement of my understanding and consent, one for Archbishop Paul Philippe, one for the Pope.

Evening. A turning point in the weather. The heavy rain clouds, broke up a bit in the morning. There were patches of sun, a few short showers late in the afternoon. It is turning cold. I noticed that my woodchuck had buried himself completely, covering up the entrance to his hole, and had gone to sleep for the winter in his bed of leaves. I wish him a happy sleep! And today is very autumn-like – cold clouds flying, trees half bare, wet leaves lying around everywhere, the broad valley beautiful and lovely. The wonderful, mysterious, lonely sense of an autumn evening. It is not the autumn of Rilke's poems, something hard, solid, yet more mysterious.

Thinking of Hildegard Goss-Mayr and the impression she made: perhaps she is something like what I have always thought Joan of Arc might be like. There is a strength and purity about her, though I imagine Joan must have been physically very rugged, as some French peasant girls are!

As to Solentiname – as far as national desires go, I am content with this hermitage, want nothing else for myself. It would be a great sacrifice to leave it. But if God asks this I will certainly go, for the grace of exile, the unknown, and to help other people find what I have found in solitude. But *later!*

October 25, 1965

Crispin and Crispinian are gone from the office – of course! I always liked them because they were connected with Kent – and Shakespeare [*Henry V,* Act 4, Scene 3]. However, it is not likely to expect them to appeal to modern people.

Some regard Ottaviani's intervention on war – to be utterly banned – as surprising in a conservative. But was it not precisely *because* he is so conservative that he made such a stand? It is the *traditional* Christian stand, otherwise he would never have taken it. The modern view is on the contrary quite different: either it takes a purely pragmatic view of war, or else opposes it on economic and sociological grounds – which is really no opposition.

An advance copy of *Seasons of Celebration* came Saturday. A book club took it and produced a completely idiotic blurb about it. As usual I see the defects when the book is finally in print – ! Though in going over manuscript of *Barth's Dream* I see much must be cut from Part II. It is a good book in general, but there are wordy parts.

Enjoyed the passage of Isaac of Stella on his island solitude (Sermon XIV) again today. I should really write an article on him.

October 29, 1965. Saints Simon and Jude

I was finally right in the heart of Isaac of Stella – the translation of his "island loneliness" into the metaphysic of being and nothingness of the Sexagesima sermons. Hit very hard [by] a lot of ambiguities in expression, but an unquestionably deep and austere intuition, and very modern. But deeply mystical. Profound implications for my own prayer and solitude opened up. (Prayer of Christ on the Cross!)

Outside – great confusion and tension. The Peace movement people are burning draft cards on T.V. This has shocked and unnerved the public so that, for security, they are beginning to support the Vietnam war and there are ugly signs of hostility and pressure against the Peace Movement, especially the Catholic Peace Fellowship, and the Berrigans – this in the national press. I am afraid the CPF is too anxious to be a Catholic CORE, in peace movement. Good or bad? I can't judge. It seems to me burning the draft cards is a bit aggressive and provocative and will do no good, only so-lidify hatreds and hostilities, without communicating a real message. It is not genuine non-violence.

October 30, 1965

Brother Alberic got (rare) copy of [John of] Ford's life of Wulfric of Hasel-bury [*Wulfric of Haselbury*, 1933] from the Library of Congress and, having finished, passed it on to me. I find it very rich indeed. Must work on it. Will get pictures of parts of it. A great theology of mystical life – and solitary life – fine, balanced, optimistic, Biblical. How much I need it!

I find more and more the power – the dangerous power – of solitude working on me. The easiness of wide error. The power of one's own inner ambivalence, the pull of inner contradiction. How little I know myself re-ally. How weak and tepid I am. I need to work hard, and I don't know how – hence I work at the wrong things. I see that in the first two months I got off to a nearly false start with too much excited reading of too many things, and my life has been grossly overstimulated for a solitary (in community, all right). Especially I worked too hard, too obsessively on the book, too fran-tic a pace for a solitary (again, in community solitude seems crowded and hopped up to me). Everything has meaning, dire meaning, in solitude. And one can easily lose it all in following the habits one has brought out of com-mon life (the daily round). One has to start over and receive (in meekness) a new awareness of work, time, prayer, oneself. A new tempo – it has to be in one's very system (and is not in mine I see).

And what I do not have I must pray for and wait for. Also need of fasting (though I know I must watch out!). Stomach has been at times wildly upset, usually after going down to monastery for Mass and dinner – particularly if I talk to someone (Father Abbot, Dan [Walsh], etc.). Yet it was very pacify-ing to talk to Cardenal, Hildegard Goss-Mayr, etc. There is still great con-flict in me, more than I thought. Hence the need for real silence and peace. Use the early hours for it. (But mere keeping still does not do it.) Have put breakfast later, meditate longer (hour and a half) with some Bible before eating. Reading slower and less. Writing fewer letters, though letters are *not* a problem now. (Except that awful business with Tadié. She is being good and patient now.)

November 1, 1965. All Saints

It has been a splendid and poignant feast, one of the greatest I can remem-ber in my nearly twenty-four years here. The concelebrated Mass was, for the first time, what I think the new liturgy means to be. Lots of new changes – all that was sung was in English except the canon. For the first time I felt that it was a real success, that everybody was really caught up in it, that it was a real celebration in which everyone was involved. If this is what they will have every day, then I think it will be excellent. Daily concelebration begins Wednesday, with a new schedule, but this does not affect me in the hermitage. I will continue to say Mass at 10:30 in the Library chapel and concelebrate on Sundays and big feasts. Some of the melodies seemed first rate to me. Brother Chrysostom as "Psalmist" was excellent. It was a great celebration. Everyone was lifted up by it. The community was really united, I thought.

A brilliant, cool afternoon. I climbed the Lake Knob then went down into that quiet, pine-filled hollow I have always liked, read a little, sat in the sun, meditated, chewed. The woods were half bare, but the last maples were splendid. Everything was very silent, and I saw no one whatever except a novice in the distance, on the road, as I came back past the waterworks and cut back into the woods to the empty, very silent hermitage.

November 3, 1965

The comet! I heard about it yesterday in the monastery, went out to see it this morning, and went just at the right time. It is magnificent, appearing just at the ineffable point when the first dim foreshadowing light (that is not light yet) makes one suspect the sun will rise. Precisely the *point vierge* [virgin point]! This great sweep of pure silent light points to the sun that will come – it takes in a good area of sky right out over the valley in front of the hermitage. I walked down the path to see it well. It was splendid. I interrupted reading Isaac of Stella's Fourteenth Sermon on God's light and His joy in His creation.

Last Thursday the Pope promulgated several Council Documents – on Bishops, Education, Priestly training, Non-Christian religions, Religious. I have not seen all the latter, only excerpts, but they are disappointing. Have not read the one on Bishops yet, which is important. Non-Christian religions – satisfactory I think. Certainly good that it clearly says we accept whatever is true in Buddhism, for instance.

November 4, 1965

Turned in *Wulfric of Haselbury* yesterday. There were fine things in it, and I want pictures of some of it. On the other hand this business of skipping through miracles with a suspended judgment and an eye open for historical sidelights is emptying and deadening. And I am not up to a completely devout and credulous acceptance of *all* in a medieval saint's life on its own terms. The battle over his body (with the Cluniac monks breaking down the walls of his anchorage and tossing out the corpse) is enough indication that this was a different world, and one in which we certainly no longer live (for better or for worse).

Today, a few quotes from Heidegger got me back on a serious and contemporary track. I cannot go long evading our contemporary confrontation with what is beyond logic, and my task is in *this*. However, in Isaac of Stella one feels a certain awareness of the "ontological reality" of the void and the *nihil* (nothingness out of which we are made is more than a mere logical supposition).

Cloudy this morning. No comet.

November 5, 1965

Old fashioned idea: that the solitary life and indeed the Christian life is a struggle with invisible powers. All this is discussed even by monks. Yet is the Bible so far wrong? I think I experience it more and more: as to what these powers are, who can clearly say: but one experiences their persuasion, their use of our weakness to prompt us to choices which, if followed out logically, would wreck us totally. So much more than mere "prudence" is needed – and infinitely more than simple "personal responsibility – autonomy – authenticity," etc. A superficial existentialism can be a disaster. I see it in my writings, once they are printed. Just my arrogant tone, and then extreme statements that could do harm, faults of perspective perhaps, and how can I complain if I am criticized? Yet I am often criticized for not being radical *enough*. Obviously I am a complex, alienated person myself and this can upset everybody. I must meanwhile go on seriously working out my own problems, but without seeking the transient satisfaction of laying down the law. That is why I am most satisfied with the article on the "Council and Religious Life" in *New Blackfriars*. There is no question that I am writing too much and this is the source of the trouble. And part of this is my inability to say "no" to those who request articles, reviews, prefaces, blurbs, etc. However, I do say no sometimes, I admit. But not as often as I should.

Riches! The comet. I went out and though there was mist I saw it as it first began to appear. Later it became more definite and quite bright (what I am seeing is the reflection of the comet's tail for it is now past the sun). A most beautiful and moving thing this great spear in the sky pointing down to the horizon where the sun will not appear yet for an hour and a half. As I watched, under the oaks, with acorns dropping around me, the bell rang in church for the preface and consecration. Three meteorites flashed across the sky in fifteen minutes. Two army transports growled and blinked across the comet's path, and the stag cried out in the dark field beyond my hedge. Riches! I recited Psalm 18, *coeli enarrant* [the heavens proclaim]– with joy.

November 7, 1965

Jim Douglass sent a letter with a clipping in it about a pacifist who burned himself to death in front of the Pentagon – it must have been last Tuesday, All Souls' Day! It was a protest against the Viet Nam war. They will probably try to write him off as a nut, but he seems to have been a perfectly responsible person, a Quaker, very dedicated. What can one say of such a thing? Since I do not know the man, I do not know that his motives were necessarily wrong or confused – all I can say is that objectively it is a terrible thing. Certainly it is an awful sign, and perhaps there had to be such a sign, but what if a lot of really pathological characters now do the same and confuse it, making everything merely another mish mash of absurdities. Certainly the sign was powerful because incontestable and final in itself (and how frightful!). It broke through the undifferentiated, uninterpretable noises, and it certainly must have hit many people awful hard. But in three days it becomes again contestable and in ten it is forgotten. O God, what a tragic world we live in! Meanwhile the Catholic Workers are all burning their draft cards . . .

I went out on the porch before dawn to think of these things, and of the words of Ezekiel (22:30). "And I sought among them for a man that might set up a hedge and stand in the gap before me in favor of the land that I might not destroy it, and I found none." And while I was standing there quails began to whistle all over the field and in the wood. I had not heard any for weeks and thought sure they were all dead, for there have been hunters everywhere. No, there they are! Signs of life, of gentleness, of helplessness, of providence, of love. They just keep on existing and loving and making more quails and whistling in the bushes.

November 8, 1965

There has been no rain for almost three weeks. The woods have been getting very dry. And I have been told of the monotonous succession of bright, hot days, walking among the stiff, paper leaves. I have been hoping and praying for rain. So this morning when I went out at dawn and saw the sky dark with clouds I was very happy. The air smelled wet and the pine needles in particular smelled strong and sweet. There may have been a light rain in the night. But at the end of the morning there was a good rain, while I was saying Mass (no server showed up so I said it alone in joy, with pauses where I felt like pausing). Then another good rain in the afternoon after I got back to the hermitage. The misty valley and wet woods filled me with joy.

I have been preparing *Raids on the Unspeakable* for printing. A collection of short pieces some of which I am mostly rewriting. But today I wrote a few letters instead – to Eshelman in Peru, for example, and Sister Pascal in Haiti. The proofs of the Postulants' Guide. came and I was pleased with them – another innocent reason for contentment. Ping Ferry says there is a true air of war fever out there. I do not doubt it – but I hear only very little news. At Santa Barbara five of the drawings (signatures) were sold at the exhibit in the Museum.

November 11, 1965. St. Martin

A sad day. Learned this morning, again by special delivery letter from Jim Douglass (a day late) that a kid from the *Catholic Worker* [Roger Laporte] burned himself alive in front of the U.N. Building. This is fantastic and horrible. He was an ex-seminarian evidently. I cannot understand the shape of things in the Peace Movement or the shape of things at all in this country. What is happening? Is everybody nuts? This took place last Monday.

I am so disturbed by the events, and especially the suicide at the U.N., that I sent a telegram to Dorothy Day and this telegram to Jim Forest of the Catholic Peace Fellowship.

"Just heard about suicide of Roger Laporte. While I do not hold Catholic Peace Fellowship responsible for this tragedy, current developments in Peace Movement make it impossible for me to continue as sponsor for Fellowship. Please remove my name from list of sponsors, letter follows."

This thought came when I was asking Father Abbot permission to send the telegrams and naturally he was much in favor, but afterwards I wondered if I had been too hard on Jim and the Catholic Peace Fellowship. But with things as crazy as they are I cannot let my name be used by an outfit as unpredictable as that is, with kids likely to do anything at any moment. The CPF is right in the middle of the draft card burning and now this. Five from *Catholic Worker* burned their cards. One burnt himself. Totally awful, the suicide at least.

Yesterday Dan Walsh said a newspaper man in Louisville was trying to get in contact with me – perhaps it had something to do with this affair.

Sometimes I wish it were possible simply to be the kind of hermit who is so cut off he knows *nothing* that goes on, but that is not right, either.

The world has never been so sick. Demonstrations. Counter-demonstrations. And all of it in the realm of signs and gestures, agitation – meaning what? The war in Viet Nam goes on and the only effect of the demonstrations is that the general run of people get scared and accept the war because at least it is familiar!

At supper – read a few pages [in *Les Grandes Amitiés: Souvenirs,* reprinted 1965] of Raïssa Maritain on [Ernest] Psichari and his conversion. His delight at his progress toward Catholicism in the desert. All that is so familiar and comforting. Before World War I, written during World War II when all the issues were clear. And now nothing is clear – and as for Psichari himself, his love of the army and so on – it is seen to be an illusion. Was all that was clear equally an illusion? It is so comforting to read of him coming back to Mother Church, and to the continuity of centuries of Christendom. But where is all that now? What a void! We need a grimmer faith than he did!

November 12, 1965

This morning in my *lectio* came to Chapter 32 of Ezekiel – again the wonderful and awful solemnity of those scenes as all the kings go down into the abyss uncircumcised and killed by the sword. Is there some key to the mentality of our country and of our time? If there is I wish I had it and could open up something of a new understanding. It is badly needed, because the first thing we lack is insight. The most obvious and terrible thing about us is that we have almost infinite power and we are completely blind. The judgment of God hangs over us and we cannot understand.

Today – fasted, chopped wood (pungent smelling hard red oak logs down by the stile, where leaves are thick on the path). – Finished [Sacheverell] Sitwell on *Monks, Nuns and Monasteries* and wrote a review for the *Critic.*[9] I find more and more in Rilke, a very rich poet whom I barely looked at years ago when I was supposed to be reading poetry. Did I even in fact ever read much poetry in those days? It was cloudy, misty, sun coming and going. The trees are bare. The landscape begins to get ready for winter. It is deer season but I hope it will soon be over.

November 13, 1965

This morning where I was saying Prime under the pine trees in front of the hermitage, I saw a wounded deer limping along in the field, one leg

[9] "Holy Camp," *The Critic* 24 (February-March 1966): 68–70.

incapacitated. I was terribly sad at this and began weeping bitterly. And something quite extraordinary happened. I will never forget standing there weeping and looking at the deer standing still looking at me questioningly for a long time, a minute or so. The deer bounded off without any sign of trouble.

Victor Hammer got permission to come and see me, and he and Carolyn and I had a very pleasant visit sitting in the sun by the pine wood in St. Malachy's field. They came by the new turnpike that just opened two weeks ago (that really was a fast job!). Spoke of a big blackout (power failure) in New York. I can't seem to get much information about the comet. He is still working on his Resurrection picture. He looked very well in fact. Deliberately did not talk of peace movement and the Viet Nam War. We spoke of [Lewis] Mumford, who has a new book out. Victor is writing some autobiographical notes. Talked of da Vinci, etc.

November 15, 1965. Feast of Dedication

Pleasant afternoon yesterday (Sunday) going no further than the brow of the hill a hundred yards before the hermitage and looking out on the valley or down to the dim monastery in autumn shadow, through the bare trees.

I continue with Rilke (and talked to novices of him yesterday) – often I can't stand his mental climate when it is too adolescent. But when he is out of that, above it, beyond it, he is a great artist. Also it falls often short of the real depth and clarity of vision. He is blocked by cleverness, by emotion, by clogging sensuality, from really mystical apprehension (except perhaps in some lines of the *Duino Elegies* – but I am working on the *Neue Gedichte*). When he is objective (in his own way of being objective), he is great. Perhaps at his greatest in his Olive Garden poem – the agony of Gethsemani, which Catholics have probably read with severe displeasure as a denial of faith. Is it, though? Is it perhaps not a deeper realization of the loneliness of Gethsemani and a key to Rilke's "unchristian" spirit, or a pointer to a solution – that he obscurely could not have a Mediator "outside," he had to be completely identified with Christ, all is not perfectly "pure" but it is nevertheless all the more true. Did not Christ take upon himself the utter, inadequate forlornness of the unbeliever? But I admit I am getting into the tone and music of Rilke, and sensing the differences of mood and intonation (v.g., in "*Gesang der Frauen an den Dichter*" ["Song of Women to the Poet"] – lovely and funny).

Evening – The concelebration was happy and beautiful for today's feast. At dinner they are reading the Council's Constitution on Pastoral Duties of

Bishops which is very fine. I went for a walk to St. Malachy's field – windy, grey skies, meditation. In the evening read of Psichari's conversion and death in Raïssa Maritain. Tomorrow is the twenty-seventh anniversary of my own baptism. There is nothing more important than the gift of Catholic Faith – and keeping that faith pure and clear. Psichari had this. Today it is Péguy with his problems and ambiguities who is more popular – and people like Rilke who will not hesitate to sacrifice the purity of faith for an aesthetic effect. I do not underestimate the sincerity and difficulty of those who have problems of faith, for whom God is so easily "dead" all at once. But for my own part, the gift has been too great to be trifled with. The faith is not something that can be set aside while one is putting on a display of cleverness. One feels that this purity of faith suffers much more than it did then – there is a lot of good will; idealism, but much confusion and a sort of "why shouldn't I believe this if I want to?" attitude. You pick your faith like your clothes!!

November 20, 1965

Naomi Burton was here, brought a long *New Yorker* article by Ved Mehta on the God is dead theologians. I read it hurriedly in one sitting – a useful survey though I think he failed to see Tillich from the "inside," so to speak. Learned from this article that Tillich died October 22. Naomi and I went over the long manuscript of *Conjectures* (the title *Barth's Dream* is dropped), made changes, cut here and there. Rode down toward Rolling Rock River in her rented Monza, and beyond, in the high lands to the south – woods, long views on the top, along the bushy peneplain. We agreed that I should refuse to write prefaces as far as possible and not do anthologies. Had a good visit with her.

Letters came from Dan Berrigan, Jim Forest, Dorothy Day. Good letters. I can see that in the trial they have gone through (death of Roger Laporte), there has been much purity of love. Dan is now being shipped out by superiors. A statement on draft card burning by Tom Cornell is lucid. However, I have to clarify my own position since people are identifying me with the card burners. While I respect their conscience, I don't think this is the most valid or helpful kind of statement at the moment and I will have to give some idea where I stand. This in turn shows that there is a certain incompatibility between my solitary life and active involvement in a movement.

November 21, 1965. Last Sunday after Pentecost

Unfortunately there is not that peace on earth. And it is imprudent to argue with pacifists. Again – along with the same question of the telegrams and letters about the Peace Movement and my attempted resignation from the Catholic Peace Fellowship – a long, melodramatic, hectoring letter from [John] Heidbrink of the Fellowship of Reconciliation. The burden of it is that I am a bastard, a traitor, etc. – all couched in Christian language. Also that the dedicated life of those working actively in the world (like himself and Jim Forest) is vastly superior to the life of ease and evasion which I am living in a hermitage "quilted in mist"! The letter was somewhat incredible and in some ways quite funny. But its self-complacency irritated me, especially since that was what he was accusing *me* of!

However, it was certainly a mistake to send that telegram. But a salutary one. I am learning from the experience. I am through with any playing with peace movements. It is no game. Remains to be seen what will work out with the Catholic Peace Fellowship. I suppose it is not important to me if they insist on keeping me (for my name). I don't want to quarrel with them and Jim Forest at least is an excellent and competent person. I think they are doing good work – apart from card-burning which they do not "sponsor" – but Tom Cornell is nevertheless the next most important member of the Catholic Peace Fellowship.

November 22, 1965

One of the images in Heidbrink's letter. Having portrayed my worthless evasion as hermit, he then dangles before me the man I "might become" if, turning from this utter waste, I would marshall all I have led into the cloister and lead them back into the world . . . back into his world of Bonhoefferish-Robinsonian concern, in which I would be welcomed and appointed a Scoutmaster. He speaks of being a "man for others" (the Robinson Term). His letter evidently manifests what this means to him. To be "for" me means for him to mind my business without understanding it, to propose to me his own fantasies, and get me to harmonize with his own rhetoric. It is the same empty Protestant fussiness that drove me out of Zion Church thirty years ago.

November 27, 1965

At midnight I woke up, and there was a great noise of wind and storm. Rain was rolling over the roof of the hermitage heavy as a freight train. The porch was covered with water and there was a lot of lightning. Now at dawn the sky is clean and all is cold again (yesterday warm). Yesterday I read some articles on psychedelics. There is a regular fury of drug-mysticism in this country. I am in a way appalled. Mysticism has finally arrived in a characteristic American mode. One feels that this is certainly it. The definitive turn in the road taken by American religion. The turn I myself will not take (don't need to!). This leaves my own road a lot quieter and more untroubled I hope. Certainly the great thing as I see it now is to get out of all the traffic: peace movement traffic, political traffic, Church traffic, "consciousness-altering" traffic, Zen traffic, monastic reform traffic. All of it! Big peace protest in Washington (against Viet Nam war) today. I am fasting and praying for them, and offering no hosannas of my own.

Rilke stayed at the Eden in Zurich, where we stayed, and he was dying in the Valois when we went through Switzerland in the summer of 1926. "We are members of a world which, producing movement upon movement, force upon force, seems to be plunging irresistibly into a less and less visible state, and we are dependent on that superior visibility of the past if we want to present an image of the muted splendor that still surrounds us." Rilke. Remarkably true. Note the invisibility of so many American cities – whole sections of Louisville are zero.

November 29, 1965

This morning I really opened the door of the *Duino Elegies* and walked in (previously I have only peeked in through the windows and read fragments here and there). For one thing I got the *sound* of the German really going, and got the feel of the First Elegy as a whole. (Did this before to a lesser extent with the Eighth.) I think I needed this hill, this silence, this frost, to really understand this great poem, to live in it – as I have also in *Four Quartets*. These are the two modern poems, long poems, that really have a great deal of meaning for me. Like Lorca (whom I have not read for years –). Others I simply like and agree with. Auden, Spender to some extent. Dylan Thomas in an entirely different way. But the *Duino Elegies* and *Four Quartets* talk about my life itself, my own self, my own destiny, my Christianity, my vocation, my relation to the world of my time, my place in it, etc. Perhaps Neruda's *Residence on Earth* and of course Vallejo will eventually do this but with *Residence* I have, once again, only looked through the windows (still I might get with that later and even give talks on it).

December 1, 1965

When I got up it was about thirty on the porch and now at dawn it is down to twenty-one. These are the coldest hours – meditation, *lectio*, and hot tea with lemon and a good fire. I am reading [Paul] Evdokimov [*La Femme et le salut du monde*, 1958] – after tea – and then the *Duino Elegies*. The *Elegies* I am just reading, without comment, especially the German, aloud, to try to get the magnificent substance of sound and to think in the German (it is a language I can't think in, as I can French and Spanish). I will go over it again for notes later. The Leishman-Spender [James Blair Leishman and Stephen Spender] translation is the best piece of translating done for Rilke. Rilke's long wait for the *Elegies* sobers me not a little.

Meanwhile – down to the ridiculous! – the postulants' guide, in final proof stage, should be ready for Christmas, and suddenly Brother Ralph in the bookstore is raising objections about the price (comes to about twenty-seven cents a copy) and wanting to get quotations from another printer!! What strange ways of thinking monks have! And this is a level-headed one, too. The other picture book (Peter Geist has done a fine design) will probably meet the same kind of obstacles! What an absurd way to live!

December 2, 1965

"La croix est faite de nos faiblesses et de nos défaillances, elle est construite par nos ego et surtout par nos ténèbres profondes et l'inavouable et complice laideur, bref par toute la complexité qui est à ce moment précis le moi authentique." ["The cross is made up of our weaknesses and our failures, it is constructed by our ego and above all by our profound gloom and unspeakable and culpable ugliness, in short by all the complexity that is at this time the real I."]

I experience the truth of this very real and exact insight of Evdokimov. Still in regard to the Catholic Peace Fellowship – about which nothing is settled, I see how much there was that was inauthentic (i.e., false, spurious) in my own initial enthusiasm for identification with peace activities, the *Catholic Worker*, etc. It was in reality selfish and naïve at the same time. And I did not foresee that necessarily they and I could hardly go along forever in agreement, living in totally different circumstances. Yet I do agree with their ideal in general – not with all its particular implementations. One could go on analyzing interminably. I must accept this result of my own inner-contradictions and trust God to bring a solution in which His will may be done by me and all of them too. Right now, still informed only by vague snatches of rumor, I am in the painful position of being simply unable to judge one way or another. And I don't know what to do next – hence I must be content not to act at all, when I would very much like to settle everything in a big sweep.

Fortunately Brother Ralph changed his mind about the printer and withdrew his objections. That is one less trouble. In solitude these things get magnified beyond all reason. I am too sensitive, too insecure. Absolute need for a more real *faith*.

Meanwhile I woke up in the night thinking of the name: Wera Ouckama Knoop!

December 3, 1965

I discovered that the storm last Friday night (see November 27th) really tore up Lawrenceburg, which is not far from here. It took off roofs, killed three people, tore off the side of a whiskey store house.

Today decided I would remain a sponsor of Catholic Peace Fellowship – i.e., let them use my name – if it were made clear that I do not automatically support each new political move they make. I think they will see that this is in the press. I certainly want to support their professed aims – education, information, help of Conscientious Objectors, etc., but not necessarily their bids for publicity and political action. It is to me clear that these repeated manifestos, agitations, picketings, card burnings, meetings, etc. are getting to be in many respects a meaningless routine. There is an atmosphere of fuss and fury, perhaps also much that is valid and alive for some who are in it. For me it would be merely an exercise in naïveté to pretend to keep up with it all and be involved in it. Hence I am from now on disengaged from immediate action – or at least from identification with any special program or movement. If any special action is required of me I will take it personally, and not in a parade.

A great event – a new presence! Arrival of a lovely Byzantine ikon (from Salonika – ?) about 1700. The most beautiful I have ever seen (except in photos of course). The Holy Mother and child and then on panels that open out, St. Nicholas and St. George, St. Demetrius and St. Charlandros – whoever that is. It was sent as a gift by Marco Pallis and I was moved, *bouleversé* [disturbed], by its arrival. How magnificent it is in its simplicity. I never tire of gazing at it. It will change my whole attitude. Already after supper instead of continuing with light reading (Raïssa Maritain), I got out the Greek New Testament!! Beautiful letter from Marco Pallis with it.

December 4, 1965

Hardware in space. There are about 180 capsules whirling around the earth out of 375 which have so far been put in orbit by the U.S. and U.S.S.R. Thirteen more orbiting around the sun, seven smashed up on the moon. And now one little French capsule whirling around too, saying nothing in any language, but "adding prestige."

December 5, 1965. Second Sunday of Advent

The bells from the Abbey are all absurd. Angelus at 3:45 – a bell for an of-fice at 5:45, etc. The darkness is alive with inappropriate bells. Probably due to the abolition of Prime – they have doubtless moved Lauds. I will find out when I go down for concelebration.

Last evening at supper I began [Jacques] Ellul's *L'Illusion politique*. It is some comfort to find someone who agrees with my position. I must be res-olutely non-political, provided I remain ready to speak out when it is needed. However, I think this book too may turn out insufficient and naïve (philosophically weak perhaps. I am not far into it). But he is basically right in attacking the modern superstition that "what has no political value has no value at all" – "A man who does not read the newspapers is not a man." And to be apolitical is to be excommunicated as a sorcerer. That the deep-est communion of man with man is in political dedication.

December 7, 1965

In the midst of the trials and distractions – (the trouble with Catholic Peace Fellowship, then the letter of Joel Orent demanding to see me to talk about his dissertation, etc., etc.) – I realize dimly that there is something else try-ing to break through into my awareness. Clearly all this fussing about defin-ing my position on this or that contemporary issue is secondary (what I held in regard to *ends* is clear. As to immediate political means I am in no posi-tion to judge!). It has its place – but I see how foolish it would be to become involved in it as if it were of primary importance.

What is primary? God's revelation of Himself to me *in Christ* and my re-sponse of faith. In the concrete, this means, for me, my present life in soli-tude, acceptance of its true perspectives and demands, and the work of slow reorientation that goes on. Each day, a little, I realize that my old life is breaking loose and will eventually fall off, in pieces, gradually. What then? My solitude is not like Rilke's ordered to a poetic explosion. Nor is it a mere deepening of religious consciousness. What is it then? What has been so far only a theological conception, or an image, has to be sought and loved. "Union with God!" So mysterious that in the end man would perhaps do anything to evade it, once he realizes it means the *end* of his own Ego-self-realization, once for all. Am I ready? Of course not. Yet the course of my life is set in this direction.

It turned into a rough day. I have had to drink buttermilk to restore the bacteria to my intestines but the buttermilk itself finally knocked me out with a terrible attack of diarrhea that laid me out for the morning and left me sagging for the rest of the day (it is a fast day anyway!).

December 11, 1965

Wednesday the Council closed. Nothing has been read about it yet in refectory, but I have heard various things. Everything was finished. The Schema on the Church and the World finally passed with the part on conscientious objection weakened, but the strong statement against total war unmitigated in spite of the efforts of Cardinal Spellman and Archbishop Hannon. Really this Council has been a great thing. Now we will really begin to see what it has meant for the Church! As far as I am concerned the document I like best is the Constitution (Decree?) on Revelation – and the one on the Church. Have not seen the one on the Church and the World, but am already busy on "Redeeming the Time" (the section on it in the book for Burns Oates). I am repeatedly thankful for this Council, for having lived at this time, for having learned so much from it. Certainly my own attitude to "the world" will have to be modified. I have too easily and unthinkingly used the old *contemptus mundi* line as an evasion. However, this does not mean I do not remain a hermit. But it changes my attitude, anyway. Rightly so.

De Gaulle was not elected on the first vote, there will be a second. General surprise! Serious situation in Africa since last month where Rhodesian white racists have taken over and broken off from England to run a little racist state of their own. Shocking appeal to values of "Christian civilization." Good protest by Rhodesian bishops read in refectory today. Otherwise I have not heard much about it.

Letter from Dorothy Day today. We agree. Dan Berrigan is, I discover, the center of a political storm – has been sent to South America by the superiors. Evidently they want to get him away from the Peace Movement. But they deny this. Hot and loud protest.

In addition to all that – more news, no less interesting but probably less accurate – from Andy Boone.

1. That some woods near here were set alight by sparks from a flying meteorite which landed in Pennsylvania and came from "the comet."

2. That two deer have been found dead around here, not shot, but just dead. Poisoned by chemicals?

3. That the white oaks are being devoured by worms that are *not* being devoured by birds, because "they ain't no more birds."

4. That all the streams are poisoned by fallout.

5. That sycamores are dying all over the country. This he got from Father Arnold.

December 13, 1965

I do not yet have the text of the Decree on the Church and the World, but I am reading and thinking and marking time on the manuscript of "Redeeming the Time." It is fruitful. A grace of the Council for me will have been this beginning of a change from a radically negative anti-science and anti-technology attitude to something more open and humane. For example when the big SAC B52 flew low over the hermitage under the low ceiling of clouds it was possible for me to think of it as part of my own world, not just as "*their* damn plane." Although that does not imply approval of the bomb, still, it is *my* world that builds the planes and flies them and there is something admirable about all that: it has at least good possibilities.

December 16, 1965

Yesterday – went in town. (First time in four months, since hospital.) Rainy, misty day. Early Mass (served by Brother Denis). Read an article by Van der Leeuw in an *Eranos Jahrbuch* in University of Louisville library – and some Prose Poems of Baudelaire. Lunch with Jim Wygal at Cunningham's, then went out to his place in Anchorage (he did 100 m.p.h. in his new Impala on the new Interstate parkway). Then, watched on TV the meeting in space of Gemini 7 and Gemini 6. Actually what was shown was a series of maps and "simulations" but I was watching at the time when 6 began catching up to 7 over the Indian Ocean and got within a few feet of 7 beyond Hawaii. They were orbiting together over Brazil when I left. A fantastic thing! The only live stuff were occasional unintelligible voices of astronauts talking to Houston, Texas. All this I went into as a deliberate exercise of the new "worldliness" – in other words to be able to see these things without defensiveness and criticism, though also without ga-ga optimism. This is the world I live in and I am part of it. Why act as if I had a better world of my own to offer as an alternative? Apparently the reason for the blackout in the Eastern States last month was a failure in a computer. There was another blackout in Texas for the same reason. So the machines are not infallible either.

But what is the meaning of this space business? I am afraid I am still not too convinced there is point to it. If it is all a form of gigantic play, well and good. It is a bit expensive, no doubt. But what does it mean? I wonder if anyone really knows, or even asks. It is first something that has to be done because now we can do it. And there was a tiny bit of escalation in Viet Nam – because we can do that too. Bombing of power plant in Haiphong. They are getting closer to Hanoi. And what does this mean? Certainly not that we are "winning" or that in this way we can force anyone to negotiate on our own terms. As to all the marches and protests – they change nothing.

December 18, 1965

I seem to be living in a shower of boomerangs which I thoughtlessly threw out into space one, two, three years ago not knowing what they were. All of them have something to do with my writing about "the world" and my desire for witness and "engagement." Purpose of the boomerangs – to convince me of the large part of illusion and myth there was in all this. For example now – the Eight Freedom Songs. Bad poems, written at the request of a young Negro singer [Robert Laurence Williams], for a fittingly idealistic project which was more or less improvised and without order. He brought in Alex Peloquin as a composer, then went himself to Ireland and instead of coming back to sing the songs stayed there to be a success in a show called "Gails of Laughter." Alexander Peloquin, carrying the ball at high speed and telling no one (of us) about it went on to do a symphony for Eileen Farrell with the Eight Songs. Now Robert Williams is (rightly) disgusted at what has happened to his songs (which no longer have much to do with Negroes!) and blames me for betrayal, for cynically treating the sorrows of the Negro as something to exploit, etc. I did not know what Alexander Peloquin was doing. He came here in the summer, then left and has not written a word.

December 21, 1965. St. Thomas

While I was saying Mass, at my Communion, I heard the bells ring for an agony and guessed they were for Brother Gerard (they rang for *thee!*) and he died about an hour later. Father Amandus-Roger made me a sign, coming late to his dinner. Another of the old Brothers, the past dying. Brother Gerard was from Europe, was long a gardener, tailor, etc., and was said to have visions.

A distant relative sent an old snapshot taken when he and his wife visited Douglaston thirty years ago. It shows them with Bonnemaman [Martha Jenkins][10] and myself – and the back porch of the house, and the birch tree. There is Bonnemaman as I remember her – within two years of dying. And

[10] Merton's grandmother, Martha Baldwin Jenkins (1865–1937).

there am I: it shakes me! I am the young rugby player, the lad from Cambridge, vigorous, light, vain, alive, obviously making a joke of some sort. The thing that shakes me: I can see that that was a different body from the one I have now – one entirely young and healthy, one that did not know sickness, weakness, anguish, tension, fatigue – a body totally assured of itself and without care, perfectly relaxed, ready for enjoyment. What a change since that day! If I were wiser, I would not mind but I am not so sure I am wiser: I have been through more, I have endured a lot of things, perhaps fruitlessly. I do not entirely think that – but it is possible. What shakes me is that – I wish I were that rugby player, vain, vigorous, etc. and could start over again!! And yet how absurd. What would I ever do? The other thing is that those were, no matter how you look at it, better times! There were things we had not heard of – Auschwitz, the Bomb, etc. (Yet it was all beginning, nevertheless.)

And now what kind of a body! An arthritic hip; a case of chronic dermatitis on my hands for a year and a half (so that I have to wear gloves); sinusitis, chronic ever since I came to Kentucky; lungs always showing up some funny shadow or other on ex-rays (though not lately); perpetual diarrhea and a bleeding anus; most of my teeth gone; most of my hair gone; a chewed-up vertebra in my neck which causes my hands to go numb and my shoulder to ache – and for which I sometimes need traction; when you write it down it looks like something, and it is true, there is no moment any more when I am not *aware* that I have something wrong with me and have to be careful! What an existence! But I have grown used to it – something which thirty years ago would have been simply incredible.

December 25, 1965. Christmas Day

Yesterday was too much like spring – warm, sunny, windy. I felt torpid in the afternoon, but forced myself to write a few letters, to try and make some inroads on the enormous pile, which I will not try to dispose of! The mail situation is one I accept as impossible to handle. Besides, Brother Dunstan, my typist, seems to have got himself steamed up spiritually and is having a breakdown – so he will not be able to work on the manuscript I have been busy with in the last few days – "Redeeming the Time" – on the Constitution about the Church in the world. The Constitution itself is not bad. Good chapter on war.

Last night when I woke up to go down for Midnight Mass, I found it storming with rain and huge winds in the dark woods. The walk down was exciting. Coming back the rain had stopped. I came up through the field and was glad to get into the silence of the hermitage which made more sense than ever. I made my thanksgiving quietly, said Lauds and had a snack and some wine (the last of what Brother Clement gave me a couple of months ago) and so went back to bed for a couple of hours. Got up again, said Prime and read E[dwin] A[rcher] Burtt's book [*In Search of Philosophic Understanding*, 1966] which he sent. It is clear and informative. And Schlier. Now I am going to get back to Rilke (volumes to be returned to University of Kentucky in a few days). It is the kind of day I like, and like Christmas to be too: dark, cloudy, windy, cold with light rain blowing now and then. I have had wonderful Christmases (Christmas weeks) here with this kind of winter weather, unforgettable. Days not too bad for walking out on the wooded knobs, cold and lonelier than ever and full of apparent meaning. They talk to me of my vocation.

The midnight Mass, concelebrated, was decent, and I was glad to be there (we shouted a great carol as recessional hymn). I felt the community was fully *in* it. Really the only reason I went was for the Community and for the Sacrament, not for any joy or light I would get out of such a ceremony. It is hard to hear the reading of the Word, we are behind the reader and the acoustics are bad. The singing is O.K. but too much of the same – all is by Father Chrysogonus and too many solos by Brother Chrysostom, who seems tired. They always overdo a good thing. And the whole community celebration is still spoiled for me by the sense of a certain falsity and willfulness (instead of faith) which some infect into it. As if there were a kind of perverse and intense determination to make certain self-deceptions come true and as if that were faith. (This of course in conjunction with, supported by, real faith. The parasitism of willful consolation and self-imposed meanings, forced upon simple faith. Monstrous, or potentially monstrous, mental gavottes.) Yet at the same time, I was moved by the simplicity and sincerity of Brother Cuthbert kneeling before the crib.

But anyway I did not get the awful depression that I have had a couple of times at Christmas in recent years. Thank God for that! Perhaps this comes from my thinking about death that has opened out with the last days of Advent – seeing death as built into my life and accepting it in and with life (not trying to push it out of life, keep it away from contaminating a life supposedly completely other than it. Death is flowering in my life as a part and fulfillment of it – its term, its final chord).

Second time in bed I had a curious, somewhat sexual dream about Naomi [Burton Stone], which says something of my ambivalence toward her perhaps and my sense of her ambivalence toward me. In a way I guess we love each other, and we are both so complicated – and so devout, maybe (or she is anyway) that it gets funny, and is very inhibited, or rather not. I feel it and bear it as another bloody nuisance, like my psychosomatic sickness.

December 30, 1965

End of a year. Should one have something to say about a "year"? I have no need to be obsessed with time here, though I don't pretend to be lost in eternity either. Days go by. The moon of Ramadan which was new on Christmas Eve is growing fat, and I will save the fasting till after New Year – a token fast with the Moslems. Must write to Abdul Aziz.

The business with Jim Forest and Catholic Peace Fellowship is settled charitably. Dorothy Day wrote a splendid card. These are authentic Christians and I feel very indebted to solitude and nothingness. Automatic and compulsive routines that are simply silly – and I don't take them seriously. All the singing, the "speaking in tongues," etc. Funny. I see how easily I could go nuts and don't especially care. I see the huge flaws in myself and don't know what to do about them. Die of them eventually, I suppose, what else can I do? I live a flawed and inconsequential life, believing in God's love. But faith can no longer be naïve and sentimental. I cannot explain things away with it. Need for deeper meditation. I certainly see more clearly where I need to go and how (surprising how my prayer in community had really reached a dead end for *years* and stayed there – fortunately I could get out to the woods and my spirit could breathe). Still, Gethsemani too has to be fully accepted. My long refusal to fully identify myself with the place is futile (and identifying myself in some forlorn and lonesome way would be worse). It is simply where I am, and the monks are who they are: not monks but people, and the younger ones are more truly people than the old ones, who are also good in their own way, signs of a different kind of excellence that is no longer desirable in its accidentals. The essence is the same.

Renounce accusations and excuses.

Brother Alberic is to type the manuscript on the Council Constitution on Church and World since Brother Dunstan got himself steamed up spiritually and had better rest.

I continue with Rilke, seeing his greatness and his limitations. His poetic solitude is not what I am here for, but it says something too. So he is no mystic. But he *is* a poet. Is that a small thing?

To work quietly and intelligently for peace. And above all to pray.

December 31, 1965

7 a.m. – still completely dark. Heavy rain clouds, warm wind waving the forest and loud in the pines. To the south – not east – a thin red line along the top of the ridge. In the east all is blocked with heavy weather.

Night. 7 p.m. Rain beginning to fall. Dark and warm all day. Year ends.

Things I am especially thankful for –

Chapter decree permitting hermitage, and my official move to hermitage.

Finishing Chuang Tzu book.

End of the Council. Pope Paul's visit to the U.N.

Victor Hammer better and able to come over again.

Other events.

Sickness in the spring and early summer. My stomach is a bit better finally.

Selma – demonstrations etc. Viet Nam worse.

Difficulty over the Catholic Peace Fellowship – settled now.

Concelebrations began – then whole new schedule (after I moved out to hermitage).

What will next year bring? I expect perhaps more sickness. More trouble in Asia (escalation of the war?). Less writing – more thought – more meditation and reading. *Conjectures* should come out in the summer, *Mystics and Zen Masters* before that. I want to go now and prepare a good book on prayer. But I have no real plans, except to live and free the reality of my life and be ready when it ends and I am called to God. Whenever that may be!

Deus misereatur nostri et benedicat nobis! [God have mercy on us and bless us!]

Some Personal Notes

End of 1965

To ask for no more books, writings, etc. for at least three months – even from monastic library. To get through what I have first and get it off the shelves (did not keep this for more than three or four weeks!). I.e., to cut down on the ceaseless movement of books back and forth, mail coming in, magazines half read and passed on, etc., etc.

I come here to die and love. I come here to be created by the Spirit in Christ.

I am called here to grow. "Death" is a critical point of growth, or transition to a new mode of being, to *maturity* and fruitfulness that I do not know (they are in Christ and in His Kingdom). The child in the womb does not know what will come after birth. He must be born in order to live. I am here to learn to face death as my birth.

This solitude – a refuge under His wings, a place to hide myself in His Name, therefore a sanctuary, where the grace of Baptism remains a conscious, living, active reality, valid not only for me but for the whole Church. Here, planted as a seed in the cosmos, I will be a Christ seed, and bring fruit for other men. Death and rising in Christ.

Relics – St. Mary of Carmel Hermitage

St. Theresa of Avila	–	Oct. 15
St. Paul	–	June 30
Charbel Makhlouf	–	Dec. 24
St. Peter Damian	–	Feb.
St. John of the Cross	–	Nov. 24
St. Bede	–	May 26
St. Romuald	–	Feb. 11
St. Gregory Nazianzus		
St. Louis	–	Aug. 25
St. Nicholas of Flue		

Need to be "confirmed" in vocation by the Spirit (speaking through the Church, i.e., the abbot and community = council at least). This ordains me to be the person I am and to have the particular place and function I have, to be myself in the sense of choosing to tend toward what God wants me to be, and to orient my whole life to being the person He loves. Too often I have been simply the person, or the individual, who is indifferent to His love, and who therefore in practice ignores it as the great option and possibility for each man. (We are all "loved in general," but we have to personally accept a *special* love of God for ourselves.)

Now is the time to see what great strength comes out of silence – and not without struggle.

Obedience to God means first of all *waiting*, having to wait, *sustine Dominum* [waiting for the Lord]. The first thing then is to accept the fact that one will have to *wait*. Otherwise obedience is undermined by an implicit condition that destroys it.

To say I am a child of God is to say, before everything else, that I grow. That I begin. A child who does not grow becomes a monster. The idea "Child of God" is therefore one of living growth, becoming, possibility, risk, and joy in the negotiation of risk. In this God is pleased: that His child grows in wisdom and grace.

God is the Father who fights to defend and rescue His child. The life of the Child of God is not in the "development of spirituality" but in obedience to the Good Shepherd who seeks him, knowing he is lost. It is in solitude that we recognize, with a shock, how lost we have been, and that now we are found, rescued, recovering conscience, returning to ourselves, to Truth, carried by Him who has sought and found us.

I can see how weak and disorganized I have been. Though God has often given me understanding, I have not been able to act on it with the full force of my being, because I have been too dispersed, too occupied, too "clever," and too much engaged in conflict and self-defense in a matter that was, certainly, not propitious for real depth and seriousness (at least in my case). Now it all becomes abundantly clear!

Therefore, clear necessity for *one* task above all now: collection and direction of inner strength upon what I know of God's will, to let it move me completely, and to move with it. (If there is any confusion of motives this is *impossible*.)

"Christ is risen, my joy!" In this way St. Seraphim of Sarov greeted those who came to him. The whole sense of this new life, life in the Spirit, is here! Encounter – Truth – the Joy of the Spirit, the presence of the Risen Kyrios.

The Lord was crushed under the weight of my sins, so I must now also consent to feel their burden, and console Him by the belief that in this "death" the Holy Spirit will miraculously transform my death into His life.

Adam was tempted to believe in himself as individual. He believed. And so became an "ego" confronting himself as stranger in millions of other isolated "egos." Each ego was enclosed in itself and condemned to struggle in vain against an inevitable death, while trying to affirm itself as immortal. Seeing there is no solution to this conflict, Adam, the ego, forgets it in work and fun. What is the key to this mystery? The self-affirmation of the ego means *loss of the Holy Spirit*. In the Spirit we are fully persons, become fully related to God and man in love. Without the Spirit, the possibility of true love and freedom is not realized and we are pseudo-persons (individuals).

In the community I prepared for solitude. Now in solitude I realize at once that my true preparation is for the transfigured common life of the Kingdom of God. In the Spirit, no man is alone. Unfortunately, human community often stifles the Spirit and keeps men isolated in their individuality, while *claiming* to produce transcendent unity.

Correspondence: examine the question of "false intimacy" – temptation to answer "sincere" fan mail which presents, in all simplicity, a confident and a seemingly authentic bid for friendship. But conditions do not permit the realization of a true intimacy. (Yet not altogether false either.) I have always avoided this kind of correspondence, with very few exceptions (some of which have turned out well, e.g., the Olmsteads. I am very fond of them).

Trials and difficulties in the life change nothing of the facts. To remain in solitude is to remain in love and freedom of direct obedience to God and not return to safety and security of a tissue of "works" and conventions (and conveniences!). When one has the vocation, then one becomes confronted with a choice equivalent to that of Grace vs. Law in Galatians.

One thing is certain: if I merely look upon solitude and "eremiticism" as a culminating monastic ideal, I will find only the delusions that are so frustrating everywhere else. The last thing in the world I want is to "be a hermit." The image of the bearded man half-blind with tears, living in a cave, is not enough. (The grace of compunction which this figure is supposed to typify is something else again!) I come into solitude to hear the words of God, to wait in expectation of a Christian fulfillment, to understand myself in relation to a community that doubts and questions itself, and of which I am very much a part. I come into solitude not to "attain to the heights of contemplation," but to rediscover painfully for myself and for my brothers the true eschatological dimension of our calling. No easy solution is permissible. This is a hard way and a way of faith, in which I must struggle to come into the right relation of obedience to the words of God constantly present in my heart, and rest in God who moves in the ground of my being, to make me grown in Him.

"*Haec dicit Dominus: State super vias et videte et interrogate de semitis antiquis quae sit via bona et ambulate in ea et invenietis refrigerium animabus vestris.*" ["Thus says the Lord: Stand on the roads and see and inquire concerning the old paths, which may be the good road, and walk upon it and you will find refreshment for your souls."] *Jeremiah 6:16*

"*Probatorem dedi te in populo meo robustum et scies et probabis viam eorum.*" ["I have given you as a sturdy tester in my people and you will know and test their path."] *Jeremiah 6:27*

Whole areas of my life meaningless – lava – not incorporated with any scheme – fighting for expression. Verbalizing won't do, it is pretense – or not the verbalizing I am in the habit of. Try some other! Try to anyway maybe. Why? Perhaps the Zen way is better – (silence until the whole thing breaks and then there is one enigmatic word for all of it).

I want to be = honest – simple – non-aggressive – pure in heart. Why I am not? Because I feel myself threatened. How? – I am vulnerable, insufficient, I need help, but if I ask for it as I need it, I will be rejected – another form of "help" will be offered, "they" will offer "help" at a price: pseudo-help. Granting of favors. Quid pro quo. The kind of help you get in a whore house. (Maybe that's what I want.)

The self-revelations of others: you see they are exerted and embarrassed by things that do not merit all that energy. Same with this? Yet in fact I *feel* it.

Alan Ginsberg – I had his name corrected in the piece for *Harper's*. Is what he says he feels so important – even to him? Is there any meaning to it? That's what I mean about myself. Actually, the search is bogging down in individualism, "no issue." You can search for 100 years and never come up with anything but more crap. (Diarrhea – a dynamism of helplessness. Acting out my despair.) (*What is this despair?* I don't know.)

What one needs to do. To find the place where *prejudice* is falsifying interpretation of life, is imposing a fiction and blocking real relationship, love, honesty.

Too much emphasis on purity of *conscience* can result in corruption of *consciousness*. Begin first with consciousness – and this means foregoing self, and manifestation of life. Direct vision.

Business and Madame Tadié. Sense of being obliged to play a game in which I have no interest, the rules of which I do not know – a game which is also very ambiguous because of the mentality of Marie Tadié. There are really *two* games. One the game of business itself. The other the game of her megalomania, her concept of her relationship with me (which is not clear to me), etc. Very annoying to be dominated by this woman. I am extremely sorry for her husband now! What hell he must go through. This second game, she herself does not fully know she is playing it. She puts it all into business and acts out. God deliver me! Chief ambiguity: under pretext of "helping" me she is exploiting me ruthlessly. The purpose of "the game" is to enable her to do this with a good conscience. I am afraid to tell her this because it would cause a typhoon. I want to break the whole thing off and can't because after all she has been a "good agent." I want to put all business in the hands of the publishers, and she does not want to have this happen – which looks fishey to me. The publishers have got to handle it. They are at least interested and that can give them a reason for putting up with all this stupid trouble.

Why is it an impasse to me? Very much anxiety? Perhaps because there is something I want that I can't let go of? I can't think what!! Something is keeping me from acting with full detachment and freedom in this, however.

Things come to the one who is open. If I am blocked it is because I block myself – i.e., am not open to what is "coming" (and perhaps unavoidable – but it brings my greatest good). What matters is not that "things come" independent of my volition, but that I can choose to be open or not. I can receive it or not.

The willfulness of Marie Tadié collides with and arouses my own willfulness. If there were nothing there . . . Now is the time to learn. Probably a great deal of it boils down simply to monastic poverty, detachment from the world, etc. All this is too ambiguous now with the new tendencies. I listen to these too much perhaps.

Tadié again – she is extremely sensitive to and looking for signs of (personal and emotional) rejection. Sin provokes rejection and it is by clamping on to and accusing evidences of it that she maintains and strengthens her hold, in so far as I am not in a position to drop her completely after all the admittedly good work she has done (and in which I am not that interested). A peculiar sado-masochistic tangle. I must learn to handle it by insight, objectivity, not just evasion. That is one of the things she desires and fears – evidence that I am fed up, want nothing more to do with her. And that is precisely what I "want" her to feel, provided I can cover it up nicely. That is what I have to get along without.

There is no evading the fact that I am in solitude for real purification and this is no easy matter. It is not simply that occasions of sin and sinful wishes are removed (they are not totally removed), the wishes themselves have to be rooted out. This is inescapable. Unless it is faced, there is no remaining in solitude. Only with special grace can this work be done.

But what are the real wishes?

"Dedisti metuentibus te significationem ut fugiant a facie eius." ["You have given *significatio* to those that fear you, that they may flee from his face."] For St. Athanasius this *significatio* is insight.

I am much more stable and peaceful when I read the Bible and the ancients, and not too much modern stuff, or exclusively that. The coherence of Isaac of Stella for instance, and the solidity of Latin and the modes of thought imposed by Latin. In modern books the mind runs ahead of itself, is crowded with images and information, is excited, incoherent, the result of agitation without depth – roots not solid.

"The will can be bent to evil; that is natural to it by nature of its origin from Nothingness." *St. Thomas*, De Veritate, *A 22, 6 ad 3*

Importance of this principle of faith: "we should not *trust in ourselves but in God who raises the dead*," II Corinthians 1:29. Must think this out more deeply and make it more truly the cornerstone – especially the last part. For if I *have in mind* the resurrection (rather than simply trusting God as Creator, Providence, etc.) much new light and strength comes from this in particular.

This morning I got up eager to pray and then could hardly pray at all (October '65).

Monastic Peace
Monastic Vocation and Modern Thought
Climate Monastic Prayer
Obedience and Monastic Renewal
Eremiticism
Baroque Monasticism
Revise – Notes on Prayer from P.W.
Work – Fall 1965. Winter 1966.
Isaac of Nineveh
Celtic Monasticism

Book = other pieces to go with "Climate of Monastic Prayer" article – for *Katallagete*.

(articles still not done   –   Grimlaic
Navigatio Brendani
Philosophic Roots of Non Violence for
   Gandhi Marg.
Franciscan Eremiticism – John of Ford?

Preface to *Johnston – Cardenal –* Wu for *"Redeeming the Time."*
Study on Cassian?

  Directory for Cardenal   Text for Gethsemani Picture Book
    Collectanea   Hallaj
   Reviews   Eremiticism for Monastic Studies

Seasons of Celebration sent to

Eileen Curns	acknowledged
Sister Thérèse	
[Lentfoehr]	acknowledged
[Hans Urs] Von Balthasar	
Dorothy Day	acknowledged November 24
Little Brothers	Detroit
M. Schroen	acknowledged
Hildegard Goss-Mayr	

Chuang Tzu   November 30

Art Fillmore	acknowledged
[Ludovico] Silva	
[José] Coronel [Urtecho]	

sent later

[Victoria] Ocampo	
[Jacques] Maritain	
Marco Pallis?	
[Robert] Giroux	acknowledged
[Raymond] Roseliep	
[Ray] Livingston	

When I see how few acknowledged a book I am less guilty about not answering when total strangers send their "works."

Need to resist glut of reading in early morning, stimulated by coffee, etc. – Prolong meditation and deep reading before taking any drink or food and then read less and more quietly.

Cross of sensitivity around sunrise – Lauds demanded this!

Problem of over-defensiveness manifesting itself in disease.

Question of the need to feel "justified" in the eyes of men. Value of my life called into question by someone who really has no sympathy for this sort of thing, thinks it a waste and an evasion – and in calling into question my solitude, calls everything else into question also. So I have to "be questioned" like this. I am subject to "examination," and this implies, in its mild way, something analogous to an official torture – "examined" on a little rack of someone else's objectivity, taken apart by him, etc. It is natural to want to explain and try to get him to see what he does not see, and does not want to see probably: the value of it for me as subject. That is first the question. It is not the authenticity of this value that is being really examined, but whether it is *just* for anyone to enjoy such a thing (the answer being "no" before the examination begins, so that guilt is a foregone conclusion).

(In the night blessing of orthodox liturgy) *"La journée vécue se présente d'emblée comme une parcelle de l'Histoire Sainte, de l'économie divine du salut où l'homme a accompli sa tâche à lui confiée par Dieu."* ["The day one has just lived is seen without qualification as a parcel of Sacred History, of the divine economy of salvation, where man has accomplished the task entrusted to him by God."] *[Paul] Evdokimov*

Directory – for Cardenal

office – Night vigils – anticipate evening before?

In any case – important to have Lauds at sunrise (begin before sunrise so Mass will start around Sunrise).

Charity and *organization*. Illusion of setting up an organization first instead of letting the ground work be done by authentic and a total *charity* (i.e., forestalling problems that would test and incite to charity – that charity which can alone prove the group worthy of survival). (Institutional idolatries in those breaking away to make new foundations on their own lines.)

Making others willing to see other and vital perspectives – and let go of obsessions and illusions with a merely partial view. Patterns of meaning – *how* held and *how* lived (background of philosophical struggles – existentialism vs. positivism).

Contrast non-violence in civil rights with non-violence in peace movement.

Creative Protest.

1. Non-violence to be used not as a mere tactic – to gain publicity, to create an image, etc. nor as apocalyptic demonstration (pathology enters into both).

2. Witness to living alternatives which are depreciated and which are in fact *essential* for the survival of a society.

3. Spirit of *response* and dialogue. Reaction is not response. (Reaction to objects – response to persons.) Response awakens dormant truth in the other, perhaps a truth of which he has despaired. Response awakens *hope* in the other, not mistrust. Hope in the validity of the alternatives we offer.

4. There will certainly be disruption, etc., because of fear of the consequences of accepting this. But where it is clear that the "witness" is creating only hatred and mistrust, then it is failing.

5. Problems of non-violence in America. What is the fear of the squares? Weakness of non-violence protest in its "best" aspect. (Fear of being overwhelmed with *weak*ness that destroys identity – war as an identity builder), fear of self-destruction.

6. Doubtless, entirely new approach needed in peace movement.

These notes written during argument with pacifists of FOR (Fellowship of Reconciliation), etc., after Roger Laporte burned himself to death outside the U.N. (November 9 or 10) and Jim Douglass was upset – asking me to write about the peace movement – while I was not able to get information. Thought of resigning as sponsor of Catholic Peace Fellowship – realizing always that the way to shut up is to stop talking: recognize when it becomes incontestable *evil* to do so (no more explanations required by charity!).

Difficulties I have had to face this last month (mid-October to mid-November 1965) are mostly due to things I have *said*. A degree of absurdity in this. And yet not. That a solitary should be tried by the consequences of speaking – and speaking in public. (And by the consequent inner struggle to determine whether or not I was justified in speaking.) Was I justified in saying *all* I said? Obviously no. Some of it was imprudent and emotional (telegram and letter to the CPF, etc.). These consequences must now be met and accepted with humility and realism – and difficult exercise of judgment. Acceptance of dialogue, obviously – this has imposed itself. I have opened a "conversation" that is in some respects bitter (Heidbrink). I trust Jim Forest to respond intelligently anyway: but there *is* this question of their interest in using my name, and to this they will cling mightily. (Calling me a traitor for withdrawing.) Yet the withdrawal on my part is dictated by the needs of my life. I can't be a militant in the peace movement and a hermit at the same time. Especially since I can't agree with all that various members of the CPF and *CW* (*Catholic Worker*) are doing or may do – if I am called to account for them. Meanwhile – I have motives to appreciate the value of shutting up, and will have to get there by talking. Absurd. But it has to be done.

Jacques Ellul on the "contemporary" political man. *"Il a la conviction de vivre en homme libre précisément parce qu'il vit dans l'instant. . . . Obéir au moment semble être la liberté. Prendre parti brusquement dans la dernière querelle c'est la vocation politique du citoyen le plus libre. Étonnante confusion, ne pas voir à quel point l'obéissance à l'instant, la réaction à l'actualité sont les plus radicales négations possibles de la liberté."* ["He has the conviction of living as a free man precisely because he lives in the present instant. . . . To obey the present moment appears to be freedom itself. Taking sides abruptly in the latest quarrel is defined as the political vocation of the freest citizen. What astonishing confusion, not to see to what extent obeying the moment and reacting to the latest events are the most radical possible negations of freedom."]

L'Illusion politique, *63–64 (December 10, 1965)*

I understand a dream I sometimes have – of having to play a role in a play – and not being prepared, not knowing the lines. Do I foolishly *choose* these roles?

Need for distance, for the development of a new unexplored consciousness, which has nothing directly to do with the strategies of active movements and the proving of an activist conscience – yet is not akin to their struggles. Direct and militant participation is supremely ambiguous. Maybe if I am involved in agony of my choice the ambiguity will be fruitful. I have plenty of pains of my own.

Psychosomatic symptoms, expressing perhaps doubt and *reaction* instead of secure faith and trusting *response*.

My need for genuine interior freedom is now urgent. Yet this is something I am helpless to enter except through the Cross, and I must try to see and accept the Cross of conflict – to renounce myself by renouncing "my" answers and by restraining the urge to answer, to *reply* – in order that I may silently respond, or obey. In this kind of obedience there is never a full understanding of what one has to do – this does not become clear until the work has been done.

Victor Frankl's point that in the camps the prisoners who wanted to keep human had to take on their suffering itself as a task (individually and together) in order to give it meaning.

Even when writing the inadequate "statement" on Peace and Protest, realized the big hole in it. The short version ok for public, says little. But I realize that I don't know what to say. Actually it is clear to me that the philosophy, if any, behind most of the peace movement is exactly the sort of thing I am protesting against – the rationalistic and utilitarian spirit, the Bertrand Russell type of humanism. What does it end in? The drab valuelessness of the welfare life: (admittedly better than the Fascism and fanaticism, say, of racist areas). Of course one can't generalize and I don't know what the younger ones are thinking. Anyway, I see that my job is to get loose from the mental tangle I got in by wanting too much to identify myself with a particular movement and with groups in it. They are not my dish – the mode of operation is not my way and there is all the nonsense in it that I am always declaiming against.

I have used a lot of existentialist terms. I can already see how nauseated I will be with them when they become vulgar currency (Commitment, authenticity, etc.) and they are already vulgar. I am nauseated by the Secular City syndrome. But forget it – in a year there will be another nausea. What is the use of being in the silence of true words and letting in this noise? Yet I do not see quite how to manage the situation. With patience, it will arrange itself.

For me – the betrayal I have to look out for is that which would consist simply in attaching myself to "a cause" that happens to be operating at this time, and getting involved, and letting myself be carried along with it, simply making appropriate noises from time to time, at a distance.

The world embraced in the monstrous benignity and youthfulness of the American consciousness – a consciousness infinitely proliferated through its machines. Proliferated rather than identified. Does the horror of everyone amount to a recognition that all can easily be reduced by this mysterious persuasion? Who knows – maybe it will succeed, and the world will actually be American in ten years' time. Then indeed we will have new problems.

Drugs and the expansion of the "American" consciousness. Now the optimism is psychedelic. The drugged smile, the plenteous myth and witticisms. The eager irresponsibility. The cautious filing away of records. (CIA experimented with drugs but did not tell.) The American psychic orgasm. Now available to all. For a limited time only. Clip coupon and send.

Points for Ernesto Cardenal January 1966

1. Question of dysentery, etc.: to be further studied; see if stomach can be completely cured by time.

2. Book to finish for Doubleday.

3. Need for more time here to get into solitary life.

4. By correspondence can get good idea of their difficulties and so on.

5. Possibility of change here after Norway foundation. Suggestion – that they apply to Rome *only in mid 1967*.

Blessed are they that hunger and thirst for justice . . .

Ernesto Cardenal is here, talking of his foundation – and his desire to have me there (October 1965).

First – facts.

1. The really unusual and I think inspired movement among influential lay intellectuals who desire a contemplative community in Nicaragua – sense of terrible need for such a community and such a life in the Latin American Church.

2. They are willing to make great sacrifices and do extraordinary things to get this going – their hearts are very much in it. Certainly the Holy Spirit is breathing here and it is a work needed by the Church.

3. They have repeatedly tried to get a foundation made from Gethsemani and failed.

4. Ordinary Trappist foundations do not do well in Latin America.

5. More a need of a new kind of community – something more like the Little Brothers – and founded, as this will be, by people of the country.

6. May need someone to direct and instruct them and they want me. As far as I am concerned I think I must accept – though I doubt if there is any possibility of getting permission to go.

7. They are willing to go so far as to send a delegation to the Pope himself to get his personal approval. Is this the best way? It is the only way left that might work. Personally I believe Dom James Fox, in his obsessive refusal of everything like this, is stifling the Spirit.

What would be my part in the project if I went?

1. To have a hermit and contemplative life while also acting as Spiritual Father.

2. To give direction and occasional conference on monastic life, asceticism, etc.

3. Occasional conference to retreatants, and to help with direction of poets, etc. who would come.

advantages –

1. Participation in a work inspired by the Holy Spirit in response to a call of charity from a church needing this kind of service, in the love of Christ – to bring something more of His word to them. (As opposed to being

simply held in cold storage here, to preserve static "image" of this community – though I have a happy, comfortable, quiet life in the hermitage) love – *true agape*, first and principal advantage.

2. Exile – poverty – solitude – risk greater simplicity.

3. Flight from the wrath that is to come!!

4. Contact with abandoned and primitive people – reparation for sins of colonialization and injustice to the Indians, etc.

"Notre tâche consiste uniquement à travailler à la réalisation de la forme divine en nous livrant à elle. Nous n'avons pas besoin de nous débattre, de nous contrôler sans cesse, de faire toujours de nouveaux projets, de poursuivre constamment de nouveaux buts. Nous ne trouverons jamais le repos, mais bien au contraire nous serons acculés au désespoir." ["Our task consists solely in working to realize the divine form by turning ourselves over to it. We do not need to be always striving, always checking to see how we're doing, always creating new projects, always pursuing new goals. Along this path we shall never find rest; on the contrary, we will find ourselves backed up against despair."]

Casel. Cf. Matthew 6:27, 32–34

"S'abandonner à Dieu, remplir la mesure de Dieu, donc s'enraciner en lui tout entier, voilà ce qui conduit à la vraie perfection. . . . Nous prouverons que nous sommes ressemblants à Dieu si justement nous ne faisons pas de puis à la manière des hommes, si nous ne comptons pas sur nos propres oeuvres. . . . Nous aurons à nous laisser former à la mesure incommensurable de Dieu . . . dont les profondeurs échappent à toute mesure." ["To abandon oneself to God, to fill the measure of God, therefore to become wholly rooted in him: this is what leads to true perfection. . . . We will prove that we are in the likeness of God precisely if we do not make any change in the manner of men, if we do not count on our own works. . . . We will have to let ourselves be formed according to the incommensurable measure of God . . . whose depths escape every measure."]

Casel

NB. The Prodigal story in Rilke obviously has no *religious* intentions. Hence there is no point in complaining that he debases the Gospel parable. Simply starting from the Parable he retraces the ideas in a purely human and psychological project, an existentialist apprehension of man's being as an object, as *Dasein*. And the weaknesses of existentialism are evident here. Still the insight is valuable. That the whole question of reconciliation of God our Father is entirely different and deeper question. However, it *does* affect our relation with other men.

I gave advice to the novices and monks about Rilke (about reading direct without afterthought). I can take my own advice reading his story of the Prodigal at the end of *Malte* [*The Notebooks of Malte Laurids Brigge*]. Must one make frightful noises over this story? Stop it from getting in the windows, or doors, or even on the porch – leave it outside with a disgraceful tag on it? Or risk understanding it? Why does everyone immediately see in such stories only something to excommunicate? It seems to me this Prodigal has something to be remembered, something to start from, simply because we have it in us. Why not recognize what is ours and start from there – why excommunicate ourselves, for sheer fear of being excommunicated by them?

Maybe the Prodigal had a real need of communion – too pure a need perhaps – and perhaps it turned to evasion. Others were at fault also. It is true Rilke never grew up. But then, what are all the noises people make today about being "grown up"? Look at *them!*

"*Tous ceux qui portent en eux le témoignage que Jésus a donné de Dieu et de lui-même et qui en font leur propre témoignage, sont des prophètes: Dieu habite en eux et leur bouche dit les paroles de Dieu.*" ["All those who bear within themselves the witness which Jesus bore to God and to himself, and who make of this their own witness, these are prophets: God dwells in them and their mouth speaks the words of God."] *Casel*

The more I think of this truth the more I think also of my own fallibility, of man's fallibility and of the untrustworthiness of human causes. In all humility and fully conscious of my limitations I must listen to His Word and respond as fully as I can without imposing upon it a further direction, the orientation of a human and political plan. The answer is not the "plan," but Christ. Yet one may work with a plan as long as it is not opposed to Christ.

The problem of psychedelics – questions of "consciousness-alteration" as an end in itself (?). My stand on this (provisionally) is that of St. John of the Cross on all questing for "experiences." Not drugs but night, not visions but *nada* [nothing]. Psychedelics resulting in part from a too rigid use of Zen koans – an efficacious means to enlightenment. Once this principle is admitted, then, if there is a quicker, cheaper, easier means . . .

How true it is that I think with my hands. Jotting things down, writing and rewriting, Drawing (not often). If I had a piano . . . yet I think I tend to use music as non-thinking. Perhaps I write to *slow down* my reading and reflect more. In the hermitage I read much more slowly, take more time, cover less ground. In the morning, with two and half hours of reading, I still read very little, and the time is gone like a half hour. There is no quantitative estimate of this time. It is simply a "period of reading" with its own quality.

Need to avoid quick judgments, "imprinting" final conceptualizations and decisions. Leave the mind open and fallow, to receive other seeds later perhaps. Another advantage of solitude and not an advantage.

Schwatzbedürfnis[1] of the solitary – singing, talking, etc. Pleasant, like a bird maybe. Free, idiotic. To indulge one's own idiocy without fear of criticism – what a luxury.

Dreams – Night of Saturday-Sunday (Fourth Sunday of Advent, 1965), I have a little water or "coffee" – in a bowl. By stirring it, perhaps it will be drinkable coffee. I stir it, but is like lukewarm muddy water to look at and there are insects in it, which I can pick and throw out. But I see really I must find fresh water and make new coffee.

"Je lis, j'écris, je voudrais un silence encore plus profond et la solitude, même douloureuse, avec Dieu." ["I read, I write, I would like to have an even deeper silence, and solitude, even painful, with God."]

Abbé [Jules] Monchanin, December 1941

"To complete at a stroke the task that was ordained from the center of my heart . . ." *Rilke*

That is what I am beginning to see for myself, but only beginning. My running after "causes" has been a delusion, though some things had to be said. He [Rilke] worked harder and more honestly than I have ever begun to, to hear the orders coming from the center.

My own personal task is not simply that of poet and writer (still less commentator, pseudo-prophet), it is basically to *praise* God out of an inner center of silence, gratitude and "awareness." This can be realized in a life which apparently accomplishes nothing. Without centering on accomplishment or non-accomplishment, my task is simply the breathing of this gratitude from day to day, in simplicity, and for the rest turning my hand to whatever comes, work being part of praise, whether splitting logs or writing poems, or best of all simple notes. And there will remain occasional necessary letters.

A purely Rilkean solitude would be the worst of temptations for me (because so easy to yield to!). It is as a protection against this that I have my present cross and trouble (about Peace movement).

If everything centers on my obligation to respond to God's call to solitude, this does not mean simply putting everything out of my mind and living as if only God and I existed. This is impossible anyway. It means rather

---

[1] Literally "the need to chat," but the experience is of talking to oneself or, even more likely, to objects, animals, etc., when no other human is present.

learning from what contacts and conflicts I still have, how deep a solitude is required of me. This means *now* the difficult realization that I have relied too much on the support and approval of others – and yet I do need others. I must now painfully rectify this. That is to say – there is a sense in which *some* of god's answers must come to me from others, even from those with whom I disagree, even from those who do not understand my way of life. Yet it would be disastrous to seek merely to placate these people – the mere willingness to do so would make me deaf to whatever real message they might have. To do this job rightly is beyond my power. Prayer is all I have left – and patient, humble (if possible) obedience to God's will. One thing is certain – I do not possess my answers ready at hand in myself. (It almost seems an axiom that a solitary should be one who has his own answers . . .) But I cannot simply seek them from others either. The problem is in learning to go for some time, perhaps for long periods – *with no answer!!*

December 2, 1965

Yet there is the problem of the climate of pseudo-charismatic action in politics now. Reason is irrelevant, what one must do is follow this or that movement which incarnates "the Spirit." Not to listen to the consensus, not to reverberate properly, is to be relegated to outer darkness. This kind of irrationality ends in wild symbolic action and immolations. That is why I want none of it, and will be very circumspect about listening to prophets or wanting to be one.

December 4, 1965

One of the trouble spots – my afternoon work – (the time to write, etc.). When I am trying to finish something I am too full of passion – and when I am not driving into something full-force I feel guilty and restless. Yet if I take time simply to study and prepare work quietly, with moments of meditation, the afternoon is well spent and fruitful, and I really enjoy it too. This is what I need more of. Work in which I am aware that I am in silence. When I am driving at it, I would not know I was in a silent and solitary place.

Absurdity of the Robinson-Cox God-is-dead secular-city theology with simply being in the news in the most superficial possible manner. Well, they are in the news. An essentially ephemeral and pointless theology, but in the present sense contemporary. A theology of pure distraction, gossip, unadulterated by reflection.

Proposing to myself more and more seriously a year of silence and study to prepare for a book on spiritual experience. More than a year. (Probably have to write occasional essays and reviews. Poems would not be excluded.) Now I reflect – an important aspect of this would be finally opening up to science, to the scientific outlook (in which silence will always be imposed by my ignorance). Here – a kind of humility, very important, which I have neglected. December 13.

"Et semper ex intimo pectore corde et vi peccatores et paenitentes nos esse profiteamur ne de aliqua re quamvis in nobis pia videatur, in elatione extollamur; sed nostra et aliarum deflemus peccata, quoniam propterea abiecimus mundum et ad hunc devenimus locu." ["Let us always confess from our innermost breast, heart and strength that we are sinners and penitents, lest we be puffed up with pride at seeing some sign of piety in ourselves; but let us rather weep for our own and others' sins, because this is why we renounced the world and came to this place."]

Blessed Rodolfus, Consuetudines Camaldulenses [Customs of the Camaldolese]

"Humanity is asleep, concerned only with what is useless living in a wrong world. Believing that one can excel: this is only habit and usage, not religion. . . . Do not prattle before the people of the path, rather consume yourself. You have only perverted knowledge and religion if you are upside down in relation to reality. A man is wrapping his net around himself. A lion (the man of the way) bursts his cage asunder."

Sanai (an Afghan Sufi), Twelfth century A.D.

". . . *être efficace pour l'autre par son silence."* [". . . to be efficacious for others through one's silence."] *Evdokimov*

"Acquiers la paix intérieure et une multitude d'hommes trouveront leur salut auprès de toi." ["Acquire interior peace and a whole host of men will find their salvation in you."] *Saint Seraphim de Sarov – in Evdokimov*

"A work of art is good only if it has sprung from necessity. In this nature of its origin lies its judgment. There is no other." Rilke. Applying this to my own books – whether they are works of art or not: I would say the following came from a kind of necessity. *Chuang Tzu – Guilty Bystander –* Some of the poems in *Emblems –* Philosophy of Solitude in *Disputed Questions –* Thoughts in Solitude – *Sign of Jonas. Seven Storey Mountain –* Thirty poems. And that's about it. The rest is trash. So is this too in a way. Or rather the rest is journalism. I would say the writing on Zen was "necessary" too. And some of *Behavior of Titans.* December 18.

Abba Arenius. "The monk is a stranger in a foreign land; let him not occupy himself with anything and he will find rest."

Index